Windows® 11

by Andy Rathbone

for
dummies®
A Wiley Brand

Windows® 11 For Dummies®

Published by: **John Wiley & Sons, Inc.,** 111 River Street, Hoboken, NJ 07030-5774, www.wiley.com

Copyright © 2022 by John Wiley & Sons, Inc., Hoboken, New Jersey

Published simultaneously in Canada

For general information on our other products and services, please contact our Customer Care Department within the U.S. at 877-762-2974, outside the U.S. at 317-572-3993, or fax 317-572-4002. For technical support, please visit https://hub.wiley.com/community/support/dummies.

Wiley publishes in a variety of print and electronic formats and by print-on-demand. Some material included with standard print versions of this book may not be included in e-books or in print-on-demand. If this book refers to media such as a CD or DVD that is not included in the version you purchased, you may download this material at http://booksupport.wiley.com. For more information about Wiley products, visit www.wiley.com.

Library of Congress Control Number: 2021948051

ISBN 978-1-119-84647-5 (pbk); ISBN 978-1-119-84648-2 (ePDF); ISBN 978-1-119-84649-9 (epub)

SKY10029803_101421

Table of Contents

Introduction

Welcome to *Windows 11 For Dummies*, the world's best-selling book about the latest Windows version, Windows 11!

This book's popularity probably boils down to this simple fact: Some people want to be Windows whizzes. They love interacting with dialog boxes. Some randomly press keys in the hope of discovering hidden, undocumented features. A few memorize long strings of computer commands while washing their hair.

And you? Well, you're no dummy, that's for sure. But when it comes to Windows and computers, the fascination just isn't there. You want to get your work done, stop, and move on to something more important. You have no intention of changing, and there's nothing wrong with that.

That's where this book comes in handy. Instead of making you a whiz at Windows, it merely dishes out chunks of useful computing information when you need them. Instead of becoming a Windows expert, you'll know just enough to get by quickly, cleanly, and with a minimum of pain so that you can move on to the more pleasant things in life.

TIP

HOW I WROTE THIS BOOK

How did this book arrive in your hands so quickly after Microsoft released the latest version of Windows, Windows 11? No, I didn't crank it out in two weeks. While creating Windows 11, Microsoft shipped early releases to people who signed up for its Windows Insider's program (https://insider.windows.com). This gave Microsoft a way to test new features before shipping them to the public. And it gave me a chance to write about features before they were released.

I pored over each early release, writing sections of the book in advance. Then, when Microsoft released its final, approved version to the Windows Insider members, I went over every section, screenshot, and step-by-step instruction to make sure the book's instructions matched Microsoft's final release.

A few weeks later, when Microsoft released Windows 11 to the public, the publisher was able to release this book, as well.

And you'll be able to do that whether you're dealing with a touchscreen tablet, laptop, or desktop computer.

About This Book

Don't try to read this book in one sitting; there's no need. Instead, treat this book like a dictionary or an encyclopedia. Turn to the page with the information you need and say, "Ah, so that's what they're talking about." Then put down the book and move on.

Don't bother trying to memorize all the Windows jargon, such as Select the Menu Item from the Drop-Down List Box. Leave that stuff for the computer enthusiasts. In fact, if anything technical comes up in a chapter, a road sign warns you well in advance. Depending on your mood, you can either slow down to read it or speed on around it.

Instead of fancy computer jargon, this book covers subjects like these, all discussed in plain English:

>> Keeping your computer safe and secure

>> Making sense of the new Windows 11 Start menu

>> Finding, starting, and closing programs and apps

>> Locating the file you saved or downloaded last week

>> Setting up a computer or tablet for the family to share

>> Copying information to and from a disc or flash drive

>> Saving and sharing files from your smartphone or digital camera

>> Printing or scanning your work

>> Linking two or more computers with a network to share the internet, files, or a printer

>> Fixing Windows when it's misbehaving

There's nothing to memorize and nothing to learn. Just turn to the right page, read the brief explanation, and get back to work. Unlike other books, this one enables you to bypass the technical hoopla and still complete your work.

How to Use This Book

Windows 11 will most definitely leave you scratching your head at some point. It's the most complicated version of Windows ever released to the public, so take pride in the fact that you're strong enough to persevere.

When something in Windows leaves you stumped, use this book as a reference. Find the troublesome topic in this book's table of contents or index. The table of contents lists chapter and section titles and page numbers. The index lists topics and page numbers. Page through the table of contents or index to the spot that deals with that particular bit of computer obscurity, read only what you have to, close the book, and apply what you've read.

If you're feeling adventurous and want to find out more, read a little further in the bulleted items below each section. You can find a few completely voluntary extra details, tips, or cross-references to check out. There's no pressure, though. You aren't forced to discover anything that you don't want to or that you simply don't have time for.

If you have to type something into the computer, you'll see easy-to-follow bold text like this:

Type **Mail** into the Search box.

In the preceding example, you type the word *Mail* and then press the keyboard's Enter key. Typing words into a computer can be confusing, so a description follows that explains what you should be seeing on the screen.

When I describe a key combination you should press, I describe it like this:

Press Ctrl+B.

That means to hold down your keyboard's Control key while pressing your keyboard's B key. (That's the shortcut key combination that applies bold formatting to selected text.)

Whenever I describe an email address or filename, I present it this way:

```
notepad.exe
```

And website addresses appear like this:

```
www.andyrathbone.com
```

This book doesn't wimp out by saying, "For further information, consult your manual." Windows doesn't even come with a manual. This book also doesn't contain information about running specific Windows programs, such as Microsoft Word or Excel. Windows is complicated enough on its own! Luckily, other *For Dummies* books mercifully explain most popular programs.

Don't feel abandoned, though. This book covers Windows in plenty of detail for you to get the job done. Plus, if you have questions or comments about *Windows 11 For Dummies,* feel free to drop me a line on my website at www.andyrathbone.com. I answer a reader's question each week, either personally or online.

Finally, keep in mind that this book is a *reference.* It's not designed to teach you how to use Windows like an expert, heaven forbid. Instead, this book dishes out enough bite-sized chunks of information so that you don't *have* to learn Windows.

Touchscreen Owners Aren't Left Out

Although Windows 11 comes preinstalled on all new Windows desktop PCs and laptops, Microsoft also aims Windows 11 at owners of *touchscreens.* Tablets, some laptops, and desktop monitors come with screens you can control by touching them with your fingers.

If you're a new touchscreen owner, don't worry. This book explains where you need to touch, slide, or tap your fingers in all the appropriate places.

If you find yourself scratching your head over explanations aimed at mouse owners, remember these three touchscreen rules:

>> **When told to *click,* you should *tap.*** Quickly touching and releasing your finger on a button is the same as clicking it with a mouse.

>> **When told to double-click, *tap twice.*** Two touches in rapid succession does the trick.

>> **When told to *right-click* something, *hold down your finger on the item.* Then, when an icon appears, *lift your finger.*** The right-click menu appears onscreen. (That's what would have happened if you'd right-clicked the item with a mouse.) While you're looking at the pop-up menu, tap any of its listed items to have Windows carry out your bidding.

If you find touchscreens to be cumbersome while you're sitting at a desk, you can always add a mouse and keyboard to your touchscreen tablet. They work just fine. In fact, a mouse and keyboard almost always work better than fingers on the Windows desktop, even in Windows 11. (They're almost mandatory on small Windows tablets.)

And What about You?

Chances are good that you already own Windows 11. You know what *you* want to do with your computer. The problem lies in making the *computer* do what you want it to do. You've gotten by one way or another, perhaps with the help of a computer guru — for instance, a friend at the office, a relative, or perhaps a neighbor's teenager.

But when your computer guru isn't around, this book can be a substitute during your times of need.

Icons Used in This Book

It just takes a glance at Windows to notice its *icons*, which are little push-button pictures for starting various programs. The icons in this book fit right in. They're even a little easier to figure out.

Watch out! This signpost warns you that pointless technical information is coming around the bend. Swerve away from this icon to stay safe from awful technical drivel.

This icon alerts you about juicy information that makes computing easier: a new method for keeping the cat from sleeping on top of your tablet, for example.

Don't forget to remember these important points (or at least dog-ear the pages so that you can look them up again a few days later).

The computer won't explode while you're performing the delicate operations associated with this icon. Still, wearing gloves and proceeding with caution is a good idea.

NEW

This icon alerts you to areas where Windows 11 behaves quite differently from the previous version, Windows 10.

Beyond the Book

Like every *Windows For Dummies* book, this one comes with a free Cheat Sheet that brings together some of the most commonly needed information for people struggling with Windows. It describes how Microsoft changes Windows 11 after its release, and it offers keyboard shortcuts as well as tips on using Windows 11 on a touchscreen. To get the Cheat Sheet, head for www.dummies.com and, using the Search box, search for **Windows 11 For Dummies Cheat Sheet.**

Where to Go from Here

Now you're ready for action. Give the pages a quick flip and scan a section or two that you know you'll need later. Please remember, this is *your* book — your weapon against the computer nerds who've inflicted this whole complicated computer concept on you. Please circle any paragraphs you find useful, highlight key concepts, add your own sticky notes, and doodle in the margins next to the complicated stuff.

REMEMBER

The more you mark up your book, the easier it will be for you to find all the good stuff again.

1

Windows 11 Stuff Everybody Thinks You Already Know

IN THIS PART . . .

Understand the changes in Windows 11.

Navigate and customize the new Start menu.

Store files in the cloud with OneDrive.

Chapter **1**

What Is Windows 11?

C hances are good that you've heard about *Windows:* the boxes and windows that greet you whenever you turn on your computer. In fact, millions of people worldwide are puzzling over Windows as you read this book. Most new computers and laptops sold today come with Windows preinstalled, ready to toss colorful boxes onto the screen.

This chapter helps you understand why Windows lives inside your computer, and I introduce Microsoft's latest Windows version, *Windows 11.* I explain how Windows 11 differs from previous Windows versions, and why parts of Windows 11 and its gang of apps can change behind your back.

What Is Windows, and Why Are You Using It?

Created and sold by a company called Microsoft, Windows isn't like your usual software that lets you calculate income taxes or send angry emails to politicians. No, Windows is an *operating system*, meaning it controls the way you work with your computer. It's been around since 1985, and the latest incarnation is called *Windows 11*, shown in Figure 1-1.

FIGURE 1-1:
Although
Windows 11 looks
different on
different PCs,
it usually looks
much like this.

The name *Windows* comes from all the little windows it places on your computer screen. Each window shows information, such as a picture, a program, or a baffling technical reprimand. You can place several windows onscreen simultaneously and jump from window to window, visiting different programs. Or you can enlarge one window to fill the entire screen.

When you turn on your computer, Windows jumps onto the screen and begins supervising any running programs. When everything goes well, you don't really notice Windows; you simply see your programs or your work. When things don't go well, though, Windows often leaves you scratching your head over a perplexing error message.

In addition to controlling your computer and bossing around your programs, Windows comes with a bunch of free programs and *apps* — mini-programs. These programs and apps let you do different things, such as write and print letters, browse the internet, play music, and send your friends dimly lit photos of your latest meal.

SEPARATING THE ADS FROM THE FEATURES

TIP

Microsoft touts Windows as a helpful companion that always keeps your best interests in mind, but that description isn't really true. Windows always keeps *Microsoft's* interests in mind.

For example, Microsoft uses Windows to plug its own products and services. *Microsoft Edge*, the new Windows web browser, opens with links to Microsoft's own websites. The browser's Favorites area, a place for you to add *your* favorite web destinations, comes stocked with *Microsoft* websites.

Windows 11 places a link to OneDrive, its online storage service, in every folder. But Microsoft isn't as quick to mention that you must pay a recurring fee when you reach your storage limit.

Advertisements appear on the Start menu, as well as the Windows *lock screen*, the screen that appears when you haven't used your PC for a while.

The Maps app uses the Microsoft Bing mapping service, rather than Google Maps or another competitor.

Microsoft also wants you to start buying *apps* rather than traditional programs. Apps are sold only through the bundled Microsoft Store app, and Microsoft takes a cut of each sale.

Simply put, Windows not only controls your computer but also serves as a Microsoft advertising vehicle. Treat these built-in advertising flyers as a salesperson's knock on your door.

And why are you using Windows 11? Well, you probably didn't have much choice. Nearly every computer, laptop, or Windows tablet sold after October 2021 comes with Windows 11 preinstalled. A few people escaped Windows by buying Apple computers (those nicer-looking computers that cost a lot more). But chances are good that you, your neighbors, your boss, and millions of other people around the world are using Windows.

>> Microsoft wants Windows 11 and its gang of apps to run on nearly *everything*: PCs, laptops, tablets, video game consoles, and even yet-to-be-invented gadgets. That's why Windows 11 includes many large buttons for easier poking with fingers on touchscreens. Windows 11 can also run *apps*, small programs usually found on smartphones and tablets, in windows on a desktop PC.

>> To confuse everybody, Microsoft never released a Windows 9. Microsoft skipped a version number when moving from Windows 8.1 to Windows 10.

>> To confuse everybody even *more*, Microsoft said Windows 10 would be the last version of Windows. Six years later, Microsoft began pushing Windows 11.

NEW

>> For years, the desktop's Start menu lived in your screen's lower-left corner. Windows 11 moves the Start menu, as well as the Windows key that launches it, to the screen's bottom center. (I explain how to change it back to its old, lower-left corner home in Chapter 2.)

What's New in Windows 11?

Microsoft views Windows 11 as a one-size-fits-all computing solution that runs on laptops and desktop PCs (shown earlier in Figure 1-1) as well as on touch-screens, including tablets, shown in Figure 1-2.

Windows 11 looks and behaves almost identically on each device, and it brings a bonus: Its apps and programs will run on a Windows 11 tablet, PC, and laptop.

NEW

Besides aiming to run on everything but clock radios, Windows 11 brings these changes to your computer:

>> **Start button and menu:** Windows 11 moves the Start button and menu from its traditional lower-left corner to the center of the screen. The revamped Start menu sports a few rows of icons, but leaves out the animated tiles found in Windows 10. Look closely, and you'll notice the Start menu now sports rounded corners, as do all other desktop windows. Flip ahead to Chapter 2 for more information on the Start button and menu.

FIGURE 1-2:
Windows 11
drops the Tablet
mode found in
Windows 10.

» **Hardware requirements:** Previous Windows versions worked fairly well on older PCs, even those up to ten years old. Windows 11 breaks that model, unfortunately. If your computer is older than three years, you probably won't be able to upgrade it to Windows 11. I explain how to see if your PC can upgrade to Windows 11 in Chapter 22.

» **Settings app:** Have you mastered Windows 10's Settings menu? Erase that memory, because the new Settings app contains a new layout with new switches in new places. Head for Chapter 12 for oodles of Settings menu tips and tricks.

» **Apps on the desktop:** *Apps,* which are small programs from the world of phones and tablets, consumed the full screen in Windows 8 and 8.1. Windows 11 lets you choose whether to run apps full screen or within desktop windows. (Microsoft says Windows 11 will let you download and run apps designed for Android smartphones sometime in 2022.) I cover apps and programs in Chapter 6.

» **File Explorer:** File Explorer, which lets you find, store, and manage files, receives a new, slimmed down look. The ribbon of menu options across the top has vanished, replaced by a single row of unnamed icons. I cover the new File Explorer in Chapter 5.

>> **Teams Chat:** When everybody jumped onto Zoom for video chats during the pandemic, Microsoft decided to push its own Teams app for people to hold online meetings. The chat portion of Microsoft's Teams program now comes built into Windows 11, and I cover it in Chapter 10.

NEW

>> **Your Phone:** The newly revamped Your Phone app lets you send and receive your phone's messages from the keyboard of your desktop PC, all wirelessly. You can browse your phone's latest photos from your desktop, make phone calls, and even run apps. I cover the Your Phone app in Chapter 17.

>> **Widgets:** *Widgets* are simply a strip of little windows that update automatically to show the latest news, weather, or other informational tidbits. They leap onto the screen with a click on its taskbar icon, a process I cover in Chapter 3.

Unlike previous Windows versions, Windows 11 no longer feels like two operating systems crammed into one computer. It feels like a single operating system that can handle both tablets and desktop PCs.

TIP

Windows 11 is a free upgrade for people owning fully patched Windows 10 computers that meet the stringent new hardware requirements required to run it. To see if your current PC qualifies, download and run Microsoft's PC Health Check app at `https://aka.ms/GetPCHealthCheckApp`. Chances are, you'll need to buy a new PC with Windows 11 preinstalled.

What's Missing from Windows 11?

Windows 11 offers many new features, described in the previous section and covered throughout this book. However, it dropped just as many features found in Windows 10. Here's the rundown on the features left behind from Windows 11:

>> **Compatibility:** Windows 10 could run on many older PCs, making it popular with owners of old Windows 7 PCs. Windows 11, by contrast, requires newer PCs with the latest technology. Chances are, you'll have to buy a new PC. (I had to buy a new PC just to write this book!)

>> **Timeline:** Windows 10 kept track of which programs and files you worked with for the past 30 days. A click of the Timeline button let you jump back to see them all, letting you quickly and easily jump back to, say, an unfinished file from last week. Windows 11 removes the feature, offering no replacement.

>> **Movable taskbar:** The Windows taskbar normally lives along the screen's bottom edge. Previous Windows versions let you move that taskbar to any edge you wanted. With Windows 11, the taskbar now remains affixed to the bottom of your desktop, with no option to move it.

- **Synced wallpaper:** In Windows 10, owners of Microsoft accounts see their wallpaper appear whenever they log onto a Windows 10 PC. To the dismay of computer decorators, Windows 11 killed that feature.

- **Tablet mode:** Designed specifically for tablets with touchscreens, Tablet mode quickly spaced your icons farther apart to accommodate thick fingertips. The Start screen and programs always filled the entire screen. Windows 11 dumps Tablet mode because Windows 11 is automatically finger-friendly.

- **Live Tiles on the Start menu:** In Windows 10, the Start menu sometimes resembled a moving marquee, with animated tiles that changed to show different things. Windows 11 ditches the animated tiles in favor of a simpler menu that merely shows static icons. You can no longer create folders on the Start menu for storing related items, either.

- **Internet Explorer:** Microsoft's elderly browser, Internet Explorer, disappeared completely from Windows 11, replaced by the new browser, Microsoft Edge.

- **Cortana:** Microsoft fired its little robot that tried to help you work but mostly got in the way. You can still launch the Cortana app from the Start menu, should you miss it, but otherwise, Cortana won't bother you.

- **Paint 3D:** Paint 3D let you design three dimensional models for 3D printers to create using layers of plastic. Few people used it, and even fewer will notice that it's missing.

- **Skype:** Microsoft paid billions for Skype, an app for making inexpensive (or free) phone calls using the internet. But Microsoft let the app languish. Now, it's replaced by Teams, a program for creating online meetings. Microsoft added the chat portion of Teams into Windows 11 to compete with Zoom, which zoomed in popularity during the pandemic.

TECHNICAL STUFF

WHAT'S A TPM CHIP?

Short for Trusted Platform Module, TPM is a computer chip that places an extra layer of security over your PC. However, most older PCs lack a TPM chip, meaning they can't be upgraded to Windows 11.

Some older PCs come with TPM chips, but the manufacturer left them turned off. To see if your PC has a compatible TPM chip and whether it can be turned on, download Microsoft's PC Health Check app, available at https://aka.ms/GetPCHealthCheckApp.

> **» OneNote:** Windows 10 came with OneNote, an app for taking notes much like a virtual school notebook. OneNote vanished from Windows 11, but compulsive note takers like me can still install it for free from the Microsoft Store.

Why Does Windows 11 Keep Changing?

Windows 10 updated itself seemly at whim, much to the detriment of people who preferred their PCs to look and behave the same whenever they sat at the keyboard. Who wants a computer with a confusing new doodad tossed in overnight?

Microsoft aims to ease that confusion by updating Windows 11 only once a year, thank goodness.

Apps, by contrast, can still be updated whenever the app's creator decides that it's time for a change.

Microsoft sends many of these updates automatically to your computer through Windows Update; you don't need to jump through hoops to find and install them.

Similarly, your apps update themselves automatically through the Microsoft Store. They constantly add features, squash bugs, and sometimes even change their names.

You may not notice these changes in the apps, as well as in Windows 11 itself. Indeed, most of them just fix hundreds of annoying bugs, making Windows 11 run and install more smoothly and safely.

So, when Windows 11 or its apps change overnight, don't think it's your fault. Microsoft constantly tweaks Windows 11, and Windows and its apps will keep changing for years to come.

Can My Current PC Run Windows 11?

If you want to upgrade to Windows 11, your old computer will probably complain. Unlike Windows 10, Windows 11 usually requires a PC sold within the past two or three years.

If you have a technogeek in your family, have him or her translate Table 1-1, which shows the Windows 11 hardware requirements you can find written in the fine print for new computers.

TABLE 1-1   ## The Windows 11 Hardware Requirements

Architecture	x86 (64-bit)
Processor	1 gigahertz (GHz) or faster with 2 or more cores on a compatible 64-bit processor or System on a Chip (SoC). (Unlike previous Windows versions, Window 11 no longer comes in a 32-bit version.)
Memory (RAM)	At least 4GB
Graphics Card	DirectX 12 graphics device with Windows Display Driver Model (WDDM) 2.X driver
HDD free space	At least 20GB
Firmware	Unified Extensible Firmware Interface (UEFI) with secure boot enabled
Internet connection and Microsoft account	Windows 11 Home edition requires internet connectivity and a Microsoft account to set up and use some features.

In common language, Table 1-1 simply says that most computers sold in the past two or three years can be upgraded to Windows 11 with little problem. If your computer is older than that, you're out of luck.

TIP

Don't know what version of Windows runs on your current PC? If clicking the Start button brings a Start menu, right-click the menu's Computer entry, and choose Properties. The screen that appears lists your Windows version.

If there's no Start button, you're running Windows 8. And if clicking your Start button fills the screen with a bunch of colorful tiles, you're running Windows 8.1.

Finally, if *right-clicking* your Start menu brings a large pop-up menu, you're running Windows 10 or 11. Choose the menu's Settings entry, and scroll down to the About section. Your version of Windows, either Windows 10 or Windows 11, is listed in that section's Windows Specifications area.

The Different Flavors of Windows 11

NEW

Microsoft offers several versions of Windows 11, but you'll probably want only one: the aptly titled "Home" version.

Small businesses will choose Windows 11 Pro, and large businesses will want Windows 11 Enterprise.

Here are some guidelines for choosing the version you need:

» If you'll be using your PC at home or in your small business, pick up **Windows Home.**

» If you need to connect to a domain through a work network — and you'll know if you're doing it — you want **Windows Pro.**

» If you're a computer tech who works for businesses, go ahead and argue with your boss over whether you need **Windows Pro** or **Windows Enterprise.** The boss will make the decision based on whether it's a small company (Windows Pro) or a large company (Windows Enterprise).

» If you're a daring soul at a business, watch for Microsoft to release **Windows 365.** This program represents a daring experiment where Windows runs speedily in the cloud, bypassing the limits of your slow and aging PC.

For more details about upgrading to Windows 11, visit Microsoft's Windows website at www.windows.com.

Chapter **2**

Starting with the Start Menu

The Windows 11 Start menu doesn't look much like the Start menu in older versions of Windows. Instead of living in the bottom-left corner, it lives in the bottom *center* of your screen. But although its position and design have changed, the Start menu's basic mechanics remain the same.

Click the Start button, and the Start menu rises, listing the apps and programs installed on your PC. Click an app or program, and it leaps to the screen, ready for action.

In this chapter, I explain how to figure out this odd new Start menu. Whether you're using a tablet or desktop PC, this chapter shows how to make the Start menu do its main job: launch your apps and programs.

TIP

If you're using a touchscreen computer, substitute the word *tap* when you read the word *click.* Tapping twice works like *double-clicking.* And when you see the term *right-click,* touch and hold your finger on the glass; lift your finger when the right-click menu appears.

Being Welcomed to the World of Windows

Starting Windows is as easy as turning on your computer — Windows leaps onto the screen automatically with a flourish. But before you can begin working, Windows stops you cold: It displays what's called a *lock screen*, shown in Figure 2-1, with no entrance key dangling nearby.

Windows 11 provides a calm and creative space to pursue your passions.

Like the image that you see?

12:59
Thursday, July 8

FIGURE 2-1: To move past this lock screen, press a key on the keyboard or drag up on the screen with your mouse or finger.

Introduced back in Windows 8, the lock screen appears before you can sign in to your computer with your account name.

How do you unlock the lock screen? The answer depends on whether you're using a mouse, keyboard, or touchscreen:

>> **Mouse:** On a desktop PC or laptop, click any mouse button.

>> **Keyboard:** Press any key, and the lock screen slides away. Easy!

>> **Touch:** Touch the screen with your finger and then slide your finger *up* the glass. A quick flick of the finger will do.

When you're in the door, Windows wants you to *sign in*, as shown in Figure 2-2, by clicking your name and passing the security check.

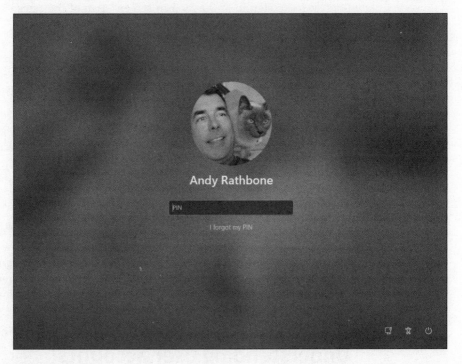

When facing the Sign In screen, you have several options:

>> **If you see your name or email address listed, type your password or PIN, or use a Windows Hello fingerprint reader or camera.** After verifying your identity, Windows lets you in and displays your Start menu, just as you last left it. (I describe how to set up Windows Hello in Chapter 14.)

>> **If you don't see your name, but you have an account on the computer, look in the screen's lower-left corner.** There, Windows displays a list of all the account holders. You may see the computer owner's name.

>> **If you bought a new computer, use the account you created when turning on your computer for the first time.** As part of its setup process, Windows guides you through creating a Microsoft account on your computer.

>> **No account?** Then find out who owns the computer and beg that person to set up an account for you.

If you need more information about user accounts, including creating new ones, managing old ones, flip ahead to Chapter 14.

Don't *want* to sign in at the Sign In screen? Two of the screen's bottom-corner buttons offer these other options:

>> **The little figurine,** shown in Figure 2-2 and the margin, customizes Windows for people with physical challenges in hearing, sight, or manual dexterity, all covered in Chapter 12. If you choose this button by mistake, click or touch on a different part of the screen to avoid changing any settings.

>> **The little round button,** shown in Figure 2-2 and the margin, lets you shut down or restart your PC, as well as put it to sleep — a power-saving state that quickly awakes. (If you've accidentally clicked the button and shut down your PC, don't panic. Press the power button on your PC's case, and your PC returns to this screen.)

Even while locked, as shown earlier in Figure 2-1, your computer's screen displays current information in its lower-right corner. Depending on how your PC is configured, you may see the time and date; your wireless internet signal strength (the more radio waves in the icon, the better your connection); battery strength (the more colorful the icon, the better); your next scheduled appointment; a count of unread email; and other items.

Understanding user accounts

Windows allows several people to work on the same computer, yet it keeps everybody's work separate. To do that, it needs to know who's currently sitting in front of the keyboard. When you *sign in* — introduce yourself — by clicking your username and typing your password, as shown in Figure 2-2, the Windows Start menu and desktop appear as you left them, ready for you to make your own personalized mess.

When you're done working or just feel like taking a break, sign out (explained later in this chapter, in the "Exiting Windows" section) so that somebody else can use the computer. Later, when you sign back in, your own files will be waiting for you.

REMEMBER

Although you may turn your work area into a mess, it's your *own* mess. When you return to the computer, your letters will be just as you saved them. Sue hasn't accidentally deleted your files or folders while playing *Words with Friends.* Bob's Start menu still contains links to his favorite ukulele websites. And nobody will be able to read your email.

Until you customize your username picture, you'll be a silhouette. To add a photo to your user account, open the Start menu and click your username. (It's the icon directly over the Start button.) Choose Change Account Settings from the pop-up menu. When the Settings menu's Your Info page appears, click the Open Camera button to take a quick shot with your computer's built-in camera. Still wearing your pajamas? Then choose the Browse Files button to choose a photo already stored in your Pictures folder.

Keeping your account private and secure

Because Windows lets many people use the same computer, how do you stop Diane from reading Rob's love letters to Miley Cyrus? How can Grace keep Josh from deleting her *Star Wars* movie trailers? Using a *password* solves some of those problems, and Windows offers other security solutions, as well.

In fact, security is more important than ever in Windows because some accounts can be tied to a credit card. By typing a secret password when signing in, you enable your computer to recognize *you* and nobody else. When you protect your account, nobody can access your files. And nobody can rack up charges for computer games while you're away from home.

Also, if your computer is stolen, a strong password keeps the thieves from logging in to your account and stealing your files.

TIP

To change a password on a Microsoft account, visit your account's website at https://account.microsoft.com. After signing in, choose the Change Password option near your account name.

Holders of Local accounts, by contrast, can follow these steps on their own PC to set up or change the password:

1. **Click the Start button and then click the Settings icon.**

When the Start menu appears, click the Settings icon (shown in the margin) near the menu's top-left corner. The Settings app appears.

2. **Click the Accounts icon (shown in the margin). When the Accounts pane appears, click the words Sign-in Options along the pane's left edge.**

Options for signing in to your computer appear.

3. **Click the Password button, shown in Figure 2-3. Then click the Change button.**

You may need to type your existing password to gain entrance. Don't see a Password or Change button? Then you have a Microsoft account, and need to change your password online at https://account.microsoft.com.

4. **Type a password that will be easy to remember.**

TIP

   Choose something like the name of your favorite vegetable, for example, or your dental floss brand. To beef up its security level, capitalize some letters and embed a number or two in the password, like **iH8Turnips** or **Floss2BKleen.** (Don't use these exact two examples, though, because they've probably been added to every password cracker's arsenal by now.)

5. **If asked, type that same password into the Retype Password text box so Windows knows you're spelling it correctly.**

6. **In the Password Hint box, type a hint that reminds you — and only you — of your password.**

   Windows won't let you type in your exact password as a hint. You have to be a bit more creative.

7. **Click the Next button and click Finish.**

   Do you suspect you've botched something during this process? Click Cancel to return to Step 3 and either start over or exit.

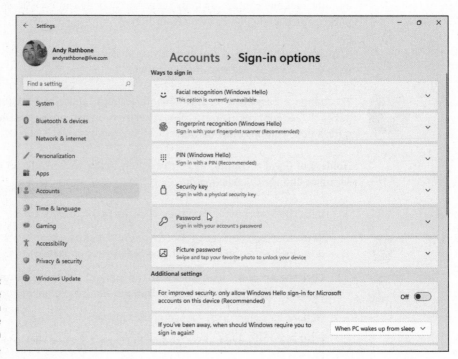

FIGURE 2-3:
Click the Password section and then click the Change button when it appears.

After you've created the password, Windows begins asking for your password whenever you sign in.

REMEMBER

>> Passwords are case-sensitive. When typed in as passwords, the words **Caviar** and **caviar** are considered different.

>> Afraid that you'll forget your password someday? Protect yourself now: Flip ahead to Chapter 14, where I describe how to make a Password Reset Disk, which is a special way of resetting forgotten passwords for local accounts.

>> When you change your Microsoft account password on your PC, you also change it on your Xbox, your Windows tablet, and every other device where you sign in with a Microsoft account. (I cover Microsoft accounts in this chapter's next section.)

>> Windows also allows you to create a picture password in Step 4, where you drag a finger or mouse pointer over an onscreen photo in a certain sequence. Then, instead of entering a password, you redraw that sequence on the sign-in picture. (Picture passwords work much better on touchscreen tablets than desktop monitors.)

>> Another option that you may see in Step 4 is to create a PIN. A *PIN* is a four-or-more character code like the ones you punch into Automated Teller Machines (ATMs). The disadvantage of a PIN? There's no password hint. Unlike Microsoft accounts, your PIN only works on the computer where it was created; it's not stored online, where hackers may find it.

TIP

>> Tired of constantly entering your password? Connect a Windows 11 compatible fingerprint reader or camera to your PC. (Some laptops, tablets, and keyboards have them built in.) Your computer quickly lets you in after you either scan your fingertip or gaze into your PC's camera. I describe how to sign in with Windows Hello in Chapter 14.

>> Forgotten your password *already?* When you type a password that doesn't work, Windows automatically displays your hint (if you created one), which should help to remind you of your password. Careful, though — anybody can read your hint, so make sure it's something that makes sense only to you. As a last resort, insert your Password Reset Disk, a job I cover in Chapter 14.

I explain much more about user accounts in Chapter 14.

Signing up for a Microsoft account

Whether you're signing in to Windows for the first time, trying to access some apps, or just trying to change a setting, you'll eventually see a screen similar to the one in Figure 2-4.

You can sign in to your computer with either a *Microsoft* account or a *Local* account. Although a Microsoft account makes Windows much easier to work with, each type of account serves different needs:

>> **Local account:** This account works fine for people using traditional Windows programs on the Windows desktop. However, Local account holders can't store files on OneDrive, where they're available from other PCs and devices. Local account holders can't buy apps from the Microsoft Store app, either.

>> **Microsoft account:** Required to access many of Microsoft's services, a Microsoft account consists of simply an email address and a password. Microsoft account holders can store files on the internet with OneDrive, download apps from the Microsoft Store, and monitor their children's online activities. When you log in online to any PC with your Microsoft account, you find your email, browser favorites, OneDrive files, and settings automatically waiting for you.

You can sign in with a Microsoft account in one of these two ways; I've listed the simplest method first:

>> **Use an existing Microsoft account.** If you already have an account with Hotmail, MSN, Xbox Live, Outlook.com, or Windows Messenger, you already have a Microsoft account and password. Type in that email address and password at the screen shown in Figure 2-4, and then click the Sign In button.

>> **Sign up for a new Microsoft account.** Click the words Microsoft Account, shown in Figure 2-4, and Microsoft takes you to a website where you can create your own Microsoft account. You can use any email address for a Microsoft account. You simply enter that email address, create a new password to go with it, and wham: You've created a Microsoft account.

Until you sign in with a Microsoft account, the nag screen in Figure 2-4 will haunt you whenever you try to access a Windows feature that requires a Microsoft account. (I explain how to convert a Local account into a Microsoft account in Chapter 14.)

TIP

When you first sign in to your new account, Windows may ask whether you want to find other PCs, devices, and content on your network. If you're using a home or work network, click the Yes button. (That lets you print to network printers, for example, as well as share files with other networked computers.) If you're connecting to a *public* network, perhaps at a hotel, coffee shop, or airport, click the No button.

Figuring Out the Windows 11 Start Menu

In Windows, everything starts with the Start button and its Start menu. Whether you're ready to blow up spaceships, do your taxes, or check your email, you start by clicking the Start button (shown in the margin) along the bottom edge of your screen: The Start menu leaps up with a list of your apps and programs, shown in Figure 2-5.

In theory, you spot the name or icon for your desired app or program and click it; the app launches, and you're off to work. In reality, finding what you want on the Windows 11 Start menu can be a little more confusing, especially if you've grown accustomed to the Windows 10 Start menu.

In Windows 11, the Start menu contains the following four parts:

>> **Search box:** This box lives across the top of the Start menu. Type what you're searching for — a name of a file, folder, or even some words contained in that file — into the Search box, and Windows will try to find it, whether it's on your PC or the internet.

>> **Pinned:** Windows displays a selective list of "pinned" apps in this section. To see *all* your apps, click the All Apps icon in the section's upper-right corner. I explain how to pin your *own* favorite apps here in this chapter's "Adding or removing Start menu items" section.

>> **Recommended:** Here, Windows lists your recently opened files, whether they be documents, photos, or videos.

>> **User Account name and Power:** The Start menu's bottom section lists your user account name. Opposite the name, the power button awaits. Click it to put your computer to sleep, restart it, or shut it down for the day.

Pinned   Search box

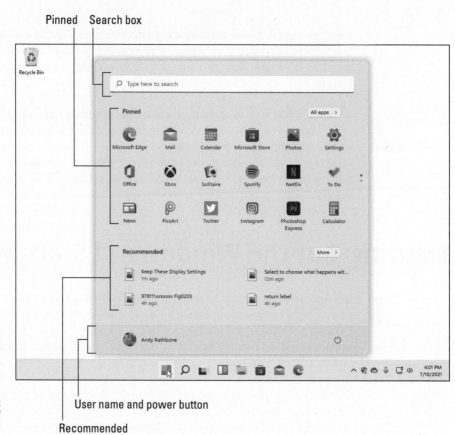

FIGURE 2-5:
The Start button
is always the
left-most icon on
your taskbar,
which lives along
the bottom of
the screen.

User name and power button

Recommended

TIP

Try the following tricks to make the Start menu feel a little more like home:

>> Keyboard fans can fetch the Start menu by pressing the ▦ key on their keyboard.

>> To launch a program or app, or to retrieve a recently used file, click or tap its name or icon. The program leaps to the screen.

All apps >

>> If you are unable to spot your desired program or app listed on the Start menu, click the All Apps button that lives across from the word *Pinned.* The Start menu changes to show all your apps sorted alphabetically.

>> On a touchscreen, navigate the Start menu with your finger: Tap an icon, and Windows launches the corresponding app or program.

The Start menu in Windows 11 looks quite different from the one found in previous versions of Windows. But it functions in a similar way: It lets you launch your programs and open your files.

Launching a Start menu program or app

All apps >

Windows stocks your Start menu's upper edge with *apps*, which are small programs for performing simple tasks. In fact, Windows now refers to *all* Windows programs as apps. To see *all* the apps and programs installed on your PC, click the All Apps button near the Start menu's upper-right corner. An alphabetical list of every installed program and app appears, ready for a mouse click or finger tap.

Each name on the Start menu is a button for starting an app or a traditional Windows program. Of course, Windows complicates things by offering several ways to launch an app or a program:

>> **Mouse:** Move the mouse pointer over the icon, and click the left mouse button.

>> **Keyboard:** Press the arrow keys until a box surrounds the desired icon. Then press the Enter key. (Press the Tab key to jump between different sections of the Start menu.)

>> **Touchscreen:** Tap the icon with your finger.

No matter which app you've chosen, it jumps onto the screen, ready to inform you, entertain you, or, if you're lucky, do both.

I explain the Start menu's built-in apps later in this chapter. If you feel like digging in, you can begin downloading and installing your own by clicking the Start menu's Microsoft Store icon. (I explain how to download apps in Chapter 6.)

Finding something on the Start menu

You can scour the Start menu until your eagle eyes spot the program, app, or icon you need, and then you can pounce on it with a quick mouse click or finger tap. But when the thrill of the hunt wanes, Windows offers several shortcuts for finding apps and programs hidden inside a crowded Start menu.

WHAT'S AN APP?

TIP

Short for *application,* apps herald from the world of *smartphones,* which is what people call cellphones that are powerful enough to run small programs. The newfangled Windows apps differ from traditional Windows programs in several ways:

- Unless preinstalled on your computer, Windows apps come from one place: the Microsoft Store app. The Microsoft Store app, one of several apps preinstalled on Windows, lets you download more apps. Once downloaded, the apps automatically install themselves on your computer. Many apps are free, but others cost money.

- In earlier Windows versions, only *Windows* apps can run on Windows. Windows 11 mixes that up by letting you also install apps from Android smartphones. (Or at least that's what Microsoft says will happen sometime in 2022.)

- Windows 11 apps run on your Windows 11 PC, laptop, and tablet. Some also run on an Xbox video game console.

- Most apps perform small tasks, usually in a way that works well on touchscreens. Some apps make it easier to visit websites such as Facebook. Others let you play games, listen to internet radio, track your car's mileage, or find nearby restaurants that are still open.

- Although most apps are fairly simple to use, their simplicity brings limitations. Unlike desktop programs, many apps don't let you copy words, photos, files, or web links. There's often no way to share an app's contents with a friend.

In an effort to sound young and hip, Windows now refers to traditional desktop programs as *apps.* Don't be surprised to hear most people still use the term *program* to describe older software designed for the Windows desktop, such as Photoshop or TurboTax.

In particular, look for these Start menu sections:

» **Pinned:** Windows stocks the Start menu's Pinned area with icons for popular apps and programs, as well as ads for new ones. I explain how to add or remove pinned items later in this chapter's "Adding or removing Start menu items" section.

» **Recommended:** When you open the Start menu, the menu automatically stocks the list's bottom edge with your most recently installed apps or documents. Click one to launch it and start working.

All Apps: The Start menu's top section lists apps that have been pinned to the section, much like pinning things to a map. However, Microsoft pinned the apps there, not you, so you might not see what you want. To see *all* the apps on your PC, click the All Apps button (shown in the margin) to see an alphabetical list of every app and program on your PC.

TIP

Chances are good that you'll spot your desired item on the Start menu without much digging. But when an app or program proves to be particularly elusive, try these tricks:

>> After opening the Start menu, keyboard owners can simply begin typing the name of their desired app or program, like this: **facebook.** As you type, Windows lists all the apps matching what you've typed so far, eventually narrowing down the search to the runaway.

>> If the apps you see don't reflect the way you work, it's time to customize the Start menu to meet your needs. Head for this chapter's upcoming "Customizing the Start menu" section for a heads up.

Viewing, closing, or returning to open apps

It's fairly easy to move from one open app to another. Because they're all open in windows on your desktop, you just click the app you want: It pops to the forefront, ready for work. (For more details about the desktop, flip ahead to Chapter 3.)

But what if the windows overlap, and you can't spot the one you want?

Whether you're running Windows on a PC, laptop, or tablet, you can bring any missing app to the forefront by following these two quick steps:

1. **Click or tap the Task View button.**

   The screen clears, and Windows displays miniature views of your open apps and programs, as shown in Figure 2-6.

2. **Tap or click any thumbnail to return the app or program to full size.**

These three tips can help you keep track of your running apps as well as close the ones you no longer want open:

>> Currently running apps and programs also appear as icons on the *taskbar,* the narrow strip along the bottom of the screen. (I cover the taskbar in Chapter 3.) Icons for apps that are open on the desktop have a little line or dot beneath them.

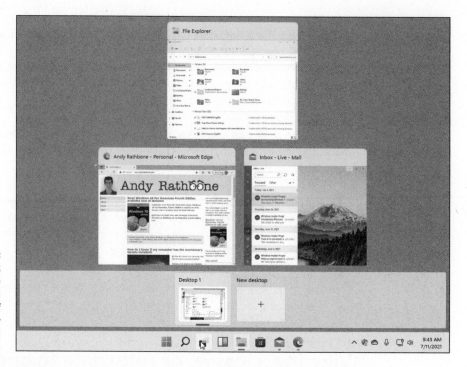

FIGURE 2-6:
Click the Task
View button to
see thumbnail
views of each of
your currently
running apps and
programs.

>> To close an unwanted app shown in thumbnail view, click or tap the X that appears in its upper-right corner. (The X only appears when your mouse pointer hovers over the thumbnail.) With a mouse, you can also right-click the app's thumbnail, and choose Close from the pop-up menu.

>> After you close an app, the miniature views of the other running apps remain onscreen, letting you either switch to them or close them. Or to leave the Task View mode, click or tap the desktop, away from the windows.

Getting to know your free apps

The Windows Start menu comes stocked with several free apps, each represented by an icon. Every icon sports a label beneath it, helping you know what's what.

NEW

Windows 11 only shows *icons* on the Start menu. It no longer shows the animated "live tiles" found in Windows 10.

Here are some of the most popular Windows 11 apps, ready to be launched at the click of a mouse or touch of a finger:

>> **Alarms & Clock:** This offers a world clock, timer, and stopwatch, but you'll probably visit for the alarm clock. It lets you set different wakeup times for every day of the week.

>> **Calculator:** With a toggle among standard, scientific, and a variety of converter modes, this app will please grade schoolers, math majors, chefs, and physicists.

>> **Calendar:** This app lets you add your appointments or grab them automatically from calendars you've already created through your online accounts. It works in tandem with the Mail app, and I cover them both in Chapter 10.

>> **Camera:** Covered in Chapter 17, the Camera app lets you snap photos with the camera built into most laptops, tablets, and some desktop PCs.

>> **File Explorer:** This app helps you manage your files by moving, copying, deleting, or searching for them. I cover all those tasks in Chapter 5.

>> **Get Help:** Click here to begin your journey through Microsoft's official technical support channels, all covered in Chapter 21.

>> **Get Started:** This program walks you through Windows 11, but also introduces Microsoft's paid services, like OneDrive.

>> **Groove Music:** Covered in Chapter 16, this app plays music stored on your PC and on OneDrive, Microsoft's built-in online storage service.

>> **Mail:** Covered in Chapter 10, the Mail app lets you send and receive email from most email accounts, including. Windows Live, Outlook, Yahoo!, and Google. When you enter your account's name and password, the Mail app sets itself up and automatically adds your contacts.

>> **Maps:** Handy for trip planning, the Maps app brings up a version of Microsoft Bing Maps.

>> **Microsoft Edge:** The browser in Windows 11, Microsoft Edge, replaces Internet Explorer. (Internet Explorer no longer appears in Windows 11.) I cover Microsoft Edge and web browsing in Chapter 9.

>> **Microsoft Solitaire Collection:** This collection of irresistible time wasters includes FreeCell and other games.

>> **Microsoft Store:** Covered in Chapter 6, the Microsoft Store is the only way to add more apps on your Start menu. The Microsoft Store also carries some programs you can install on your Windows desktop and Android phone, covered in Chapter 3.

>> **Mixed Reality Portal:** This app lets people wear funny-looking expensive headsets and pretend they're living in a 3D movie.

» **Movies & TV:** Microsoft's video storefront lets you rent or buy movies and TV shows, as covered in Chapter 17. The app also lets you watch videos you've taken with your camera or smartphone.

» **Office:** Click this advertisement to sign up for Microsoft's online version of Office. Called Office 365, it offers online versions of Word, Excel, PowerPoint, and others, all available through an annual fee.

» **OneDrive:** This term describes the Microsoft internet cubbyhole where you can store your files. By storing them online in OneDrive, covered in Chapter 5, you can access them from nearly any internet-connected computer, phone (both Android and Apple), or tablet.

» **Photos:** Covered in Chapter 17, the Photos app displays photos stored in your computer, as well as on OneDrive, your internet storage space.

» **Scan:** This delightfully simple program bypasses the complicated software bundled with most scanners to do one thing well: Scan your document.

» **Settings:** This takes you to the Windows 11 Settings app, which contains almost all the settings found in the Control Panel from earlier Windows versions. (I cover the Settings app in Chapter 12.)

» **Teams Chat:** This subset of Teams runs inside the Microsoft Edge browser so you can send messages and hold video chats with friends or coworkers.

» **Tips:** Drop by here to see flashcards listing steps for performing simple tasks in Windows 11.

» **Video Editor:** This simple video editor lets you crop videos or stitch photos and videos together with music to create slideshows.

» **Voice Recorder:** The name says it all. When the app appears, click the Microphone icon to begin recording; click the icon again to stop. The app lists your recordings, named by recording date and time, along its left edge for easy retrieval. (Right-click any recording's name to share, delete, or rename it, as well as to see its location in File Explorer.)

» **Weather:** This weather station forecasts a week's worth of weather in your area, but only if you grant it permission to access your location information. (Unless your computer has a GPS — Global Positioning System — the app narrows down your location by closest major city rather than street address.)

» **Windows Security:** Click this to access the built-in antivirus program. Flip ahead to Chapter 11 for more details.

» **Your Phone:** This newly revamped app helps you link your newer model Android phone with Windows to send and receive texts, access your contacts, make phone calls, see notifications, and even see your phone's screen on your PC. I cover the Your Phone app in Chapter 12.

TIP

I explain in Chapter 3 how to choose which apps and programs handle which tasks, but here's a temporary hint: Right-click a file and choose Open With. A menu appears, letting you choose which program should handle the job. The change takes place immediately.

Your Start menu may offer icons for programs that aren't already on your PC. Click the app to install it, and Microsoft receives a commission.

Adding or removing Start menu items

Microsoft dumped a random assortment of icons on the Windows 11 Start menu's *Pinned* area — the rows of icons that fill the top half of the Start menu. The resulting jumble consumes lots of real estate, includes advertisements, and is probably not tailored to *your* personal interests or work habits. This section shows how you can fix that shortcoming by removing, or *unpinning*, the extra icons from the Pinned area of the Start menu, and adding, or *pinning*, the ones you use most often.

TIP

Removing icons from the Start menu is easy, so you can begin there. To remove an unwanted or unused icons from the Start menu, right-click it and choose Unpin from Start from the pop-up menu. The unloved icon vanishes without fuss, freeing up some prime real estate. (This doesn't *uninstall* the app or program, mind you; any unpinned items can still be found in the Start menu's All Apps area.)

On a touchscreen, hold down your finger on the unwanted icon. When the pop-up menu appears, choose Unpin From Start to remove the icon.

After removing the unwanted items, spend some time *adding* items to the Start menu, making them as easy to reach as a pencil holder on an office desk.

To add programs or apps to the Start menu, follow these steps:

| All apps > |

1. **Click the Start button and when the Start menu appears, click the All Apps button, shown in the margin.**

   The Start menu presents an alphabetical list of all your installed apps and programs, even those you've just unpinned from the Start menu.

2. **Right-click the item you want to appear on the Pinned area of the Start menu; then choose Pin to Start.**

   Each selected item appears as a new Start menu icon. Repeat until you've added all the items you want. Unfortunately, you must right-click and pin each item separately. Windows doesn't let you select and add several items simultaneously.

3. **From the desktop, right-click desired items and choose Pin to Start.**

The Start menu icons aren't limited to apps and programs. From the desktop or even within File Manager, right-click any oft-used folder, file, or other item you want added to the Start menu and then choose Pin to Start from the pop-up menu.

When you're through, the Pinned area of your Start menu will have grown considerably with all your newly added destinations.

TIP

Can't find a newly installed app? Chances are good that it's hiding in the Start menu's All Apps area. If you want it visible in the Pinned area near the Start menu's top edge, you need to pin it there yourself.

After you've stuffed your Start menu's Pinned area with your favorite desktop destinations, head to this chapter's "Customizing the Start menu" section to finish organizing. When you finish, you'll have created a Start menu that meets your needs.

Customizing the Start menu

The Start menu contains mostly *icons* — little pictures that represent apps on your PC. The icons consume a lot of space, but they're not very organized. How can you find your favorite stuff?

Give yourself a fighting chance by organizing your Start menu. The following steps begin with a small dose of organization: removing unwanted apps and adding your own favorite apps to the Start menu's Pinned area. These steps won't uninstall any apps; they all remain safely on your PC. However, the Start menu's Pinned area will be full of apps that match your *own* interests.

But no matter how organized you want to be, follow these steps to begin turning that haphazard Start menu into your own organized list:

1. **Remove icons you don't need from the Pinned area.**

Spot an icon you don't need? Right-click it and choose Unpin from Start from the pop-up menu. Repeat until you've removed all the icons you don't use. (On a touchscreen, hold down your finger on an unwanted app and then tap Unpin from Start from the pop-up menu.)

REMEMBER

Choosing Unpin from Start doesn't *uninstall* the app or program; removing the icon merely removes that item's "start" button from the Start menu's Pinned area. In fact, if you accidentally remove the icon for a favorite app or program, you can easily put it back in Step 3.

2. **In the Start menu's Pinned area, move related icons next to each other.**

As an example, you might want to keep your people-oriented apps — Mail and Calendar — next to each other, and perhaps on the top row, as shown in Figure 2-7. To move an icon to a new location, move the mouse pointer over the icon, and then hold down the left mouse button as you drag the icon to the desired spot. As you drag the icon, other icons automatically move out of the way to make room for the newcomer.

TIP

On a touchscreen, hold down your finger on the app; when the pop-up menu appears, drag the app to its new position.

When you've dragged an app's icon to the desired spot, lift your finger or release the mouse button to set the icon into its new place.

NEW

Windows 11 no longer lets you change an icon's size on the Start menu. It also lacks the ability to place icons into groups of folders.

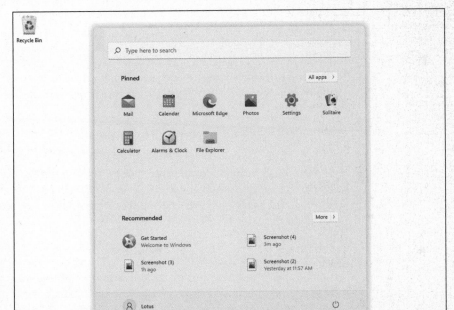

FIGURE 2-7: Your Start menu may be easier to work with when the Pinned area only shows your own favorite icons.

3. **Add icons for apps, programs, folders, and files you need.**

I explain how to add icons for apps, programs, folders, and files earlier, in this chapter's "Adding or removing Start menu items" section.

TIP

Newly added items appear at the bottom of the Start menu's Pinned area. To move an icon quickly to the top, right-click it and choose Move to Top from the pop-up menu.

After you purge any unwanted icons, rearrange the remaining icons, and add new icons for items you need, your Start menu may meet your needs. If so, stop. You're done!

PERSONALIZING THE START MENU

The Windows 11 Settings app offers additional ways to tweak the Start menu. I cover the Settings app in Chapter 12, but this sidebar applies particularly to the Start menu.

To find the Start menu settings, click the Start button, choose the Settings icon, and click the Settings app's Personalization button. When the Personalization page appears, click Start in the left pane, and the Start menu's options spill out to the right.

The Start menu section offers these options:

- **Show recently added apps:** A boon for those who hate to organize things, leave this on, and newly installed apps will automatically appear in the Start menu's Pinned area.

- **Show most used apps:** Another perk for the lazy, leave this on: The Start menu automatically stocks your Start menu's Pinned area with your most-used apps.

- **Show recently opened items in Start, Jump Lists, and File Explorer:** Leave this turned on so you can return to favorite destinations, both listed on the Start menu and on the taskbar's Jump Lists, covered in Chapter 3, as well as atop File Explorer's left corner.

- **Folders:** The Start menu's bottom edge normally lists your account name, a lot of empty space, and a power button. Click here to fill that empty space with links to your favorite folders and other things. You can add or remove links to Settings, File Explorer, Documents, Downloads, Music, Pictures, Videos, Network, and Personal Folder, which opens to show links to all your most popular folders.

There's no right or wrong way to set these settings. Stick with the default settings or experiment to see which settings work for you. The settings are all on-and-off toggle switches, so you can always return and flip the toggle again if a change doesn't meet your needs.

Exiting from Windows

Ah! The most pleasant thing you'll do with Windows all day could very well be to stop using it. Exiting Windows brings a hurdle to the process, however: You must decide whether to Sleep, Shutdown, or Restart your computer.

The answer depends on how long you're abandoning your computer. Are you simply stepping away from the computer for a few moments, or are you through working for the day?

I cover both scenarios — a temporary sojourn and leaving your computer for the day — in the next two sections.

If you don't want to trudge through a manual to figure out how to turn off your PC, here's the quickest way to turn it off:

1. **Click the Start button and then click the Power icon (shown in the margin) near the Start menu's lower-right corner.**

2. **Choose Shut Down from the pop-up menu.**

3. **If the computer protests, saying you'll lose unsaved work, choose Sleep instead.**

The following two sections deal with the finer points of what's become a complex chore.

TIP

Power users enjoy this quick shut down trick after they've saved their work: Right-click the Start button, choose Shut Down or Sign Out from the pop-up menu, and choose Shut Down from the pop-up menu.

Temporarily leaving your computer

Windows offers three options when you're leaving your computer temporarily, perhaps to reheat some fish in the office microwave and sneak back to your cubicle before anybody notices. To make the right choice among the various "temporary leave" scenarios in Windows, follow these steps:

1. **Click the Start button to fetch the Start menu.**

2. **Click your user account picture from the Start menu's lower-left corner.**

   From the menu that appears, shown in Figure 2-8, you can choose one of these options:

   - *Change Account Settings:* This option whisks you straight to the Settings app, where you can tweak your account's settings. You can change your user account photo, for example, or change an account password.

- *Lock:* Meant to add privacy while you take short trips to the water cooler, this option locks your PC, veiling your screen with the lock screen picture. When you return, unlock the screen by pressing any key and then typing your password. Windows quickly displays your work, just as you left it. To lock your computer quickly, press ▦ +L.

- *Sign Out:* Choose this option when you're through working at the PC and somebody else wants to have a go at it. Windows saves your work and your settings and then returns to the lock screen, ready for the next person to log on.

- *Another account:* Below your name, as shown in Figure 2-8, Windows lists names of any other accounts on the computer. If one of those people wants to borrow the computer for a few minutes while you're grabbing some coffee, let them choose their name from the list. When they type in their password, their customized screen appears, ready for them to work. When they sign out and you log back in, all your work reappears, just as you left it.

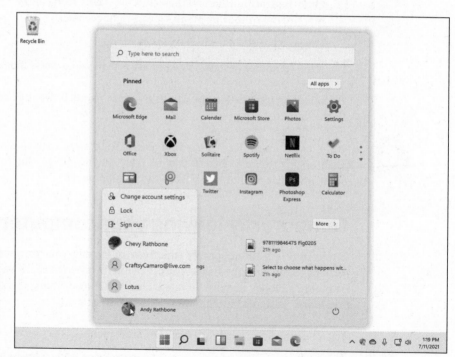

FIGURE 2-8:
Click your account name near the Start menu's lower-left corner to choose from these options.

Each of these options lets you give up your computer for a little while, but leaves it waiting for your return.

If you're finished for the day, though, you're ready for the next section.

Leaving your computer for the day

When you're done computing for the day — or perhaps you just want to shut down the laptop while on the subway or that flight to Rome — Windows offers three ways to handle the situation.

Follow this step to choose from the available options:

 Click the Start button and click the Power icon (shown in the margin).

The Power icon's pop-up menu offers three settings, as shown in Figure 2-9.

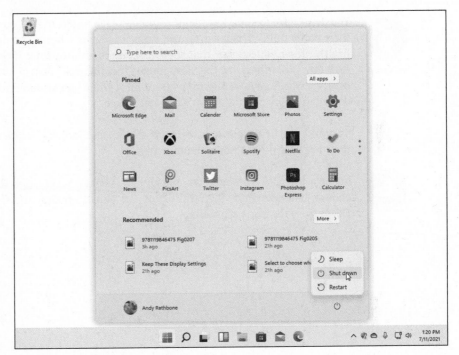

FIGURE 2-9:
The Power icon's pop-up menu options include Sleep, Shut Down, and Restart.

Here's the rundown on your options:

>> **Sleep:** The most popular choice, this saves your work in your PC's memory *and* on its hard drive and then lets your PC slumber in a low-power state. Later, when you return to your PC, Windows quickly presents everything — even your unsaved work — as if you'd never left. And if the power goes out, your PC will still wake up with everything saved, but it will take a few more seconds.

>> **Shut Down:** This option turns off your computer completely. It's just like Restart but without turning back on again. And if you're worried about preserving battery life on a laptop or tablet, it's your best choice.

>> **Restart:** Choose this option as a first cure when something weird happens (a program crashes, for example, or Windows seems dazed and confused). Windows turns off your computer and then starts itself anew, hopefully feeling better. (Patches from Windows Update, as well as newly installed programs, occasionally ask you to restart your PC.)

That should be enough to wade through. But if you have a little more time, here are some other facts to consider:

REMEMBER

You don't *have* to shut down your computer each night. In fact, some experts leave their computers turned on all the time, saying it's better for their computer's health. Other experts say that their computers are healthier if they're turned *off* each day. Still others say the Sleep mode gives them the best of both worlds. However, *everybody* says to turn off your monitor when you're done working. Monitors definitely enjoy cooling down when not in use.

To avoid overheating issues, turn off tablets and laptops before storing them in their bags for more than an hour or two.

TIP

To turn off your computer as quickly as possible, right-click the Start button, choose "Shut Down or Sign Out" from the pop-up menu, and then choose Shut Down from the pop-out menu.

Chapter **3**

The Traditional Desktop

After you turn on your PC and type in your user name and password, the Windows desktop fills the screen, ready for work. For the most part, the Windows 11 desktop works the same way it's worked for the past decade. It's where you arrange your work in onscreen windows and make things happen.

The Windows 11 new Start menu and its gang of apps bring many changes, but the desktop works much like the familiar workhorse of yesteryear. This chapter shows you how to make the desktop do your bidding.

Finding the Desktop and the Start Menu

The Windows 11 Start menu may look drastically different from its predecessors, but the *desktop*, shown in Figure 3-1, is almost indistinguishable from the one in Windows 7.

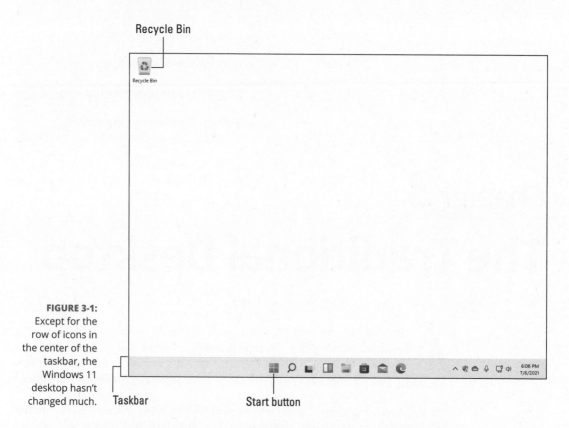

Recycle Bin

Taskbar Start button

FIGURE 3-1:
Except for the row of icons in the center of the taskbar, the Windows 11 desktop hasn't changed much.

The Windows 11 desktop runs most of the Windows programs that ran on your old Windows 7, Windows 8, or Windows 8.1 computer. Exceptions are antivirus programs, security suites, high-performance video games, and some utility programs. Those don't usually transfer well from one Windows version to another.

Unlike Windows 8 and Windows 8.1, Windows 11 runs apps within a window on the desktop.

WORKING ON THE DESKTOP WITH A TOUCHSCREEN

Windows 11 dumped the Tablet mode by automatically adding a little more space between icons, and widening the buttons and borders that appear on the desktop. Here's how to control the desktop with your fingers in Windows 11:

- **Select:** To select something on the desktop, tap it with a fingertip. If the pad of your index finger is too large, try tapping with your pinky finger.

- **Double-click:** To double-click something, tap it twice. Again, your fingertip works best.

- **Right-click:** To right-click an item, press your fingertip gently on it and wait for a small square to appear onscreen. When the square appears, remove your finger, and the pop-up menu stays on the screen. Then you can tap the option you want to choose from the menu.

If your fingertip still seems too wide for delicate desktop window maneuvers, buy a Bluetooth mouse and keyboard for your tablet. They turn your tablet into two computers: one that uses lightweight apps for casual computing and another with a full Windows desktop for doing some *real* work.

For more portability, try a Bluetooth pen. Bluetooth pens give you pinpoint precision for grabbing hard-to-reach items on a tablet's desktop.

Working with the Desktop

The desktop lets you run several apps and programs simultaneously, each living within its own little *window.* That separation lets you spread several programs across the screen, sharing bits of information among them.

When first installed, Windows starts with the freshly scrubbed, nearly empty desktop shown earlier in Figure 3-1. After you've been working for a while, your desktop will fill up with *icons* — little buttons that load your files with a quick double-click. Many people leave their desktops strewn with icons for easy access.

Other people organize their work: When they finish working on something, they store their files in *folders,* which are places for storing similar items, that I cover in Chapter 4.

No matter how you use the desktop, it comes with three main parts, labeled earlier in Figure 3-1:

>> **Start button:** To launch a program, click the Start button. It's the first icon on the right of the *taskbar*, that strip that runs along the bottom of your desktop. When the Start menu appears, click the name or icon for the app or program you want to run.

I cover the Start menu and all its quirks in Chapter 2. (Flip back to that chapter if you want to remove or rearrange the Start menu's app icons.) For easy access to your favorite programs, place them on your desktop's taskbar (described below).

>> **Taskbar:** Resting lazily along the bottom edge of your screen, the taskbar shows icons for the apps and programs you currently have open, as well as icons for launching a few favored programs. (Hover your mouse pointer over a program's icon on the taskbar to see the program's name or perhaps a thumbnail photo of that program in action.) I describe how to add your favorite programs' icons to the taskbar later in this chapter's "Customizing the taskbar" section.

>> **Recycle Bin:** The desktop's *Recycle Bin,* that wastebasket-shaped icon, stores your recently deleted files and folders for easy retrieval. Whew!

I cover these items later in this chapter and throughout the book, but the following tips will help you until you page ahead:

>> PC and laptop owners can start new projects directly from the Windows desktop: Right-click a blank part of the desktop, choose New Item, and choose the project of your dreams from the pop-up menu, be it loading a favorite program or creating a folder to store new files. (The New Item menu even lists some of your computer's programs, sparing you a journey back to the Start menu.)

REMEMBER

>> Are you befuddled about a desktop object's reason for being? Timidly rest the pointer over the mysterious doodad, and Windows often pops up a little box explaining what that thing is or does. Right-click the object, and the ever-helpful Windows usually tosses up a menu listing nearly everything you can do with that particular object. This trick works on most icons and buttons found on your desktop and its programs.

WARNING

>> All the icons on your desktop may suddenly disappear. To bring your work back to life, right-click your empty desktop and choose View from the pop-up menu. Then make sure the Show Desktop Icons menu option has a check mark so that everything stays visible.

Launching apps with the Start menu

The Start button lives on the left edge of your taskbar, that icon-filled strip centered along the desktop's bottom edge. A click or tap of the Start button fetches the Start menu, which lists your installed apps and programs. When the Start menu appears, you click the app or program you'd like to run.

I cover the Start menu in Chapter 2, but here's a quick step-by-step on how to open the Start menu and launch an app or program:

1. **Click the Start button, the left-most icon on your taskbar.**

   The Start menu appears, as shown in Figure 3-2.

   The Start menu automatically lists names of your most recently accessed apps and programs in its bottom edge. Above them, the Start menu displays icons of popular apps installed on your computer.

FIGURE 3-2:
You can launch apps and programs from the Start menu.

2. **If you see the app or program you want to launch listed on the Start menu, click it.**

   Click a name or an icon, and the app or program opens in a window on your desktop, ready for action.

Don't see the name of the app or program you want to launch? Click the All Apps button in the Start menu's upper-right corner to see an alphabetical list of all your apps and programs. From here, you have several choices:

» If you don't see your desired app's name, scroll down the list of names by clicking in the bar just to the right of the names. (I describe how to scroll with a scroll box in Chapter 4.)

» If the app you want to launch doesn't appear on the list, chances are good that it's not installed on your computer. To download it, open the Microsoft Store app, which I cover in Chapter 6.

You can also fetch the Start menu by pressing the key on your keyboard or tablet.

 After you've opened an app or program, you'll eventually want to close it, a task I cover in Chapter 4. (But here's a spoiler: To close an app, move your mouse pointer to the app's upper-right corner and click the little X, shown in the margin.)

I explain more about the Start menu, including how to customize it to meet your needs, in Chapter 2.

Jazzing up the desktop's background

To jazz up your desktop, Windows covers it with a pretty picture known as a *background*. (Many people refer to the background simply as *wallpaper*.)

TIP

Already looking at a photo you want to appear as your background? Right-click it and choose Set As Desktop Background from the pop-up menu. Your photo quickly splashes itself across your desktop to create a new background.

When you tire of the built-in scenery, feel free to replace it with a picture stored on your computer:

1. **Click the Start button, and choose the Settings icon.**

   The Settings icon resembles a gear. Click it, and the new Windows 11 Settings app appears. (I cover the Settings app in Chapter 12.)

2. **From the left column of the Settings app, click the Personalization icon, and from the right column, click the Background section.**

   The Personalization section of the Settings app opens to the Theme section. Scroll down and click the Background button; the Background section appears.

3. **From the Personalize Your Background section, click Picture from the adjacent drop-down menu. Below that menu, click the Browse Photos button, shown in Figure 3-3, and double-click your desired photo.**

Found a keeper? Double-click the photo, and you're done; your change takes place immediately. Or, if you're still searching, move to the next step.

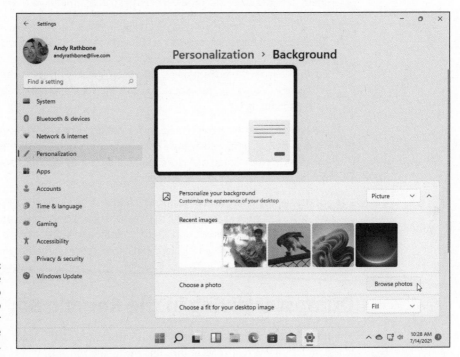

FIGURE 3-3:
Click the Browse Photos button to choose a photo from another folder for the background.

4. **Navigate to your Pictures folder.**

Most people store their digital photos in their Pictures folder, either on their PC or on OneDrive. (I explain how to browse folders, as well as OneDrive, in Chapter 5.)

5. **Click different pictures to see how they look as your desktop's background.**

When you find a background you like, you're done. The change takes place automatically. Exit the Settings app with a click in its upper-right corner, and your chosen photo drapes across your desktop, like wallpaper beneath your desktop's icons and open windows.

TIP

Here are some tips on changing your desktop's background:

>> Options listed on the Background page's Choose a Fit For Your Desktop Image menu let you choose whether the image should be *tiled* repeatedly across the screen, *centered* directly in the middle, or *stretched* to fill the entire screen. The Tile, Fill, and Fit options work best with small photos by repeating or enlarging them to fit the screen's borders. Feel free to experiment; you'll want different options for different sized photos.

>> The Microsoft Edge web browser can borrow most pictures found on the internet for a background. Right-click the website's picture and choose Save Picture As from the pop-up menu. Microsoft sneakily offers to copy the image into your Pictures folder, where you can choose it as a background in Step 4 of the preceding list.

>> If a background photograph makes your desktop icons too difficult to see, splash your desktop with a single color instead: In Step 3 of the preceding list, click Solid Color instead of Picture. When the colored squares appear, click one to splash its color across your desktop.

>> To change the entire *look* of Windows, choose Themes from the Personalization window's left edge in Step 2. The right pane lets you customize your computer's look by clicking the Background, Color, Sounds, and Mouse Cursor sections, and then changing them to your liking. I explain more about themes in Chapter 12.

Dumpster diving in the Recycle Bin

The Recycle Bin, that wastebasket icon in the upper-left corner of your desktop, works much like a *real* recycle bin. Shown in the margin, it lets you retrieve the discarded desktop files you thought you'd never need.

You can dump something from the desktop or File Explorer — a file or folder, for example — into the Recycle Bin in either of these ways:

>> Simply right-click the unwanted item and choose Delete from the pop-up menu. Windows asks cautiously if you're *sure* that you want to delete the item. Click Yes, and Windows dumps it into the Recycle Bin, just as if you'd dragged it there. Whoosh!

>> For a quick deletion rush, click the unwanted object and poke your Delete key.

Want something back? Double-click the Recycle Bin icon to see your recently deleted items. Right-click the item you want and choose Restore. The handy little Recycle Bin returns your precious item to the same spot where you deleted it.

(You can also resuscitate deleted items by dragging them to your desktop or any other folder; drag 'em back into the Recycle Bin to delete them again.)

TIP

The Recycle Bin can get pretty crowded. If you're searching frantically for a recently deleted file, tell the Recycle Bin to sort everything by the date and time you deleted it: Right-click an empty area inside the Recycle Bin and choose Sort By. Then choose Date Deleted from the pop-up menu.

TIP

To delete something *permanently,* just delete it from inside the Recycle Bin: Click it and press the Delete key. To delete *everything* in the Recycle Bin, right-click the Recycle Bin icon and choose Empty Recycle Bin.

To bypass the Recycle Bin completely when deleting files, hold down Shift while pressing Delete. Poof! The deleted object disappears, ne'er to be seen again — a handy trick when dealing with sensitive items, such as credit-card numbers or bleary-eyed selfies.

The Recycle Bin serves as an intelligent wastebasket, though. Here are a few other ways it shines:

>> The Recycle Bin icon changes from an empty wastepaper basket to a full one (as shown in the margin) as soon as it's holding any deleted file or files.

>> The Recycle Bin holds only items deleted from the *desktop, and your files and folders*. It doesn't retain information deleted from apps or programs.

>> Your Recycle Bin keeps your deleted files until the garbage consumes about 5 percent of your computer's available space. Then it automatically purges your oldest deleted files to make room for the new. If you're low on hard drive space, shrink the bin's size by right-clicking the Recycle Bin and choosing Properties. Decrease the Custom Size number to purge the bin more quickly; increase the number, and the Recycle Bin hangs onto files a little longer.

WARNING

>> The Recycle Bin saves only items deleted from your computer's *own* drives. That means it won't save anything deleted from a memory card, phone, MP3 player, flash drive, or digital camera.

>> Already emptied the Recycle Bin? You might still be able to retrieve the then-trashed-now-treasured item from the Windows File History backup, covered in Chapter 13.

WARNING

If you delete something from somebody else's computer over a network, it can't be retrieved. The Recycle Bin holds only items deleted from your *own* computer, not somebody else's computer. (For some awful reason, the Recycle Bin on the other person's computer doesn't save the item either.) Be careful, and make sure every computer in your house has a backup system in place.

Bellying Up to the Taskbar

Whenever more than one window sits across your desktop, you face a logistics problem: Programs and windows tend to overlap, making them difficult to spot. To make matters worse, programs such as web browsers and Microsoft Word can contain several windows apiece. How do you keep track of all the windows?

The Windows solution is the *taskbar* — a special area that keeps track of your currently running programs and their windows. Shown in Figure 3-4, the taskbar lives along the bottom of your desktop, constantly updating itself to show an icon for every currently running app or desktop program.

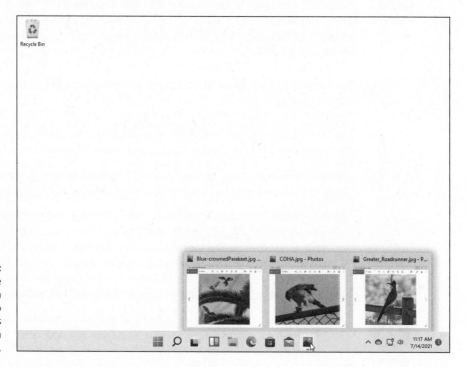

FIGURE 3-4:
Move the mouse pointer over a taskbar icon to see that app's currently open files.

The taskbar remains accessible along the screen's bottom edge, even when apps or the Start menu fill the screen.

TIP

The taskbar also serves as a place to launch your favorite programs. By keeping your favorite programs' icons in sight and one quick click away, you're spared a detour to the Start menu.

Not sure what a taskbar icon does? Rest your mouse pointer over any of the taskbar icons to see either the program's name or a thumbnail image of the program's contents, as shown in Figure 3-4. In that figure, for example, you can see that the Photos app displays three photos.

From the taskbar, you can perform powerful magic, as described in the following list:

>> To play with a program listed on the taskbar, click its icon. The window rises to the surface and rests atop any other open windows, ready for action. Clicking the taskbar icon yet again minimizes that same window.

REMEMBER

>> Whenever you load an app or program, its icon automatically appears on the taskbar. If one of your open windows ever gets lost on your desktop, click its icon on the taskbar to bring it to the forefront.

>> To close an app or program listed on the taskbar, right-click its icon and choose Close from the pop-up menu. The program quits, just as if you'd chosen its Exit command from within its own window. (The departing program thoughtfully gives you a chance to save your work before it quits and walks off the screen.)

>> Taskbar icons with a thin underline along their bottom edge let you know that their app or program is currently running.

NEW

>> Traditionally, the taskbar lives along your desktop's bottom edge, but earlier Windows versions let you move it to any edge you want. That feature disappeared from Windows 11; the taskbar now stays firmly affixed to the screen's bottom edge.

>> Can't find an open app or window? Click the taskbar's Task View icon (shown in the margin) to see thumbnails of *all* your open apps and programs. Click the one you want to revisit, and it rises to the top of the screen.

>> You can quickly jump to the taskbar page in the Settings app by right-clicking the taskbar and choosing Taskbar Settings.

>> If the taskbar keeps hiding below the screen's bottom edge, rest the mouse pointer to the screen's bottom edge until the taskbar surfaces. Then right-click the newly revealed taskbar and choose Taskbar Settings. When the Settings app opens to the Personalization page, scroll down to the Taskbar section. Click it to fetch the Taskbar page, and then click the Taskbar Behaviors menu and click the Automatically Hide The Taskbar option to remove its check mark.

TIP

You can add your favorite apps and programs directly to the taskbar: From the Start menu, right-click the favored program's name or icon, and choose Pin To Taskbar from the pop-up menu. The program's icon then lives on the taskbar for easy access, just as if it were running. Tired of the program hogging space on your taskbar? Right-click it and choose Unpin From Taskbar from the pop-up menu.

Shrinking windows to the taskbar and retrieving them

Windows spawn windows. You start with one window to write a letter of praise to your local deli. You open another window to check an address, and then yet another to ogle an online menu. Before you know it, four windows are crowded across the desktop.

To combat the clutter, Windows provides a simple means of window control: You can transform a window from a screen-cluttering square into a tiny button on the taskbar along the bottom of the screen. The solution is the Minimize button.

 See the three buttons lurking in just about every window's upper-right corner? Click the *Minimize button* — the button with the little line in it, shown in the margin. Whoosh! The window disappears, and is instead represented by its little icon on the taskbar, located as always at the bottom of the screen.

 To make a minimized program on the taskbar revert to a regular, onscreen window, just click its icon on the taskbar. Pretty simple, huh?

REMEMBER

It *is* simple, if you keep these things in mind:

>> Can't find the taskbar icon for the window you want to minimize or maximize? If you hover your mouse pointer over the taskbar icon, Windows displays a thumbnail photo of that program or the program's name.

>> If one program has several open files, say, Microsoft Word, then hover your mouse pointer over the Microsoft Word icon: A list appears, showing thumbnails of each open file. Click a thumbnail to return to that particular file.

>> When you minimize a window, you neither destroy its contents nor close the program. And when you click the window's name on the taskbar, it reopens to the same size you left it, showing its same contents.

Switching to different tasks from the taskbar's Jump Lists

The Windows taskbar doesn't limit you to opening programs and switching between windows. You can jump to other tasks, as well, by right-clicking the taskbar's icons. Right-clicking the File Explorer icon, for example, brings up a quick list of your recently visited folders, as shown in Figure 3-5. Click any folder on the list to make a quick return visit. Similarly, right-click the Edge app to see the last few websites you've visited.

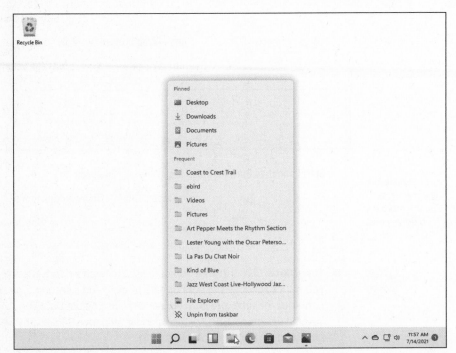

FIGURE 3-5:
Right-click File
Explorer to see a
clickable list of
recently visited
locations.

Called *Jump Lists*, these pop-up menus add a special trick to the taskbar: They let you quickly jump to previously visited locations, letting you work more efficiently.

Jump List items work any time, even when a program is closed. As long as a program's icon appears on the taskbar, you can access its Jump List. So even if you haven't opened File Explorer, for example, you can still right-click its taskbar icon and jump to a recently visited folder.

Clicking the taskbar's sensitive areas

Like a crafty card player, the taskbar comes with a few tips and tricks. For example, here's the lowdown on the icons near the taskbar's right edge, shown in Figure 3-6, known as the *Action Center*. Different items appear in the Action Center depending on your PC, your programs, and your PC's settings, but you'll probably encounter some of these:

>> **Show Desktop:** This small strip nestled against the taskbar's far-right edge instantly minimizes all open windows when you click it. Click it again to put the windows back in place. Windows 11 makes this strip nearly invisible, but it's still there; just point at the far-right edge. When the words Show Desktop appear, you're in the right place to click and minimize all your open windows.

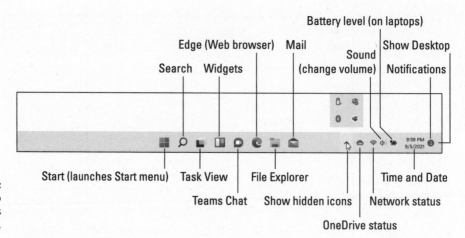

FIGURE 3-6:
Click the arrow to
see the taskbar's
hidden icons.

>> **Time/Date:** Click the time and date area to fetch a handy monthly calendar. If you want to change the time or date or even add a second time zone, right-click the time and date area and choose Adjust Date and Time, a task I cover in Chapter 12. Above the calendar, Windows 11 lists any waiting *notifications*, described later in this list.

>> **Bluetooth:** Click this to see your options for connecting wirelessly with Bluetooth, commonly used with mice, keyboards, and nearby speakers.

>> **Safely Remove Hardware:** Before unplugging a storage device, be it a tiny flash drive, a portable music player, or a portable hard drive, click here. That tells Windows to prepare the gadget for unplugging.

>> **Notifications:** When a small dot appears to the left of taskbar's time and date area, that means a notification awaits to tell you about newly arrived emails, upcoming appointments, and other tidbits. (A number inside the dot lists the number of waiting notifications.)

>> **Wired Network:** Found mostly on desktop PCs, this icon appears when you're connected to the internet or other PCs through a wired network. Not connected? The icon turns into a circle with a line through it.

>> **Wireless Network:** This appears when your PC is wirelessly connected to the internet or other network. The more waves you see on the icon, the more powerful your wireless signal. (I explain how to connect to wireless networks in Chapter 9.)

>> **Volume:** Click or tap the tiny speaker icon to adjust your PC's volume, as shown in Figure 3-7. Or right-click the volume icon and choose Open Volume Mixer to fetch a mixing panel. (Mixers let you adjust separate volume levels for each program, handy for keeping your music player's volume louder than your other programs' annoying beeps.) The volume slider also shows a list of

"Quick Action" icons that once lived in the Windows 10 Action Center; I cover those in this chapter's next section, "Seeing the Action Center and Notifications."

» **Task Manager:** Coveted by computer technicians, this little program can end misbehaving programs, monitor background tasks, track your PC's performance, and do other stuff of techie dreams.

» **Windows Update:** When you spot this icon, click it: Windows Update wants you to restart your computer so it can finish installing an update.

» **OneDrive:** When your computer is synchronizing its files with OneDrive (your internet storage space), little round arrows almost cover this icon.

» **Power, Outlet:** This shows that your laptop or tablet is plugged into an electrical outlet and is charging its battery.

» **Power, Battery:** Your laptop or tablet is running on batteries only. (Rest your mouse pointer over the icon to see how much power remains.)

» **Arrow:** Sometimes the taskbar hides things. If you see a tiny upward-pointing arrow at the start of the taskbar's notification area, click it to see a few hidden icons slide up and out. (Check out the later "Customizing the taskbar" section for tips and tricks on whether icons should hide from you.)

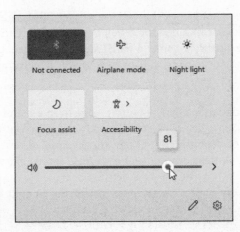

FIGURE 3-7: Slide the lever to adjust the volume.

You can pick and choose which notification icons should always be visible by right-clicking a blank portion of the taskbar and choosing Taskbar Settings. When the Taskbar Settings page appears, click Taskbar Corner Overflow, and choose which icons should appear by sliding their on/off toggles. (Turn on as many as will fit comfortably.)

NEW

WHERE IS CORTANA?

In earlier Windows versions, Cortana, Microsoft's personal assistant, struck up conversations about computer tasks. Some loved Cortana, but most must have felt it was an intrusion. So Microsoft removed Cortana from Windows 11. If you miss Cortana, bring it back by clicking the Start button, typing **Cortana,** and pressing Enter.

A window appears, where you sign in with your Microsoft account. Finish by giving Cortana access to your information, which allows Cortana to check your calendar, contacts, location, and search history. Armed with that information, Cortana can manage your appointments as it assists with your life.

As digital butlers go, Cortana lacks references from past employers, leading to a trust issue. Some people feel comfortable with robots managing parts of their lives, and others, understandably, are less comfortable with the thought.

Since Microsoft hid Cortana in Windows 11, the digital assistant will probably be phased out of Windows soon. Don't become too attached.

Seeing the Action Center and Notifications

NEW

Windows 11 brings *big* changes to the taskbar's icon-filled right edge. Back in Windows 10, the taskbar contained an *Action Center* icon. A click on the Action Center fetched the Notifications pane: a panel along the screen's right edge that listed bits of information alerting you to new email, appointments, results of security scans, and other news.

Nestled along the Notifications pane's bottom edge lived a list of icons that toggled handy settings. One quick click could quickly put your laptop into Airplane mode, for example; a click on the Night Light toggle dimmed your laptop's screen for working in poorly lit areas, saving your eyes from screen glare.

Windows 11 dumped the Action Center icon, preferring to split its job into two separate sections, as described in the following sections.

Viewing notifications

In Windows 11, a click on the taskbar's time and date area fetches not only a calendar, but a list of notifications above it, as shown in Figure 3-8. If no notifications await, you simply see the calendar, with nothing listed above it.

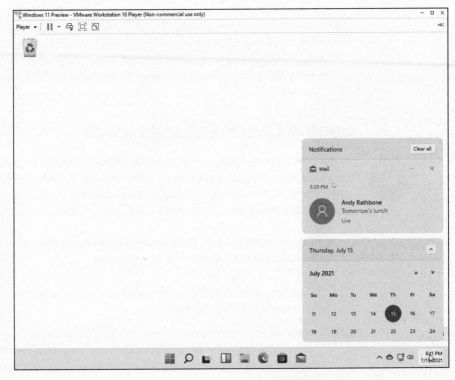

FIGURE 3-8:
Click the time and
date area to see
the Notifications
pane, which
displays current
information
about both your
life and your
computer.

Notifications may list information about your latest emails, for example, as well as times of upcoming appointments, news headlines, virus scan results, and other informational tidbits.

They first appear as a flash in the lower-left corner of your screen, hoping your eyes will dart to it and absorb it. Then they disappear, piling up in the Notifications pane.

Notifications can be dealt with in a variety of ways:

» Ignore them. You needn't even look at the Notifications pane. The notifications will simply pile up unread, with no damage done. Unless it's a reminder for a forgotten-but-upcoming appointment, a notification usually is more informational than urgent.

» Clear them all. If you grow weary of seeing a pile of notifications, click the Clear All button in the Notifications pane's upper-right corner. Whoosh, gone!

» Close any single notification by clicking the X in its upper-right corner.

» Stop seeing a particularly nagging notification by clicking the three dots next to the X in the notification's upper-right corner. When the drop-down menu appears, select Turn Off All Notifications from that app or program.

>> To choose which apps can bug you with notifications, click the three dots next to the X in any notification's upper-right corner. When the drop-down menu appears, click Go To Notification Settings. There, toggle switches let you choose which apps can and can't disturb you with their latest news.

Seeing Quick Settings icons

NEW

At the bottom of the Navigation pane, Windows 10 places its Quick Action icons: handy toggle switches for commonly used settings. Windows 11 shows those icons when you click the Sound or Network icons (located on the far right edge of the taskbar). And Windows 11 calls them *Quick Settings* icons.

Shown earlier in Figure 3-7, these icons appear most often, although Windows 11 lets you customize them to meet your own needs:

>> **Network or WiFi:** This displays information about your current network connections, including the internet.

>> **Bluetooth:** When turned on, this lets your PC communicate with other Bluetooth devices within range (about 30 feet). Common Bluetooth gadgetry includes speakers, smartphones, and smartwatches. I cover Bluetooth in Chapter 12.

>> **Location:** This lets you toggle your computer's knowledge of your geographic location, handy when looking at apps with maps or weather reports.

>> **All Settings:** A click here fetches the Windows 11 Settings app, a huge panel of organized switches, which replaces Control Panel found in older Windows versions. (You can also reach the Settings app by clicking the Start button and clicking the Settings icon.)

The available icons vary according to your model of computer or tablet.

TIP

You can customize the Quick Settings' bank of icons by clicking the little pencil icon in the section's lower-right corner. When pushpins appear next to the other icons, click a pushpin to remove an icon. To add an unlisted icon, click the word Add; a pop-up list offers other icons you can add with a click on their name.

Watching Widgets

NEW

Windows 11 introduces *Widgets*: a panel filled with news about weather, sports, world events, stocks, and other tidbits of up-to-the-minute information that already appear on our phones, websites, TVs, radios, and wristwatches.

To see the Widgets in Windows 11, click the Widgets icon (shown in the margin) from its home on the taskbar. A panel appears along the screen's left edge, shown in Figure 3-9, showing information.

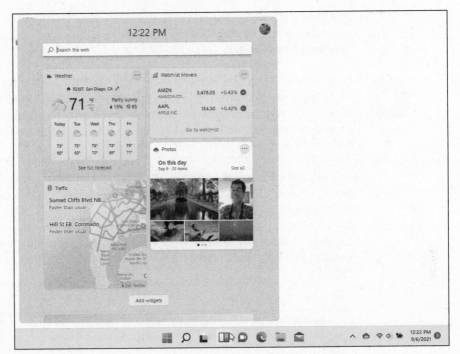

FIGURE 3-9:
Click the taskbar's
Widgets icon,
and the Widgets
panel appears.

The Widgets fill themselves automatically with information gathered from the internet, and there's not much you can do with them. Here are a few tricks, though, to make the Widgets match your interests:

>> A click on the Add Widgets button lets you customize the panel with even more informational boxes: upcoming appointments, for example, current traffic information, or a to-do list.

>> To customize a particular Widget, click the little three dots in that Widget's upper-right corner. A menu appears, letting you customize the stocks that appear in the Watchlist Movers window, for example.

Behind the scenes, though, Widgets provides Microsoft with a way to know your interests, which make you more valuable to advertisers. And in today's technology-based world, that's increasingly important stuff.

Customizing the taskbar

Windows offers a whirlwind of options for the lowly taskbar, letting you play with it in more ways than a strand of spaghetti and a fork.

And that's especially important if you don't care for the new Start menu: By stocking the taskbar with icons for oft-used programs, you can avoid unnecessary trips to the Start menu.

NEW

First, the taskbar comes preloaded with icons for five apps: the new Widgets app (breaking news headlines), File Explorer (your file browser), Microsoft Edge (the Windows 11 web browser), the Microsoft Store app (for downloading apps and programs), and the Mail app. All but the first four taskbar icons are movable, so feel free to drag them to any order you want.

You can add your own favorites to the taskbar, as well. When you spot a favored program's icon on the Start menu, right-click the icon, and choose Pin To Taskbar from the next pop-up menu.

For even more customization, right-click a blank part of the taskbar and choose Taskbar Settings. The Taskbar page appears in the Settings app, as shown in Figure 3-10.

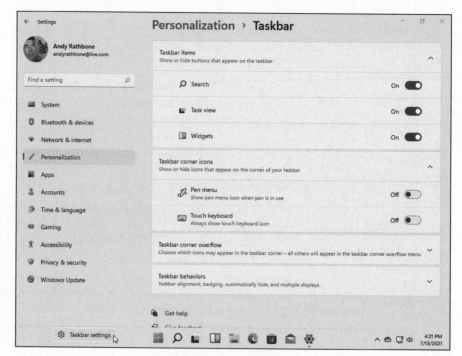

FIGURE 3-10:
Right-click a blank portion of the taskbar and choose Taskbar Settings to customize the taskbar's appearance and behavior.

Table 3-1 explains the most-used taskbar settings, as well as my recommendations for them.

TABLE 3-1   **Most-Used Taskbar Settings**

Setting	My Recommendations
Taskbar items	These toggle switches let you add or remove the Search, Task View, and Widgets options. I read way too much news already, so I turn off the entire Widgets panel with a click of its toggle.
Taskbar Corner Icons	On and off toggle switches live here, designed mostly for touchscreens, that let you add icons for a digital pen and touchscreen keyboard. I keep these turned off on my desktop PC, but turned *on* on my tablets.
Taskbar Corner Overflow	Another bundle of toggle switches let you choose which tiny icons should appear on your taskbar's far right edge, and which should be hidden, only to pop up when you click the little upward pointing arrow next to those icons. This is a personal choice, but I don't like hidden icons, so I let them all show.
Taskbar Behaviors	I ignore this overwhelming number of toggles except for one: In Taskbar Alignment, I choose left, which moves the currently centered icons and Start button back to the left corner, where they've lived for years.

Feel free to experiment with this section's many toggle switches until the taskbar looks right for you. Your changes take place immediately. Don't like the change, or don't notice a big difference? Click the toggle switch again to reverse your decision.

Again, most of these toggles boil down to personal preference; there's no standard right or wrong for everybody. People who run Windows 11 on very wide monitors often prefer seeing their taskbar icons centered rather than along the traditional left side.

Setting Up Virtual Desktops

TECHNICAL
STUFF

Most people work with the same set of windows, over and over. Some people type into a word processor all day; others enter numbers into boxes. Because these people stick with one program, they can easily fire up their PC and begin working.

Others work on a wide variety of tasks and programs, and they meticulously arrange their programs and windows for the easiest access. To please the meticulous, Windows 11 continues with the Virtual Desktops introduced in Windows 10. They're a simple way of organizing and switching between entire *groups* of windows.

You can create one desktop for writing, for example, complete with a word processor, notepad, and procrastinator's toys. A second desktop can be arranged for video gaming, and a third can contain a browser stocked with favorite websites that constantly update in the background. At work, add a fourth for Facebook, so you can quickly switch back to your work desktop when the boss walks by.

Virtual desktops let you switch among these desktops quickly and easily, saving you the time it takes to rearrange the programs and windows to your liking.

To create virtual desktops and work between them, follow these steps:

1. **Click the taskbar's Task View icon.**

   A click or tap on the Task View icon, shown in the margin, and the screen clears, showing thumbnails of all your currently open windows. Just above the Task View icon, shown in Figure 3-11, you see a miniature view of your desktop. To the right of it, a blank window shows the words New Desktop.

2. **Click the words New Desktop, and your empty new desktop fills the screen.**

   The thumbnail expands into a new desktop. The new desktop is a replica of your original desktop but without any open programs or windows.

FIGURE 3-11:
Click the taskbar's Task View icon, and the words New Desktop appear above the taskbar.

That's it. You've created a second virtual desktop and switched to it. Windows keeps your other desktop tucked away until you want to switch back to it with a return click on the Task View icon.

Some people love virtual desktops. Other people find the whole concept needless and confusing. But whether you love or hate virtual desktops, these tips will come in handy:

>> To switch between desktops, click the Task View icon. When your miniature virtual desktop windows appear along the taskbar's top edge, as shown in Figure 3-12, click the one you want.

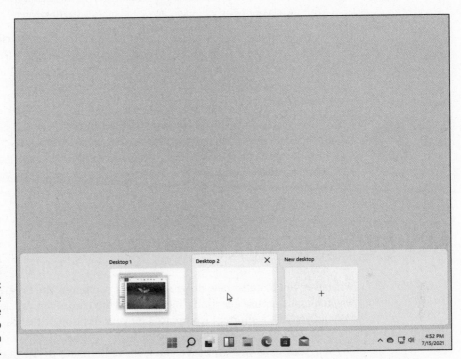

FIGURE 3-12:
When the thumbnail of the second desktop appears, switch to it with a click.

>> To see a virtual desktop's currently open windows, click the Task View icon. When the miniature desktops appear along the taskbar's top edge, rest (or *hover*) your mouse pointer over a miniature desktop; the screen changes to show thumbnails of *that* desktop's open windows. To revisit a window on any desktop, just click the window's thumbnail.

>> To close an unwanted desktop, click the Task View icon, and then click the X (shown in the margin) in that miniature desktop's thumbnail. (Hover your mouse pointer over the miniature desktop, and the X appears.) Any open windows on that desktop will be dumped onto your original, "real" desktop. That's important: You won't lose any unsaved work by accidentally closing a virtual desktop.

>> To create even more virtual desktops, click the Task View icon. From the screen that appears, click the plus sign (shown in the margin) in the center of the miniature desktop.

>> Keyboard lovers can add a desktop by holding the Windows key and then pressing Ctrl+D. Your current desktop immediately disappears, replaced by a new, empty desktop. (Pressing ⊞+Tab opens the Task View mode, letting you see all your open windows, as well as any virtual desktops.)

>> To move an open window from one virtual desktop to another, click the Task View icon to see the thumbnails of your open virtual desktops. Then drag the desired window down to the desired desktop thumbnail along the screen's bottom edge. (Right-clicking a desired window fetches a pop-up menu that lists all your virtual desktop options.)

NEW

>> Keen-eyed upgraders from Windows 10 will notice the lack of a sliding bar along the screen's right edge in Figures 3-11 and 3-12. Windows 10 let you slide that bar up or down to revisit apps and websites you opened in the last 30 days. Known as *Timeline*, the feature is no longer included in Windows 11.

Making Programs Easier to Find

Whenever you install a new program on your computer, the program usually asks way too many obtuse questions. But perk up your ears when you see this question: "Would you like a shortcut icon placed on your desktop or taskbar?"

Say yes, please, as that will save you from dashing out to the Start menu to find the program's icon.

But if your favorite programs don't yet have icons on the desktop or taskbar, put them there by following these steps:

1. **Head to the Start menu, and click the All Apps button in the upper-right corner.**

As you scroll up or down, an alphabetical list of icons for all your apps and programs scrolls up or down as well.

2. **Right-click the name of any program or app you want to appear on the taskbar, choose More from the pop-up menu, and choose Pin To Taskbar from the second pop-up menu.**

If you're using a touchscreen, hold down your finger on the desired app icon for a second or two. Then lift your finger, tap the word More, and tap the Pin To Taskbar option on the pop-up menu.

Now, instead of heading to the Start menu, you can launch your oft-used apps with a click on their taskbar icon.

After you've stocked your taskbar with icons, pretend they're numbered, from left to right. (Skip the Start, Search, Widgets, and Task View icons, which don't count.) Pressing ▦+1 from the desktop opens the first program; ▦+2 opens the second program; and so on. You've created automatic shortcuts!

Don't care for the Search, Widgets, or Task View icons? Windows 11 won't let you move them, but you can *hide* them: Right-click the unwanted icon and choose Hide From Taskbar from the pop-up menu.

Chapter **4**

Basic Desktop Window Mechanics

The Windows Start menu simply contains icons and an occasional button. It's easy to see what you're poking at with a finger or mouse.

The Windows desktop, by contrast, includes lots of movable windows, each with miniscule, monochrome buttons, tiny lettering, unlabeled buttons, and pencil-thin borders. The windows come with way too many parts, many with confusing names that programs expect you to remember. To give you a hand, this chapter provides a lesson in basic windows anatomy and navigation.

You eventually need to know this stuff because windows tend to overlap on the desktop; you need to manually push and prod them into view. And if you think you already know this stuff from Windows 10, think again: Windows 11 brings drastic changes to File Explorer.

I've dissected each part of a window so you know what happens when you click or touch each portion. By all means, use this book's margins to scribble notes as you move from the fairly simple Start menu to the powerful yet complicated Windows desktop.

Dissecting a Typical Desktop Window

Figure 4-1 places a typical window on the slab, with all its parts labeled. You might recognize the window as File Explorer's Quick Access section, the first area that appears when you open File Explorer.

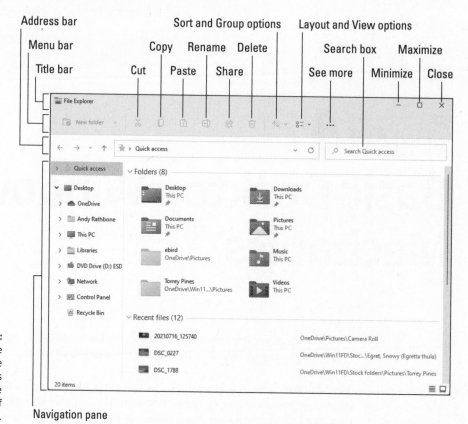

Just as boxers grimace differently depending on where they've been punched, windows behave differently depending on where they've been clicked. The next few sections describe the main parts of the File Explorer window in Figure 4-1, how to click them, and how Windows jerks in response.

> » Windows veterans remember their My Documents folder, that stash for almost all their files. Windows now calls it simply the Documents folder. (No matter what it's called, you're still supposed to stash your files inside it.) Similarly, Microsoft dropped the "My" from the Music, Videos, and other oft-used folders.

>> In Windows 10, a thick, control-filled panel called the Ribbon lives atop every folder. Windows 11 replaces the Ribbon with dimly lit, gray icons with no names. Most of the cryptic new icons don't even reveal their name when you hover a mouse pointer over them. Luckily, I've labeled them all in Figure 4-1.

>> Windows no longer shows libraries in the Navigation pane. Most people won't miss them. If you do, put them back: Right-click a blank place inside the Navigation pane and choose Show Libraries from the pop-up menu.

>> Windows no longer shows Homegroups in the Navigation pane, either. There's no way to put them back. I cover alternative networking and file-sharing solutions in Chapter 15.

>> Windows is full of little oddly shaped buttons, borders, and boxes. You don't need to remember all their names, although that would give you a leg up on figuring out the scholarly Windows Help menus. When you spot an odd portion of a window, just return to this chapter, look up its name in Figure 4-1, and read its explanation.

>> You can deal with most things in Windows by clicking, double-clicking, or right-clicking. Hint: When in doubt, always right-click.

>> Navigating desktop windows on a touchscreen computer? For some touching tips, drop by the sidebar in Chapter 3 on touching desktop programs on a Windows tablet.

>> After you click a few windows a few times, you realize how easy it is to boss them around. The hard part is finding the right controls for the *first* time, like figuring out the dashboard on that rental car.

Tugging on a window's title bar

Found atop nearly every window (see examples in Figure 4-2), the title bar usually lists the program name and, if applicable, the file, folder, or section that it's currently displaying. For example, Figure 4-2 shows the title bars living atop File Explorer (top) and the Settings app (bottom).

Although mild-mannered, the mundane title bar holds hidden powers, described in the following tips:

>> To find the window you're currently working on, look at the title bar along the window's top edge. One title bar will usually be slightly darker than the other, and its window casts a gray shadow over the other windows. See how File Explorer (Figure 4-2, top) casts a slight shadow over the Settings app's title bar (Figure 4-2, bottom)? That distinguishes that window from windows you *aren't* working on. By glancing at all the title bars on the desktop, you can tell which window is awake and accepting anything you type.

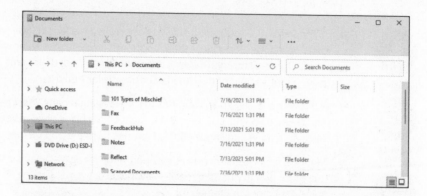

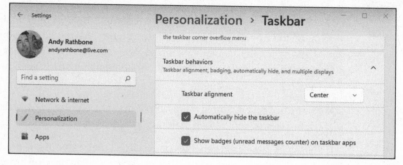

FIGURE 4-2:
A title bar across
the top of File
Explorer (top) and
the Settings app
(bottom).

>> Windows 11 isn't consistent with its title bars. Most programs have them, but some apps don't show title bars at all, much less show them in different colors. Windows 11 continues that trend toward monotone confusion.

>> On the positive side, title bars make convenient handles for moving windows around your desktop. Move the mouse pointer to a blank part of the title bar, hold down the mouse button, and move the mouse around: The window follows along as you move your mouse. Found the right location? Let go of the mouse button, and the window sets up camp in its new spot.

>> Don't see a title bar across a window's top edge? Microsoft still put it there, but sneakily made it invisible. To reposition that window, aim the mouse pointer at the window's top, where the title bar *should* be, and drag the window to its new place on your desktop.

>> Double-click a blank portion of the title bar, and the window leaps to fill the entire desktop. Double-click it again, and the window retreats to its previous size.

>> All programs and apps place three buttons on the right end of every title bar. From left to right, they let you Minimize, Restore (or Maximize), or Close a window, topics all covered in the "Maneuvering Windows Around the Desktop" section, later in this chapter.

TIP

DRAGGING, DROPPING, AND RUNNING

Although the phrase *drag and drop* sounds as if it's straight out of a Mafia guidebook, it's really a nonviolent mouse trick used throughout Windows. Dragging and dropping is a way of moving something — say, an icon on your desktop — from one place to another.

To *drag,* put the mouse pointer over the icon and *hold down* the left or right mouse button. (I prefer the right mouse button.) As you move the mouse across your desk, the pointer drags the icon across the screen. Place the pointer/icon where you want it and release the mouse button. The icon *drops,* unharmed.

Holding down the *right* mouse button while dragging and dropping makes Windows toss up a helpful little menu, asking whether you want to *copy* or *move* the icon.

Helpful Tip Department: Did you start dragging something and realize midstream that you're dragging the wrong item? Don't let go of the mouse button — instead, press Esc to cancel the action. Whew! (If you've dragged with your right mouse button and already let go of the button, you can take another exit: Choose Cancel from the pop-up menu.)

>> Don't see those three buttons at the top of the title bar? In another odd move, Microsoft sometimes makes them invisible. They'll appear if you point the mouse where the buttons should be, which is the window's upper-right corner.

Navigating folders with a window's Address bar

Directly beneath every open folder's title bar or menu bar lives the *Address bar,* shown near the top of the folder in Figure 4-3. Web surfers will experience déjà vu: The Windows Address bar is lifted straight from the top edge of web browsers and glued atop every open folder.

FIGURE 4-3:
An Address bar.

The Address bar's four main parts, described from left to right in the following list, perform four different duties:

» **Backward and Forward buttons:** These two arrows track your path as you forage through your PC's folders. The Backward button backtracks to the folder you just visited. The Forward button brings you back.

» **Down Arrow button:** Click this extraordinarily tiny arrow to see a drop-down list of folders you've visited previously. You can click any listed folder for a quick revisit.

» **Up Arrow button:** Click the Up Arrow button to move up one folder from your current folder. For example, if you've been sorting files in your Documents folder's "Stuff" folder, click the Up arrow to return to your Documents folder.

» **Address:** Just as a web browser's Address bar lists a website's address, the Windows Address bar displays your current folder's address — its location inside your PC. For example, the Address bar shown in Figure 4-3 shows two words: This PC, and Documents. Those words tell you that you're looking inside the Documents folder on This PC. (That's *your* PC, as opposed to somebody else's PC.) Yes, addresses are complicated enough to warrant an entire chapter: Chapter 5.

» **Search box:** Every Windows folder sports a Search box. Instead of searching the internet, though, it rummages through your current folder's contents. For example, if you type the word **carrot** into a folder's Search box, Windows digs through that folder's contents and retrieves every file or folder mentioning *carrot.* (For more tips on finding things, flip ahead to Chapter 7.)

TIP

In the Address bar, notice the little arrows between the words *This PC* and *Documents.* The arrows offer quick trips to other folders. Click any arrow — the one to the right of the word *Documents,* for example. A little menu drops down from the arrow, letting you jump to any other folder inside your Documents folder.

Figuring out your folder's new Menu bars

Desktop windows have more menu items than an Asian restaurant. To keep everybody's minds on computer commands instead of a tasty seaweed salad, Windows places menus and icons on a strip that lives atop every folder. (See Figure 4-4.)

NEW

In Windows 11, these new menus and icons replace the Ribbon, a menu-filled strip found in earlier Windows versions.

FIGURE 4-4:
The Pictures
folder's
Menu bar.

The menus change depending on the window's contents, as well as the items you select in that folder. Click on a photo in a folder, for example, and the far right option changes to Set as Background: a quick way to splash that photo across your desktop.

Just as restaurants sometimes run out of specials, a window sometimes isn't capable of offering all its menu items. Any unavailable options are *grayed out*, like the Paste option in Figure 4-4. But if you click on the More icon — the three dots on the bar's far right edge in Figure 4-5 — you can see additional items that don't fit on the menu.

FIGURE 4-5:
Click the More
icon to see
additional
options.

TIP

Make the window wider by stretching its edges outward, and more options appear on the Menu bar, described later in this chapter's "Boring borders" section.

You needn't know much about the Menu bar because Windows automatically places the correct buttons atop each program's window. Open a photo, for example, and the Menu bar quickly spouts a new icons for rotating upside-down photos.

If a button's meaning isn't immediately obvious, hover your mouse pointer over it; a little message usually explains the button's purpose.

Quick shortcuts with the Navigation pane

Look at most "real" desktops, and you'll see the most-used items sitting within arm's reach: the coffee cup, the stapler, and perhaps a few crumbs from the coffee room snacks. Similarly, Windows gathers your PC's most frequently used items and places them in the Navigation pane, shown in Figure 4-6.

FIGURE 4-6:
The Navigation pane offers shortcuts to places you visit most frequently.

Found along the left edge of every folder, the Navigation pane contains several main sections: Quick Access, OneDrive, and This PC. (On PCs connected through a network, you'll see an entry for Network, as well.) Click any of those sections — Quick Access, for example — and the window's right side quickly shows you the contents of what you've clicked.

Here's a more detailed description of each part of the Navigation pane:

» **Quick Access:** Formerly called *Favorites,* these locations serve as clickable shortcuts to your most frequently accessed locations in Windows. The little "pin" icon next to their name means they're pinned to that area, and they won't disappear.

- **Desktop:** A quick click here brings you right back to your desktop, where most people store their favorite files and folders.

- **Downloads:** Click this shortcut to find the files you've downloaded while browsing the internet. Ah, that's where they ended up!

- **Documents:** A perennial favorite, this folder stores most of your work: spreadsheets, reports, letters, and other things you've created.

- **Pictures:** Another popular destination, this takes you to photos you've shot yourself or saved from the internet.

- **Recently accessed areas:** The Quick Access area automatically places links to your most frequently accessed folders. Since they lack pins next to them, they're temporary. If Windows notices that you visit other places more often, those new places will replace the older ones.

» **OneDrive:** This online storage space was handed to you by Microsoft when you created a Microsoft account. (Without a Microsoft account, it's simply another folder on your PC.) Because OneDrive is password-protected and online, it's tempting to fill it with favorite files for access from any PC, phone, or other internet-connected device. But when your stored files exceed your 5GB free storage limit, Microsoft asks for your credit card to pay for the extra space. I cover OneDrive at the end of Chapter 5.

» **This PC:** This section lets you browse through your PC's folders and hard drives. (Many of these commonly used storage areas live in the Quick Access area of the Navigation pane, as well.) The This PC section holds these areas:

- **Desktop:** Click this to see the files and folders stored on your desktop.

- **Documents:** This opens the Documents folder, a convenient repository for letters, forms, and reports.

- **Downloads:** Downloaded a file from a website? Then look in here to be reintroduced.

- **Music:** Yep, this shortcut jumps straight to your Music folder, where a double-click on a song starts it playing through your PC's speakers.

- **Pictures:** This shortcut opens your Pictures folder, the living quarters for all your digital photos.

- **Videos:** Click here to visit your Videos folder, where a double-click on a video opens it for immediate viewing.

- **Local Disk (C:):** A holdover for old techies, this entry lets you crawl through the hundreds of folders on your PC. Unless you know specifically what item you're seeking, though, you probably won't find it. Stick with the other destinations instead.

- **Disc Drives:** If your PC includes extra disc drives, like DVD drives, icons for those appear here. Insert a flash drive into your USB port, and its icon appears here, as well.

>> **Network:** After you create a network from the PCs in your home, their names appear here. I cover networks in Chapter 15.

Here are a few tips for making the most of your Navigation pane:

>> To avoid treks back to the Start menu, add your own favorite places to the Navigation pane's Quick Access area: Right-click a favorite folder and choose Pin To Quick Access from the pop-up menu. (Similarly, right-click any unwanted listing in the Quick Access area and remove it by choosing Unpin From Quick Access.)

>> If you've connected to a network at home or work, the pane's This PC section may include those other computers' music, video, and photos (which are sometimes referred to as *media*). Click those computers' icons to access those goodies as if they were stored on your own computer.

>> Old-time Windows owners may notice that Windows 11 doesn't show libraries in the Navigation pane. Libraries still exist, but they're hidden in the background. To bring them back into view, click a blank portion of the Navigation pane and choose Show Libraries from the pop-up menu. (You must also manually add the Public folders to each library to return them to the glory days of Windows 7.)

Moving inside a window with its scroll bar

The scroll bar, which resembles a cutaway of an elevator shaft (see Figure 4-7), rests along the edge of all overstuffed windows. And in Windows 11, those elevator shafts are narrower than ever. Sometimes they don't appear until you hover your mouse pointer over a window's border.

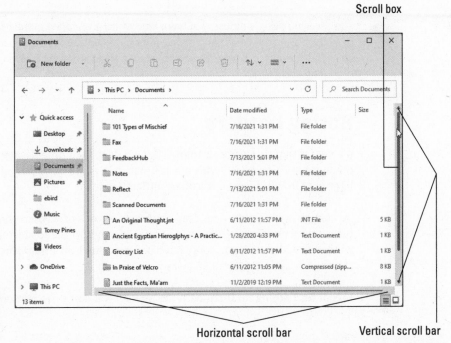

Scroll box

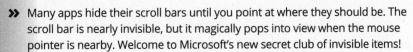

FIGURE 4-7:
Horizontal
and vertical
scroll bars.

Horizontal scroll bar

Vertical scroll bar

Inside the shaft, a little elevator (technically, the *scroll box*) rides along as you move through the window's contents. In fact, by glancing at the box's position in the scroll bar, you can tell whether you're viewing items in the window's beginning, middle, or end.

By clicking in various places on the scroll bar, you can quickly view different parts of things. Here's the dirt:

>> Click inside the scroll bar in the direction you want to view. On a *vertical* scroll bar, for example, click above the scroll box to move your view up one page. Similarly, click below the scroll box to move your view down a page.

>> Many apps hide their scroll bars until you point at where they should be. The scroll bar is nearly invisible, but it magically pops into view when the mouse pointer is nearby. Welcome to Microsoft's new secret club of invisible items!

>> Don't see a scroll bar or a box in the bar, even when you point your mouse at the screen's border? Then you're already seeing everything that the window has to offer; there's nothing to scroll.

>> To move around in a hurry, drag the scroll box inside the scroll bar. As you drag, you see the window's contents race past. When you see the spot you want, let go of the mouse button to stay at that viewing position.

» Are you using a mouse that has a little wheel embedded in the poor critter's back? Spin the wheel, and the elevator moves inside the scroll bar, shifting your view accordingly. It's a handy way to explore an icon-packed folder or long document.

Boring borders

A *border* is that thin edge surrounding a window, including desktop windows containing apps. Compared with a scroll bar, it's really tiny. And since it's usually light gray in Windows 11, it's often difficult to see.

To change a window's size, drag the border in or out. (When the mouse pointer turns into a two-headed arrow, you're in the right place to start dragging.) Some windows, oddly enough, don't have borders. Stuck in limbo, their size can't be changed — even if they're an awkward size.

Except for tugging on them with the mouse, you don't use borders much.

TIP

WHEN ONE JUST ISN'T ENOUGH

Normally, you can select only one thing at a time in Windows. When you click another file, for example, Windows deselects the first file to select the second. If you want to select several files or folders simultaneously, try these tricks:

- To select more than one file or folder, hold down the Ctrl key and click each item you want. Each item stays highlighted. On a tablet, hold your finger down on a file or folder to select it. (You may see check boxes appear around adjacent files or folders, letting you select multiple items by clicking their check boxes.)

- To select a bunch of adjacent files from a list inside a folder, click the first file you want. Then hold down Shift and click the last file you want. Windows immediately highlights the first file, last file, and every file in between. Pretty sneaky, huh? (To weed out a few unwanted files from the middle, hold down Ctrl and click them; Windows unhighlights them, leaving the rest highlighted.)

- Finally, when grabbing bunches of files or folders, try using the "lasso" trick: Move the mouse pointer to an area of the screen next to one item and, while holding down the mouse button, move the mouse until you've drawn a lasso around all the items. After you've highlighted the files or folders you want, let go of the mouse button, and they remain highlighted. (On tablets, your finger works as a mouse when lassoing items.)

Maneuvering Windows Around the Desktop

A terrible dealer at the poker table, Windows tosses windows around your desktop in a seemingly random way. Programs cover each other or sometimes dangle off the desktop. The following sections show you how to gather all your windows into a neat pile, placing your favorite window on the top of the stack. If you prefer, lay them all down like a poker hand. As an added bonus, you can change their size, making them open to any size you want, automatically.

Moving a window to the top of the pile

Windows says the window atop the pile that's getting all the attention is called the *active* window. Being the active window means that it receives any keystrokes you or your cat happen to type.

You can move a window to the top of the pile so that it's active in any of several ways:

>> Move the mouse pointer until it hovers over any portion of your desired window; then click the mouse button. Windows immediately brings the window to the top of the pile.

>> On the taskbar (located along the bottom of the desktop), click the icon for the window you want. Chapter 3 explains what the taskbar can do in more detail.

TIP

>> Hold down the Alt key while tapping and releasing the Tab key. With each tap of the Tab key, a small window pops up, displaying a thumbnail of each open window on your desktop. (You also see thumbnails of open Start menu apps.) When your press of the Tab key highlights your favorite window, let go of the Alt key, and your window leaps to the forefront.

>> A click of the Task View button (shown in the margin) also places miniature views of each window on the screen, even if they're on different virtual desktops. Click the desired miniature window, and it rises to the top, ready for action. I cover the Task View button and virtual desktops in Chapter 3.

NEW

Windows 10 offered a solution for cluttered desktops: You could hold down your mouse pointer on your desired window's title bar and give it a few quick shakes; Windows drops the other windows down to the taskbar, leaving your main window resting alone on an empty desktop. Windows 11 dropped that feature, for some shaky reason.

Moving a window from here to there

Sometimes you want to move a window to a different place on the desktop. Perhaps part of the window hangs off the edge, and you want it centered. Or maybe you want one window closer to another.

In either case, you can move a window by dragging and dropping its *title bar*, that thick bar along its top. (If you're not sure how dragging and dropping works, see the sidebar "Dragging, dropping, and running," earlier in this chapter.) When you *drop* the window in place, the window not only remains where you've dragged and dropped it, but it also stays on top of the pile — until you click another window, that is, which brings *that* window to the pile's top.

Here's a historical tidbit: Title bars used to always contain the *title* of the app or program, hence, the name *title bar*. Now, many apps leave out the title. Nevertheless, you can still tug those apps around by dragging their title bar, just as before.

Making a window fill the whole desktop

Sooner or later, you'll grow tired of all this multiwindow mumbo jumbo. Why can't you just make one window fill the screen? Well, you can.

To make any desktop window grow as large as possible, double-click its *title bar*, that bar along the window's topmost edge. The window leaps up to fill the entire desktop, covering up all the other windows.

To reduce the pumped-up window back to its former size, double-click its title bar once again. The window quickly shrinks to its former size, and you can see things that it covered.

» If you're morally opposed to double-clicking a window's title bar to expand it, you can click the Maximize button. Shown in the margin, it's the middle of the three buttons in the upper-right corner of every window.

» When a window is maximized to fill the desktop, the Maximize button turns into a Restore button, shown in the margin. Click the Restore button, and the window returns to its smaller size.

» Need a brute force method? Then drag a window's top edge until it butts against the top edge of your desktop. The shadow of the window's borders will expand to fill the desktop; let go of the mouse button, and the window's borders fill the desktop. (Yes, simply double-clicking the title bar is faster, but this method impresses any onlookers from neighboring cubicles.)

Too busy to reach for the mouse? Maximize the current window by holding down the ▦ key and pressing the up-arrow key. (Hold down the ▦ key and press the down-arrow key to return to normal size.)

Closing a window

When you're through working in a window, close it: Click the little X in its upper-right corner. Zap! You're back to an empty desktop.

If you try to close your window before finishing your work, be it a game of Solitaire or a report for the boss, Windows cautiously asks whether you'd like to save your work. Take it up on its offer by clicking Yes and, if necessary, typing in a filename so that you can find your work later.

Making a window bigger or smaller

Like big lazy dogs, windows tend to flop on top of one another. To space your windows more evenly, you can resize them by dragging and dropping their edges inward or outward. It works like this:

1. **Point at any corner with the mouse arrow. When the arrow turns into a two-headed arrow, you can hold down the mouse button and drag the corner in or out to change the window's size.**

2. **When you're happy with the window's new size, release the mouse button.**

   The window settles down into its new position.

Neatly placing windows side by side

The longer you use Windows, the more likely you are to want to see two windows side by side. For example, you may want to copy things from one window into another or compare two versions of the same file. By spending a few hours with the mouse, you can drag and drop the windows' corners until they're in perfect juxtaposition.

If you're impatient, Windows lets you speed up this handy side-by-side placement in several ways:

>> For the quickest solution, drag a window's title bar against one side of your desktop; when your mouse pointer touches the edge of the desktop, let go of the mouse button. Repeat these same steps with the second window, dragging it to the opposite side of the desktop.

TIP

>> If you drag a window to fill one edge of the screen, Windows immediately shows thumbnails of your minimized windows. Click the thumbnail of the window you'd like to see fill the screen's other half.

>> To place four windows onscreen simultaneously, drag the title bar of each window to a different corner of the screen. Each window resizes itself to grab its own quarter of the screen.

>> To make the current window fill the desktop's right half, hold the ⊞ key and press the right-arrow key. To fill the desktop's left half, hold the ⊞ key and press the left-arrow key.

NEW

>> Windows 11 adds yet *another* way to organize open windows. Hover your mouse pointer over the window's Maximize button and a grid appears, shown in Figure 4-8. The grid shows different ways to organize your windows. Click a spot on the grid; it lights up, and you're set: Your window quickly resizes itself and jumps there. This works best for people with large monitors with a lot of space for windows. The more space on your desktop, the more spaces you see on the grid.

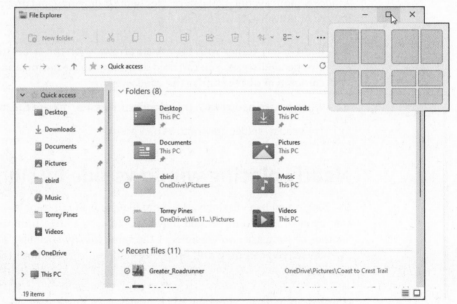

FIGURE 4-8:
Click the spot on the grid where the window should position itself.

Making windows open to the same darn size

Sometimes a window opens to a small square; other times, it opens to fill the entire desktop. But windows rarely open to the exact size you want. Until you discover this trick, that is: When you *manually* adjust the size and placement of a window, Windows remembers that size and always reopens the window to that same size. Follow these three steps to see how it works:

1. **Open your window.**

The window opens to its usual unwanted size.

2. **Drag the window's corners until the window is the exact size and in the exact location you want. Let go of the mouse to drop the corner into its new position.**

Be sure to resize the window *manually* by dragging its corners or edges with the mouse. Simply clicking the Maximize button won't work.

3. **Immediately close the window.**

Windows memorizes the size and placement of a window at the time it was last closed. When you open that window again, it should open to the same size you last left it. But the changes you made apply only to the program you made them in. For example, changes made to the File Explorer window will be remembered only for *File Explorer,* not for other programs you open.

Most windows follow these sizing rules, but a few renegades may misbehave, unfortunately.

> » **Navigating drives, folders, and flash drives**
>
> » **Creating and naming folders**
>
> » **Selecting and deselecting items**
>
> » **Copying and moving files and folders**
>
> » **Writing to CDs and memory cards**
>
> » **Understanding Windows OneDrive**

Chapter 5

Storing and Organizing Files

By leaving their paper-strewn oak desktops and moving to computers, people hoped things would be much easier. Important papers would no longer slide behind the desk or languish in dusty drawers. Thirty years later, though, we know the truth: Computers come with just as many nooks, crannies, and hiding places as did the desks they replaced . . . maybe even more.

In Windows, File Explorer serves as your computerized file cabinet. Plug a flash drive or portable hard drive into your computer, and File Explorer appears, ready for you to start rustling through folders.

You're stuck with File Explorer whenever you need to find folders inside your computer, *outside* your computer on plug-in drives and digital cameras, and even in some storage spots on the internet called *clouds*.

Whether you're using a touchscreen tablet, a laptop, or a desktop PC, files and folders still rule the computing world. And unless you grasp the Windows folder metaphor, you may not find your information very easily.

This chapter explains how to put File Explorer to work. (You may recognize it as *Windows Explorer*, its name from older Windows versions.) This chapter also explains how to use OneDrive, your cloud storage space, to store files away from your computer and on the internet, instead.

Along the way, you ingest just enough Windows file management skills for you to save and retrieve your work without too much discomfort.

NEW

MANAGING FILES ON A TOUCHSCREEN

Simply put, a finger is larger than a tiny mouse pointer. That simple size difference led previous Windows versions to come with a special Tablet mode. In Windows 10, for example, Tablet mode includes big buttons and finger-friendly apps that fill the screen, hiding the desktop.

With Windows 11, Microsoft finally figured out a way to ditch Tablet mode: What you see on a desktop PC is almost identical to what you see on a tablet. But on a tablet, the icons now *automatically* space themselves far enough for finger control.

Whether running on a tablet, laptop or wide-screen desktop PC, Windows 11 looks and behaves nearly the same. Or at least, that's what Microsoft says; your finger-sliding mileage may vary. File Manager, in particular, can still be cumbersome on a touchscreen.

If Windows 11 still seems difficult to control with your fingers, consider investing in an inexpensive and portable Bluetooth (wireless) mouse for clicking the controls. And, to remove the tablet's onscreen keyboard that blocks much of your view of the desktop, consider buying a portable Bluetooth keyboard or pen as well.

If you want your tablet to double as a desktop PC, buy a *docking station* instead. A docking station lives on your office desk and lets you permanently attach a monitor, wired mouse, and wired keyboard. Then, when you slide your tablet into a docking station, it's nearly indistinguishable from a desktop PC.

To avoid a docking station, consider buying a touchscreen laptop with a hinge that folds backward. Then you can prop it on a table like a PC monitor, allowing you to easily attach a full-sized keyboard, mouse, or even a full-sized keyboard with a trackball.

Browsing the File Explorer File Cabinets

To keep your programs and files neatly arranged, Windows cleaned up the squeaky old file cabinet metaphor with whisper-quiet Windows icons. Inside File Explorer, the icons represent your computer's storage areas, allowing you to copy, move, rename, or delete your files before the investigators arrive.

 To open File Explorer, shown in Figure 5-1, and begin rummaging around inside your computer, click the File Explorer icon. Shown in the margin, it's near the middle of the taskbar's row of icons along the bottom of your screen.

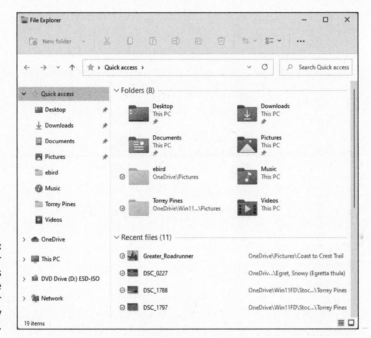

FIGURE 5-1:
The File Explorer window displays popular storage areas and your most recently opened files.

In previous versions of Windows, File Explorer opened to show your computer's largest file cabinets, called *drives* or *disks* in computer lingo. Windows 11 goes one step further.

NEW

Instead of dropping you off at the drives and forcing you to dig for your files, the Windows 11 File Explorer tries to be more helpful. It simply lists your most popular folders along the top, in its Folders section. For example, it shows Documents, where you store most of your files, and Downloads, the holding tank for everything you download from the internet. (You also see shortcuts to your Music, Videos, and Pictures folders, as well as your Desktop.)

Below those main folders, in the Recent Files section, File Explorer may list short-cuts to the items you've opened most recently. If you worked on a spreadsheet yesterday, for example, find it again by opening File Explorer: A link to that spreadsheet lives in the Recent Files section, ready to be reopened with a double-click.

Seeing your main storage folders and recently opened files may be all you need to start working. But if you need to see *all* your computer's storage areas, click the words This PC in the pane along the left edge. File Explorer opens to a similar view, but with your computer's storage areas — hard drives, disk drives, flash drives, and similar holding tanks — listed below them, shown in Figure 5-2.

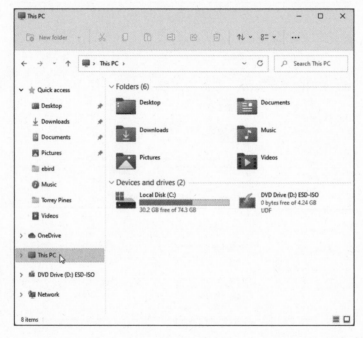

FIGURE 5-2:
Click This PC
to see your
computer's
storage areas,
which you can
open to find
your files.

The File Explorer images shown in Figure 5-2 will look slightly different from the ones on your PC, but you should still see the same basic sections:

>> **Navigation pane:** The handy Navigation pane, that strip along every folder's left edge, lists shortcuts to different storage spaces on your PC, on OneDrive, and on any other connected computers. (I cover the Navigation pane in Chapter 4.)

>> **Folders:** When opened, File Explorer lists shortcuts to your main storage folders, as well as your *computing history,* a list of recently accessed folders and files. Unless you're starting a brand-new project, you can probably find your most recent work here.

>> **Devices and Drives:** Shown in Figure 5-2, this area lists your PC's storage areas and devices. (The term *devices* usually refers to gadgets plugged into your PC.) Every computer has at least one hard drive. Double-clicking a hard drive icon displays its files and folders, but you can rarely find much useful information when probing that way. No, your most important files live in your Documents, Music, Pictures, and Videos folders, which appear near the top of Figure 5-2.

Notice the hard drive bearing the little Windows icon (shown in the margin)? That means that Windows 11 lives on that drive. If you click the Layout and View icon from the top menu and select Tiles, a multicolored line appears next to each drive's icon. The more colored space you see in the line, the more files you've stuffed onto your drive. When the line turns red, your drive is almost full, and you should think about deleting some unwanted files, uninstalling some unused programs, or upgrading to a larger drive.

You may also see some detachable gadgetry attached to your computer. Here are some of the more common items:

- **CD, DVD, and Blu-ray drives:** As shown in Figure 5-2, Windows places a short description next to each drive's icon. For example, *CD-RW* means the drive can store files on *CDs* but not DVDs. *DVD-RW* means that it can both read and store files onto DVDs *and* CDs. A *BD-ROM* drive can read Blu-ray discs, but it can store files only to CDs and DVDs. And the ever-so-versatile *BD-RE* and *BD-R* drives can read and store files onto Blu-ray discs, DVDs, *and* CDs.

  Writing information to a disc is called *burning.* Copying information from a disc is called *ripping.*

- **Flash drives:** The icon for some flash drive brands resembles the actual flash drive. Most flash drives simply show a generic icon like the one in the margin.

TIP

Windows doesn't usually display icons for your computer's memory card readers until you've inserted a card into them. To see icons for your *empty* card readers, open File Explorer, click the Layout and View Options icon, and click Show from the drop down menu. Finally, select the Hidden Items option from the drop-down menu. To hide them again, take a few breaths, and then repeat these steps.

- **iPads, phones, and MP3 players:** Android phones, iPads, and iPhones usually receive a generic icon of a hard drive, tablet, or MP3 player. Some let you copy photos to and from the device; others don't. If you own an iPhone or iPad, you need the Apple iTunes software (www.apple.com/itunes) that runs on the Windows desktop. Windows can't copy songs to and from an iPhone or iPad by itself. (I cover MP3 players in Chapter 16.)

- **Cameras:** When plugged into your computer's USB port, digital cameras usually appear as camera icons in the File Explorer window. To import your camera's photos, turn on your camera and set it to its View Photos mode rather than its Take Photos mode. Then right-click the camera's icon in File Explorer and choose Import Pictures and Videos from the pop-up menu. After Windows walks you through the process of extracting the images (see Chapter 17), it places the photos in either your Pictures folder or OneDrive's Picture folder.

If you plug a digital camcorder, phone, or other gadget into your PC, the File Explorer window often sprouts a new icon representing your gadget. If Windows neglects to ask what you'd like to do with your newly plugged-in gadget, right-click the icon to open a list of everything you can do with that item. No icon? Then you need to install a *driver* for your gadget, a precipitous journey detailed in Chapter 13.

To see the contents of an item listed in File Explorer, perhaps a flash drive or your digital camera, double-click it. To back out of that view, click the left-pointing arrow (shown in the margin) above the Navigation pane.

TIP

Tip for tablets: When you read the word *click,* substitute *tap.* Similarly, *right-click* means *touch and hold.* And the term *drag and drop* means *slide your finger along the screen as if your finger is the mouse pointer and then lift the finger to drop the item.*

Getting the Lowdown on Folders

This stuff is dreadfully boring, but if you don't read it, you'll be just as lost as your files.

A *folder* is a storage area, just like a real folder in a file cabinet. Windows divides your computer's hard drives into many folders to separate your many projects. For example, you store all your music in your Music folder and your pictures in your Pictures folder. That lets both you and your programs find them easily.

NEW

Windows gives you several main folders for storing your files. For easy access, they live in the This PC section of the Navigation pane along the left side of every folder. Shown earlier, Figure 5-2 shows your main storage areas: Desktop, Documents, Downloads, Music, Pictures, and Videos. (Microsoft removed the 3D Objects folder, a head-scratcher found in Windows 10.)

Keep these folder facts in mind when shuffling files in Windows:

>> You can ignore folders and dump all your files onto the Windows desktop. But that's like tossing everything into your car's back seat and pawing around to find your sunglasses a month later. Organized stuff is much easier to find.

>> If you're eager to create a folder or two (and it's pretty easy), page ahead to this chapter's "Creating a New Folder" section.

>> The Windows 11 web browser, Microsoft Edge, conveniently drops all your downloaded files into your Downloads folder. Until you delete them, every file you download from the internet lives on inside that folder.

>> File Explorer folders use a tree metaphor. File Explorer shows an icon for a drive which, when clicked on, branches out into folders. Click on a folder, and it branches out into even *more* folders. Keep clicking inside those folders, and eventually, you reach files, which represent the leaves on your computerized tree.

TECHNICAL STUFF

Peering into Your Drives, Folders, and Other Media

Knowing all this folder stuff not only impresses computer store employees but also helps you find the files you want. (See the preceding section for a lowdown on which folder holds what.) Put on your hard hat and get ready to go spelunking among your computer's drives and folders as well as your CDs, DVDs, and smartphones. The following sections are your guide.

Seeing the files on a drive

Like everything else in Windows, disk drives are represented by buttons or *icons*. File Explorer also shows information stored in other areas, such as phones, digital cameras, networked gadgetry, portable hard drives, flash drives, and scanners. (I explain these icons in the section "Browsing the File Explorer File Cabinets," earlier in this chapter.)

Opening an icon usually lets you access the device's contents and move files back and forth, just as with any other folders in Windows.

When you double-click a hard drive icon in File Explorer, for example, Windows promptly opens the drive to show you the folders packed inside. But how should Windows react when you insert something new into your computer, such as a CD, DVD, or flash drive?

Earlier versions of Windows tried to second-guess you. When you inserted a music CD, for example, Windows automatically began playing the music. Today's newer, politer Windows, by contrast, asks how you prefer it to handle the situation, as shown by the pop-up notification in the lower-right corner of Figure 5-3.

FIGURE 5-3:
Windows asks how it should handle newly inserted items.

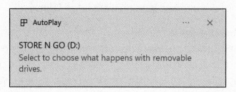

When that message appears, choose it with a click of the mouse. A second message appears, as shown in Figure 5-4, listing every way your PC and its gang of apps and programs can handle that item.

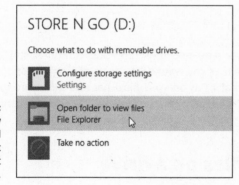

FIGURE 5-4:
Choose how Windows should react the next time you insert that item.

Choose an option — Open Folder To View Files, for example — and Windows fires up File Explorer to display your newly inserted drive's contents. The next time you plug that drive into your PC, your computer won't bother asking; it will automatically summon File Explorer and display your drive's folders.

But what if you change your mind about how Windows should treat a newly inserted item? Then you need to change how Windows reacts: In the This PC section of File Explorer, right-click the inserted item's icon, choose Show More Options, and choose Open AutoPlay. Once again, Windows shows the message from Figure 5-4 and asks you to plot the future course.

TIP

Adjusting the AutoPlay settings comes in particularly handy for USB thumb drives. If your flash drive carries a few songs, Windows may want to play them, slowing your access to your flash drive's other files. To prevent that, select the AutoPlay option, Open Folder to View Files.

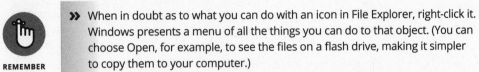

REMEMBER

» When in doubt as to what you can do with an icon in File Explorer, right-click it. Windows presents a menu of all the things you can do to that object. (You can choose Open, for example, to see the files on a flash drive, making it simpler to copy them to your computer.)

» If you double-click an icon for a CD, DVD, or Blu-ray drive when no disk is in the drive, Windows stops you, gently suggesting that you insert a disk before proceeding further.

» Spot an icon under the heading Network Location? That's a little doorway for peering into other computers linked to your computer — if there are any. You find more network stuff in Chapter 15.

Seeing what's inside a folder

Because folders are really little storage compartments, Windows uses a picture of a little folder to represent a place for storing files.

To see what's inside a folder, either in File Explorer or on the Windows desktop, just double-click that folder's picture. A new window pops up, showing that folder's contents. Spot another folder inside that folder? Double-click that one to see what's inside. Keep clicking until you find what you want or reach a dead end.

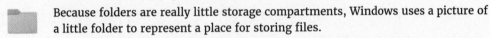

Reached a dead end? If you mistakenly end up in the wrong folder, back your way out as if you're browsing the web. Click the tiny Back arrow (shown in the margin) at the window's top-left corner. That shows you the contents of the folder you just left. If you keep clicking the Back arrow, you end up right where you started.

The Address bar provides another quick way to jump to different places in your PC. As you move from folder to folder, the folder's Address bar — that wide word-filled box at the folder's top — constantly keeps track of your trek.

Notice the little arrows between the folder names. Those little arrows provide quick shortcuts to other folders and windows. If you try clicking any of the arrows, menus appear, listing the places you can jump to from that point. For example, click the arrow after Music, shown in Figure 5-5, and a menu drops down, letting you jump quickly to your other folders.

TECHNICAL STUFF

WHAT'S ALL THIS PATH STUFF?

A *path* is merely the file's address, similar to your street address. When a letter is mailed to your house, for example, it travels to your country, state, city, street, and (with any luck) apartment or house. A computer path does the same thing. It starts with the letter of the disk drive and ends with the file's name. In between, the path lists all the folders the computer must travel through to reach the file.

For example, look at the Downloads folder. For Windows to find a file stored in my Downloads folder, it starts from the computer's C: drive, travels through the Users folder, and then goes through the Andy folder. From there, it goes into the Andy folder's Downloads folder. (Microsoft Edge follows that path when saving your downloaded files.)

Take a deep breath and exhale slowly. Now add in the computer's ugly grammar: In a path, the Windows disk drive letter is referred to as C:\. The disk drive letter and colon make up the first part of the path. All the other folders are inside the big C: folder, so they're listed after the C: part. Windows separates these nested folders with something called a *backslash,* or \. The downloaded file's name — *Tax Form 3890,* for example — comes last.

Put it all together, and you get C:\Users\Andy\Downloads\Tax Form 3890. That's my computer's official path to the *Tax Form 3890 file in Andy's Downloads folder.* Of course, on your computer, you can substitute your own username for *Andy.* (Microsoft account usernames usually start with the first few letters of the linked Microsoft account email address.)

This stuff can be tricky, so here it is again: The letter for the drive comes first, followed by a colon and a backslash. Then come the names of all the folders leading to the file, separated by backslashes. Last comes the name of the file itself.

Windows automatically puts together the path for you when you click folders — thankfully. But whenever you click the Browse button to look for a file, you're navigating through folders and traversing along the path leading to the file.

TIP

Here are some more tips for finding your way in and out of folders:

>> Sometimes a folder contains too many files or folders to fit in the window. To see more files, click that window's scroll bars along a window's bottom or right edges. (I cover scroll bars in your field guide, Chapter 4.)

>> While burrowing deeply into folders, take note of the little arrows in File Explorer's upper-left corner, just to the left of the Address bar. Click the little downward-pointing arrow, and a menu drops down, listing the folders you've plowed past on your journey. Click any name to jump quickly to that folder.

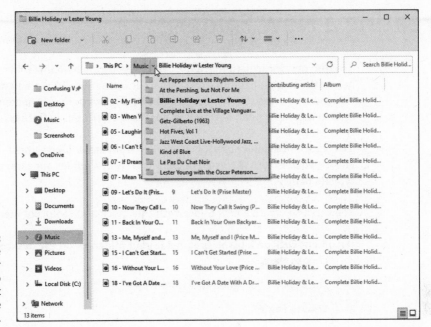

FIGURE 5-5:
Click the little
arrow after
Music to jump to
any place that
appears in the
Music folder.

» Click the Up Arrow button, located just to the left of the Address bar, to move your view up one folder. Keep clicking it, and you'll eventually wind up at someplace recognizable: your desktop.

» Can't find a particular file or folder? Instead of aimlessly rummaging through folders, check out the Start menu's Search box, which I describe in Chapter 7. The Search box can automatically find your lost files, folders, email, and nearly anything else hiding in your PC, as well as on the internet.

» When faced with a long list of alphabetically sorted files, click anywhere on the list. Then quickly type the first letter or two of the filename you're looking for. Windows immediately jumps up or down the list to the first name beginning with those letters.

TECHNICAL STUFF

» Libraries, a sort of super folder introduced in Windows 7, vanished in Windows 8.1: Microsoft dropped them from the Navigation pane, and they're still missing from Windows 11. If you miss them, add them back by right-clicking a *blank* portion of the Navigation pane and choosing Show Libraries from the pop-up menu.

Creating a New Folder

To store new information in a file cabinet, you grab a manila folder, scrawl a name across the top, and start stuffing it with information. To store new information in Windows — notes for your autobiography, for example — you create a new folder, type in a name for the new folder, and start stuffing it with files.

To create a new folder quickly, click New from any folder's upper-left corner, and choose Folder from the drop-down menu: A new folder appears, ready for you to type its name.

You can also create a new folder with this quick and foolproof method:

1. **Right-click on a blank spot inside your folder (or on the desktop) and choose New.**

    The all-powerful right-click shoots a menu out the side.

2. **Choose Folder.**

    When you choose Folder, shown in Figure 5-6, a new folder quickly appears, waiting for you to type a new name.

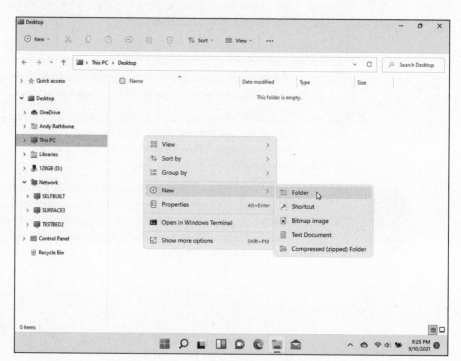

FIGURE 5-6: Right-click where you want a new folder to appear, choose New, and select Folder from the menu.

3. Type a new name for the folder.

A newly created folder bears the boring name of New Folder. When you begin typing, Windows quickly erases the old name and fills in your new name. Done? Save the new name by either pressing Enter or clicking somewhere away from the name you just typed.

 If you mess up the name and want to try again, right-click the misnamed folder, choose the unlabeled Rename icon (shown in the margin) along File Explorer's top edge, and start over.

>> Certain symbols are banned from folder (and file) names. The "Using legal folder names and filenames" sidebar spells out the details, but you never have trouble when using plain old letters and numbers for names.

>> Shrewd observers notice that in Figure 5-6, Windows offers to create many more things than just a folder when you click the New button. Right-click inside a folder anytime you want to create a new shortcut or other common item.

TIP

USING LEGAL FOLDER NAMES AND FILENAMES

Windows is pretty picky about what you can and can't name a file or folder. If you stick to plain old letters and numbers, you're fine. But don't try to stick any of the following characters in there:

 : / \ * | < > ? "

If you try to use any of those characters, Windows bounces an error message to the screen, and you have to try again. Here are some illegal filenames:

    1/2 of my Homework
    JOB:2
    ONE<TWO
    He's no "Gentleman"

These names are legal:

    Half of my Term Paper
    JOB=2
    Two is Bigger than One
    A #@$%) Scoundrel

» Cautious observers may remark that their right-click menu looks different than the one shown in Figure 5-6. There's nothing wrong; programs and apps often add their own items to the right-click menus, making the menu look different on different PCs.

Renaming a File or Folder

 Sick of a filename or folder name? Then change it. Just right-click the offending icon and choose the Rename icon (shown in the margin) from the top edge of the pop-up menu. Windows highlights the file's old name, which disappears as you begin typing the new one. Press Enter or click the desktop when you're done, and you're off.

Or you can click the filename or folder name to select it, wait a second, and click the name again to change it. Some people click the name and press F2; either way, Windows automatically lets you rename the file or folder.

» When you rename a file, only its name changes. The contents are still the same, the file is still the same size, and the file is still in the same place.

TIP

» To rename large groups of files simultaneously, select them all, right-click the first one, and click the Rename icon. Type in the new name and press Enter, and Windows renames that file. However, it also renames all your other selected files to the new name, adding numbers as it goes: cat, cat(2), cat(3), cat(4), and so on. It's a handy way to rename a group of photographs after a special event.

» Renaming some folders confuses Windows, especially if those folders contain programs. And please don't rename your main folders: Downloads, Documents, Pictures, Music, or Videos. (That can cause under-the-hood problems that you don't want to deal with.)

TECHNICAL STUFF

» Windows won't let you rename a file or folder if one of your programs currently uses it. Sometimes closing the program fixes the problem. Other times, you need to restart your PC. This releases the program's clutches so that you can rename the file or folder.

Selecting Bunches of Files or Folders

Although selecting a file, folder, or other object may seem particularly boring, it swings the doors wide open for further tasks: deleting, renaming, moving, copying, and performing other file-juggling tricks discussed in the rest of this chapter.

To select a single item, just click it. To select several files and folders, hold down the Ctrl key when you click the names or icons. Each name or icon stays highlighted when you click the next one.

To gather several files or folders sitting next to each other in a list, click the first one. Then hold down the Shift key as you click the last one. Those two items are highlighted, along with every file and folder sitting between them.

TIP

Windows lets you *lasso* desktop files and folders, as well. Point slightly above the first file or folder you want and then, while holding down the mouse button, point at the last file or folder. The mouse creates a colored lasso to surround your files. Let go of the mouse button, and the lasso disappears, leaving all the surrounded files highlighted.

Here are a few things you can do with a bunch of files you've selected:

>> You can drag and drop armfuls of files in the same way that you drag a single file.

>> You can also simultaneously cut or copy and paste these armfuls into new locations using any of the methods described in the "Copying or Moving Files and Folders" section, later in this chapter.

>> You can delete these armfuls of goods, too, with a press of the Delete key. (They all drop into the Recycle Bin and are available for emergency retrieval.)

TIP

To quickly select all the files in a folder, choose Select All from the folder's See More menu: three dots in the folder's upper-right corner. (No menu? Then select them by pressing Ctrl+A.) Here's another nifty trick: To grab all but a few files, press Ctrl+A, and while still holding down Ctrl, click the ones you don't want.

Getting Rid of a File or Folder

Sooner or later, you'll want to delete a file that's no longer important — yesterday's lottery picks, for example, or a particularly embarrassing digital photo. To delete a file or folder, right-click its name or icon. Then click the Delete icon (shown in the margin) from the top edge of the pop-up menu. This surprisingly simple trick works for files, folders, shortcuts, and just about anything else in Windows.

To delete in a hurry, click the offending object and press the Delete key. Dragging and dropping a file or folder to the Recycle Bin does the same thing.

WARNING

You can delete entire folders, including any files or folders stuffed inside those folders. Just be sure you select the correct folder before you delete it and all its contents. Deleted something by mistake? It's waiting to be recovered in the Recycle Bin.

NEW

» Unlike earlier Windows versions, Windows 11 doesn't toss a box in your face, asking whether you're *sure* you want to delete the file. If you prefer being asked, right-click the Recycle Bin, choose Properties, and place a check mark next to Display Delete Confirmation Dialog, then click the OK button to save your change.

» Be extra sure that you know what you're doing when deleting any file that depicts a little gear in its icon. These files are usually sensitive hidden files that belong to apps or programs, and the computer wants you to leave them alone. (Other than that, they're not particularly exciting, despite the action-oriented gears.)

DON'T BOTHER READING THIS HIDDEN TECHNICAL STUFF

TECHNICAL STUFF

You're not the only one creating files on your computer. Programs often store their own information in a *data file*. They may need to store information about the way your computer is set up, for example. To keep people from confusing those files for trash and deleting them, Windows hides them.

However, if you want to play voyeur, you can view the names of these hidden files and folders:

1. **Open any folder and click the Layout and View icon from along the top edge, and choose Show from the drop-down menu.**

    Yet another menu appears, showing different ways you can view that folder's files.

2. **Click the option named Hidden Items.**

These steps expose the hidden files alongside the other filenames. Be sure not to delete them, however: The programs that created them will gag, possibly damaging them or Windows itself. To avoid trouble, repeat these steps to clear the Hidden Items option and drape the veil of secrecy back over those important files.

>> Icons with little arrows in their corners (like the one in the margin) are shortcuts, which are push buttons that merely load other files. (I cover shortcuts in Chapter 6.) Deleting shortcuts deletes only a button that loads a file or program. The file or program itself remains undamaged and still lives inside your computer.

>> As soon as you find out how to delete files, trot off to Chapter 3, which explains several ways to *un*delete them. (**Hint for the desperate:** Open the Recycle Bin, right-click your file's name, and choose Restore.)

Copying or Moving Files and Folders

To copy or move files to different folders on your hard drive, it's sometimes easiest to use your mouse to *drag* them there. For example, here's how to move a file to a different folder on your desktop. In this case, I'm moving the `Traveler` file from the `House` folder to the `Morocco` folder.

1. **Align the two windows next to each other.**

I explain this in Chapter 4. If you skipped that chapter, try this: Click the first window and then hold the ▦+key and press the right-arrow key. To fill the screen's left half, click the other window, hold the ▦+key, and press the left-arrow key.

2. **Hover the mouse pointer over the file or folder you want to move.**

In my example, I hover the mouse pointer over the `Traveler` file.

3. **While holding down the right mouse button, move the mouse until it points at the destination folder.**

As you see in Figure 5-7, I'm dragging the `Traveler` file from the House folder to the Morocco folder.

Moving the mouse drags the file along with it, and Windows explains that you're moving the file, as shown in Figure 5-7. (Be sure to hold down the right mouse button the entire time.)

REMEMBER

Always drag icons while holding down the *right* mouse button. Windows is then gracious enough to give you a menu of options when you position the icon, and you can choose to copy, move, or create a shortcut. If you hold down the *left* mouse button, Windows sometimes doesn't know whether you want to copy or move.

4. **Release the mouse button and choose Copy Here, Move Here, or Create Shortcuts Here from the pop-up menu.**

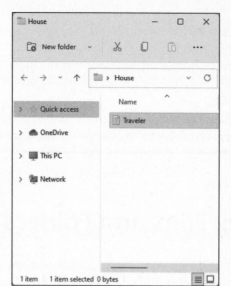
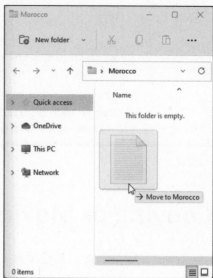

FIGURE 5-7:
To move a file or folder from one window to another, drag it there while holding down the right mouse button.

When dragging and dropping takes too much work, Windows offers a few other ways to copy or move files. Depending on your screen's current layout, some of the following onscreen tools may work more easily:

>> **Right-click menus:** Right-click a file or folder and choose either the Cut or Copy icons, depending on whether you want to move or copy it. Then right-click inside your destination folder and click the Paste icon. It's simple, it always works, and you needn't bother placing any windows side by side.

>> **File Explorer commands:** In File Explorer, click your file or folder, and then click either the Copy or Move icon from the top of File Explorer. Then click inside that item's destination and click the Paste icon to neatly deposit the item into its new location.

>> **Navigation pane:** Described in Chapter 4, this panel along File Explorer's left edge lists popular locations: drives, networks, OneDrive, and oft-used folders. That lets you drag and drop items into a folder on the Navigation pane, sparing you the hassle of opening a destination folder.

WARNING

After you install a program on your computer, don't ever move that program's folder. Programs wedge themselves deeply into Windows. Moving the program may break it, and you'll have to reinstall it. However, feel free to move a program's *shortcut*. (Shortcut icons contain a little arrow in their lower-left corner.) If you no longer need the program, head to the Start menu, right-click the unloved app, and choose Uninstall from the pop-up menu.

Seeing More Information about Files and Folders

Whenever you create a file or folder, Windows scrawls a bunch of secret hidden information on it, such as the date you created it, its size, and even more trivial stuff. Sometimes Windows even lets you add your own secret information, including reviews for your music files or thumbnail pictures for any of your folders.

You can safely ignore most of the information. Other times, tweaking that information is the only way to solve a problem.

To see what Windows is calling your files and folders behind your back, right-click the item and choose Properties from the pop-up menu. Choosing Properties on a song, for example, brings up bunches of details, as shown in Figure 5-8. Here's what each tab means:

TIP

TECHNICAL STUFF

>> **General:** This first tab (far left in Figure 5-8) shows the file's *type* (an MP3 file of the song "Gut Bucket Blues"), its *size* (6.54MB), the program that *opens* it (in this case, the Groove Music app), and the file's *location*.

Want a different program to open your file? Right-click the file, choose Properties, and click the Change button on the General tab, shown in Figure 5-8. A list of your computer's available music players appears, letting you choose your preferred program.

>> **Security:** On this tab, you control *permissions,* which are rules determining who may access the file and what they may do with it. System administrators earn high wages mostly for understanding this type of stuff.

>> **Details:** True to its name, this tab reveals arcane details about a file. On digital photos, for example, this tab lists EXIF (Exchangeable Image File Format) data: the camera model, f-stop, aperture, focal length, and other items loved by photographers. On songs, this tab displays the song's *ID3 tag* (IDentify MP3), which includes the artist, album title, year, track number, genre, length, and similar information.

>> **Previous Versions:** After you set up the Windows File History backup system, this tab lists all the previously saved versions of this file, ready for retrieval with a click. I cover File History in Chapter 13.

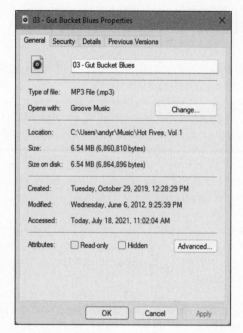

Normally, these tidbits of information remain hidden unless you right-click a file or folder and choose Properties. But what if you want to see details about all the files in a folder, perhaps to find pictures taken on a certain day? For that, switch your folder's view to Details by following these steps:

1. **Click the Layout and View Options tab along the folder's top edge.**

   A menu drops down, listing the umpteen ways a folder can display your files.

2. **In the Layout group, select Details, as shown in Figure 5-9.**

   The screen changes to show your files' names, with details about them stretching to the right in orderly columns. A small dot appears next to your folder's current view, in this case, Details, shown in Figure 5-9.

Try all the views to see which view you prefer. (Windows remembers which views you prefer for different folders.)

REMEMBER

>> If you can't remember what a folder's toolbar buttons do, rest your mouse pointer over a button. Windows usually displays a helpful box summing up the button's mission.

>> Feel free to switch among the different views until you find the one that fits what you're trying to accomplish, be it to see a particular photo's creation date or see thumbnails of every photo in a folder. Different views work better for different folders; there's no "right" view. Experiment, and choose the one you most prefer.

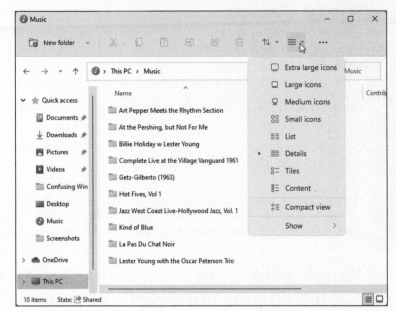

FIGURE 5-9:
To see details about files in a folder, click the Layout and View Options icon and select Details.

>> Folders usually display files sorted alphabetically. To sort them differently, right-click a blank spot inside the folder and choose Sort By. A pop-up menu lets you choose to sort items by size, name, type, and other details. Or click the Sort and Group Options button (shown in the margin) that lives atop every folder to see the same options.

TIP

>> When the excitement of the Sort By menu wears off, try clicking the words at the top of each sorted column. Click Size, for example, to reverse the order, placing the largest files at the list's top.

TIP

>> Feel free to add your own columns to Details view: Right-click a column header you don't need, and a drop-down menu appears, letting you choose a different criterion. (I always add a Date Taken column to my photos, so I can sort my photos by the date I snapped them.)

Writing to CDs and DVDs

Most computers today write information to CDs and DVDs by using a flameless approach known as *burning.* To see whether you're stuck with an older drive that can't burn discs, first remove any discs from inside the drive. Then from the desktop, click the taskbar's File Explorer icon and look at the icon for your CD or DVD drive.

Because computers always speak in secret code, here's what you can do with the disc drives in your computer:

>> **DVD-RW:** These drives both read and write to CDs *and* DVDs.

>> **BD-ROM:** These can read and write to CDs and DVDs, plus they can read Blu-ray discs.

>> **BD-RE:** Although these have the same icon as BD-ROM drives, they can read and write to CDs, DVDs, *and* Blu-ray discs.

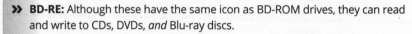

If your PC has two CD or DVD burners, tell Windows which drive you want to handle your disc-burning chores: Right-click the drive, choose Properties, and click the Recording tab. Then choose your favorite drive in the top box.

TECHNICAL
STUFF

Buying the right kind of blank CDs and DVDs for burning

Stores sell two types of CDs: CD-R (short for CD-Recordable) and CD-RW (short for CD-ReWritable). Here's the difference:

>> **CD-R:** Most people buy CD-Rs because they're very cheap and they work fine for storing music or files. You can write to them until they fill up; then you can't write to them anymore. But that's no problem because most people don't want to erase their CDs and start over. They want to stick their burned disc into the car's stereo or stash it as a backup.

>> **CD-RW:** Techies sometimes buy CD-RWs for making temporary backups of data. You can write information to them, just as you can with CD-Rs. But when a CD-RW fills up, you can erase it and start over with a clean slate — something not possible with a CD-R. However, CD-RWs cost more money, so most people stick with the cheaper and faster CD-Rs.

DVDs come in both R and RW formats, just like CDs, so the preceding R and RW rules apply to them, as well. Most DVD burners sold in the past few years can write to any type of blank CD or DVD.

Buying blank DVDs for older drives is chaos: The manufacturers fought over which storage format to use, confusing things for everybody. To buy the right blank DVD, check your computer's specifications sheet to see what formats its DVD burner needs: DVD-R, DVD-RW, DVD+R, or DVD+RW.

TECHNICAL
STUFF

>> Discs come rated by their speed. For faster disc burning, buy the largest number "x" speed you can find, usually 52x for CDs and 16x for DVDs.

>> Blank CDs and DVDs are cheap; borrow one from a neighbor's kid to see whether it works in your drive. If it works fine, buy some of the same type.

>> Blank Blu-ray discs cost much more than CDs or DVDs. Luckily, Blu-ray drives aren't very picky, and just about any blank Blu-ray disc will work.

>> For some odd reason, Compact Discs and Digital Video Discs are spelled as discs, not disks.

>> Although Windows can handle simple disc-burning tasks, it's extraordinarily awkward at duplicating discs. Most people give up quickly and buy third-party disc-burning software. I explain how Windows creates music CDs in Chapter 16.

>> It's currently illegal to make duplicates of movie DVDs in the United States — even to make a backup copy in case the kids scratch up the new Disney DVD. Windows can't copy DVDs on its own, but some programs on websites from other countries can handle the job. They can even copy the DVD's contents to your PC, so you can watch the movie without needing the DVD itself.

Copying files to or from a CD or DVD

TECHNICAL STUFF

Very few people copy information to or from CDs or DVDs these days. It's much more convenient to use flash drives, covered in the next section. Still, for those people who still use those old-school discs, this section may come in handy.

CDs and DVDs once hailed from the school of simplicity: You simply slid them into your CD player or DVD player, and they played. But as soon as those discs graduated to PCs, the problems started. When you create a CD or DVD, you must tell your PC *what* you're copying and *where* you intend to play it: Music for a CD player? Photo slideshows for a TV's DVD player? Or files to store on your computer?

If you choose the wrong answer, your disc won't work, and you've created yet another coaster.

Here are the Disc Creation rules:

>> **Music:** To create a CD that plays music in your CD player or car stereo, flip ahead to Chapter 16. You need to fire up the age-old Windows Media Player program and burn an *audio CD*.

>> **Photo slideshows:** Windows doesn't include the Windows DVD Maker bundled with Windows Vista and Windows 7. To create photo slideshows on a DVD, you need a third-party program. If one didn't come with your computer, you need to purchase one.

If you just want to copy *files* to a CD or DVD, perhaps to save as a backup or to give to a friend, stick around.

Follow these steps to write files to a new blank CD or DVD. (If you're writing files to a CD or DVD that you've written to before, jump ahead to Step 4.)

1. **Insert the blank disc into your disc burner and push in the tray. Then click or tap the Notification box that appears in the screen's lower-right corner.**

2. **When the Notification box asks how you'd like to proceed, click the box's Burn Files to a Disc option.**

Windows displays a Burn a Disc window and asks you to create a title for the disc.

If the Notification box disappeared before you could click on it, eject your disc, push it back in, and have your hand ready on the mouse. (Alternatively, you can bring back the Notification box by right-clicking the disc drive's icon in File Explorer and choosing the Open Autoplay option.)

3. **Type a name for the disc, describe how you want to use the disc, and click Next.**

Unfortunately, Windows limits your CD's or DVD's title to 16 characters. Instead of typing **Family Picnic atop Orizaba in 2021**, stick to the facts: **Orizaba 2021**. Or just click Next to use the default name for the disc: the current date.

Windows can burn the files to the disc two different ways. To help you decide which method will work best for you, the Windows menu offers two options:

- **Like a USB flash drive:** This method lets you read and write files to the disc many times, a handy way to use discs as portable file carriers. Unfortunately, that method isn't compatible with some CD or DVD players connected to home stereos or TVs.

- **With a CD/DVD player:** If you plan to play your disc on a fairly new home stereo disc player that's smart enough to read files stored in several different formats, select this method.

Armed with the disc's name, Windows prepares the disc for incoming files.

4. **Tell Windows which files to write to disc.**

Now that your disc is ready to accept the files, tell Windows what information to send its way. You can do this in any of several ways:

- Drag and drop your files and/or folders into the drive's File Explorer window.

- Right-click the item you want to copy, be it a single file, folder, or selected files and folders. When the pop-up menu appears, choose Send To and select your disc burner from the menu. (The pop-up menu lists the disc's title you chose in Step 3.)

- Drag and drop files and/or folders on top of the burner's icon in File Explorer.

- Tell your current program to save the information to the disc rather than to your hard drive.

No matter which method you choose, Windows dutifully looks over the information and copies it to the disc you inserted in the first step. A progress window appears, showing the disc burner's progress. When the progress window disappears, Windows has finished burning the disc.

5. Close your disc-burning session by ejecting the disc.

When you're through copying files to the disc, push your drive's Eject button (or right-click the drive's icon in File Explorer and choose Eject). Windows closes the session, adding a finishing touch to the disc that lets other PCs read it.

TIP

If you try to copy a large batch of files to a disc — more than will fit — Windows complains immediately. Copy fewer files at a time, perhaps spacing them out over two discs.

TIP

Most programs let you save files directly to disc. Choose Save from the File menu, and select your CD burner. Put a disc (preferably one that's not already filled) into your disc drive to start the process.

TIP

DUPLICATING A CD OR DVD

Windows doesn't include any way to duplicate a CD, DVD, or Blu-ray disc. It can't even make a copy of a music CD. (That's why so many people buy CD-burning programs.)

But it can copy all of a CD's or DVD's files to a blank disc by using this two-step process:

1. Copy the files and folders from the CD or DVD to a folder on your PC.

2. Copy those same files and folders back to a blank CD or DVD.

That gives you a duplicate CD or DVD, which is handy when you need a second copy of an essential backup disc.

You can try this process on a music CD or DVD movie, but it won't work. (I tried.) It works only when you're duplicating a disc containing data files.

Working with Flash Drives and Memory Cards

Digital camera owners eventually become acquainted with *memory cards* — those little plastic squares that replaced the awkward rolls of film. Windows can read digital photos directly from the camera after you find its cable and plug it into your PC. But Windows can also grab photos straight off the memory card, a method praised by those who've lost their camera's cables.

The same holds true for smartphones, which also use the cards, as well as some audio recorders and digital gaming devices.

The secret is a *memory card reader* — a little slot-filled box that stays plugged into your PC. Slide your memory card into the slot, and your PC can read the card's files, just like reading files from any other folder. Some tablets, laptops, and PCs include built-in memory card readers.

Most office supply and electronics stores sell memory card readers that accept most popular memory card formats: Compact Flash, SecureDigital High Capacity (SDHC), Micro-SecureDigital High Capacity (SDHC), Micro-SecureDigital Extended Capacity (SDXC), and a host of other tongue twisters. Some computers even come with built-in memory card readers on the front of their case.

The beauty of card readers is that there's nothing new to figure out: Windows treats your inserted card just like an ordinary folder. Insert your card, and a folder appears on your screen to show your digital camera photos. The same drag-and-drop and cut-and-paste rules covered earlier in this chapter still apply, letting you move the pictures or other files off the card and into your Pictures folder.

 Flash drives — also known as *thumb drives* — work just like memory card readers. Plug the flash drive into one of your PC's USB ports, and the drive appears as an icon (shown in the margin) in File Explorer, ready to be opened with a double-click. Skip back to this chapter's "Copying or Moving Files and Folders" section for step-by-step instructions on transferring the flash drive's contents to your PC.

WARNING

» First, the warning: Formatting a card or flash drive wipes out all its information. Never format a card or flash drive unless you don't care about the information it currently holds.

>> Now the procedure: If Windows complains that a newly inserted card isn't formatted, right-click its drive and choose Format. (This problem happens most often with brand-new or damaged cards.)

>> Most smartphones and tablets contain memory card slots, as well. Their cards work the same as the ones found in digital cameras.

OneDrive: Your Cubbyhole in the Clouds

When you're sitting in front of your computer, you naturally store your files inside your computer. It's the easiest place to put them. When you leave your computer, you can bring along important files by stashing them on flash drives, CDs, DVDs, and portable hard drives — if you remember to grab them on the way out.

But how can you access your files from your computers if you've forgotten to bring along the files? How can you grab your home files from work, and vice versa? How can you view an important document or hear some favorite tunes while traveling? How can you grab your PC's files with your smartphone?

Microsoft's answer to those questions is called *OneDrive*. It's your own private file storage space on the internet, and it's built into Windows. With OneDrive, your files are available from any computer with an internet connection. You can even grab them from phones or tablets from Apple or that run Android: Microsoft offers a free OneDrive app for both operating systems.

If you change a file stored on OneDrive, that updated file is available on *all* your computers and devices. OneDrive automatically keeps everything in sync. You only need the following things in order to put OneDrive to work:

>> **Microsoft account:** You need a Microsoft account in order to upload, view, or retrieve your files from OneDrive. Chances are good that you created a Microsoft account when you first created your account on your Windows PC. (I describe Microsoft accounts in Chapter 2.)

>> **An internet connection:** Without an internet signal, either wireless or wired, your web-stashed files remain floating in the clouds, away from you and your computer. (You can avoid that problem by choosing to keep all your OneDrive files stored on your computer as well as the cloud.)

>> **Patience:** Uploading files takes longer than downloading files. Although you can upload small files fairly quickly, larger files such as digital photos or movies take much longer to upload.

For some people, OneDrive offers a safe internet haven, sometimes called the *cloud*, where they can always find their most important files. For others, OneDrive brings another layer of complication, as well as another possible hiding place for that missing file.

The following sections explain how to access OneDrive from within Windows, as well as from a web browser on any other PC or device. They also explain how to tweak OneDrive's many settings so it works perfectly on both desktop PCs, laptops, and small tablets with limited storage space.

Setting up OneDrive

Windows places a link to OneDrive in every folder's Navigation pane, where it's easily accessible. There, OneDrive works like any other folder but with one exception: Files and folders you place inside your OneDrive folder are also copied to your OneDrive storage space on the internet.

That can create a problem: Today's smaller phones, tablets, and laptops don't include much storage space. OneDrive, by contrast, can hold *lots* of files. Some smaller computers, usually small tablets, don't have enough room to keep a copy of *everything* you've packed away on your desktop PC's OneDrive folder.

To meet everybody's needs, OneDrive can work in these three ways:

>> **All files:** The simplest option, and the one chosen by most desktop PC owners, this puts all your OneDrive files on both the internet and your PC. Then it keeps them all in sync: Update a file on your PC, and it's updated on the internet, and vice versa. It's a convenient way to keep your most important files instantly accessible and always backed up.

>> **Some files:** Designed for devices with limited amounts of storage like some tablets and laptops, this lets you pick and choose which folders should live only on OneDrive and which should also be stored on your computer, too.

>> **Files On Demand:** The best option for people with limited storage space, this lets your PC display names of *all* your OneDrive files and folders. Then, when you open a file or folder, Windows quickly downloads it to your device for you to display its contents. It requires an internet connection, and it's a little slower, but it lets you access any of your OneDrive files without them all hogging your PC's storage space.

When you first click the OneDrive folder on a new PC, Windows begins the setup process, described in the steps listed below. If you've already set up OneDrive, but want to change its settings, skip ahead to the next section, "Changing your One-Drive settings."

To set up OneDrive on a new PC, follow these steps:

1. **From the taskbar, click the File Explorer icon and click the OneDrive icon in the folder's left edge.**

   Since this is the first time you've set up OneDrive on the computer, OneDrive displays an opening screen.

2. **If asked, sign in with your Microsoft account and password.**

   Only Local account holders need to sign in; Microsoft account holders already sign in when they sign into their user account. (I describe how to convert a Local account into a Microsoft account in Chapter 14.)

TIP

   Local account holders can sign in with any Microsoft account. They don't need to convert their account to a Microsoft account.

   After you enter a Microsoft account name and password, a window appears, pointing out the location of your OneDrive folder.

3. **If you want to change where to store your OneDrive files, click the Change Location button. Otherwise, click the Next button.**

   If you're using a desktop PC with plenty of storage space, just click the Next button. OneDrive will store all your OneDrive files on your C: drive, which normally has plenty of room.

   Inexpensive tablets and laptops, by contrast, contain very limited storage space. To add more storage, many tablet owners buy a memory card and slide it into their tablet's memory slot. If you've bought and inserted a memory card into your tiny tablet, click this window's Change Location button and tell OneDrive to save its files on your tablet's memory card instead of the default C: drive. (The memory card is often called the D: drive.)

   If an advertisement appears, asking you to increase your storage for a monthly fee, click the words Not Now. (You can always change your mind later.)

4. **If asked, choose which folders to sync to your PC.**

   OneDrive lists your existing OneDrive folders, if you have any, as shown in Figure 5-10.

5. **Select the files and folders you'd like to keep synced between your PC and OneDrive, and click the Next button.**

   OneDrive gives you two options, which you can change later:

   - **Sync All Files and Folders in my OneDrive:** Unless you have a reason not to, select this option to keep all your OneDrive files mirrored on your PC's or tablet's memory card. Most desktop PCs won't have a problem with this option, and it's the most trouble-free way to access OneDrive.

- **Sync Only These Folders:** Select this option on tablets or PCs with very little storage. If you select this option, place a check mark next to the folders you consider to be essential enough to warrant storage both on your PC and OneDrive.

6. **Click Next to save your changes.**

OneDrive leaves you with an Open my OneDrive Folder button, which you can click to see the results of your file syncing decisions.

FIGURE 5-10:
Place a check mark next to the folders you want to stay on both your computer *and* OneDrive.

Feel free to sync different folders on different computers. For example, you can choose to sync only the essentials on your small tablet — perhaps just your photos. On a desktop PC with large storage, you can choose to sync everything.

Changing your OneDrive settings

Windows usually guesses your correct settings when you first set up OneDrive. To revisit your OneDrive settings and ensure that they're set correctly for your particular computer or other device, follow these steps:

1. **From the taskbar's notification area, right-click the OneDrive icon and choose Help & Settings, and then choose Settings from the pop-up menu.**

You may need to click the little upward-pointing arrow in the notification area to see the OneDrive icon (shown in the margin). I cover the taskbar's notification area — the tiny icon-filled area to the taskbar's far right — in Chapter 3.

OneDrive's Settings window appears, as shown in Figure 5-11, open to the Account tab.

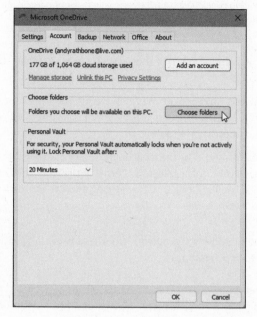

FIGURE 5-11:
The Microsoft
OneDrive Settings
window lets you
change how
OneDrive
communicates
with your
computer.

2. **To change which files should live both on your PC and on OneDrive, click the Choose Folders button.**

   The Sync Your OneDrive Files to This PC window opens, listing all your OneDrive folders, as shown previously in Figure 5-10.

3. **Make any changes, and click the OK button.**

   This area lets you adjust which of your PC's folders live only on your PC, only on the internet, or on both.

The Microsoft OneDrive Settings window opens to the Account tab, shown in Figure 5-11, but all the tabs are worth exploring:

>> **Settings:** A check box here lets you tell OneDrive to start syncing automatically when you log in to Windows. This area also lets you turn on the OneDrive Files On Demand, a feature I cover in this chapter's next section. (I keep all these check boxes turned on.)

>> **Account:** This tab lets you choose which OneDrive folders should be available to your PC, as well as how much space OneDrive is consuming. (If you go over 5GB, you've hit the storage limit, and Microsoft asks you to subscribe to one of its paid plans.)

>> **Backup:** This backs up your most important folders: Desktop, Documents, and Pictures. It also offers to store your camera's or phone's photos to OneDrive whenever you connect those devices to your PC. It's quite handy, but it fills OneDrive quickly, so you'll eventually run out of storage and have to pay. (I did.)

>> **Network:** Designed for people without speedy internet connections, this lets you control how quickly OneDrive should sync. Unless you have good reason, keep this set to Don't Limit.

>> **Office:** This tab lets you control how OneDrive interacts with documents created in Office, Microsoft's suite of software that includes Outlook, Word, Excel, and other popular programs.

>> **About:** Probably tossed in by the legal department, this offers links to Microsoft's pages of boring legalese: Its Terms of Use and its Privacy and Cookies policies. For OneDrive troubleshooting information, click the Get Help with OneDrive link.

When you click the window's OK button, OneDrive begins syncing your files and folders according to your changes.

Microsoft gives everybody 5GB of free OneDrive storage space, but you can increase that amount by paying a monthly fee. Microsoft begins reminding you of that unfortunate fact as your storage limit nears.

TIP

The Account tab shown in Figure 5-11 also shows your amount of available One-Drive storage space and offers a Manager Storage link in case you're running low on space.

Opening and saving files from OneDrive

When you first sign into Windows 11 with a new Microsoft Account, Windows stocks your OneDrive with two empty folders: Documents and Photos.

To see the two folders, open any folder. Don't have a folder open? Then click the File Explorer icon (shown in the margin) on the taskbar. OneDrive is listed in the folder's Navigation pane along the left edge. Click the word OneDrive, and One-Drive's contents spill out into the folder's right side. You can see the two empty folders, named Documents and Photos. If you already have a OneDrive account, you see your existing OneDrive folders instead. You have nothing new to learn with OneDrive; its folders work like any other folder on your computer:

>> To view the contents of a OneDrive folder, double-click it. The folder opens to show its contents.

>> To edit a file stored in a OneDrive folder, double-click it. The file opens in the program that created it.

>> To save something new inside a OneDrive folder, save it to a folder inside OneDrive — its Documents folder, for example. Don't just save it to the Documents folder on your PC.

>> To delete something from OneDrive, right-click it and choose Delete. The item moves to your desktop's Recycle Bin, where it can be retrieved later if necessary.

No matter what changes you make to your files and folders in your computer's OneDrive folder, Windows automatically changes the internet's copies to match as soon as your computer finds an internet connection.

Later, when you visit OneDrive through anything with a web browser — your smartphone, tablet, or even another PC — your up-to-date files are waiting for you to peruse.

OneDrive also comes in handy in situations like these:

TIP

>> By storing a shopping list on OneDrive, you can add needed grocery items while sitting at your PC. Then, when you're at the store, you can view that up-to-date shopping list on your smartphone. (Microsoft makes OneDrive apps for iPhones and Android phones.)

>> Want to copy a few favorites to your OneDrive folder? I describe how to copy and move files between folders earlier in this chapter.

>> To share a OneDrive file or folder with friends, right-click it, choose Show More Options from the pop-up menu, and choose Share from the next menu. A window appears, where you can enter the email addresses of the friends. When your friends receive and click the emailed link, they'll have access to your OneDrive-stored file or folder.

TIP

>> Many people keep a few desert island discs on OneDrive. Whenever you have an internet connection, the Groove Music app, covered in Chapter 16, automatically lists and plays any music you store on OneDrive. (The old school Media Player program, by contrast, plays only the music stored physically on your PC.)

Understanding which files live on OneDrive, your PC, or both places

Windows lets you see the names of every file and folder you've stored on One-Drive. Then you can quickly open a OneDrive file or folder even if it's not stored locally on your PC. OneDrive simply grabs the file from the internet and places it onto your computer. (This depends on your having a working internet connection at the time, of course.)

OneDrive's Files On Demand feature lets you see all your files on all your devices. Yet it lets you save space on devices that don't have much storage space. For example, you can sync your entire music collection only on devices with lots of storage spaces. But your device that lacks storage can still see the music and, if you have an internet connection, play it whenever you like.

You can even see thumbnails of more than 300 different file types — even if they're not stored on your computer.

To turn on OneDrive Files On Demand, follow these steps:

1. **From the taskbar's notification area, right-click the OneDrive icon, choose Help & Settings from the pop-up menu, and choose Settings from the next menu.**

   You may need to click the little upward-pointing arrow in the notification area to see the OneDrive icon (shown in the margin). I cover the taskbar's notification area — the tiny icon-filled area to the taskbar's far right — in Chapter 3.

   OneDrive's Settings window appears, as shown earlier in Figure 5-11, open to the Account tab.

2. **Click the Settings tab, and in the Files On Demand section, select the Save Space and Download Files as You Use Them check box.**

3. **Click the OK button to close the window.**

Now, even though your OneDrive files aren't saved on your PC, you can see their names, as shown in Figure 5-12.

The key to understanding OneDrive Files On Demand is to look at the three little icons next to each file's name, shown in Figure 5-12. Here is what each icon means:

>> **Online only:** This file is available online only; you need an internet connection to access it.

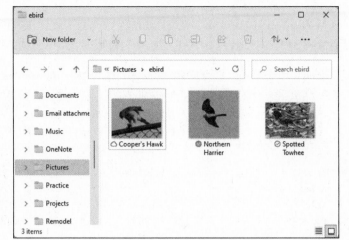

FIGURE 5-12:
OneDrive Files On
Demand shows
the name of
every stored file
and folder, as
well as its status.

>> **Locally available:** You've opened an online only file, so now it's available on your PC. Any edits you make also change the copy stored on OneDrive. If you need to free up space and remove it from your PC, right-click it and choose Free Up Space. (A copy remains on OneDrive, and the file's icon on your PC changes to Online Only.)

>> **Always keep on this device:** Files and folders with this icon are always available on your PC, even without an internet connection.

To change the status of a file or folder, right-click it. There, you can choose between these three settings:

>> **View Online:** This downloads your file or folder to your PC and opens it for you to view or edit.

>> **Always Keep On This Device:** This also downloads the file or folder to your PC. However, it doesn't open it. It's handy mostly for grabbing folders that you always want to have available, even without an internet connection.

>> **Free Up Space:** This deletes the file from your device, which frees up storage space. It keeps that file stored on OneDrive though, where you can fetch it again whenever you have an internet connection.

TIP

These tips will help you discover whether OneDrive Files On Demand is worth turning on and how to use it on different devices:

>> If your device has plenty of storage space, as do most desktop PCs, don't bother with Files On Demand. Simply choose Make All Files Available, described earlier in this chapter's "Setting up OneDrive" section.

>> If your device doesn't have much storage, but you want to see the names of all your OneDrive files and folders, turn on OneDrive Files On Demand. Then, when you have an internet connection and need a file or folder, just open it, as if it lived on your PC. Windows quickly downloads and opens it.

>> If you store a few Desert Island Discs of music on OneDrive, turn on OneDrive Files On Demand, but set those particular folders to be Always Keep on This Device. That way you can see every file and access them when you have an internet connection, but you still play your favorite music without an internet connection.

By assessing your needs, your device's storage limits, and the availability of your internet connection, you can customize OneDrive's Files On Demand feature to meet the storage capacity of all your devices.

Accessing OneDrive from the internet

Sometimes you may need to access OneDrive when you're not sitting in front of your computer. Or you may need to reach a OneDrive file that's not synced on your PC. To help you in either situation, Microsoft offers OneDrive access from any web browser.

When you need your files, drop by any computer, visit the OneDrive website at `https://OneDrive.live.com`, and, if asked, sign in with your Microsoft account name and password. The OneDrive website appears, shown in Figure 5-13.

After you sign in to the OneDrive website, you can add, delete, move, and rename files, as well as create folders and move files between folders. You can even edit some files directly online. (OneDrive even contains a Recycle Bin for retrieving mistakenly deleted OneDrive files, whether they were deleted online or on your phone, PC, or other device.)

It's much easier to manage your files directly from the folder on your computer. But if you're away from your computer, the OneDrive website provides a handy fallback zone.

The OneDrive website also lets you share files by emailing people links to them, making it a handy way to share folders.

TIP

You can also share OneDrive files with friends directly from your PC: Right-click the file or folder you want to share, and choose OneDrive, then choose Share from the pop-up menu. A window appears, where you can enter the email address of who should receive a link to the shared item. When the recipient clicks the link in the email, they're taken online to view the file or folder's contents.

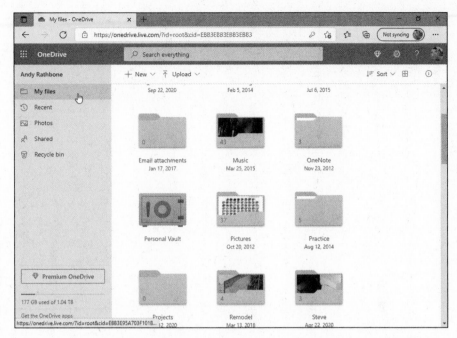

FIGURE 5-13:
You can access
your OneDrive
files from any
computer or
device with a web
browser.

If you find yourself using OneDrive regularly, take note that Microsoft offers free
OneDrive apps for Apple, and Android smartphones and tablets. OneDrive simplifies file sharing among all your gadgets.

**TECHNICAL
STUFF**

OneDrive'S PERSONAL VAULT

A Personal Vault is a fancy term for what looks and acts like a regular OneDrive folder,
but with one big difference: To open it, you need to pass a second layer of security. That
makes it perfect for storing sensitive files that should be seen by others.

That security could be as simple as running your fingertip over a fingerprint reader or
looking into a camera. (I cover Windows Hello fingerprint readers and face cameras in
Chapter 14.) You can also enter a PIN, or a secret code sent to you through email or a
phone message.

After 20 minutes of inactivity, the Personal Vault automatically locks itself, keeping your
most sensitive files secure yet accessible.

2

Working with Programs, Apps, and Files

IN THIS CHAPTER

» Opening a program, an app, or a document

» Changing which program opens which document

» Installing, uninstalling, and updating apps

» Creating a shortcut

» Cutting, copying, and pasting

Chapter **6**

Playing with Programs, Apps, and Documents

In Windows, *apps* and *programs* are your tools: Load a program or an app, and you can add numbers, arrange words, and shoot spaceships.

Documents, by contrast, are the things you create with apps and programs, such as tax forms, heartfelt apologies, and lists of high scores.

This chapter explains the basics of opening apps and programs from the Start menu in Windows. It explains how to find, download, and install a new app from the Start menu's Microsoft Store app. It also shows you where to find an app's menus. (Microsoft mysteriously hid most of them.)

As you flip through this chapter's pages, you figure out how to make your preferred program open your files. You also create desktop shortcuts — buttons that let you quickly load favorite files, folders, and programs.

The chapter ends with the section "Absolutely Essential Guide to Cutting, Copying, and Pasting." Put this one trick under your belt, and you'll know how to manipulate words in a word processor, move files between folders, copy files from your camera to your PC, and send files to and from flash drives.

Starting an App or Program

 Windows 11 moves the Start button and menu to the center of the taskbar, that icon-filled strip along the bottom of your screen. A click of the Start button (shown in the margin) brings you the Start menu's latest incarnation.

I explain the new Start menu, shown in Figure 6-1, in Chapter 2; head there for tips on how to customize the menu by adding, moving, or removing icons to ensure you find things more easily.

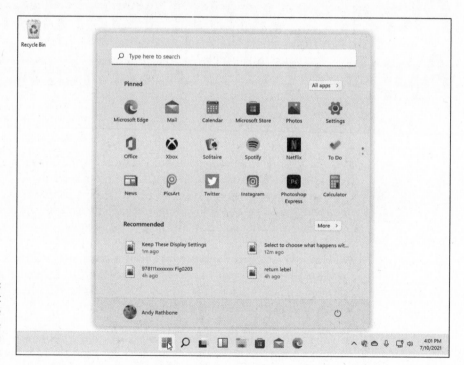

FIGURE 6-1:
On the Start menu, click the icon for the program you want to open.

If you just want to launch a program or app, follow these steps:

1. Open the Start menu.

Summon the Start menu by clicking or tapping the Start button near the middle of the taskbar. If your hands are already on the keyboard, just press the Windows key ().

The Start menu appears, as shown previously in Figure 6-1, bringing a list of your apps and programs. In fact, the Start menu automatically updates itself to display the names of your most recently used programs, apps, or files. (To return to one, just click its name.)

NEW

Windows 11 no longer has a Tablet mode, so the Start menu no longer fills the entire screen on tablets and touchscreen monitors. Instead, Windows 11 automatically expands the space between icons, making them easier targets for fumbling fingers. Other than that, Windows 11 looks identical on tablets, laptops, and desktop PCs.

2. If you spot the icon for your app or program, choose it with a mouse click or, on a touchscreen, a tap of a finger.

Don't see an icon for your sought-after app on the Start menu's list? Move to the next step.

3. Page down the Start screen's right side to see more icons.

Nestled along the Start menu's right edge are two buttons, stacked on top of each other. Click the lower button, shown in the margin, and the Start menu reveals another page of icons. Repeat to see more pages; when no more icons appear, you're seeing the Start menu's last row of icons. Similarly, clicking the top button moves up a page.

On touchscreens, you can view the icons hidden below the screen's edge by sliding your finger up the screen over the icons.

TIP

Still don't see your program or app listed? Head for Step 4.

4. View *all* your apps by clicking the All Apps button.

To keep its list of apps and programs manageable, the Start menu's icon-filled section doesn't list every program or app on your computer.

All apps >

To reveal them *all,* click the All Apps button in the upper-right corner of the Start menu. All your installed apps and programs suddenly appear, sorted alphabetically.

If you *still* can't find your program on the admittedly crowded Start menu, follow these tips for other ways to open an app or a program:

NEW

>> Click inside the Search box, located along the top edge of the Start menu. As you type the first letter, the Search box expands into its own window and begins presenting a list of names containing that letter. Type a second or third letter, and the list of matches shrinks accordingly to match that sequence. When the window lists your desired app or program, open it with a click (or a tap on a touchscreen). I explain the new Search box in Chapter 7.

>> Double-click a shortcut to the program. Shortcuts, which often sit on your desktop, are handy, disposable buttons for launching files and folders. (I explain more about shortcuts in this chapter's "Taking the Lazy Way with a Desktop Shortcut" section.)

>> While you're on the desktop, you may spot the program's icon on the taskbar — a handy strip of icons lazily lounging along your desktop's bottom edge. If so, click the taskbar icon, and the program leaps into action. (I cover the desktop's taskbar, including how to customize its row of icons, in Chapter 3.)

>> Right-click on a blank portion of the Windows desktop, choose New, and select the type of document you want to create. Windows loads the correct program for the job.

Windows offers other ways to open an app or program, but the preceding methods usually get the job done. (I cover the Start menu more extensively in Chapter 2, and the desktop is the star of Chapter 3.)

Opening a Document

Like Tupperware, the Windows desktop is a big fan of standardization. Almost all Windows programs load their documents — often called *files* — the same way:

1. **Click the word File on the program's *menu bar,* that row of staid words along the program's top.**

   If your program hides its menu bar, pressing the Alt key often reveals it.

   Still no menu bar? Then your program might have a *Ribbon,* a thick strip of multicolored icons along the window's top. If you spot the Ribbon, click the tab or button in its leftmost corner to let the File menu tumble down.

2. **When the File menu drops down, choose Open.**

Windows gives you a sense of déjà vu with the Open window, shown in Figure 6-2. It looks (and works) just like your Documents folder, which I cover in Chapter 5.

There's one big difference, however: This time, your folder displays only files that your particular program knows how to open — it filters out all the others.

3. **Hover the mouse pointer on the document you want to open (shown in Figure 6-2), click the mouse button, and click the Open button.**

TIP

On a touchscreen, tap the document to open it. The program opens the file and displays it on the screen.

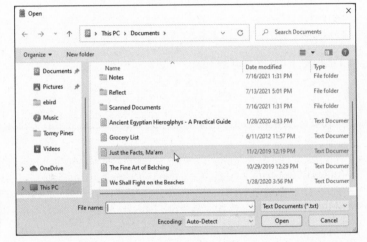

FIGURE 6-2: Double-click the filename you want to open.

Opening a file works this way in most Windows programs, whether written by Microsoft, its corporate partners, or the teenager down the street.

TIP

›› To speed things up, double-click a desired file's name; that opens it immediately, automatically closing the Open window.

›› Humans store things in the garage, but computers store their files in neatly labeled compartments called *folders*. (Double-click a folder to see what's stored inside. If you spot your file, open it with a double-click.) If browsing folders gives you trouble, the folders section in Chapter 5 offers a refresher.

>> If your file isn't listed by name, start browsing by clicking the buttons or words shown along the left side of Figure 6-2. Click the words `OneDrive` or `This PC`, for example, to search the folders and their files stored inside those places.

>> When you open a file and change it, even by accident, Windows usually assumes that you've changed the file for the better. If you try to close the file, Windows cautiously asks whether you want to save your changes. If you updated the file with masterful wit, click Yes. If you made a mess or opened the wrong file, click No or Cancel.

TIP

>> Confused about any icons or commands along the Open window's top or left side? Rest your mouse pointer over the icons, and a little box announces their occupations.

TECHNICAL STUFF

WHEN PROGRAMMERS FIGHT OVER FILE TYPES

When not fighting over fast food, programmers fight over *formats* — ways to pack information into a file. To tiptoe around the format wars, most programs let you open files stored in several different types of formats.

For example, look at the drop-down list box in the bottom-right corner of Figure 6-2. It currently lists all `Text Documents (*.txt)`, the format used by the Notepad text editor built into Windows. To see files stored in *other* formats, click in that box and choose a different format. The Open box quickly updates its list to show files from that new format instead.

And how can you see a list of *all* your folder's files in that menu, regardless of their format? Select All Documents from the drop-down list box. That switches the view to show all of that particular folder's files. Your program probably can't open them all, though, and it will choke while trying.

For example, Notepad may include some digital photos in its All Documents view. But if you try to open a photo, Notepad dutifully displays the photo as obscure coding symbols. (If you ever mistakenly open a photo in a program and *don't* see the photo, don't try to save what you opened. If the program is like Notepad, saving the file ruins the photo. Simply turn tail and exit immediately with a click on the Cancel button.)

Saving a Document

Saving means to send the work you just created to a place for safekeeping. Unless you specifically save your work, your computer thinks that you've just been fiddling around for the past four hours. You must specifically tell the computer to save your work before it will safely store it.

Thanks to Microsoft snapping leather whips, a Save command appears in nearly every Windows program no matter which programmer wrote it. Here are a few ways to save a file:

>> Click File on the top menu, and choose Save. (Pressing the Alt key, followed by the F key and the S key, does the same thing.)

>> Click the Save icon (shown in the margin).

>> Hold down Ctrl and press the S key. (*S* stands for *Save.*)

If you're saving something for the first time, Windows asks you to think up a name for your document. Type something descriptive using only letters, numbers, and spaces between the words. (If you try to use one of the "illegal" characters I describe in Chapter 5, the Windows Police step in, politely requesting that you use a different name.)

REMEMBER

>> You can save files to any folder, recordable CD or DVD, or even a flash drive. But files are much easier to find down the road when they stay in one of your four main folders: Documents, Music, Pictures, or Videos. (Those folders are listed on the left edge of every folder — in the *Navigation pane* — making it easy to place files inside them.)

>> Choose descriptive filenames for your work. Windows gives you 255 characters to work with. A file named *January 2022 Fidget Spinner Sales* is easier to relocate than one named *Stuff.*

>> If you want to access your current file from other devices, perhaps your phone, tablet, or another PC, save it to the Documents folder on OneDrive: Choose OneDrive from the Save window's left edge, and then choose the OneDrive Documents folder. Then click the Save button.

>> Most programs can save files directly to a recordable CD or DVD. Choose Save from the File menu, and choose your preferred drive from the right pane's This PC section. Put a disc (preferably one that's not already filled) into your disc-writing drive to start the process.

WHAT'S THE DIFFERENCE BETWEEN SAVE AND SAVE AS?

TIP

Huh? Save as *what*? A chemical compound? Nah, the Save As command just gives you a chance to save your work with a different name and in a different location.

Suppose that you open the *Ode to Jazz* file and change a few sentences. You want to save your new changes, but you don't want to lose the original words either. Preserve *both* versions by selecting Save As and typing the new name, *Tentative Additions to Ode to Jazz.*

When you're saving something for the *first* time, the Save and Save As commands are identical: Both make you choose a fresh name and location for your work.

Perhaps just as important, the Save As command also lets you save a file in a different *format.* You can save your original copy in your normal format, but you can also save a copy in a different format for a friend clinging to older software that requires a format from yesteryear.

>> A few newer programs spare you the chore of clicking the Save button: They save your work automatically as you type. Microsoft's OneNote note-taking program and many Start menu apps save your work automatically, so they lack a Save button.

REMEMBER

>> If you're working on something important (and most things are important), click the program's Save command every few minutes. Or use the Ctrl+S keyboard shortcut. (While holding down the Ctrl key, press the S key.) Programs make you choose a name and location for a file when you *first* save it; subsequent saves are much speedier.

Choosing Which Program Should Open Which File

Most of the time, Windows automatically knows which program should open which file. Open a file, and Windows tells the correct program to jump in and let you view its contents.

But sometimes Windows doesn't choose your preferred program. For example, the new app-loving Windows tells the Start menu's Groove Music app to play your music. You may prefer that the desktop's Windows Media Player handle the music-playing chores instead.

When the wrong program opens your file, here's how to make the *right* program open it instead:

1. **Right-click your problematic file, and choose Open With from the pop-up menu.**

   As shown in Figure 6-3, Windows lists a few capable programs, including ones you've used to open that file in the past.

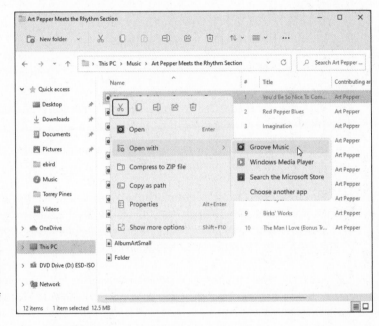

FIGURE 6-3:
Windows lists some programs that opened that type of file in the past.

2. **Click the Choose Another App option.**

   The window that appears, as shown in Figure 6-4, lists more apps, and the currently assigned apps appears at the top of the list. If you spot your favorite apps, double-click to tell it to open your file. (Make sure the Always Use This App to Open Files check box is selected so you don't need to repeat these steps.) Then click OK. You're done!

   Don't see the apps you want or need to open the file? Move to Step 3.

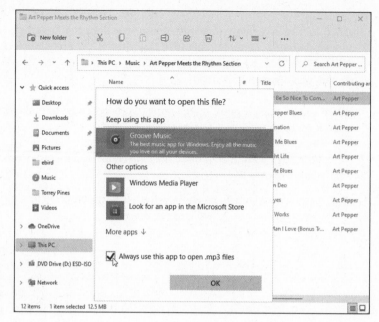

FIGURE 6-4:
Choose the app
you want, and
select the check
box at the
bottom.

3. **Click the words Look for An App in the Microsoft Store, and click the
OK button.**

The Microsoft Store app appears, leaving you at a virtual shelf stocked with
apps capable of opening the file.

If you install a new app or program to open a particular file, the newcomer usually
assigns itself the rights to open that type of file in the future. If it doesn't, head
back to Step 1. This time, however, your newly installed app or program appears
on the list. Choose it, and you've *finally* finished.

REMEMBER

» In a bit of revisionist history, Windows now uses the term *app* when referring
to both traditional desktop programs and Start menu apps. Be mindful of the
Windows terminology when on the desktop. If Windows says an action will
affect your apps, it will also affect your desktop programs.

» Windows lets you choose your default app from the Start menu as well.
From the Start menu, click the Settings icon, shown in the margin. When the
Settings app appears, click the Apps icon from the left pane. From the Apps
window, choose Default Apps from the right pane. Click any app's name, and a
list appears for you to hand the reins to a different program.

» Sometimes you'll want to alternate between different apps or programs when
working on the same file. To do so, right-click the file, choose Open With, and
select the program you need at that time. Just be sure to leave the Always
Open with this App box unchecked.

>> Occasionally, you can't make your favorite program open a particular file because it simply doesn't know how. For example, Windows 11 can't play DVD movies. Your only solution is to install a DVD playing program or app from the Microsoft Store.

>> If somebody says something about "file associations," feel free to browse the technical sidebar "The awkward world of file associations," which explains that awful subject.

THE AWKWARD WORLD OF FILE ASSOCIATIONS

TECHNICAL STUFF

Every Windows program slaps a secret code known as a *file extension* onto the name of every file it creates. The file extension works like a cattle brand: When you double-click the file, Windows eyeballs the extension and automatically summons the proper program to open the file. Notepad, for example, tacks on the three-letter extension .txt to every file it creates. So Windows associates the .txt extension with the Notepad program.

Windows normally doesn't display these extensions, isolating users from such inner mechanisms for safety reasons. If somebody accidentally changes or removes an extension, Windows won't know how to open that file.

If you're curious about what an extension looks like, sneak a peek by following these steps:

1. **Click the Layout and View tab icon atop any folder and choose Show from the drop-down menu.**

   A drop-down menu quickly appears, showing different ways to view that folder's contents. Choose Show from the menu and click File Name Extensions Items.

   The files inside the folder immediately change to show their extensions — a handy thing to know in technical emergencies.

2. **Repeat these steps to stop showing the File Name Extensions.**

Unless you're a techie, you shouldn't allow Windows to show file name extensions. And please don't change a file's extension unless you know exactly what you're doing. Windows will forget which program to use for opening the file, potentially leaving the file inaccessible.

Navigating the Microsoft Store

 Apps, which are mini-programs specialized for single tasks, come from the world of *smartphones* (computerized cellphones). And, like the apps from smartphones, apps come only from an App store. In Windows, they come from the Microsoft Store app, available with a click on the taskbar's Microsoft Store icon (shown in the margin). (Earlier versions of Windows called the store the *Windows Store.*)

Although the terms "app" and "program" are often interchangeable, apps differ from traditional desktop programs in several ways:

» Windows allows apps to run within desktop windows rather than consuming the entire screen as they did in some earlier Windows versions.

» Apps are tied to your Microsoft account. That means you need a Microsoft account to download a free or paid app from the Store app.

» When you buy an app from the Microsoft Store app, you can usually run it on up to ten PCs or devices — as long as you're signed in to those PCs or devices with your Windows account. (Some apps may raise or lower that number.)

» Newly installed apps consume just one Start menu icon. Newly installed programs, by contrast, often sprinkle several icons onto your Start menu.

Apps and programs can be created and sold both by large companies and hobbyists working in their spare time. It's difficult to tell beforehand which one will give you the most support should things go wrong.

Although programs and apps look and behave differently, Microsoft unfortunately refers to both as *apps.* You might run across this terminology quirk when dealing with older programs, as well as newer programs created by companies not hip to Microsoft's new lingo.

Adding new apps from the Microsoft Store app

When you're tired of the apps bundled with Windows or you need a new app to fill a special need, follow these steps to bring one into your computer.

 If you miss the OneNote app bundled with Windows 10 but left behind in Windows 11, here's your chance to get it back. Plus, it gives you some practice in downloading an app.

TIP

1. **Click the Start button, and click the Microsoft Store app from the Start menu.**

   The Microsoft Store app jumps to the screen, as shown in Figure 6-5. If you prefer, you can also click the Microsoft Store app (shown in the margin) from the taskbar that always runs along the bottom of your screen.

   Although the Microsoft Store changes its layout frequently, it usually opens to show its Spotlight category along the top edge, where Microsoft highlights a few chosen apps. Keep scrolling down the window to see links to popular apps, as well as apps that are trending, or rising in popularity.

   To see more, point near the Microsoft Store app's left edge to see the top few apps in each category: Apps, Gaming, and Entertainment. (You can also buy or rent movies and computer gadgets from the Microsoft Store app.)

2. **To narrow your search, choose a category by clicking its name.**

   The Store lists its offerings based on your chosen category.

TIP

   Save some time by scrolling down to the "Top Free Apps" section, if you spot one. If you spot an interesting free app, click it. When the Install button appears, click the button to install the app and get the hang of the process. (Similarly, to buy a paid app, click the button that lists its price.)

   Didn't find the right app? Head to the next step.

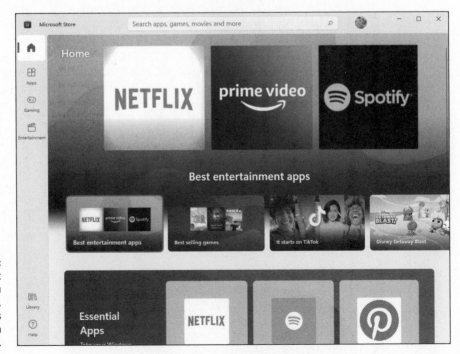

FIGURE 6-5:
The Microsoft Store app lets you download free, trial, or paid apps to launch from your Start menu.

3. **Search for a particular app by typing a keyword into the Search box across the upper edge and pressing Enter.**

   The Search box lives across the store's upper edge. Shown in Figure 6-6, the Search box narrows down the apps by a keyword.

REMEMBER

   Like the Microsoft Store app, almost all searchable apps include a built-in Search box.

   When you press Enter, the Microsoft Store app lists all matching apps, games, artists, albums, movies, and TV shows.

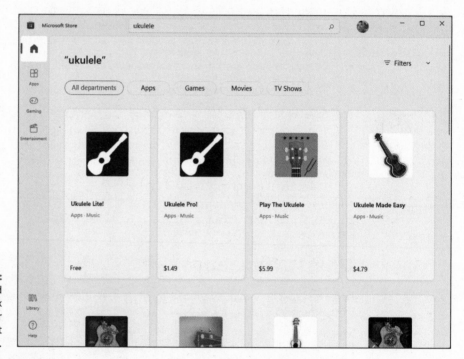

FIGURE 6-6:
Type a keyword in the Search box and press Enter to see relevant apps.

4. **Sort the listed apps.**

   The buttons along the search results top let you fine-tune your app search with a click of a button. Click the Apps button, for example, to further sort your search by only apps; similarly, the Gaming, Movies, and TV Shows buttons limit your search to those categories.

5. **Click any app to read a more detailed description.**

A page opens to show more detailed information, including its price tag, pictures, reviews left by previous customers, and more technical information.

6. **Click the Get or Price button.**

When you find a free app that you can't live without, grab it with a click on its adjacent Get button. To buy a paid app, click the button that lists its price. The price will be charged to the credit card linked to your Microsoft account. If you haven't yet entered a card, Microsoft walks you through the process.

TECHNICAL STUFF

The Microsoft Store may ask you to choose which drive to use for installing your app. Most people choose their C: drive; owners of tablets with limited storage may prefer to choose their memory card, instead, which is usually the D: drive. (Tiny tablets traditionally come with tiny C: drives.)

No matter what you download from the Microsoft Store, the new item appears on your Start menu's alphabetical All Apps list as quickly as your internet connection speed allows.

To copy an app from the All Apps list to a front-page Start menu icon, right-click the app's name and choose Pin to Start. I explain how to customize your Start menu further in Chapter 2.

NEW

Microsoft plans to offer Android apps from the Microsoft Store sometime in 2022. Supposedly, the Android apps will run in onscreen windows.

Uninstalling apps

Downloaded a dud app? To uninstall any app from the Start menu, right-click its icon. When the pop-up menu appears, click Uninstall.

Uninstalling an app removes that app only from *your* account's Start menu. Your action won't affect other account holders on your PC who may have installed the app.

Uninstalling an app also won't give you a refund on apps you've purchased, but decided they were duds.

UPDATING YOUR APPS

Programmers constantly tweak their apps, smoothing over rough spots, adding new features, and plugging security holes. Whenever you connect with the internet, Windows examines your installed apps. If any are out of date, Windows automatically downloads any waiting updates and applies the updates.

If you're using a cellular connection, don't worry: Apps don't update when you're using a metered internet connection like those found on cellphones. Windows resumes updating the apps as soon as you connect to a Wi-Fi or wired internet connection.

Don't want automatic updates, perhaps when traveling through areas with slow or expensive internet connections? You can temporarily turn off automatic updating by following these steps:

1. **From the Microsoft Store app, click your account icon and choose App Settings from the drop-down menu.**

   Your account icon is your round user account photo, located in the Microsoft Store app's upper-right corner next to the Search box.

2. **When the Settings screen appears, click to make sure the App Updates toggle is set to Off.**

   Your changes take place immediately. When you reach a more reliable internet connection, be sure to set the toggle back to On; otherwise, your apps won't update.

When the App Updates toggle is on, *all* your apps update. You can't keep individual apps from updating, unfortunately. That's why I recommend that you keep your apps set to update automatically. If you try to stop one from updating, you could miss out on security patches as well as improvements to all your other apps.

Taking the Lazy Way with a Desktop Shortcut

As you work, you'll constantly find yourself traveling between the desktop and the Start menu. When you grow tired of meandering through the woods to find a program, folder, disc drive, document, or even a website, create a desktop *shortcut* — an icon that takes you directly to the object of your desires.

Because a shortcut is a mere icon that launches something else, shortcuts are safe, convenient, and disposable. And they're easy to tell apart from the original because they have a little arrow lodged in their lower-left corner, as you can see on the folder shortcut shown in the margin.

To skip the Start menu, follow these instructions to create desktop shortcuts to your oft-used items:

>> **Folders or Documents:** From within File Explorer, right-click a favorite folder or document, and choose Show More Options. When the pop-up menu appears, choose Send To, and select the Desktop (Create Shortcut) option. The shortcut appears on your desktop.

>> **Websites:** When viewing a website in Microsoft Edge, look for the little icon in front of the website's address in the browser's Address bar. Drag and drop that little icon to your desktop for quick access later.

>> **Storage areas:** Open File Explorer with a click of its icon on the desktop's taskbar. Then, while holding down your right mouse button, drag and drop nearly anything you want to the desktop. Release the mouse button and choose Create Shortcut Here from the pop-up menu. (This works for drives, folders, files, and even network locations.)

Here are some more tips for desktop shortcuts:

>> For quick CD or DVD burning, put a shortcut to your disc drive on your desktop. Burning files to disc becomes as simple as dragging and dropping them onto the disc drive's new shortcut. (Insert a blank disc into the disc drive's tray, confirm the settings, and begin burning your disc.)

>> Want to send a desktop shortcut to the Start menu? Right-click the desktop shortcut and choose Pin to Start.

WARNING

>> Feel free to move shortcuts from place to place, but *don't* move the items they launch. If you do, the shortcut won't be able to find the item, causing Windows to panic and search (usually in vain) for the relocated goods.

>> Want to see what program a shortcut will launch? Right-click the shortcut, and click Open File Location. The shortcut quickly takes you to its leader.

Absolutely Essential Guide to Cutting, Copying, and Pasting

Windows took a tip from the kindergartners and made *cut* and *paste* an integral part of computing life. You can electronically *cut* or *copy* just about anything and then *paste* it just about anyplace else with little fuss and even less mess.

For example, you can copy a photo and paste it onto your party invitation flyers. You can move files by cutting them from one folder and pasting them into another. You can cut and paste your digital camera's photos into a folder inside your Pictures folder. And you can easily cut and paste paragraphs to different locations within a word processor.

The beauty of the Windows desktop is that, with all those windows onscreen at the same time, you can easily grab bits and pieces from any of them and paste all the parts into a brand-new window.

TIP

Don't overlook copying and pasting for the small stuff. Copying a name and an address is much faster and more accurate than typing them into your letter by hand. Or, when somebody emails you a web address, copy and paste it directly into your browser's Address bar. It's easy to copy most items displayed on websites too (much to the dismay of many professional photographers).

The quick 'n' dirty guide to cut 'n' paste

REMEMBER

In compliance with the Don't Bore Me with Details Department, here's a quick guide to the three basic steps used for cutting, copying, and pasting:

1. **Select the item to cut or copy: a few words, a paragraph, or an entire page; a file or a group of files; a web address; or just about any other item on your computer.**

2. **Right-click your selection, and choose the Cut or Copy icons from the top of the pop-up menu, depending on your needs.**

    Use *Cut* when you want to *move* something. Use *Copy* when you want to *duplicate* something, leaving the original intact.

    Keyboard shortcut: Hold down Ctrl, and press X to cut or C to copy.

3. **Right-click the item's destination, and choose Paste.**

You can right-click inside a document, folder, another program, or some other place in your computer.

Keyboard shortcut: Hold down Ctrl and press V to paste.

The next three sections explain each of these three steps in more detail.

Selecting things to cut or copy

Before you can shuttle pieces of information to new places, you have to tell Windows exactly what you want to grab. The easiest way to tell it is to *select* the information with a mouse. In most cases, selecting involves one swift trick with the mouse, which then highlights whatever you've selected.

>> **To select text in a document, website, or spreadsheet:** Put the mouse pointer or cursor at the beginning of the information you want and hold down the mouse button. Then move the mouse to the end of the information and release the button. That's it! That lassoing action selects all the stuff lying between where you clicked and released, as shown in Figure 6-7.

TIP

On a touchscreen, double-tap one word to select it. To select more than one word, double-tap the first word, but keep your finger pressed on the glass with your second tap. Then slide your finger along the glass until you've reached the area where the highlighting should stop. Done? Remove your finger to select that portion of text.

WARNING

Be careful after you highlight a bunch of text. If you accidentally press the K key, for example, the program replaces your highlighted text with the letter *k*. To reverse that calamity, choose Undo from the program's Edit menu (or press Ctrl+Z, which is the magical keyboard shortcut for Undo).

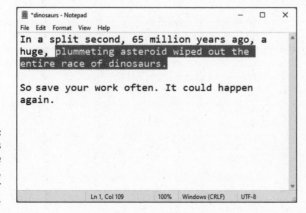

FIGURE 6-7:
Windows highlights the selected text, changing its color for easy visibility.

>> **To select any files or folders:** Simply click a file or folder to select it. To select *several* items, try these tricks:

- **If all the files are in a row:** Click the first item in the bunch, hold down the Shift key, and then select the last item. Windows highlights the first and last items as well as everything in between.

- **If the files *aren't* in a row:** Hold down the Ctrl key while clicking each file or folder you want to select.

The next section explains how to cut or copy a selected item.

>> After you select something, cut it or copy it *immediately*. If you absentmindedly click the mouse someplace else, your highlighted text or file reverts to its boring self, and you're forced to start over.

REMEMBER

TIP

SELECTING INDIVIDUAL LETTERS, WORDS, PARAGRAPHS, AND MORE

When dealing with words in Windows, these shortcuts help you quickly select information:

- To select an individual *letter or character,* click in front of the character. Then, while holding down the Shift key, press the right-arrow key. Keep holding down these two keys to keep selecting text in a line.

- To select a single *word,* point at it with the mouse and double-click. The word changes color, meaning it's highlighted. (In most word processors, you can hold down the button on its second click, and then by moving the mouse around you can quickly highlight additional text word by word.)

- To select a single *line* of text, simply click next to it in the left margin. To highlight additional text line by line, keep holding down the mouse button and move the mouse up or down. You can also keep selecting additional lines by holding down the Shift key and pressing the left-arrow key or the right-arrow key.

- To select a *paragraph,* double-click next to it in the left margin. (Your mouse pointer often turns to point at the paragraph when it's in the correct place.) To highlight additional text paragraph by paragraph, keep holding down the mouse button on the second click and move the mouse.

- To select an entire *document,* hold down Ctrl and press A. (Or choose Select All from the program's Edit menu.)

>> To delete any selected item, be it a file, paragraph, or picture, press the Delete key. Alternatively, right-click the item and choose Delete from the pop-up menu.

Cutting or copying your selected goods

After you select some information (which I describe in the preceding section, in case you just arrived), you're ready to start playing with it. You can cut it or copy it. (Or just press Delete to delete it.)

REMEMBER

This bears repeating. After selecting something, right-click it. (On a touchscreen, touch it and hold down your finger to fetch the pop-up menu.) When the menu appears, choose Cut or Copy, depending on your needs, as shown in Figure 6-8. Then right-click your destination and choose Paste.

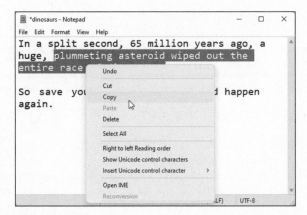

FIGURE 6-8:
To copy information into another window, right-click your selection and choose Copy.

The Cut and Copy options differ drastically. How do you know which one to choose?

>> **Choose Cut to *move* information.** Cutting wipes the selected information off the screen, but you haven't lost anything: Windows stores the cut information in a hidden Windows storage tank called the *Clipboard,* waiting for you to paste it. (Windows 11 adds a new icon, shown in the margin, for the Cut command.)

TIP

Feel free to cut and paste entire files to different folders. When you cut a file from a folder, the icon dims until you paste it. (Making the icon disappear would be too scary.) Changed your mind in mid-cut? Press Esc to cancel the cut, and the icon reverts to normal.

>> **Choose Copy to make a copy of the information.** Compared with cutting, *copying* information is quite anticlimactic. Whereas cutting removes the item from view, copying the selected item leaves it in the window, seemingly untouched. Copied information also goes to the Clipboard until you paste it. (Windows 11 places a new icon, shown in the margin, for the Copy command.)

To save a picture of your entire screen, press +PrtScr. (Some keyboards call that key *Print Screen* or *PrintScr.*) Windows quickly saves the image in a file called Screenshot inside your Pictures folder. Do it again, and the screenshot is named Screenshot (2). (You get the idea.)

Pasting information to another place

After you cut or copy information to the Windows Clipboard, it's checked in and ready for travel. You can *paste* that information nearly anyplace else.

Pasting is relatively straightforward:

1. Open the destination window, and move the mouse pointer or cursor to the spot where you want the stuff to appear.

2. Right-click the mouse, and choose Paste from the pop-up menu.

Presto! The item you just cut or copied immediately leaps into its new spot.

Or, if you want to paste a file onto the desktop, right-click on the desktop and choose Paste. The cut or copied file appears where you've right-clicked. (Windows 11 adds a new icon for Paste, shown in the margin, to the right-click menu.)

>> The Paste command inserts a *copy* of the information that's sitting on the Clipboard. The information stays on the Clipboard, so you can keep pasting the same thing into other places if you want.

>> To paste on a touchscreen, hold down your finger where you'd like to paste the information. When the menu pops up, tap Paste.

TIP

>> Some programs, including File Explorer, have toolbars along their tops, offering additional one-click access to the versatile Cut, Copy, and Paste buttons, as shown in Figure 6-9. (To keep you from having to move you hand too much, they also appear along the bottom of some pop-up menus.)

NEW

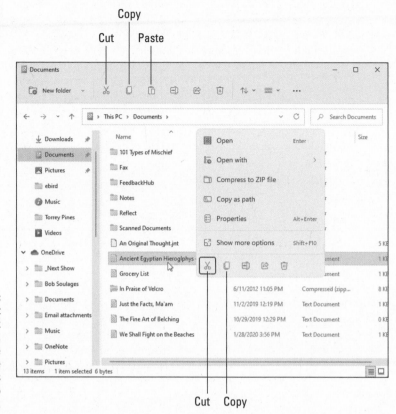

FIGURE 6-9:
Throughout
Windows 11, look
for the new Cut,
Copy, and Paste
icons along the
bottom of its
many pop-up
menus.

TIP

UNDOING WHAT YOU'VE JUST DONE

Windows offers a way for you to undo your last action, which quickly pours the spilled milk back into the carton.

Hold down the Ctrl key, and press the Z key. The last mistake you made is reversed, sparing you from further shame. (Pressing a program's Undo button, if you can find one, does the same thing.)

And if you mistakenly undo something that really should have stayed in place, press Ctrl+Y. That undoes your last undo, putting it back in place.

Chapter **7**

Finding the Lost

S ooner or later, Windows gives you that head-scratching feeling. "Gosh," you say as you drum nervous fingers, "that stuff was *right there* a second ago. Where did it go?"

When Windows starts playing hide-and-seek, this chapter tells you where to search and how to make it stop playing foolish games.

Finding Currently Running Apps and Programs

The Windows desktop lets you run apps and programs in windows, keeping everything neatly self-contained. But even then, those windows tend to overlap, hiding the ones beneath.

How do you find and return to an app or program you just used? How do you easily jump between them, perhaps glancing at a report while creating a spreadsheet?

Windows offers a quick solution to the problem: It can clear the screen, shrink all your running apps and programs into miniature windows, and show you the lineup, as displayed in Figure 7-1. Click the app or program you want, and it returns to active duty at its normal size.

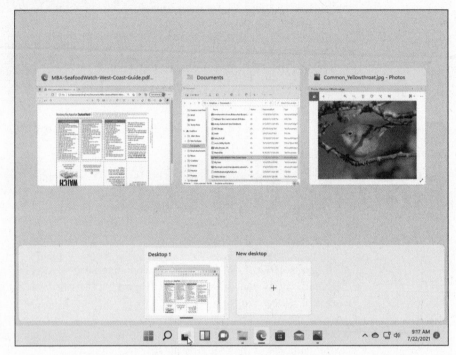

FIGURE 7-1:
Click the Task View icon to see all your currently running apps and programs.

To see the list of your recently used apps and programs (and to close unwanted ones, if desired), employ any of these tricks:

>> **Mouse:** Click the taskbar's Task View icon (shown in the margin) to see miniature windows of all your open apps. To switch to an app, click its miniature window. To close an app, right-click its thumbnail and choose Close. (You can also click the X in the thumbnail's upper-right corner.)

>> **Keyboard:** Press ▦ +Tab to see the list of your most recently used apps, as shown in Figure 7-1. Press the left- or right-arrow keys to select different miniature windows. When you've selected your desired window, press Enter, and the app fills the screen.

NEW

Windows 11 no longer allows touchscreen owners to slide their finger gently inward from the screen's left edge to see all their open apps. Well, you can still slide your finger inward, but you'll only see a monthly calendar and any waiting notifications.

The Task View icon shows your currently running apps *and* desktop programs, making it easy to return to work.

Clicking the Task View icon also lets you create a *virtual desktop*, an odd concept that gives you *more than one desktop*, that I cover in Chapter 3.

Finding Lost Windows on the Desktop

The Windows desktop works much like a spike memo holder. Every time you open a new window or program, you toss another piece of information onto the spike. The window on top is easy to spot, but how do you reach the windows lying beneath it?

If you can see any part of a buried window's edge or corner, a well-placed click fetches it, bringing it to the top.

When your window is completely buried, look at the desktop's *taskbar* — that strip along your screen's bottom edge. Spot your missing window's icon on the task-bar? Click it to dredge the window back to the top. (See Chapter 3 for details about the taskbar.)

Still can't get at that missing window? Hold down the Alt key and press Tab. Shown in Figure 7-2, Windows shows thumbnails of all your open windows, pro-grams, and apps in a strip across the screen's center. While holding down the Alt key, repeatedly press Tab, and Windows highlights a different app or window with each press of the Tab key. When your window is highlighted, let go of the Alt key, and that window appears atop your desktop.

TIP

Pressing the Task View icon, described in the preceding section, also lets you see miniature views of every open window. When you spot the window you want to bring back to the forefront, return to it with a click.

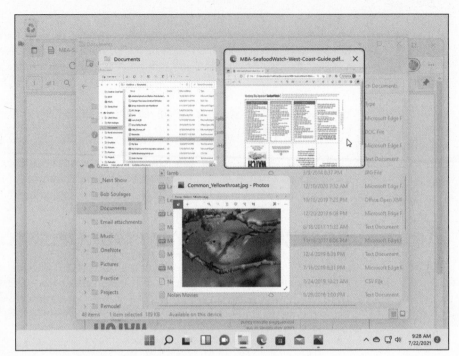

FIGURE 7-2:
Hold down the Alt
key and press Tab
repeatedly to
cycle through
your open
windows.

Locating a Missing App, Program, Setting, or File

The preceding two sections explain how to find *currently running* apps and programs. But what about things that you haven't looked at for a while?

 That's the job of the Search box, which now lives atop the Start menu. To jump immediately to the Search box, click the little magnifying glass icon, shown in the margin. (It lives next to the Start button on the taskbar.)

But whether you reach the Search box from the Start menu or from the magnifying glass icon, the Search box searches through *everything*, both on your PC and the internet. That lets you help you find wandering files, hidden settings, and informational tidbits, all with one search.

To search for missing things, follow these steps:

 1. Click the taskbar's Search icon to summon the Search window, and then type what you'd like to find.

 The Search box accepts typing as soon as you click or tap its icon. As you type, Windows immediately begins searching for matches.

For example, here's what happens when searching for Lester Young: As you begin typing letters, Windows begins listing files with matching names, as shown in Figure 7-3. After typing **Lester You** on my computer, for example, Windows found several matches and organized them in the Search window in these categories:

- **Best Match:** The Search box lists all matching terms, with the best match at the top, in this case, a folder on my PC with the music of saxophone player Lester Young.

- **Search the Web:** Beneath the best match, the Search window shows internet links to other potential matches, including a doctor with the same name.

- **Folders:** Six folders contain the term Lester Young.

- **Music:** My computer holds 13 music files with Lester Young.

As you begin typing, the Search box concentrates on speed, so it searches only for matching filenames stored on your computer and OneDrive, as well as doing a quick internet search.

If you spot your missing item, jump ahead to Step 3.

If you finish typing your complete search term but *don't* see your sought-after item on the Search list, move on to Step 2. You need to define your search more thoroughly.

2. **Limit your search to a specific category.**

   To route your search to a specific area, click one of the words just below the Search box. Choose Apps, for example, and the window lists a link to search for matching apps from the Microsoft Store, as shown in Figure 7-4.

   No matter which category you choose, Windows immediately shows any available matches. Changed your mind about a search category? Click a different word to route your search to that category, instead.

3. **Choose a matching item to open it, bringing it to the screen.**

   Click a song, for example, and it begins playing. Click a setting, and the Control Panel or Settings app appears, open to that particular setting. Click a folder, and it opens in a new window.

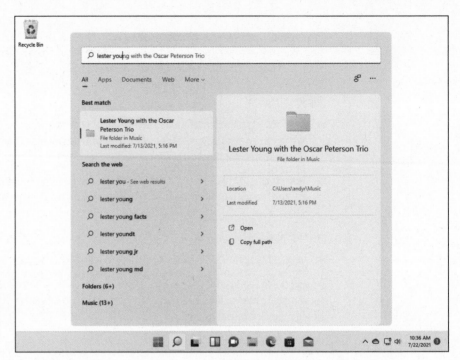

FIGURE 7-3:
The Search box searches for items both on your computer and the internet.

FIGURE 7-4:
Narrow your search further by limiting it to certain areas.

TIP

These tips can help you wring the most out of the Search feature:

>> In its emphasis on speed, the Search window lists only files with names that match your search term. While this strategy sometimes helps you find quick matches, it may not find your shopping list if you search for **oranges**. When you don't spot a sure match, finish typing your search term and click one of the icons along the top of the pane to route your search to the appropriate spot.

>> Don't press the Enter key after typing in your Search. If you do that, Windows calls up the first match, which may not be what you want. Wait to see what matches turn up and then click the desired match.

>> The Search box scours every file in your `Documents`, `Music`, `Pictures`, and `Videos` folders. That feature makes storing your files in those folders more important than ever.

>> The Search box also scours every file you store on your OneDrive space, even if those files aren't also stored on your PC.

>> Windows doesn't search for files stored in removable devices, such as flash drives, CDs, DVDs, or portable hard drives.

>> If you're searching for a common word and the Search box finds too many files, limit your search by typing a short phrase from your sought-after file: **Shortly after the cat nibbled the bamboo**, for example. The more words you type, the better your chances of pinpointing a particular file.

>> The Search box ignores capital letters. It considers **Bee** and **bee** to be the same insect.

TECHNICAL STUFF

WHERE'S CORTANA?

Windows 10 included a personal digital assistant named *Cortana*. Cortana tried to simplify your life by finding not only missing files but also helpful bits of information about you and your surroundings. In real life, though, most people found Cortana to be a nuisance who kept interrupting in a robotic attempt to be helpful.

Windows 11 still keeps Cortana around, but it no longer interferes with the Windows 11 setup process, and the Cortana icon no longer lives on the taskbar. Microsoft recently placed Cortana on its *deprecated* list, meaning it's no longer being developed and is slated for eventual removal.

If you miss Cortana, fire it up by clicking the Start button and typing **Cortana.** After you log in with your Microsoft Account, Cortana wakes up and greets you, just as it did in Windows 10.

Finding a Missing File inside a Folder

The Start menu's Search box can be overkill when you're poking around inside a single desktop folder, looking for a missing file. To solve the "sea of files in a folder" problem, Windows includes a Search box in every folder's upper-right corner. That Search box limits your search to files within that *particular* folder.

To find a missing file within a specific folder, click inside that folder's Search box and begin typing a word or short phrase from your missing file. As you type letters and words, Windows begins filtering out files that are missing your sought-after word or phrase. It keeps narrowing down the candidates until the folder displays only a few files, including, I hope, your runaway file.

When a folder's Search box locates too many possible matches, bring in some other helping hands: the headers above each column. For best results, click the word View along the folder's top edge and select Details from the drop-down menu. That lines up your filenames in one column, as shown in Figure 7-5. The first column, Name, lists the name of each file, and the adjacent columns list specific details about each file.

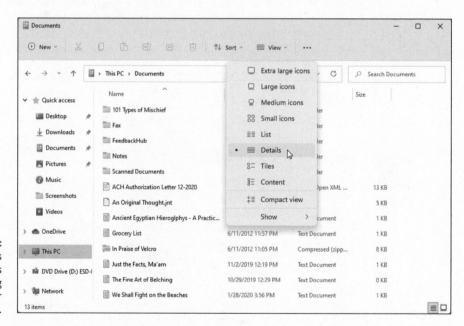

FIGURE 7-5:
Details view lets you sort your files by name, making them easier to find.

TECHNICAL STUFF

DEEP SORT

A folder's Details view (shown in Figure 7-5) arranges your filenames into a single column, with oodles of detail columns flowing off to the right. You can sort a folder's contents by clicking the word atop any column: Name, Date Modified, Author, and so on. But the sort features in Windows go much deeper, as you'll notice when clicking the little downward-pointing arrow that appears as you hover your mouse pointer over each column's name.

Click the little arrow to the right of the words *Date Modified,* for example, and a calendar drops down. Click a date, and the folder quickly displays files modified on that particular date, filtering out all the rest. Beneath the calendar, check boxes also let you view files created Today, Yesterday, Last Week, Earlier This Month, Earlier This Year, or simply A Long Time Ago. (The available check boxes change depending on the age of the files inside your currently viewed folder.)

Similarly, click the arrow next to the Authors column header, and a drop-down menu lists the authors of every document in the folder. Select the check boxes next to the author names you'd like to see, and Windows immediately filters out files created by other people, leaving only the matches. (This feature works best with Microsoft Office documents.)

These hidden filters can be dangerous, however, because you can easily forget that you've turned them on. If you spot a check mark next to any column header, you've left a filter turned on, and the folder is hiding some of its files. To turn off the filter and see *all* that folder's files, deselect the check box next to the column header and examine the drop-down menu. Click any selected check boxes on that drop-down menu to remove their check marks and remove the filter.

TIP

See the column headers, such as Name, Date Modified, and Type, atop each column? Click any of those headers to sort your files by that term. Here's how to sort by some of the column headers you may see in your Documents folder:

>> **Name:** Know the first letter of your file's name? Then click here to sort your files alphabetically. You can then pluck your file from the list. (Click Name again to reverse the sort order.)

>> **Date Modified:** When you remember the approximate date you last changed a document, click the Date Modified header. That places your newest files atop the list, making them easy to locate. (Clicking Date Modified again reverses the order, a handy way to weed out old files you may no longer need.)

>> **Type:** This header sorts files by their contents. All your photos group together, for example, as do all your Word documents. It's a handy way to find a few stray photos swimming in a sea of text files.

>> **Size:** Sorting here places your 45-page thesis on one end and your grocery list on the other.

>> **Authors:** Microsoft Word and some other programs tack your name onto your work. A click on this label sorts the files alphabetically by their creators' names.

>> **Tags:** Windows often lets you assign tags to your documents and photos, a task I describe later in this chapter. Adding the tag "Moldy Cheese" to that pungent photo session lets you retrieve those pictures by either typing the tag or sorting a folder's files by their tags.

TIP

Folders usually display about five columns of details, but you can add more columns. In fact, you can sort files by their word count, song length, photo size, creation date, and dozens of other details. To see a list of available detail columns, right-click an existing label along a column's top. When the drop-down menu appears, select More to see the Choose Details window. Click to put check marks next to the new detail columns you'd like to see, and then click OK.

Finding Lost Photos

Windows indexes your email down to the last word, but it can't tell the difference between photos of your cat and photos of your office party. When it comes to photos, the ID work lies in *your* hands, and these tips make the chore as easy as possible:

>> **Store shooting sessions in separate folders.** The Windows Photo importing feature automatically creates a new folder to store each session, named after the current date. But if you're using some other program to dump photos, be sure to create a new folder for each session. Then name the folder with a short description of your session: *Dog Walk, Kite Surfing,* or *Truffle Hunt.* (Windows indexes the folder names, making them easier to find down the road.)

>> **Sort by date.** Have you stumbled onto a massive folder that's a mishmash of digital photos? Try this quick sorting trick: Click the word View along the folder's upper edge, and choose Large Icons to make the photos morph into identifiable thumbnails. Then, from the adjacent Sort menu, choose More from the drop-down menu. From there, you can choose Date Taken. Windows sorts the photos by the date you snapped them, turning chaos into organization.

>> **Rename your photos.** Instead of leaving your Tunisian vacation photos with their boring camera-given names like DSC_2421, DSC_2422, and so on, give them meaningful names: Select all the files in your Tunisia folder by clicking the Home tab on the Ribbon and clicking the Select All button. Then right-click the first picture, choose Rename, and type **Tunisia**. Windows names them as Tunisia, Tunisia (2), Tunisia (3), and so on. (If you messed up, immediately press Ctrl+Z to undo the renaming.)

Following those simple rules helps keep your photo collection from becoming a jumble of files.

REMEMBER

Be *sure* to back up your digital photos to a portable hard drive, CDs, DVDs, or another backup method I describe in Chapter 13. If they're not backed up, you'll lose your family history when your PC's hard drive eventually crashes.

Finding Other Computers on a Network

A *network* is simply a group of connected PCs that can share things, such as your internet connection, files, or a printer. Most people use a public network every day without knowing it: Every time you check your email, your PC connects to another computer on the internet to grab your waiting messages.

Much of the time, you needn't care about the other PCs on your private network. But when you want to find a connected PC, perhaps to grab files from the PC in your family room, Windows is happy to help.

To find a PC on your network, open any folder and click Network on the Navigation pane along the folder's left edge, as shown in Figure 7-6.

Clicking Network lists every PC that's connected to your own PC in a traditional network. To browse files on any of those PCs, just double-click their names.

I walk through the steps of creating your own home network in Chapter 15.

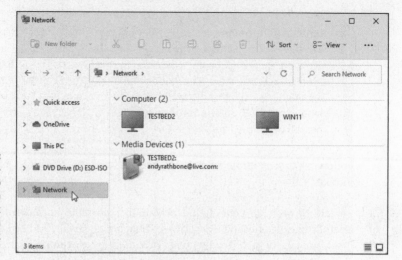

FIGURE 7-6:
To find computers connected to your PC through a network, click the Navigation pane's Network category.

» Printing files, envelopes, and web pages from the desktop

» Adjusting how your work fits on a page

» Troubleshooting printer problems

Chapter **8**

Printing and Scanning Your Work

Occasionally you'll want to take text or an image away from your PC's whirling electrons and place it onto something more permanent: a piece of paper. This chapter tackles that job by explaining all you need to know about printing.

I explain how to print just the relevant portions of a website — without the other pages, the ads, the menus, and the printer-ink-wasting images.

You discover how to print from the Start menu's gang of apps as well as from the desktop's programs.

And should you find yourself near a printer spitting out 17 pages of the wrong thing, flip ahead to this chapter's coverage of the mysterious *print queue*. It's a little-known area that lets you cancel documents *before* they waste all your paper. (I explain how to set up a printer in Chapter 12.)

When you need to turn a piece of paper or printed photo into a file on your PC, check out the last section of this chapter. It provides a rundown on the Windows Scan app. When combined with a scanner, this app transforms maps, receipts, photos, and any other paper items into digital files that you can store on your PC.

Printing from a Start Menu App

Although Microsoft now tries to pretend that Start menu apps and desktop programs are the same, apps often behave quite differently than traditional desktop programs.

Many of the apps can't print, and those that do allow printing don't offer many ways to tinker with your printer's settings. Nevertheless, when you *must* print something from a Windows app, following these steps ensures the best chance of success:

1. **From the Start menu, load the app containing information you want to print.**

    Cross your fingers in the hopes that your app is one of the few that can print.

2. **Click the app's icon for either Settings, Print, or More to see the drop-down menus, and click the Print option.**

     A click on these three striped lines, known informally as the *hamburger menu*, fetches a drop-down menu.

     Similarly, a click on an icon of three dots (shown in the margin) found in some apps also fetches a drop-down menu. (The three dots menu is sometimes called a *More* or *Expand* menu, because clicking it expands a menu to display more options.)

     Just to confuse things, some apps offer a dedicated Print icon, shown in the margin.

    Whether you click the three striped lines, the three dots, or click the Print icon, the app's Print menu appears, shown in Figure 8-1. (If the word Print isn't listed on the drop-down menu or is grayed out, that app probably isn't able to print.)

3. **When you spot your printer from the list that appears, click its name to route your work to that printer.**

    Click the Printer box, and a drop-down menu appears, listing any printers available to your computer. Click the name of the printer you want to handle the job.

     Windows 11 lets you "print" your work to a new *PDF file*, a file format that's accessible from a wide variety of phones, computers, tablets, and other devices. To print your work to a PDF file, click the name of the currently listed printer, and choose Microsoft Print to PDF from the drop-down menu.

    TIP

4. Make any final adjustments.

The Print window sometimes offers a preview of what you're printing, with the total number of pages listed above. To browse the pages you're about to print, click the Forward or Backward arrows above the preview.

Not enough options? Then click the More Settings link at the bottom of the left pane to see options offered by your particular printer model.

5. Click the Print button.

Windows shuffles your work to the printer of your choice, using the settings you chose in Step 4.

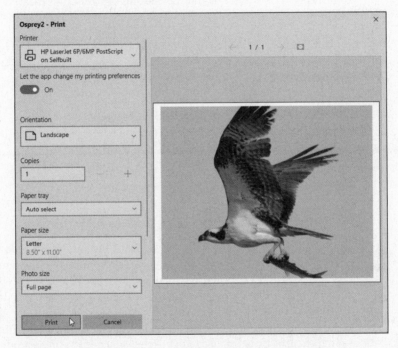

FIGURE 8-1:
Choose your print options, or click the More Settings link for additional options.

Although you can print from a few apps, you'll eventually run into limitations:

REMEMBER

» Most apps don't offer many printing options. You can't print a blank monthly calendar from your Calendar app, for example, but you can print a daily, weekly, or monthly itinerary.

» The More Settings link, described previously in Step 4, lets you choose between Portrait and Landscape mode, as well as choose a printer tray. However, you usually won't find more detailed adjustments, such as choosing margins or adding headers and footers.

In short, although you *can* print from a few apps, your results will be quick and dirty. Desktop programs, described in the rest of this chapter, usually offer much more control over printing jobs.

Printing Your Masterpiece from the Desktop

Built for power and control, the desktop offers many more options when it comes to printing your work. But that power and control often mean wading through a sea of menus.

When working from the desktop, Windows shuttles your work to the printer in any of a half-dozen ways. Chances are good that you'll be using these methods most often:

>> Choose Print from your program's File menu.

>> Click the program's Print icon, usually a tiny printer.

>> Right-click your unopened document's icon, and choose Print.

>> Click the Print button on a program's toolbar.

>> Drag and drop a document's icon onto your printer's icon.

If a window appears, click the OK or Print button, and Windows immediately begins sending your pages to the printer. Take a minute or so to refresh your coffee. If the printer is turned on (and still has paper and ink), Windows handles everything automatically, printing in the background while you do other things.

If the printed pages don't look quite right — perhaps the information doesn't fit on the paper correctly or it looks faded — then you need to fiddle around with the print settings or perhaps change the paper quality, as described in the next sections.

>> To print a bunch of documents quickly, select all their icons. Then right-click the selected icons, and choose Print. Windows quickly shuttles all of them to the printer, where they emerge on paper, one after the other.

>> When printing with an inkjet printer, faded colors usually mean you need to replace your printer's color inkjet cartridge. You can buy replacement cartridges both online and at most office supply stores.

>> Still haven't installed a printer? Flip to Chapter 12, where I explain how to plug one into your computer and make Windows notice it.

PEEKING AT YOUR PRINTED PAGE *BEFORE* IT HITS PAPER

Printing often requires a leap of faith: You choose Print from the menu and wait for the paper to emerge from the printer. If you're blessed, the page looks fine. But if you're cursed, you've wasted yet another sheet of paper.

The Print Preview option, found on many print menus, foretells your printing fate *before* the words hit paper. Print Preview compares your current work with your program's page settings and then displays a detailed picture of the printed page. That preview makes it easy to spot off-kilter margins, dangling sentences, and other printing fouls.

Different programs use slightly different Print Preview screens, with some offering more insight than others. But almost any program's Print Preview screen lets you know whether everything will fit onto the page correctly.

If the preview looks fine, choose Print to send the work to the printer. If something looks wrong, however, click Close to return to your work and make any necessary adjustments.

Adjusting how your work fits on the page

In theory, Windows *always* displays your work as if it were printed on paper. Microsoft's marketing department calls it *What You See Is What You Get*, forever disgraced with the awful acronym WYSIWYG and its awkward pronunciation: "wizzy-wig." If what you see onscreen *isn't* what you want to see on paper, a trip to the program's Page Setup window, shown in Figure 8-2, usually sets things straight.

On desktop programs, the Page Setup window offers many formatting options; on apps, by contrast, the similar Print window offers a more limited version (refer to Figure 8-1). But they both offer several ways to flow your work across a printed page (and subsequently your screen). Page Setup windows differ among programs and printer models, but the following list describes the options that you'll find most often and the settings that usually work best:

>> **Paper Size:** This option lets your program know what size of paper currently lives inside your printer. Leave this option set to Letter for printing on standard, 8.5-x-11-inch sheets of paper. Change this setting only if you're using legal-size paper (8.5 x 14), envelopes, or other paper sizes. (The nearby sidebar, "Printing envelopes without fuss," contains more information about printing envelopes.)

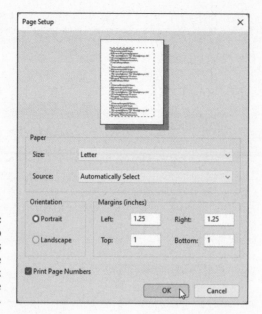

FIGURE 8-2:
The Page Setup window allows you to adjust the way your work fits onto a piece of paper.

>> **Source:** Choose Automatically Select or Sheet Feeder unless you're using a fancy printer that accepts paper from more than one printer tray. People who have printers with two or more printer trays can select the tray containing the correct paper size. Some printers offer Manual Paper Feed, making the printer wait until you slide in that single sheet of paper.

>> **Header/Footer:** Type secret codes in these boxes to customize what the printer places along the top and bottom of your pages: page numbers, titles, and dates, for example, as well as their spacing. Unfortunately, different programs use different codes for their header and footer. If you spot a little question mark in the Page Setup window's upper-right corner, click it and then click inside the Header or Footer box for clues to the secret codes.

>> **Orientation:** Leave this option set to Portrait to print normal pages that read vertically like a letter. Choose Landscape only when you want to print sideways, which is a handy way to print large photos and wide spreadsheets. (If you choose Landscape, the printer automatically prints the page sideways; you don't need to slide the paper sideways into your printer.)

>> **Margins:** Feel free to reduce the margins to fit everything on a single sheet of paper. Or *enlarge* the margins to turn your six-page term paper into the required seven pages.

>> **Printer:** If you have more than one printer installed on your computer or network, click this button to choose which printer should handle the job. Click here to change that printer's settings as well, a job discussed in the next section.

PRINTING ENVELOPES WITHOUT FUSS

Although clicking Envelopes in a program's Page Setup area is fairly easy, printing addresses in the correct spot on the envelope is extraordinarily difficult. Some printer models want you to insert envelopes upside down, but others prefer right side up. Your best bet is to run several tests, placing the envelope into your printer's tray in different ways until you finally stumble on the magic method. (Or you can pull out your printer's manual, if you still have it, and pore over the "proper envelope insertion" pictures.)

After you figure out the correct method for your particular printer, tape a successfully printed envelope above your printer and add an arrow pointing to the correct way to insert it.

Should you eventually give up on printing envelopes, try using Avery's free downloadable templates from Avery's website (www.avery.com). Compatible with Microsoft Word, the templates place little boxes on your screen that precisely match the size of your particular Avery labels. Type the addresses into the little boxes, insert the label sheet into your printer, and Word prints everything onto the little stickers. You don't even need to lick them.

Or do as I did: Buy a little rubber stamp with your return address. It's much faster than stickers or printers.

When you're finished adjusting settings, click the OK button to save your changes. (Click the Print Preview button, if it's offered, to make sure that everything looks right.)

TIP

To find the Page Setup box in some apps and programs, click the little arrow next to the program's Printer icon and choose Page Setup from the menu that drops down.

Adjusting your printer's settings

When you choose Print from many programs, Windows offers one last chance to spruce up your printed page. The Print window, shown in Figure 8-3, lets you route your work to any printer installed on your computer or network. While there, you can adjust the printer's settings, choose your paper quality, and select the pages (and quantities) you'd like to print.

FIGURE 8-3:
The Print window lets you choose your printer and adjust its settings.

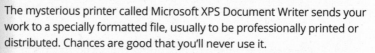

You're likely to find these settings waiting in the Print window:

TIP

>> **Select Printer:** Ignore this option if you have only one printer, as Windows will choose it automatically. If your computer has access to several printers, click the one that should receive the job. If you have a fax built into your printer, computer, or network, click Fax to send your work as a fax.

The mysterious printer called Microsoft XPS Document Writer sends your work to a specially formatted file, usually to be professionally printed or distributed. Chances are good that you'll never use it.

>> **Page Range:** Select All to print your entire document. To print just a few of its pages, select the Pages option and enter the page numbers you want to print. For example, enter **1-4, 6** to leave out page 5 of a 6-page document. If you've highlighted a paragraph, choose Selection to print that particular paragraph — a great way to print the important part of a web page and leave out the rest.

>> **Number of Copies:** Most people leave this set to 1 copy, unless everybody in the boardroom wants their own copy. You can choose Collate only if your printer offers that option. (Most don't, leaving you to sort the pages yourself.)

>> **Preferences:** Click this button to see a window like the one in Figure 8-4, where you can choose options specific to your own printer model. The Printing Preferences window's Layout and Paper/Quality tabs let you select different grades of paper, choose between color and black and white, set the printing quality, and make last-minute corrections to the page layout. (This option varies greatly according to your printer model, so yours may look different.)

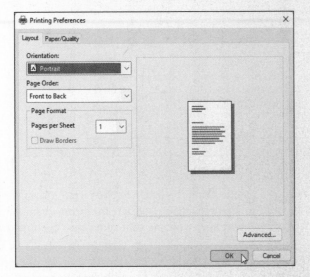

FIGURE 8-4:
The Printing
Preferences
window lets you
change settings
specific to your
printer model.

Canceling a print job

Just realized you sent the wrong 26-page document to the printer? So you panic and hit the printer's Off button. Unfortunately, many printers automatically pick up where they left off when you turn them back on, leaving you or your co-workers to deal with the mess.

To purge the mistake from your printer's memory, follow these steps:

1. **From the desktop's taskbar, right-click your printer's icon and choose your printer's name from the pop-up menu.**

   To see your printer's icon, you may need to click the little upward-pointing arrow to the left of the taskbar's icons next to the clock.

   When you choose your printer's name, the handy *print queue* window appears, as shown in Figure 8-5.

2. **Right-click your mistaken document, and choose Cancel to end the job. If asked to confirm, click the Yes button. Repeat with any other listed unwanted documents.**

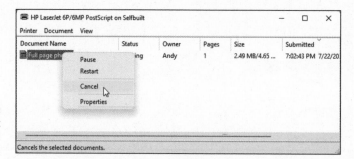

FIGURE 8-5:
Use the print
queue to cancel a
print job.

The print queue can take a minute or two to clear itself. (To speed things up, click the View menu and choose Refresh.) When the print queue is clear, turn your printer back on; it won't keep printing that same darn document.

>> The print queue, also known as the *print spooler,* lists every document waiting patiently to reach your printer. Feel free to change the printing order by dragging and dropping documents up or down the list. (You can't move anything in front of the currently printing document though.)

>> Sharing your printer on the network? Print jobs sent from other PCs sometimes end up in your computer's print queue, so you'll need to cancel the botched ones. (And networked folks who share their printer may need to delete your botched print jobs as well.)

>> If your printer runs out of paper during a job and stubbornly halts, add more paper. Then to start things flowing again, open the print queue, right-click your document, and choose Restart. (Some printers have an Online button that you push to begin printing again.)

TIP

>> You can send items to the printer even when you're working in the coffee shop with your laptop. Later, when you connect the laptop to your printer, the print queue notices and begins sending your files. (Beware: When they're in the print queue, documents are formatted for your specific printer model. If you subsequently connect your laptop to a *different* printer model, the print queue's waiting documents won't print correctly.)

Printing a web page

Although information-stuffed web pages look awfully tempting, *printing* those web pages is rarely satisfying because they look so awful on paper. When sent to the printer, web pages often run off the page's right side, consume zillions of additional pages, or appear much too small to read.

To make matters worse, all those colorful advertisements can suck your printer's color cartridges dry fairly quickly. Only four things make for successfully printed web pages, and I rank them in order of probable success rate:

>> **Use the web page's built-in Print option.** Some websites, but not all, offer a tiny menu option called Print This Page, Text Version, Printer-Friendly Version, or something similar. That option tells the website to strip out its garbage and reformat the page so that it fits neatly onto a sheet of paper. This option is the most reliable way to print a web page.

>> **Choose Print Preview from your browser's File or Print menu.** After 20 years, some web page designers noticed that people want to print their pages, so they tweaked the settings, making their pages *automatically* reformat themselves when printed. If you're lucky, a clean look in the Print Preview window confirms that you've stumbled onto one of those printer-friendly sites.

>> **Copy the portion you want, and paste it into a word processor.** Try selecting the desired text from the web page, copying it, and pasting it into a word processor. Delete any unwanted remnants, adjust the margins, and print the portion you want. I explain how to select, copy, and paste in Chapter 6.

>> **Copy the entire page, and paste it into a word processor.** Although it's lots of work, it's an option. Right-click a blank portion of the web page, and choose Select All. Right-click again, and choose Copy. Next, open Microsoft Word or another full-featured word processor, and paste the web page inside a new document. By hacking away at the unwanted portions, you can sometimes end up with something printable.

TIP

These tips may also come in handy for moving a web page from screen to paper:

>> The Microsoft Edge web browser can print. To print what you're viewing in Edge, click the browser's Settings and More icon (three dots in the upper-right corner), and choose Print from the drop-down menu.

>> For best results in the Edge browser, turn on the Reading View mode by clicking the Reading View icon (shown in the margin). Reading View strips away ads and other detritus, leaving you with a clean page to send to the printer. Unfortunately, Reading View is not available for all websites. But if it's available, you can also enable it with this shortcut key: Ctrl+Shift+R.

>> If you spot an Email option but no Print option, email the page to yourself. Depending on your email program, you may have better success printing it as an email message.

>> To print just a few paragraphs of a web page, use the mouse to select the portion you're after. (I cover the act of *selecting* things in Chapter 6.) Then choose Print from Edge's Tools menu (shown in the margin) to open the Print window, shown previously in Figure 8-3. Finally, in the Page Range box, choose the Selection option.

>> If a web page's table or photo insists on vanishing off the paper's right edge, try printing the page in Landscape mode rather than Portrait. See the "Adjusting how your work fits on the page" section, previously in this chapter, for details on Landscape mode.

Troubleshooting your printer

When you can't print something, start with the basics: Are you *sure* that the printer is turned on, plugged into the wall, full of paper, and connected securely to your computer with a cable?

If so, try plugging the printer into different outlets, turning it on, and seeing whether its power light comes on. If the light stays off, your printer's power supply is probably blown.

TIP

Printers are almost always cheaper to replace than repair. Printer companies make their money on ink cartridges, so they often sell printers at a loss.

If the printer's power light beams brightly, check these things before giving up:

>> Make sure that a sheet of paper hasn't jammed itself inside the printer. (A slow, steady pull usually extricates jammed paper. Sometimes opening and closing the printer's lid starts things moving again.)

TIP

>> Does your inkjet printer still have ink in its cartridges? Does your laser printer have toner? Try printing a test page: Click the taskbar's Search icon (the little magnifying glass), type **Control Panel**, and press Enter. From the Hardware and Sound category, choose Devices and Printers. Right-click your printer's icon, choose Printer Properties, and click the Print Test Page button to see whether the computer and printer can talk to each other.

>> If you're using a wireless printer, try connecting it to your PC with a cable. That helps you see whether the problem is your wireless connection, or the printer itself.

>> Try updating the printer's *driver,* the little program that helps it talk with Windows. Visit the printer manufacturer's website, download the newest Windows driver for your particular printer model, and run its installation program. (I cover drivers in Chapter 13.)

Finally, here are a couple of tips to help you protect your printer and cartridges:

WARNING

>> Turn off your printer when you're not using it. Older inkjet printers, especially, should be turned off when they're not in use. The heat tends to dry the cartridges, shortening their life.

>> Don't unplug your inkjet printer to turn it off. Always use the On/Off switch. The switch ensures that the cartridges slide back to their home positions, keeping them from drying out or clogging.

TIP

CHOOSING THE RIGHT PAPER FOR YOUR PRINTER

If you've strolled the aisles at an office-supply store lately, you've noticed a bewildering array of paper choices. Sometimes the paper's packaging lists its application: Premium Inkjet Paper, for example, for high-quality memos. Here's a list of different print jobs and the types of paper they require. Before printing, be sure to click the Printer's Preferences section to select the grade of paper you're using for that job.

- **Junk:** Keep some cheap or scrap paper around for testing the printer, printing quick drafts, leaving desktop notes, and printing other on-the-fly jobs. Botched print jobs work great here; just use the paper's other side.

- **Letter quality:** Bearing the words Premium or Bright White, this paper works fine for letters, reports, memos, and other things designed for showing to others.

- **Photos:** You can print photos on any type of paper, but they look like photos only on actual *photo-quality paper* — the expensive stuff. Slide the paper carefully into your printer tray so that the picture prints on the glossy, shiny side. Some photo paper requires placing a little cardboard sheet beneath it, which helps glide the paper smoothly through the printer.

- **Labels:** Avery, the paper company, offers templates that let Microsoft Word mesh with Avery's preformatted mailing labels, greeting cards, business cards, CD labels, and other items. You might also try the company's free Avery Design & Print program, available at its website (www.avery.com).

- **Transparencies:** For powerful PowerPoint presentations, buy special transparent plastic sheets designed to be used with your type of printer. Make sure the transparency is compatible with your printer, be it laser or inkjet.

Before plunking down your money, make sure that your paper is designed specifically for your printer type, be it laser or inkjet. Laser printers heat the pages, and some paper and transparencies can't take the heat.

Scanning from the Start Menu

Windows 10 removed the Scan app that came with Windows 8 and 8.1. However, you can still download it for free from the Microsoft Store. Look for the app by its new name, Windows Scan. (I explain how to get apps from the Microsoft Store in Chapter 6.)

I can't give you step-by-steps for your particular scanner because they all work slightly differently. The Windows Scan app doesn't work with some older scanners. But if your scanner is relatively new, you may find Windows Scan to be a refreshing change from the complicated software bundled with most scanners.

REMEMBER

Setting up a new scanner for the first time? Be sure to *unlock* it by sliding a lever or turning a dial on the scanner to the unlock position. That lock protects the scanner during shipping, but you must turn it off before use.

After installing the Windows Scan app from the Microsoft Store and connecting your scanner, follow these steps to scan something into your computer:

1. **From the Start menu, open the Windows Scan app.**

If you don't spot the Windows Scan app on the Start menu, click All Apps in the Start menu's upper-right corner. The Start menu lists all of its apps alphabetically. **Note:** If you don't find the Windows Scan app on your computer, you can download it for free from the Microsoft Store.

Although the Microsoft Store calls the app "Windows Scan," the app renames itself to simply *Scan* when it installs on your PC. Thanks, Microsoft.

Click the Scan app, shown in the margin, and the Scan app appears on the screen. If it complains that your scanner isn't connected, make sure you've connected the USB cable between your computer's USB port and the scanner and that the scanner is turned on.

If your scanner is plugged in and turned on, the Scan app lists your scanner's name, shown in Figure 8-6, and the *file type* used for saving your files. (The PNG file type is widely accepted by most programs.)

If the app doesn't recognize your scanner, your scanner is too old. You're stuck with your scanner's bundled software — if it works — or, unfortunately, buying a new scanner.

2. **(Optional) To change the Scan app's settings, click the Show More link.**

The app's default settings work fine for most jobs. The Show More link offers these options for specific types of scans:

- **File Type:** PNG works fine for most scans. But to create smaller, lower-resolution scans for emailing, choose JPG from this pull-down menu.

- **Color mode:** Choose Color for color items, including photos and glossy magazine pages. Choose Grayscale for nearly everything else, and choose Black and White *only* for line drawings or black-and-white clip art.

- **Resolution (DPI):** For most work, the default 300 works fine. Higher resolution scans (larger numbers) bring more detail but consume more space, making them difficult to email. Lower resolution scans show less detail but create smaller file sizes. You may need to experiment to find the settings that meet your needs.

- **Save File To:** The Scan app creates a Scan folder in your PC's Pictures folder, where it stores your newly scanned images. If you want, you can change the Scan folder's name or even create a different folder for each scanning session.

3. **Click the Preview button to make sure your scan appears correct.**

Click the Preview icon, shown in the margin, and the Scan app makes a first pass, letting you preview a scan made with your chosen settings.

If the preview doesn't look right, make sure you've made the right choice for your job in Color Mode, described in the preceding step. If the preview shows a blank white page, make sure you've *unlocked* the scanner as described in the scanner's bundled instruction sheets.

If you're scanning a smaller item that doesn't fill the entire scanner bed, look for the circle markers in each corner of the preview scan. Drag each circle inward to surround the area you want to copy.

4. **Click the Scan button. When the scan finishes, click the View button to see your scan.**

The Scan app scans your image with the settings you've chosen in the previous steps and then saves your image in your Pictures folder's Scan folder.

The Scan app works well for fast, easy scans. But because it relies on the simple, built-in Windows software, your scanner's built-in control buttons won't work.

If you want your scanner's buttons to work or you need finer control over your scans, skip the Scan app and install your scanner's bundled software. (For some scanner models, Windows Update installs the scanner's bundled software automatically as soon as you plug in the scanner.)

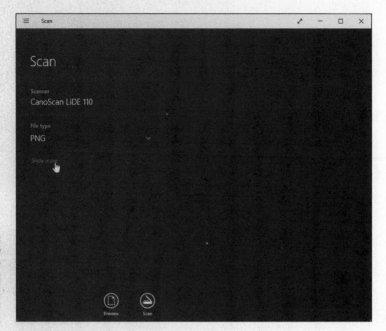

FIGURE 8-6:
Click the Show
More link for
additional
options, or click
Preview to test a
scan.

TIP

For quick-and-dirty scans, just take a picture of the document with the camera built into your phone or tablet. That won't work well for photos, but it's an easy way to keep track of receipts and invoices.

If you need more features than the Scan app offers, check out the desktop's venerable Windows Fax and Scan program. It's more complicated and requires special equipment for faxing, but it offers more features than the Scan app.

3

Getting Things Done on the Internet

Chapter **9**

Cruising the Web

Even when being installed, Windows starts reaching for the internet, hungry for any hint of a connection. After connecting, Windows quickly downloads updates to make your PC run more smoothly. Other motives are less pure: Windows also checks in with Microsoft to make sure that you're not installing a pirated copy.

To help you visit the internet, Windows 11 includes a web browser named *Microsoft Edge*, a familiar sight for Windows 10 upgraders. Fast, sleek, and recently updated with a new look, Microsoft Edge helps you move in and out of today's internet-dependent world.

This chapter explains how to find and fire up Microsoft Edge, connect with the internet, visit websites, and find what you're seeking online.

For ways to keep out the bad stuff, be sure to flip ahead to Chapter 11. It's a primer on safe computing that explains how to avoid the web's bad neighborhoods, which harbor viruses, spyware, hijackers, and other internet parasites.

What's an ISP, and Why Do I Need One?

Everybody needs three things to connect with the internet and visit websites: a computer, web browser software, and an Internet Service Provider (ISP).

You already have the computer, be it a tablet, laptop, or desktop PC. And the newly enhanced browser, Microsoft Edge, handles the software side.

That means most people need to find only an ISP. Most coffee shops, airports, and hotels let you connect wirelessly, and often for free. At home, though, you must pay an ISP for the privilege of surfing the web. When your computer connects to your ISP's computers, Windows automatically finds the internet, and you're ready to surf the web.

Choosing an ISP is fairly easy because you're often stuck with whichever ISPs serve your particular geographic area. Ask your friends and neighbors how they connect and whether they recommend their ISP. Call several ISPs serving your area for a rate quote and then compare rates. Most bill on a monthly basis, so if you're not happy, you can always switch.

>> Although ISPs charge for internet access, you don't always have to pay. More and more public businesses share their internet access for free, usually through a wireless connection. If your phone, laptop, or tablet includes wireless support, and most do, you can browse the internet whenever you're within range of a free wireless signal. (I cover wireless in the next section.)

>> Although a handful of ISPs charge for each minute you're connected, most charge from $30 to $100 a month for service. (Some also offer faster connection speeds for more money.) Make sure that you know your rate before hopping aboard, or you may be unpleasantly surprised at the month's end. Some ISPs offer bundled plans that include not only internet access, but television channels and telephone service.

>> ISPs let you connect to the internet in a variety of ways. The slowest ISPs require a dialup modem and an ordinary phone line; they're still a lifeline for some rural areas. (Satellite access also works well in rural areas.) Faster and the most popular are broadband connections: special DSL or ISDN lines provided by some phone companies, and the even faster cable modems supplied by your cable television company. Some providers offer speedy fiber optic cable. You're only limited by what's offered in your geographic area.

WHERE'S INTERNET EXPLORER?

After 25 years of live performance, Internet Explorer has finally left the building with Windows 11. Built way back in 1995, Internet Explorer carried plenty of baggage. For example, it needed specialized coding to display websites created with older technology. All that old code slowed down Internet Explorer's performance when viewing modern websites. That old code also made Internet Explorer more vulnerable to viruses and other exploits.

So Microsoft started anew with Microsoft Edge, its faster, more modern browser. If you don't care for Microsoft Edge, you're welcome to try Google Chrome (www.google.com/chrome) or Mozilla Firefox (www.GetFirefox.com) browsers. They all have their fans.

TIP

>> You need to pay an ISP for only *one* internet connection. You can share that single connection with any other computers, cellphones, smart TVs, refrigerators, thermostats, lightbulbs, personal assistants like Amazon's Alexa, and other internet-aware gadgetry in your home, office, or kitchen. (I explain how to share an internet connection by creating your own wired or wireless network in Chapter 15.)

Connecting Wirelessly to the Internet

Windows *constantly* searches for a working internet connection, whether your computer connects through a cable or scans the airwaves for a Wi-Fi (wireless) connection. If your computer finds a Wi-Fi connection that you've previously connected with, you're set: Windows quickly connects to it, passes the news along to Microsoft Edge, and you're ready to visit the web.

When you're traveling, however, the wireless networks around are often new, forcing you to find and authorize these new connections.

To connect to a nearby wireless network for the first time (whether it's one in your own home or in a public place), follow these steps:

1. **Click the taskbar's Wi-Fi icon (shown in the margin) near the clock.**

   Don't see the Wi-Fi icon? If you're not connected to the internet, you see the sad looking No internet Access icon (shown in the margin). Click that icon, instead.

   No matter which icon you click, a cluttered menu pops up listing your wireless network status in its upper-left corner, shown in Figure 9-1.

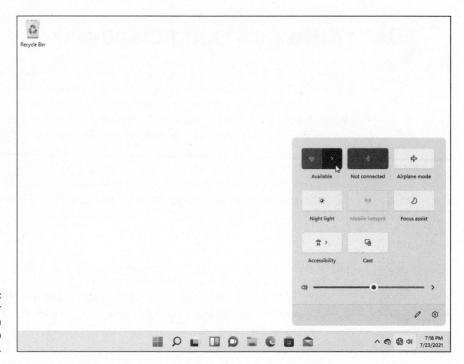

FIGURE 9-1:
Click the Wi-Fi (or
No Network) icon
to see the pop-up
menu.

2. **Click the right arrow next to the pop-up menu's Wi-Fi icon.**

   Windows lists all the nearby wireless networks, as shown in Figure 9-2.

   The networks are ranked by signal strength, with the strongest network listed at the top.

3. **Choose to connect to a network by clicking its name and clicking the Connect button that appears.**

   If you're connecting to an *unsecured network* — a network that doesn't require a password — you're finished. Windows warns you about connecting to an unsecured network, but a click or tap of the Connect button lets you connect anyway. (Don't do anything involving money or entering passwords on an unsecured connection.)

   For a more secure connection, skip the unsecured networks. Instead, ask your hotel staff, coffee shop barista, or airport staff for the password to their secure network. Then head to the next step.

   Unless you specifically don't want to connect to that network automatically, leave the adjacent Connect Automatically check box checked. This tells Windows to connect automatically to that network whenever you're within range, sparing you from following these steps each time.

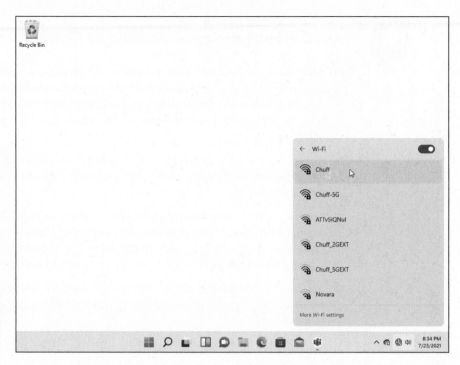

FIGURE 9-2:
Windows shows
the wireless
networks within
your range.

4. **Enter a password if needed.**

   If you try to connect to a *security-enabled* wireless connection, Windows asks you to enter a *network security key* — technospeak for *password*. If you're at home, here's where you type in the same password you entered into your router when setting up your wireless network.

   If you're connecting to somebody *else's* password-protected wireless network, ask the network's owner for the password. You may need to pull out your credit card at the front counter in some hotels and coffee shops; sometimes they charge for access.

5. **If connecting for the first time, choose whether you want to share your files with other people on the network.**

   If you're connecting on your own home or office network, choose "Yes, turn on sharing and connect to devices." Windows makes your network *private*, meaning you may safely share files with others on your private network, as well as connect to shared devices, such as printers.

   If you're connecting in a *public* area, by contrast, always choose "No, don't turn on sharing or connect to devices." Windows makes your network Public, meaning that you can connect with the internet, but other networked computers can't connect to your computer to view or access your files. This helps keep out snoops.

TIP

If you're still having problems connecting, try the following tips:

» When Windows says that it can't connect to your wireless network, it offers to bring up the Network Troubleshooter. The Network Troubleshooter mulls over the problem and then usually says something about the signal being weak. It's really telling you this: "Move your computer closer to the wireless transmitter."

» At some businesses, your browser will open to a Terms of Services agreement. There, you must agree to the company's terms before being allowed to browse further.

» If you're in a hotel room, moving your computer closer to a window may help you find a stronger wireless signal. (It might even pick up a wider variety of available wireless networks.) If you don't mind moving outside your room, then wander down to the lobby or hotel coffee shop to find a better connection.

» If you can't connect to the secured network you want, try connecting to one of the unsecured networks. Unsecured networks work fine for casual browsing on the internet.

Browsing the Web with Microsoft Edge

Built for speedy browsing of modern websites, Microsoft Edge loads quickly and displays web pages as quickly as your connection allows. Part of its speed and clean look comes from its limitations though. The browser hides its menus in order to showcase every website's content. This makes navigation challenging.

 To open Microsoft Edge, click its icon (shown in the margin) on the taskbar along the bottom of your screen. The browser opens, as shown in Figure 9-3, filling the screen with either your last-viewed site or a launch screen that shows the top news, weather, and links to popular sites.

The browser hides most of its menus behind cryptic icons, so I've called them all out in Figure 9-3 and neatly labeled them here:

 » **Tab actions:** This new icon offers three tricks from a drop-down menu. You can choose between these three things:

- Place your tabs *vertically* along the left edge instead of the top edge.

- Retrieve recently closed tabs.

- Add your current group of open tabs to a *collection*, a name for a group of tabs that can be opened with one click.

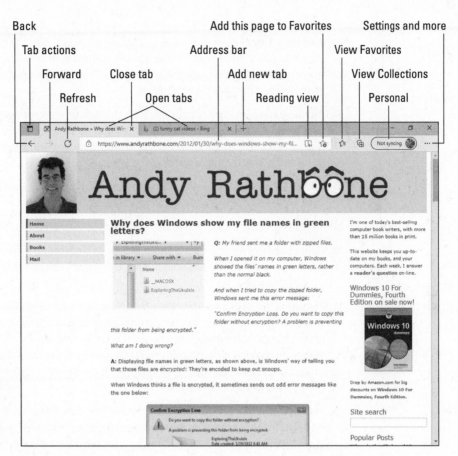

Back   Add this page to Favorites   Settings and more

Tab actions   Address bar   View Favorites

Forward   Close tab   Add new tab   View Collections

Refresh   Open tabs   Reading view   Personal

FIGURE 9-3:
Microsoft Edge
lets you view
several websites,
each in its
own tab.

» **Back:** This back-arrow icon near the upper-left corner lets you revisit the page you just visited.

» **Forward:** A click on this icon lets you return to the page you just left.

» **Refresh:** Handy when viewing sites with breaking news, this icon reloads the currently viewed page, gathering the latest material available.

» **Tabs:** Your currently open sites appear as tabs along the window's top edge, letting you revisit them with a click. (Or you can close them by clicking the X in their tab's right corner.)

» **Address bar:** Click the name of the currently displayed site, which usually appears along the site's top edge, and the Address bar appears, letting you type the address of a website you'd like to visit. Don't know where to go? Type a few descriptive words, and the browser searches for and displays possible matches. Click any match to visit the site.

>> **Add New Tab:** Clicking the plus sign icon, which lives just to the right of your currently open tab or tabs, fetches a blank window with an Address bar along the top. There, you can type either the address of a coveted website or a few search terms for the browser to fetch.

>> **Reading view:** When available, this icon changes the current website's layout to resemble a page of a book. How? When you click the icon, Microsoft Edge ditches lots of the ads and formatting, leaving only text and pertinent photos. (It's a handy way to print a website, too.)

>> **Add to Favorites:** Click the star icon to place your currently viewed page onto your list of *Favorites,* a collection of your frequently visited sites.

>> **Favorites:** This icon lets you revisit websites you've marked as Favorites.

>> **Collections:** When you save a group of tabs as a collection with the Tab Actions icon, described earlier in this list, the groups can be recalled with a click on this icon.

>> **Personal:** When this little box says, "Not Syncing," your favorite websites are saved on Microsoft Edge, but they aren't linked to your *Microsoft account.* To make your favorites to appear whenever you sign into any PC with your Microsoft account, click this button and choose Turn On Sync from the drop-down menu. (This option works best for people who own more than one desktop PC, laptop, or tablet.)

>> **Settings and more:** Clicking this icon with three dots fetches a drop-down list with options for opening a new window, changing the current website's text size, sharing a site with friends, searching for a word on the current page, printing the page, pinning the page to the Start menu, and a slew of other settings.

When you're on the go and looking for quick information, Microsoft Edge's speedy browser and its simple menus might be all you need. (If you're looking to push Microsoft Edge to its edge, click the Settings and More icon; you may be surprised at all the options.)

If you've clicked or tapped the wrong button but haven't yet lifted your finger, stop! Commands don't take effect until you complete the click on a button by *releasing* your finger. Keep holding down your finger or mouse button but slide the pointer or finger away from the wrong button. Move safely away from the button and *then* lift your finger.

Moving from one web page to another

Web pages come with specific addresses, just like homes do. *Any* web browser lets you move among those addresses. No matter which browser you use, they all let you move from one page to another in any of three ways:

>> By pointing and clicking a button or link that automatically whisks you away to another page

>> By typing a complicated string of code words (the web address) into the Address bar of the web browser and pressing Enter

>> By clicking the navigation buttons on the browser's toolbar, which is usually at the top of the screen

Clicking links

The first way to navigate the web is by far the easiest. Look for *links* — highlighted words or pictures on a page — and click them.

 For example, see how the mouse pointer turned into a hand (shown in the margin) as it pointed at the word *Books* in Figure 9-4? That hand means the thing you're pointing at (be it a word, button, or picture) is clickable. In this instance, I can click the word *Books* to see a web page with more information about that subject. The mouse pointer morphs into a hand whenever it's over a link. Click any linked word to see pages dealing with that link's particular subject.

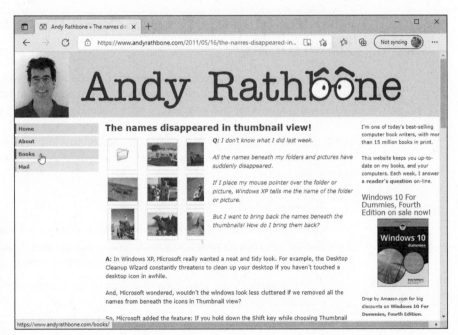

FIGURE 9-4: When the mouse pointer becomes a hand, click the word or picture to go to a web page with more information about that item.

Typing web addresses in the Address bar

The second method of web surfing is more difficult. If a friend gives you a napkin with a cool website's address written on it, you need to type the website's address into your browser's *Address bar* — the text-filled bar near the top of the browser window. You'll do fine as long as you don't misspell anything.

See the address for my website along the top of Figure 9-3? I typed **andyrathbone. com** into the Address bar. When I pressed Enter, Microsoft Edge scooted me to my website. (You don't need to type the *http://www* part, thank goodness.)

Using the Microsoft Edge menu icons

Finally, you can maneuver through the internet by clicking various icons on Microsoft Edge's stripped-down menus, as described in the previous section and Figure 9-3. Click the browser's Back arrow icon, for example, to return to a page you just visited.

TIP

Hover your mouse pointer over a confusing item in any program, and a pop-up usually appears, explaining that icon's purpose in life.

Making Microsoft Edge open to your favorite site

When you open the desktop's web browser, it needs to show you *something* right away. Well, that something can be any website you want. In computer terms, that's called your *home page*, and you can tell Microsoft Edge to use any site you want.

Naturally, Microsoft wants Microsoft Edge to open to a *Microsoft* website. To make Microsoft Edge open to your *own* favorite site, you need to jump through these convoluted hoops:

1. **Visit your favorite website or websites.**

Choose any sites you like. If you choose Google News (http://news.google.com), for example, Microsoft Edge always opens with the latest headlines from the Google News site. Feel free to open more than one favorite site in other tabs.

2. **Click the Settings and More icon in Microsoft Edge, and choose Settings from the drop-down menu.**

The Settings pane appears, listing your options.

3. **In the When Edge Starts section, click the Use All Open Tabs button, as shown in Figure 9-5.**

Choosing this option tells Microsoft Edge to remember your currently open tabs and reopen them the next time you launch the browser. To leave this page, close the tab by clicking the X in the top of the tab named Settings. Your changes take place immediately.

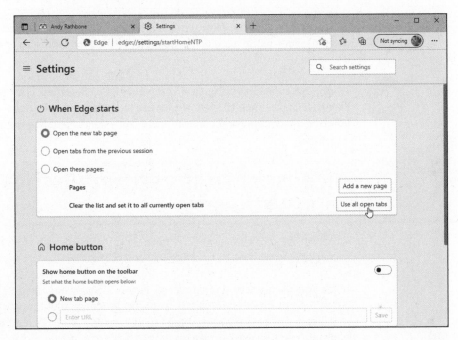

FIGURE 9-5: Click the Use All Open Tabs button.

After Microsoft Edge opens with your chosen home page or pages, you can still browse the internet, searching for topics by typing them into the Address bar or by simply pointing and clicking different links.

TIP

Just as your browser's home page is the site you see when your browser opens, a website's home page is its "cover," like the cover of a magazine. Whenever you navigate to a website, you usually start at the site's home page and begin browsing from there.

Revisiting favorite places

Sooner or later, you'll stumble across a web page that's indescribably delicious. To make sure that you can find it again later, add it to your list of favorite pages. To add the page you're currently viewing to your Favorites list, follow these steps:

1. **Click the Add to Favorites icon (shown in the margin) at the end of the site's address along the top of your Microsoft Edge browser.**

   The Favorite Added box appears, listing the site's name. (Feel free to edit the name to make it more descriptive.)

2. **Click the Done button.**

   Click the Done button, and the name is added to your Favorites list.

To return to a favorite page, click Microsoft Edge's Favorites icon (shown in the margin). Your list of added sites appears, letting you return to one with a click on its name.

TIP

To remove a disappointing site from your list of favorites, click Microsoft Edge's Favorites icon. When the list of favorite sites drops down, right-click the disappointing site's name and choose Delete from the drop-down menu.

MICROSOFT EDGE'S SECRET HISTORY OF YOUR WEB VISITS

Microsoft Edge keeps a record of every website you visit. Although Microsoft Edge's History list provides a handy record of your computing activities, it's a spy's dream.

To see what Microsoft Edge has recorded, click its Settings and More icon, and click the History link from the drop-down menu. Microsoft Edge lists the last few websites you've visited, sorted by date. (Your latest visits appear at the list's top.) By presenting the sites in the order you viewed them, Microsoft Edge makes it easy to jump back to that site you found interesting this morning, last week, or even several months ago.

To delete the entire list, click the More Options icon at the top of the list, and click Clear Browsing Data from the drop-down list.

To prune sites from your history or see older visited sites, click Open History Page at the list's top; Microsoft Edge lists every site you've visited. To delete unwanted ones, click the X next to their name, and then click the Delete button at the top of the page.

Type a website's name into the Search box atop the list; Microsoft Edge presents every page you've visited from that website, making for easy bulk deleting.

Finding things on the internet

When looking for something in a text book, you usually flip back to the index and start searching. The same holds true for the internet because you need an index to ferret out that piece of information you're after.

To help you out, Microsoft Edge lets you consult a *search engine,* a service that contains a vast index of internet sites. To search for something, head for the Address bar — that space where you normally type in the address of the website you want to visit.

Instead, though, type your search term — **exotic orchids,** for example — directly into the Address bar, and press Enter.

Microsoft Edge fires your search off to Bing, Microsoft's own search engine, and spits out names of websites dealing in exotic orchids. Click a website's name to drop by.

Don't like Bing handling your search needs? You can change that search engine to Google (www.google.com), DuckDuckGo (www.duckduckgo.com), or any other search engine you like.

Sometimes, just visiting another search engine triggers a pop-up message on your screen asking if you'd like to make that your *default* search engine. Click the Yes or Okay button if it's your favorite search engine. Otherwise, follow these complicated steps to change Microsoft Edge's Bing to your own favorite search engine:

1. **Click the Settings and More icon (shown in the margin), located in Microsoft Edge's upper-right corner, and choose Settings from the drop-down menu that appears.**

   The Settings window appears as a new tab in Microsoft Edge.

2. **From the Settings tab's left edge, click the Privacy, Search, and Services entry.**

   Yet another menu full of settings appears.

3. **In the Services section of the new settings menu, click the Address Bar and Search category.**

   The Address Bar and Search menu appears.

4. **Click the drop-down menu adjacent to the words** Search Engine Used in Address Bar, **and choose your preferred search engine from the drop-down menu.**

   Your change takes place immediately. To close the Settings tab, click the little X on the tab. (It's the same as closing a tab that shows a website.)

Microsoft Edge then replaces Bing with your newly selected search provider.

Finding More Information on a Website

Clicking a website's links lets you jump easily to other places online. But what if you want to know more about something that *doesn't* have a clickable link? For example, what if you spot an address for a paleo-diet-friendly donut shop and want to see it on a map? What if you see a term you don't understand, and you simply want more information about it?

Microsoft Edge helps you find extra information about things you find online.

Here's how it works:

1. **When visiting a web page in Microsoft Edge, select the terms you want to explore.**

   Double-click a word or term, for example, to select it; Microsoft Edge highlights your chosen selection. Or point at the beginning of a phrase, hold down the mouse button, and — while holding down the mouse button — point at the end of a phrase. Release the mouse button, and you've highlighted the entire phrase.

   I provide more detail on how to select items in Chapter 6.

2. **Right-click the highlighted information, and choose Search the Web For from the pop-up menu.**

   Microsoft Edge sends your highlighted term to your chosen search engine, searches the internet for pertinent information, and then displays it, as shown in Figure 9-6.

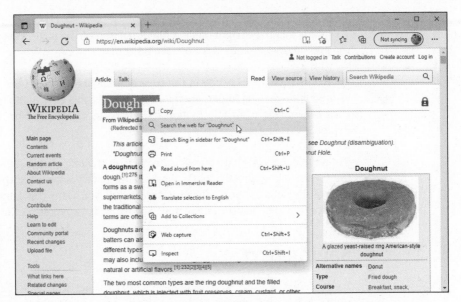

FIGURE 9-6:
Microsoft Edge lets you find information about terms found online.

Saving Information from the Internet

The internet places a full-service library inside your house, with no long checkout lines. And just as every library comes with a copy machine, Microsoft Edge provides several ways for you to save interesting tidbits of information for your personal use.

This section explains how to copy something from the internet onto your computer, whether it's an entire web page, a single picture, a sound or movie, or a program.

TIP

I explain how to print a web page (or a snippet of information it contains) in Chapter 8. But for those who hate flipping pages, try to turn on Microsoft Edge's Reader View, right-click a blank portion of the web page, and then choose Print from the pop-up menu.

Saving a web page

Hankering for a handy Fahrenheit/Centigrade conversion chart? Need that Sushi Identification Chart for dinner? Want to save the itinerary for next month's trip to Norway? When you find a web page with indispensable information, sometimes you can't resist saving a copy onto your computer for further viewing, perusal, or even printing at a later date.

To save a web page, right-click a blank portion of the page, choose Save As from the pop-up menu, and click the Save button.

 Microsoft Edge saves a copy of the coveted web page in your Downloads folder. To visit your Downloads folder, open File Explorer with a click on its taskbar icon, and click Downloads from File Explorer's left pane. (I explain how to navigate File Explorer in Chapter 5.)

Be aware, however, that your saved page won't change, even if the actual page on the internet is updated. That's why saving pages is best for things that won't change, like charts, or finalized itineraries. If you want consistently up-to-date information, just add the site to your Favorites list, covered earlier in this chapter.

Saving text

To save just a little of a web page's text, select the text you want to grab, right-click it, and choose Copy. (I explain how to select, copy, and paste text in Chapter 6.) Open your word processor, paste the text into a new document, and save it in your Documents folder with a descriptive name.

Saving a picture

As you browse through web pages and spot a picture that's too good to pass up, save it to your computer: Right-click the picture, and choose Save Image As, as shown in Figure 9-7.

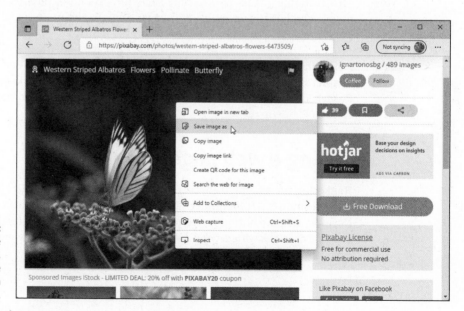

FIGURE 9-7:
Right-click the coveted picture, and choose Save Image As from the pop-up menu.

The Save As window appears, letting you enter a new filename for the picture, if desired. Click Save to place your pilfered picture in the folder of your choice, usually Downloads or Pictures.

The crowded pop-up menu shown in Figure 9-7 offers other handy options, letting you choose to open just that image in a new tab, copy the image to the Windows Clipboard for pasting into another program, or search the web for other versions of the image.

TIP

Remember the little picture by your name on the Windows Start menu? Feel free to use any picture from the internet. Right-click the new picture, and save it to your Pictures folder. Then use the Settings app (see Chapter 2) to transform that picture into your new user account picture.

Downloading a program, song, or other type of file

Microsoft Edge makes it a little easier to download files from the internet. Best yet, it's easier than ever to *find* the files after you download them.

To download something from a website, click the link to the item or click an adjacent Download button (if one is available). Microsoft Edge downloads the item and automatically places it into your Downloads folder for easy retrieval. The file usually arrives within a few seconds.

WARNING

When choosing the Download button, take some extra time to make sure you're clicking the correct button. Many sites deliberately try to confuse you into downloading something else, either spyware, a virus, or something else that gives the website a payback.

You can find your downloaded item in either of two ways:

>> **Downloads folder:** Downloaded items flow into your Downloads folder. To find them, open File Explorer (shown in the margin) from the taskbar. When File Explorer opens, click the Downloads folder listed in the program's left pane. The Downloads folder appears, showing all your downloaded items.

>> **Microsoft Edge's download queue:** Click the Settings and More icon (shown in the margin) in Microsoft Edge. When the Settings menu drops down, click the Downloads button. The Downloads tab appears, listing all your downloaded files for one-click access. You can also click the menu's Open Downloads Folder link to head straight for the Downloads folder mentioned in the preceding bullet.

Many downloaded files come packaged in a tidy folder with a zipper on it, known as a *ZIP file*. Windows treats them like normal folders, so you can just double-click them to see inside them. (The files are actually compressed inside that folder to save download time, if you care about the engineering involved.) To extract copies of the zipped files, right-click the zipped file and choose Extract All.

Chapter **10**

Being Social: Mail, Calendar, and Teams Chat

Thanks to the internet's never-fading memory, your friends and acquaintances never disappear. Old college chums, business pals, and even those elementary school bullies are all waiting for you online. Toss in a few strangers you may have swapped messages with on websites, and the internet has created a huge social network.

Windows helps you stay in touch with friends you enjoy and avoid those you don't. To manage your online social life, Windows includes two intertwined social apps: Mail and Calendar. You can pretty much guess which app handles what job.

Microsoft has improved the Mail and Calendar apps since their debut in Windows 10, and they work together quite well, vastly simplifying the chore of tracking your contacts and appointments.

NEW

The newcomer to the Windows 11 party is Teams Chat, a light version of Microsoft's Teams app. Like Zoom, a familiar video conferencing tool during the pandemic, Teams Chat lets you exchange text messages and hold video chats with friends, family, and coworkers.

This chapter describes the Windows suite of social apps, as well as how to set them up and put them to work managing your daily flow.

Adding Your Accounts to Windows

For years, you've heard people say, "Never tell *anybody* your user account name and password." Now, it seems Windows wants you to break that rule.

When you first open your Mail or Calendar apps, Windows may ask you to enter your account names and passwords from your email services, as well as services such as Google or Apple's iCloud.

It's not as scary as you think, though. Microsoft and the other networks have agreed to share your information *only if you approve it*. And should you approve it, Windows connects to all your added accounts and imports information about your contacts, email, and calendar.

And frankly, approving the information swap is a huge timesaver. When you link those accounts to Windows, your computer automatically signs in to each service, imports your friends' contact information, and stocks your apps.

To fill in Windows about your life online, follow these steps:

1. **Click the Start button. When the Start menu appears, open the Mail app.**

Click the Mail icon, usually found in the Start menu's top row, and the app opens.

The Mail app may be listed on your taskbar, that strip along the bottom of the screen. A click on the taskbar's Mail icon spares you a trip to the Start menu. If it's not there, I explain how to put any icon onto the taskbar in Chapter 3.

2. **Enter your accounts into the Mail app.**

When you first open the Mail app, it prompts you to add your email account or accounts, as shown in Figure 10-1. If you signed up with a Microsoft account that also serves as a Microsoft email address — one ending in Live, Hotmail, or Outlook, for example — that email address should already be listed at the top and set up. If that's your only email address, click it, and you're through!

To add other email accounts, click your account from the list, which includes email accounts from Google, Yahoo!, iCloud (for Apple), or Other Account (which usually means accounts from your internet service provider that use POP or IMAP for access).

To add a Google account, for example, click the word Google. Windows takes you to a secure area on Google's website, where you can authorize the transaction by entering your Gmail email address and password and then clicking Accept or Connect.

To add new email accounts later while inside the Mail app, click the Settings icon (it looks like a gear) and choose Accounts from the Settings pane.

Repeat these steps for any of your other listed accounts, authorizing each of them, if required, to share information with your Windows account.

FIGURE 10-1:
The Mail app lets you enter email accounts like Gmail, Hotmail, Outlook, Yahoo!, and others.

After you enter your accounts, Windows automatically fetches your email through your Mail app, fills the People app with your friends' contact information, and adds any appointments in your Calendar app.

Although it might seem frightening to give Windows your coveted usernames and passwords, it enriches Windows in many ways:

>> Instead of typing in your contacts by hand, they're waiting for you automatically, whether they're from your Google, Hotmail, Outlook, Apple, or Windows Live account.

>> Windows apps work well with apps and programs from other companies. Your friends' birthdays from your Google calendar, for example, show up on the Calendar app without your having to enter them.

REMEMBER

>> Don't like these newfangled Windows apps? Then ignore them. You can always spend your time on the Windows desktop instead. There, you can visit Facebook and your other accounts from your web browser the same way you've always done.

>> If you're already accustomed to firing up your browser and reading your mail on Google, Yahoo!, or any other online watering hole, you don't have to use the Mail app. You can still send and receive your mail the old-fashioned way. Or you can use a combination of both, depending on your mood, or whichever PC you happen to be using.

Understanding the Mail App

Microsoft constantly tweaks Windows 11 and its apps. It updates Windows 11 once a year, and it updates the Mail app much more frequently. Don't be surprised to see the Mail app (or any app) change subtly as Microsoft adds new features and drops old ones.

NEW

The People app, found in Windows 10, no longer lives as separate program in Windows 11. Instead, it's built directly into the Mail and Calendar app. To launch it, just click the People app icon within either of those apps. (The icon remains unchanged.)

The following sections explain how to make sense of the Mail app's menus, as well as how to compose, send, and read email. (If you haven't already imported your email accounts, skip back to this chapter's first section.)

Switching among the Mail app's views, menus, and accounts

To load the Windows Mail app, open the Start menu (by clicking the Start button on the taskbar's left edge) and then click the Mail app icon (shown in the margin).

The Mail app appears, shown in Figure 10-2, displaying email received from your primary email account — the first account you entered when setting up the app. (Chances are, it's your Microsoft account, which I describe in Chapter 2.) Figure 10-2, for example, shows the currently viewed Microsoft Live account at the pane's top. To see your mail from a different account, click that account's name along the left pane.

Currently viewed folder

Currently viewed email account

Search emails in currently viewed account

Create new email

Switch between Focused and Other

Toggle left pane

Sync emails   Select multiple emails

Menu items

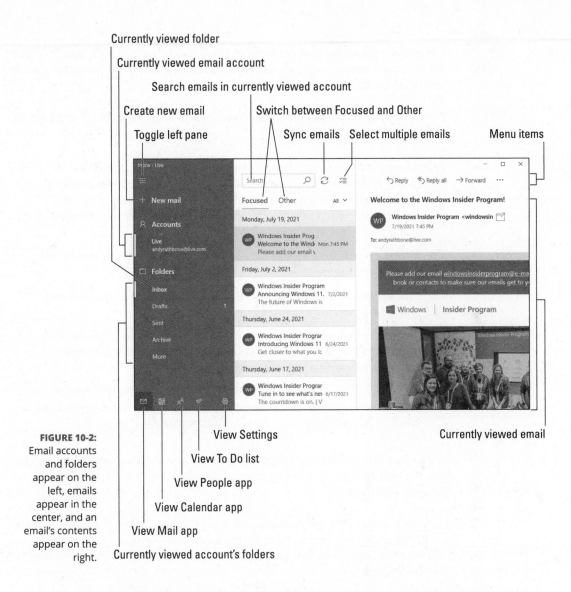

Currently viewed email

View Settings

View To Do list

View People app

View Calendar app

View Mail app

Currently viewed account's folders

FIGURE 10-2:
Email accounts
and folders
appear on the
left, emails
appear in the
center, and an
email's contents
appear on the
right.

The Mail app separates your mail into two categories: *Focused* and *Other*.

The Focused category only shows mail from people in your contacts list. The Other category, by contrast, usually contains mass-mailed newsletters and other mail from people you've never contacted. Don't forget to look in the Other category, though; you may find important messages from doctors, contractors, pet sitters, old school chums, or other people entering your life.

TIP

If you find it easier to see every piece of email in one place — your Inbox — visit the Mail app's Settings area, choose Focused Inbox, and turn off the toggle switch named Sort Messages into Focused and Other.

Beneath the name of your currently viewed email account, the Mail app lists its folders:

>> **Inbox:** Shown when you first load the Mail app, the Inbox folder lists your waiting email, with your newest email at the top. The Mail app automatically checks for new email every few minutes, but if you tire of waiting, click the Sync button (shown in the margin) atop that account's list of received emails. That action immediately grabs any waiting mail.

>> **Drafts:** If you write a message but don't send it for some reason, it waits here, ready for your further attention.

>> **Sent Items:** Click here to see the messages you've *sent* rather than received from others.

>> **Archive:** To remove an email from your Inbox, but save it for later reference, right-click the unwanted mail and choose Archive. (A click on the Archive folder lets you retrieve previously archived messages.)

>> **More:** If you don't see all your account's folders, click More to find them. A pop-out menu appears, listing them all. (In particular, peek in here to find your Deleted folder, where you can retrieve accidentally deleted emails.)

The icons along the bottom of the left pane let you switch among the Calendar app, the Mail app, the People app (your contacts), the optional To Do list, and the Mail app's settings.

Click the Settings icon, for example, and a pane appears along the right, offering all the things you can tweak inside the Mail app. The Feedback app, found in several Microsoft apps, lets you play armchair critic, advising Microsoft on how to improve its apps.

TIP

The Mail app, like most apps, changes its width depending on the size of your display and the size of the Mail window itself. On smaller monitors, or when running in a smaller window, the Mail app's left pane shrinks to a small strip showing icons instead of words, as shown in Figure 10-3. Click the Expand icon in the app's upper-left corner, and the tiny left strip expands, showing you the same left pane shown in Figure 10-2, earlier.

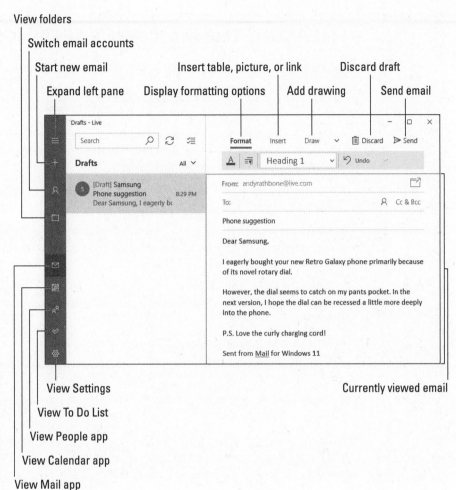

View folders

Switch email accounts

Start new email   Insert table, picture, or link   Discard draft

Expand left pane   Display formatting options   Add drawing   Send email

View Settings   Currently viewed email

View To Do List

FIGURE 10-3:   View People app

The Mail app
resizes to adjust
to different sized   View Calendar app
screens and
windows.   View Mail app

Composing and sending email

When you're ready to send an email, follow these steps to compose your letter and drop it in the electronic mailbox, sending it through virtual space to the recipient's computer:

1. **From the Start menu, open the Mail app's icon (shown in the margin) and click the New Mail icon (it's a plus sign icon) in the app's upper-left corner.**

   A new and blank email appears, awaiting your words.

**TECHNICAL
STUFF**

   If you've added more than one email account to the Mail app, first choose your return address by clicking your desired account name from the All Accounts section along the Mail app's right pane. *Then* click the New Mail icon in the program's upper-left corner.

TWEAKING THE MAIL APP'S SETTINGS

Click the little gear icon near the Mail app's lower-left corner, and the Settings pane slides into view along the app's right edge. There, you can tweak more than a dozen of the Mail app's settings. Here are some of the most useful settings:

- **Manage Accounts:** Head here to tweak the settings of your currently entered email accounts, as well as to add new accounts. After an email account's settings finally work, though, you rarely need to change them.

- **Personalization:** Interior decorators can visit here to change the Mail app's colors and background.

- **Automatic Replies:** Head here to create an "I'm sunning myself in Mazatlán for the next week" reply. The Mail app then automatically sends that reply to any email you receive while vacationing.

- **Signature:** Microsoft automatically slips the words "Sent from Mail for Windows" to every email you send. Head here to either turn off that message or change its wording.

- **Trust Center:** This oddly named and mysterious entry lets you control whether Microsoft can send you information based on your "usage and preferences." Presumably, this authorizes Microsoft's robots to send you pertinent ads.

- **About:** Handy mostly for techie troubleshooters, this area reveals the app's version number.

You may never need to set foot in the Settings area, but when things go wrong, this is usually the first troubleshooting destination.

2. **Type your friend's email address into the To box.**

   As you begin typing, the Mail app scans your contacts for both names and email addresses, listing potential matches below the To box. Spot a match on the list? Click it, and the Mail app automatically fills in the rest of the email address.

   To add another person to the list, begin typing their name in the To box as well. Unfortunately, the Mail app won't let create and save groups for emailing the same bunch of people in future mailings. Instead, you must retype everybody's name. (That's Microsoft way of forcing you to pay for Office 365, which *does* offer that feature.)

3. **Click in the Subject line, and type a subject.**

Click in the line labeled Subject, and type your subject. In Figure 10-3, for example, I added the subject "Phone suggestion." Although technically optional, the Subject line helps your friends sort their mail.

4. **Type your message into the large box beneath the Subject line.**

Type as many words as you want. As you type, the Mail app automatically corrects any noticed misspellings.

5. **If you want, add any formatting, tables, files, or photos to your email.**

The menu directly above your composed email offers four menus, each with different options:

- **Format:** This option lets you change your email's formatting by selecting portions of your email and then clicking the bold, italic, underline, or font color icons along the window's top edge. To change the font size, click the tiny downward-pointing arrow next to the underlined *U* icon. A menu drops down, letting you change the font and font size, as well as add or clear the formatting from any selected item.

- **Insert:** Click here to attach files, as I describe in this chapter's later section, "Sending and receiving files through email." This tab also lets you insert tables, pictures, hyperlinks, and *emojis* — little symbols ranging from smiley faces to vegetables.

- **Draw:** Used mainly by owners of a tablet and stylus, this option lets you add drawings to your mail.

- **Options:** Click here after composing your email to give it a final spellcheck.

Most ISPs won't send attached files totaling more than 10 to 25MB. That lets you send a song or two, a few digital photos, and most documents. It's not enough room to send any but the tiniest videos.

6. **Check your spelling, if desired.**

The Mail app does a pretty good job of correcting your spelling as you type. But to proofread more closely before sending your mail, click the Options button along the Mail app's top edge. Then choose Spelling from the drop-down menu.

The Mail app jumps to each error it finds. When it finds a problem, it highlights the word and places a drop-down menu where you can choose from potential replacements.

TIP

If the spellchecker constantly flags a correctly spelled word as being mis-spelled, choose Ignore All from the drop-down menu. That keeps the program from bugging you about a word it doesn't understand.

7. **Click the Send button along the Mail app's upper-right corner.**

 Send

Whoosh! The Mail app whisks your message through the internet to your friend's mailbox. Depending on the speed of your internet connection, mail can arrive anywhere from a few seconds to a few hours later, with a few minutes being the average.

 Discard

Don't want to send the message? Then delete it with a click of the Discard button in the Mail app's upper-right corner.

Reading a received email

When your computer is connected to the internet, the Mail app heralds the arrival of a newly received email with an announcement in the Action Center, the pane that periodically appears along the screen's right edge.

You can click that little announcement to fire up the Mail app and see the message. But if the announcement disappears before you can pounce on it with a click, follow these steps to read or respond to the message:

1. **Click the Start menu's Mail icon.**

Mail opens to show the messages in your Inbox, as shown earlier in Figure 10-3. Each subject is listed, one by one, with the newest subject at the top.

TIP

To find a particular email quickly, click the Magnifying Glass icon at the top of the email column. A search box appears alongside the icon where you can type the sender's name or a keyword into the search box. Press the Enter key to see all the matching emails.

2. **Click the subject of any message you want to read.**

The Mail app spills that message's contents into the pane along the window's right side.

3. **From here, the Mail app leaves you with several options, each accessed from the buttons along the email's top edge:**

- *Nothing:* Undecided? Don't do anything, and the message simply lingers in your Inbox folder.

↩ Reply

- *Reply:* Click the Reply button, and a new window appears, ready for you to type your response. The window is just like the one that appears when you first compose a message but with a handy difference: This window is already addressed with the recipient's name and the subject. Also, the original message usually appears at the bottom of your reply for reference.

- *Reply All:* Some people address emails to several people simultaneously. If you see several other people listed on an email's To line, you can reply to *all* of them by clicking Reply All.

- *Forward:* Receive something that a friend simply must see? Click Forward to kick a copy of the email to your friend's Inbox.

- *Archive:* Copy the message to the Archive folder for later retrieval, handy when you want to save a read mail for later reference.

- *Delete:* Click the Delete button to toss the message into your Trash or Deleted Items folder. (Different email accounts use different words for that folder.)

- *Actions:* Clicking this fetches a drop-down menu that lists any menu items above that didn't fit on your particular screen. The menu's Move option, for example, lets you move an item out of your Inbox and into a different folder. (Save and Print options appear on the Actions drop-down menu, as well.)

Some email accounts lack the Archive button, which removes a piece of mail from your Inbox and stashes it in a folder named Archive. That keeps the email out of sight, but ready for retrieval later, if desired.

The Mail app works well for basic email needs, but it has its limitations. If you're struggling to find a missing feature, it's probably not included. If you need more, Microsoft encourages you to purchase its Microsoft Office suite of programs or to pay a subscription fee to join its Office 365 mail service.

If you don't want to pay extra, you may be able to open your web browser and manage your email online, such as at Outlook (www.outlook.com), Google (www.google.com/gmail), or your ISP's own website.

WARNING

If you ever receive an unexpected email from a bank, social security, your credit card company, or any other money-related website, don't click any of the email's web links. A criminal industry called *phishing* sends emails that try to trick you into entering your name and password on a phony website. That gives your coveted information to the evil folk, who promptly steal your money. I write more about phishing schemes and how to avoid them in Chapter 11.

Sending and receiving files through email

Like a gift card slipped into the envelope of a thank-you note, an *attachment* is a file that piggybacks onto an email message. You can send or receive any type of file as an attachment.

The following sections describe how to both send and receive a file through the Mail app.

Saving a received attachment

When an attachment arrives in an email, you'll recognize it: A paperclip icon rests next to the email's subject. And when you open the email, you see a photo thumbnail or a message saying, "Download Message and Pictures."

Saving the attached file or files takes just a few steps:

1. **Right-click the attached file, and choose Open or Save.**

   The Mail app usually doesn't download the file or files until you specifically give it the command. Instead, the Mail app shows small thumbnails — placeholders for attached files — along the email's top edge.

   Choose Open from the pop-up menu, and the Mail app opens the file for viewing. If you choose to open an attached photo, for example, the Photos app appears, with the displayed photo in tow.

   To save the file, choose Save from the pop-up menu and move to Step 2.

2. **Choose a storage area to receive the saved file.**

   File Explorer's Save As window appears, shown in Figure 10-4, ready for you to save the file in your Documents folder. To save it someplace else, choose any folder listed along the Save As window's left edge. Or click the words This PC, also on the window's left edge, and begin browsing to the folder that should receive the file.

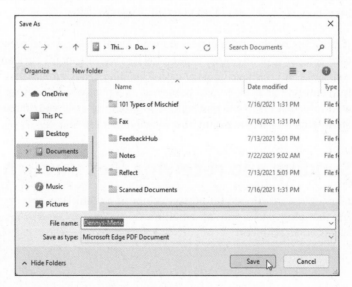

FIGURE 10-4:
Choose a folder, and click Save.

TIP

Saving the file inside one of your four main folders — Documents, Pictures, Videos, or Music — is the easiest way to ensure you'll be able to find it later. (I describe files and folders in Chapter 5.) When you choose a folder, you see a list of existing folders where you can stash your new file.

To create a new folder inside your currently viewed folder, click the New Folder button from the menu along the folder's top and, when the new folder appears, type in a name for the folder.

3. **Click the Save button in the Save As window's lower-right corner.**

   The Mail app saves the file in the folder you choose.

After you've saved the file, the attachment remains inside the email. That's because saving attachments always saves a *copy* of the sent file. If you accidentally delete or botch an edit on your saved file, you can return to the original email and save the attached file again.

Windows Security, the built-in virus checker in Windows, automatically scans your incoming email for evil file attachments. I explain more about Microsoft Security in Chapter 11. Still, if you feel suspicious about the attachment, or it arrives unexpectedly, don't download it. (Just delete the entire email.)

Sending a file as an attachment

Sending a file through the Mail app works much like saving an attached file, although in reverse: Instead of grabbing a file from an email and saving it into a folder, you're grabbing a file from a folder and saving it in an email, a process known as "attaching a file."

To send a file as an attachment in the Mail app, follow these steps:

1. **Open the Mail app, and create a new email.**

   I describe creating a new email in this chapter's earlier "Composing and sending email" section.

2. **Click the Insert tab from the Mail app's top menu, and then choose Files from the drop-down menu.**

   When you choose Files from the drop-down menu, File Explorer's Open window appears, showing the contents of your Documents folder.

   If the Documents folder contains the file you'd like to send, jump to Step 4. To send something from a different folder, move to Step 3.

3. **Navigate to the folder and file you want to send.**

Click the words This PC along any folder's left edge, and a menu appears listing your storage areas. Most files are stored in your Documents, Pictures, Music, and Videos folders.

Click a folder's name to open it and see the files lurking inside. Not the correct folder? Click the Up Arrow icon (shown in the margin) to move back out of the folder and try again.

4. **Click the file you want to send, and click the Open button.**

Click a file to select it. To select several files, hold down the Ctrl key while selecting them. Selected too many files? Deselect unwanted files by clicking their names again. When you click the Attach button, the Mail app adds the file or files to your email.

5. **Click the Send button.**

The Mail app whisks off your mail and its attachment to the recipient.

REMEMBER

When you send an attached file, you're only sending a copy. Your original stays safely on your computer. Also, most ISPs limit attachment size to 10 to 25MB. That's enough to send a few photos, but rarely enough for videos. (Share those on You-Tube or Facebook.)

Managing Your Contacts in the People App

When you enter your own email addresses into the Mail app when first setting it up, Windows also grabs email addresses for all your friends that it can find. That means the embedded People app may already be stocked with your friends' email addresses. Think of the People app as a simple address book that lists your contacts and their contact information.

Unlike earlier Windows versions, the People app doesn't live on the Start menu or taskbar. Instead, launch the People app by opening either Mail or Calendar and click the People icon, shown in the margin. The People app appears, presenting all your online friends in an alphabetical list, as shown in Figure 10-5.

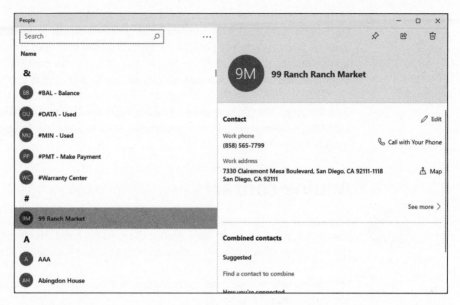

FIGURE 10-5:
The People app automatically stocks itself with contacts from your email accounts.

The People app contains two main panes: your list of contacts, and the details about the contact you've currently clicked on. Here's what you'll see:

» **Contacts:** The app presents an alphabetical list of your friends. When you click a contact's name, their details spill across the adjacent pane to the right, which offers three main options:

» **Profile:** The default view for the second pane, Profile lists your selected friend's photo and contact information.

» **Events:** Click Events to send the People app racing to the Calendar app, where it prepares a dossier of your scheduled meetings. That person's appointments then appear as clickable links to provide quick access.

» **Conversations:** Click this to see a list of clickable emails involving that person.

» **Pushpin:** When you spot a popular contact, click the pushpin icon atop the pane and choose Pin to Start to place their smiling face on a Start menu icon for easy access. Or choose Pin to Taskbar to place their face on your taskbar along the screen's bottom edge, where's it's *always* visible.

» **Edit:** To edit a contact's details — change a phone number, perhaps — click the Edit link that's next to the pencil icon. (Clicking this link also lets you add a photo to a faceless contact.)

» **Share:** Click this option to forward your contact's information to others, hopefully with your contact's approval.

The People app handles much of its upkeep automatically, updating itself with any changes you make to your online contacts, usually gathered from iCloud, Google, or your Microsoft account. That means that updates you make to contacts on your iPhone or Android phone automatically appear in the People app and vice versa.

Occasionally, though, you need to add or edit some People entries manually. The following sections explain the occasional pruning needed to keep up with your constantly evolving contacts list.

Adding contacts

TIP

Although the People app loves to add contacts automatically, you can easily add people the old-fashioned way, typing them in by hand. However, the app forces you to choose which of your online accounts should accept the new entry.

The People app will also ask permission to access your calendar and email, so it can show those items to you.

To add somebody to the People app, which makes that person available in your Mail and Calendar apps, follow these steps:

1. **Click the People icon from either the Mail or Calendar app.**

The People app appears onscreen.

2. **Click the See More icon (shown in the margin), and choose New Contact from the drop-down menu.**

3. **If asked, choose which account to use for saving new contacts.**

If you have more than two email accounts, the People app asks you to decide which account should receive the new contact. The answer hinges mainly on which smartphone you own:

- Choose your Google account if you use an Android phone so that your newly added contact appears in your Gmail contacts. From there, it also appears in your Android phone's contacts list. Similarly, iPhone owners should choose iCloud.

- Choose the Outlook account if you run the Outlook app on your iPhone or Android smartphone.

- Choose the iCloud account if you use your iPhone's built-in mail program.

4. **Fill out the New Contact form.**

   Shown in Figure 10-6, most of the choices are self-explanatory fields such as Name, Phone, Email, Address, and Other. (The Other field lets you add details such as a job title, website, significant other, or notes.)

   To add a photo, click the Add Photo button; the Photo app appears, letting you choose from a previously shot photo.

5. **Click the Save button along the window's bottom edge.**

FIGURE 10-6: Fill in contact information, and click the Save button.

The People app dutifully saves your new contact. If you spot a mistake, don't worry; you can go back and edit the information as described in the next section.

Deleting or editing contacts

Has somebody fallen from your social graces? Or perhaps someone just changed a phone number? Either way, you can delete or edit a contact manually by following these steps:

1. **Open the Mail or Calendar app and click the People icon on the Start menu.**

   The People app appears, as shown earlier in Figure 10-5.

2. **To delete a contact, right-click their name and choose Delete from the pop-up menu.**

The person disappears from both the People app and the email account that held that contact.

3. **To edit a contact, right-click the contact's name and choose Edit from the pop-up menu.**

The person's contact information appears for you to edit (refer to Figure 10-6).

4. **Click the Save button along the window's bottom edge.**

The People app updates your contacts list, both in the app itself and in the online account where that contact is stored. Edit a Gmail contact in the People app, for example, and Gmail also reflects the changes.

Managing Appointments in Calendar

After you enter your online accounts such as Gmail, Outlook, Live.com, and others, as described in this chapter's first section, you've already stocked the Calendar app with your existing online appointments.

 To see your appointments, click the Start menu's Calendar icon, shown in the margin. Or, if you're working in the Mail app, click the Calendar icon from the Mail app's lower-left corner.

When first opened, the Calendar app asks you to add your email accounts. If you previously entered your accounts into the Mail app, they already show up here.

The Calendar app opens to show any appointments associated with your linked email accounts, such as Google, iCloud, or Outlook.com. To see more or fewer days displayed, click the Day, Week, Month, or Year button along the top. If you click Week, for example, the Calendar app appears as shown in Figure 10-7.

Unless you keep all your appointments online, you'll need to edit some entries, add new ones, or delete those you can no longer attend. This section explains how to keep your appointments up to date.

TIP

No matter which view the Calendar app displays, you can flip through the appointments by clicking the little arrows near the listed month in the screen's upper-left corner. Click the right arrow to move forward in time; click the left arrow to move backward.

To add an appointment to your Calendar app, follow these steps:

1. **Click the Calendar icon on the Start menu.**

   The Calendar app appears, as shown in Figure 10-7.

   If you're in the Mail app, you can also click the Calendar app's icon in the Mail app's lower-left corner.

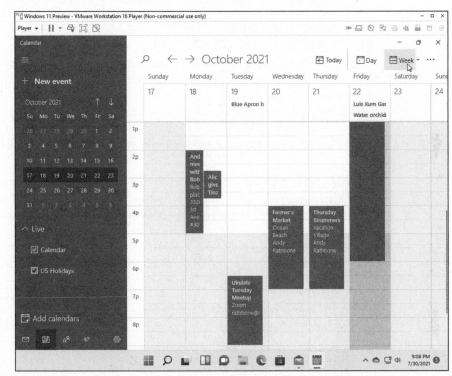

2. **Click the New Event link from the Calendar app's upper-left corner.**

   A blank event template appears, ready for you to fill in the time and place, and invite people.

3. **Fill out the Details form.**

   Shown in Figure 10-8, most of the choices are self-explanatory fields.

   The biggest challenge comes with the Details field's drop-down menu, which appears only if you've entered more than one email account into your Mail app. Which email *account* should receive the new calendar appointment? Again, the answer depends on your phone:

- Choose Gmail to send appointments to Gmail's calendar, where they appear on your Android phone.

- Choose iCloud for your iPhone.

Or you can choose Outlook. You can then download and install the Outlook app, available on both Android and iPhones. The Outlook app can sync the Calendar app's appointments with your phone.

4. **Click the Save & Close button.**

The Calendar app adds your new appointment to its own calendar, as well as to whichever account you chose in Step 3.

 To edit or delete an appointment, open it from the Calendar app. Click the Delete button (shown in the margin) from the top menu. To edit it, open it from the Calendar app, make your changes, and save your changes by clicking the Save button.

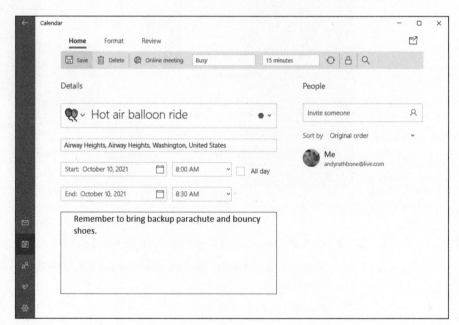

FIGURE 10-8:
Add your appointment's date, start time, duration, and other details.

Meeting Online with Teams Chat

NEW

Designed for businesses, Microsoft Teams lets workers exchange messages, hold video chats, and exchange files. It's designed to work well with other popular Microsoft products, like Word and Excel. Many office managers love how it lets them track office-related details with precision. Other employees, though, see Teams as yet another form of robotic micromanaging.

But no matter how you feel about the full-featured Teams program, Windows 11 includes what could be called "Teams Lite." Alternatively called "Teams Chat" or simply "Chat," the app includes Teams' text messaging and video chat features, but leaves out the other features found the more full-featured Teams app.

All you need to fire up the Teams Chat app in Windows 11 are a video camera, microphone, and speakers; those are standard equipment on most of today's PCs, laptops, and tablets.

This section explains how to start Teams Chat on your PC, connect with your friends, family, or even coworkers, and begin chatting, either through text messages or video.

Starting Teams Chat

The Teams Chat icon (shown in the margin) sits on the taskbar, that strip along the bottom of your screen. To load Teams Chat, follow these steps:

1. **Click the Teams Chat icon found on the taskbar, and click Get Started.**

   If your computer already has the full-featured Teams program, you may see that app's icon, instead (shown in the margin). If you have the full-featured version of Teams, you may want the full-featured book, *Microsoft Teams For Dummies,* Second Edition, by Rosemarie Withee; these steps probably won't work for you.

   The Teams Chat app from Windows 11 jumps to the screen, shown in Figure 10-9.

2. **If asked, choose the account you'd like to use for Teams Chat, enter its password, and click the Sign In button.**

   A Welcome window appears. If you're already logged on with a Microsoft account, that account appears at the top of the window; click the account name to start.

   No Microsoft account? Choose Use Another Account to be guided through the process of creating one.

FIGURE 10-9:
Click Get Started
to load Teams
Chat and begin
chatting with
friends.

3. **If asked, add your phone number, and, when you receive the confirmation code as a text message, enter the code into the Enter Code window. Then click Next.**

Enter your cell phone number, and be sure it's the correct one: Teams Chat will send you a text message to verify your identify and your account. Enter the code you receive and click Next.

4. **If asked, tell Teams Chat to sync your contacts.**

This allows Teams Chat to automatically stock itself with your contacts' information from your email program or Skype, making them easier to find for online meetings.

5. **Click the Let's Go button.**

When the Teams Chat window appears, shown in Figure 10-10, you're done and ready to start chatting and holding video chats, as described in the next two sections.

FIGURE 10-10:
Once you set up
and validate your
account, you can
begin using
Teams Chat.

Sending text messages

Sending text messages in Teams Chat works much like sending text messages on your phone, Facebook, or most other places on the internet. Here's how to load Teams Chat, find your contact, and begin chatting through text messages.

If you've never loaded Teams Chat before, jump back to the Starting Teams Chat section. You need to set up an email account and/or a phone number to start the process.

1. **Click the Teams Chat icon on the taskbar.**

   A pop-up window appears, shown earlier in Figure 10-10, with two buttons on the top:

   - *Meet:* Click the Meet button to start a *video chat*: a way to see and hear each other through your computer's camera.

   - *Chat:* Click this button to exchange text messages with somebody on Teams Chat.

2. **Click the Chat button, and, when the New Chat window appears, enter the person's name, email, or phone number in the To: box in the window's upper-left corner.**

3. **When the box appears at lower-edge of the New Chat window, type your message and press the Enter key.**

   The recipient sees your message in their Teams Chat app. When they type a message in response, it appears in your Teams Chat app window, and you can begin typing messages to each other.

The Teams Chat app looks and behaves much like the text messages you've already been sending on your smartphone, Facebook Messenger, and similar "instant messaging" programs.

TIP

Here are a few of its quirks to keep in mind:

» If you try to send a message to somebody new, that person sees an onscreen message allowing them to either accept or block your chat request. That helps weed out stalkers, weirdos, and bored teenagers.

» Before starting a video chat, as described in the next section, you may want to use the app's Chat portion first, just to make sure they're awake and ready to chat face to face.

» To end your chat, close the Teams Chat app window by clicking the X in its upper-right corner.

Holding video chats

Video chats, as opposed to text chats, send a live video of your face to the app of the other person. That lets you see each other as you talk, handy for face-to-face meetings where text messages can lose their nuance or become too long to type.

If you've never loaded Teams Chat before, jump back to this chapter's "Starting Teams Chat" section. You need to set up an email account and/or a phone number to begin the process.

Here's how to load Teams Chat, find your contact, and begin video chatting through your computers' cameras.

1. **Click the Teams Chat icon on the taskbar.**

   A pop-up window appears, shown earlier in Figure 10-11, with two buttons on the top:

- *Meet:* Click the Meet button to start a *video chat:* a way to see and hear each other through your computer's camera.

- *Chat:* Covered in the previous section, click this button to simply exchange text messages with somebody.

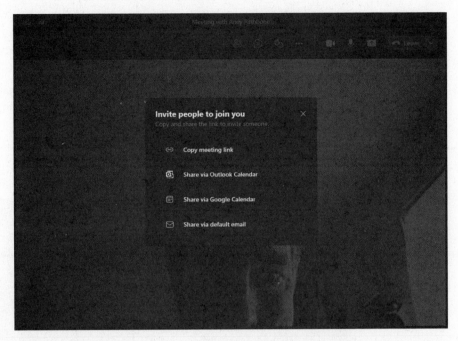

FIGURE 10-11:
Choose how to invite people to your meeting.

2. **Click the Meet button, and, when the Meeting window appears, click the Join Now button.**

At this point, the Meeting window shows only your own smiling face. When you click the Join Now button, the Invite People to Join You window appears, shown in Figure 10-11. The window lets you invite people to your lonely video chat in four ways:

- *Copy Meeting Link:* Often the easiest option, this copies a link to your Clipboard, where you can send the link to the person you'd like to see. You can email it to them, send it to them as an instant message with your phone, or write it down on paper and hand it to them. When the recipient visits that link with their web browser, they can join your meeting and begin talking.

- *Share via Outlook Calendar:* Outlook Calendar owners can use this option to share the meeting's link through Outlook Calendar.

- *Share via Google Calendar:* Similarly, Google Calendar owners can use this option to share the meeting's link through Google Calendar.

- *Share via default email:* This fetches whatever program you currently use for email. Then it opens a new mail, places the link inside, and lets you fill in the recipient's email address, ready for you to mail the video chat invitation.

At this point, you wait until somebody clicks the link you've sent. When Teams Chat appears on their screen, they click the Join Now button to start joining the meeting.

3. **When a pop-up messages appears on your screen, saying that your invited guest is "waiting in the lobby," click the Admit button to let them join your meeting.**

The other person (or people, if you've invited more than one) then appears onscreen, shown in Figure 10-12, and you can begin talking to each other.

FIGURE 10-12: When video chatting, your own face is reduced to a small square in the screen's lower-right corner.

Video chatting has a few more intricacies than simply swapping text messages, as described in the previous section. Keep these things in mind for the best video chat experience:

>> Near the upper-right edge of the Teams Chat video window, icons for both a microphone and a video camera can be toggled on or off with a click. If nobody can hear you, click the microphone icon to turn it on. Similarly, if nobody can see you — click the video camera icon to start sending video.

>> The face of your invited guest fills the screen on your PC, and your own face is reduced to the small square in the screen's lower-right corner. These are reversed on screen of the guest you've invited to the meeting.

>> If you don't want somebody to see you while wearing your hair curlers or tooth whitening strips, feel free to click the video camera icon to turn it off. Then people will only see the photo attached to your email address, as shown earlier in Figure 10-12.

>> When starting a meeting, you need to wait for everybody to receive the link and join the meeting. This is why scheduling video chats for a certain time and day works better than waiting until somebody receives your email or text message.

>> When attending a group meeting being led by somebody giving a presentation, it's common courtesy to mute your microphone by clicking the microphone icon at the screen's top edge. If you want to speak to everybody or ask a question, click the microphone icon again to unmute it.

>> When you're through chatting, leave the meeting by clicking the Leave button the upper-right corner of the Teams Chat window.

TIP

>> Be sure to feed the cat before you begin a work chat. Otherwise, your cat may become an unwitting participant at the board meeting.

Chapter **11**

Safe Computing

L ike driving a car, working with Windows is reasonably safe as long as you avoid bad neighborhoods, obey traffic signals, and don't try to steer with your feet.

But in the world of Windows and the internet, there's no easy way to recognize a bad neighborhood, find a traffic signal, or even know what's dangerous. Something that appears to be fun, innocent, or important — a friend's email, a downloaded app or program, or a message from a bank — may be a virus that infects your computer.

This chapter helps you recognize the bad streets in virtual neighborhoods and explains the steps you can take to protect yourself from harm and minimize any damage. Along the way, it introduces you to the new Windows Security section and its suite of tools that help identify and avert threats.

Understanding Those Annoying Permission Messages

After more than 20 years of development, Windows is still pretty naive. Sometimes when you run an app or program or try to change a setting on your PC, Windows can't tell whether *you're* doing the work or a *virus* is trying to move in behind your back.

The Windows solution? When Windows notices anybody (or anything) trying to change something that can potentially harm Windows or your PC, it darkens the screen and flashes a security message asking for permission, like the one shown in Figure 11-1.

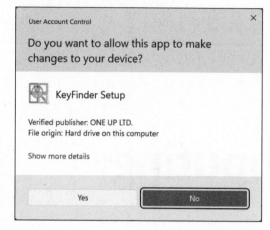

FIGURE 11-1:
Click Don't Install, Cancel, or No if a message similar to this one appears unexpectedly.

If one of these User Account Control security messages appears out of the blue, Windows may be warning you about a bit of nastiness trying to sneak in. So click Cancel, No, or Don't Install to deny it permission. But if *you're* trying to install a trusted app or program onto your PC and Windows puts up its boxing gloves, click OK, Yes, or Install instead. Windows drops its guard and lets you proceed.

If you don't hold an Administrator account, however, you can't simply approve the deed. You must track down an Administrator account holder (usually the PC's owner) and ask them to type their password.

Yes, a rather dimwitted security robot guards the front door to Windows, but it's also an extra challenge for the people who write the viruses.

Staying Safe with Windows Security

Windows Security isn't simply an antivirus app, although it includes one. It's also a handy repository for the seven biggest security features in Windows. Hopefully, though, you won't need to visit any of them: The security features all work automatically and come preset to keep you safe. In fact, if an inadvertent settings change leaves you unsafe, the app quickly notifies you and shows you which toggle switch needs to be flipped to the safer position.

To launch Windows Security, click the Start button. When the Start menu appears, click the All Apps button in the Start menu's upper-right corner. Finally, choose Windows Security from the alphabetical list of apps that appear. The app appears, shown in Figure 11-2.

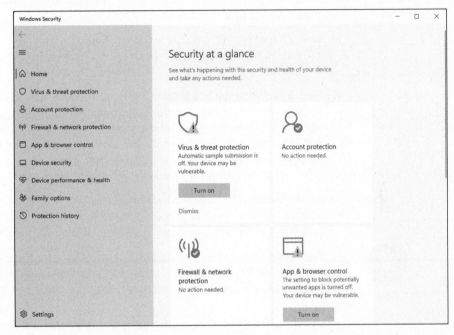

FIGURE 11-2:
The Windows Security suite of apps helps to keep your computer safe.

When you spot a green check mark next to each icon, your computer's defenses are all turned on. If you spot a red X or a yellow exclamation point, by contrast, open that icon with a click. Windows guides you directly to the switch that needs to be flipped.

Windows Security offers these categories:

>> **Virus and Threat Protection:** Covered in this chapter's next section, this area lets you access settings for Microsoft Defender Antivirus. The app runs automatically, constantly scanning your PC for threats. But you may want to visit here to run a quick, unscheduled scan if you suspect foul play.

>> **Account Protection:** Visit here to check on the security of your user account. You can also set up a fingerprint reader: A swipe of your fingertip lets you into your PC without having to type in a password.

>> **Firewall and Network Protection:** Hidden in here are settings for the Windows built-in firewall, which helps stop hackers from breaking into your

computer through the internet. It's turned on automatically, so you'll probably never need to visit here.

>> **App and Browser Control:** These settings tell Microsoft Defender to warn you if you try to download an unsafe app or file, or if the Microsoft Edge browser visits an unsafe website. I cover this subject in the "Avoiding phishing scams" section later in this chapter.

>> **Device Security:** This lets you check on the security measures built directly into your PC's hardware, including its memory chips and central processing unit (CPU).

>> **Device Performance and Health:** If Windows doesn't seem to be running correctly, visit this section. It lets you know whether your PC is running low on storage room and notifies you of any problems with *drivers:* pieces of software that let your PC talk with devices like mice, keyboards, and other computer parts. This section also alerts you to trouble with any of your apps or programs. (I devote Chapter 18 to troubleshooting Windows 11.)

>> **Family Options:** This takes you online to set up ways to control and monitor how your children use their PCs and other Windows devices. (I cover this subject in the "Setting up controls for children" section later in this chapter.)

NEW

>> **Protection History:** New to Windows 11, this section lists all the times Windows Security has found and thwarted something unsafe on your PC. It also recommends actions you should take to make your PC more secure.

If you've installed third-party antivirus or firewall apps, Windows Security provides updates on those as well.

REMEMBER

When everything is running smoothly, the icons in Windows Security bear a green check mark. The check mark turns into a red X or yellow exclamation point when something is amiss, alerting you that you should visit that category and take the recommended action.

Avoiding and removing viruses

When it comes to viruses, *everything* is suspect. Viruses travel not only through email messages, websites, apps and programs, files, networks, and flash drives, but also in screen savers, themes, toolbars, and other Windows add-ons.

To combat the problem, Windows Security includes the free Microsoft Defender Antivirus app.

Microsoft Defender Antivirus scans everything that enters your computer, whether through downloads, email, networks, messaging apps and programs, flash drives, or discs. Unless you tell it not to, the app casts a watchful eye on your OneDrive files as well.

When Microsoft Defender Antivirus notices something evil trying to enter your computer, it lets you know with a message in your screen's lower-right corner, as shown in Figure 11-3. Then the antivirus app quickly quarantines the virus before it has a chance to infect your computer. Whew!

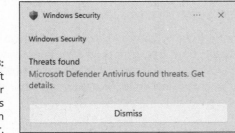

FIGURE 11-3:
Microsoft
Defender
Antivirus detects
and removes an
intruder.

Microsoft Defender Antivirus automatically updates itself to recognize new viruses, and it constantly scans your PC for threats in the background. But if your PC acts strangely, tell Microsoft Defender Antivirus to scan your PC immediately by following these steps:

1. **Click the taskbar's Windows Security icon (shown in the margin) near the clock.**

   The Windows Security suite of apps appears, shown earlier in Figure 11-2. Don't spot the app's icon on the taskbar? Then click the little upward-pointing arrow near the taskbar's right edge; a pop-up menu appears, showing the Windows Security icon.

   You can also launch Windows Security from the Settings app's Privacy and Security section. (I cover the newly updated Settings app in Chapter 12.)

2. **Click the Windows Security Virus and Threat Protection icon from the left column.**

   The Virus and Threat protection window appears.

3. **Click the app's Quick Scan button.**

   Microsoft Defender Antivirus immediately performs a quick scan of your PC.

   To perform a full scan, which takes longer but scans more files, click the Scan Options link beneath the Scan Now button. When the Scan Options window appears, click the Full Scan option and then click the Scan Now button.

TIP

To run a quick scan from the desktop, right-click the Windows Security icon on your taskbar and choose Run Quick Scan from the pop-up menu.

Even with Windows Security's suite of apps watching your back, follow these rules to reduce your risk of infection:

REMEMBER

» Open only attachments that you're expecting. If you receive something unexpected from a friend, don't open it. Instead, email or phone that person to ask whether they really sent you something. Your friend's computer might be infected and trying to infect your computer as well.

» Be wary of items arriving in email that ask for a click. For example, if you receive a message saying somebody wants to be a Facebook friend, don't click it. Instead, visit Facebook from your browser and look to see whether the person is listed on your Friend Request list. The more emailed links you can avoid, the safer you'll be.

» If you receive an important-looking email from a financial institution that asks you to click a link and type in your name and password, don't do it. Instead, visit your financial institution's website through your web browser and log in there. Chances are good that there's nothing wrong with your account, and that email was only trying to steal your username and password. (This type of scam is often called *phishing,* and I describe it further in the next section.)

» Updates for Microsoft Defender Antivirus arrive automatically through Windows Update. Windows keeps Windows Update running constantly, so you don't need to worry about keeping Microsoft Defender Antivirus updated.

WARNING

» If you prefer running a third-party antivirus app, you're welcome to do so. It will turn off Microsoft Defender Antivirus automatically as part of its install process. But don't try to keep *two* third-party antivirus apps running together, because they often quarrel.

Avoiding phishing scams

Eventually you'll receive an email from a bank, eBay, PayPal, or a similar website announcing a problem with your account. Invariably, the email offers a handy link to click, saying that you must enter your username and password to set things in order.

WARNING

Don't do it, no matter how realistic the email and website may appear. You're seeing an ugly industry called *phishing:* Fraudsters send millions of these messages worldwide, hoping to convince a few frightened souls into typing their precious account name and password.

IS MICROSOFT DEFENDER ANTIVIRUS GOOD ENOUGH?

Like several Windows versions before it, Windows 11 includes the Microsoft Defender Antivirus app. Microsoft Defender Antivirus runs quickly, updates automatically, and catches the most common malware before it invades your computer.

But is it *better* than third-party antivirus apps, including the ones that charge recurring subscription fees? The answer depends on several things.

For example, some third-party antivirus apps and programs will catch more viruses than Microsoft Defender Antivirus. However, doing that extra work can slow down your PC. Some powerful security suites throw up false alarms as well, leaving you the work of sorting out the problem. Many seem complicated and cumbersome.

Microsoft Defender Antivirus works best for people who can spot a potential virus as it arrives in the mail and avoid clicking on suspicious email attachments. People who feel more comfortable with a larger safety net will prefer a paid app or program. There's no right or wrong answer.

Instead, your answer depends on your personal comfort level. If you find a reasonably priced third-party antivirus app or program that doesn't slow down your computer too much, then stick with it. But if you feel confident in your ability to weed out most potential attackers before you click on them, Microsoft Defender Antivirus may be all you need.

How do you tell the real emails from the fake ones? It's easy, actually, because *all* these emails are fake. Finance-related sites may send you legitimate history statements, receipts, or confirmation notices, but they will never, ever email you an unexpected link for you to click and enter your password.

TIP

If you're suspicious, visit the company's *real* website by typing the web address by hand into your web browser's Address bar. Chances are good that the real site won't list anything as being wrong with your account.

Microsoft Edge uses Microsoft SmartScreen Filter technology that compares a website's address with a list of known phishing sites. If it finds a match, the SmartScreen filter keeps you from entering, as shown in Figure 11-4. Should you ever spot that screen, close the web page by clicking the words Go Back listed on the warning message.

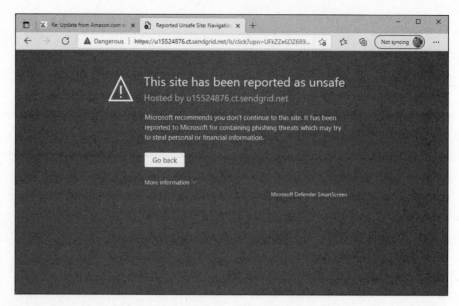

FIGURE 11-4:
Microsoft Edge
warns you when
you visit a
suspected
phishing site.

So why can't the authorities simply arrest those people responsible? Because internet thieves are notoriously difficult to track down and prosecute. The reach of the internet lets them work from any place in the world, hidden beneath a global maze of networks.

If you mistakenly enter information and then realize you shouldn't have, take these actions:

» If you've already entered your name and password into a phishing site, act immediately: Visit the real website, and change your password. Then contact the company involved and ask it for help. It may be able to stop the thieves before they wrap their electronic fingers around your account.

» If you've entered credit card information, call the card's issuer immediately. You can almost always find a toll-free, 24-hour phone number on the back of your credit card.

Setting up controls for children

A feature much-welcomed by parents and much-booed by their children, Microsoft's Family Options area in Windows Security offers several ways to monitor how children can access the computer as well as the internet.

Rather than running as a app on your computer, Microsoft's family options now work online through a Microsoft website called Family Safety. By tracking your children's activity through their Microsoft account usage, you can monitor their online activity wherever they log in to a Windows PC. The online, password-protected records stay online, where you can access them from any PC, tablet, or smartphone.

Microsoft's family options work only if both you and your children have Microsoft accounts.

To set up Microsoft's family options, follow these steps:

1. Add your children and any adults who want to monitor the children as family members when creating their user accounts.

I describe how to add family members when creating user accounts in Chapter 14. When you add family members to your PC's list of user accounts, each member receives an email inviting them to join your family network; when they accept, their accounts automatically appear on your computer.

2. Visit Microsoft's Family Safety website.

Open any browser and visit the website at https://account.microsoft.com/family. Log in with your Microsoft Account, if asked, and the site opens to show your list of family members who have accepted their invitations. Click the name of a family member, and the website, shown in Figure 11-5, lets you set limits on that child's computer behavior, as well as monitor their activity.

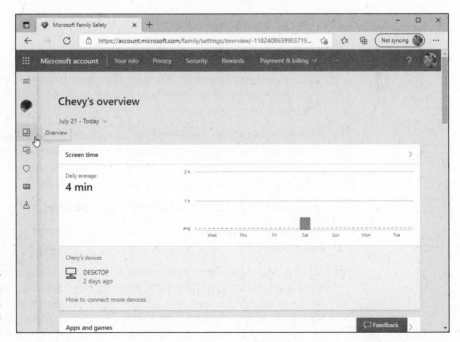

FIGURE 11-5: Microsoft's Family Safety website lets you set limits on your children's computer activity.

You can also visit the online settings by visiting Windows Security, covered earlier in this chapter, choosing Family Options, and choosing the View Family Settings link.

3. **Turn on the categories you'd like to enforce, and set the limits.**

Microsoft's family area contains a variety of categories that let you monitor or control different areas of behavior. Visit any of the categories described below, and each opens a new page with a toggle control at the top. Turn the toggle to either On or Off, and fine-tune the offered settings. (You can also turn categories Off to temporarily suspend monitoring in those areas.)

Microsoft's Family Safety website offers these categories, which apply whenever your child uses their Microsoft account to sign in to any Windows computer or tablet:

- *Overview:* A haven for time-stressed parents, the Activity area offers a quick rundown of your child's computer activity, along with an option to have the information emailed to you each week.

- *Screen Time:* Visit here to set time and day-of-the-week limits on when your child may access their PC or Xbox game system. Click the Turn Limits On button, and a grid appears for you to choose the exact hours your child is allowed to access the device.

- *Content Filters:* Visit here to control whether your child needs adult approval for spending money, as well as to block access to inappropriate apps, games, media, and websites.

- *App and Game Limits:* Set time and day-of-the-week limits on when your child may open apps and games.

- *Spending:* Want your child to be able to purchase items from the Microsoft Store app? Head here and click the button corresponding to the amount. It's withdrawn from the credit card attached to your Microsoft account and added to your child's account.

- *Find Child on a Map:* If your child has an Android smartphone with the Microsoft Family Safety app installed, this toggle switch lets you locate the device — and, hopefully, your child — on a map. (You can download the Microsoft Family Safety app from Google's App Store.)

4. **When you're done, close the window in your browser.**

Your changes take place immediately. When you're finished, just close your web browser.

Although Microsoft's family options work well, few things in the computer world are foolproof. If you're worried about your children's computer use, cast an occasional eye their way. Also, some of these options monitor your child only when they log in with their Microsoft account and use Microsoft Edge. If you spot an unfamiliar account (or a different browser) on the PC, it's time to ask some questions.

4

Customizing and Upgrading Windows 11

Chapter **12**

Customizing Settings in Windows

M ost people hate changing settings in Windows, and for good reason: They're too complicated. How do you know which setting works best? How can you even *find* the right setting? And, if you flip the wrong switch, how do you undo any peripheral damage?

Windows doesn't make this easy, unfortunately, as several things work against you. First, each app includes its own, individual batch of settings. Windows, too, contains another set of master settings known as the *Settings app.* Finally, Windows occasionally kicks you to that old switch-filled circuit box known as the Control Panel, a remnant from earlier Windows versions.

No matter which bank of switches you face, you can use them to customize the look, feel, behavior, and vibe of Windows and its apps and programs. This chapter explains how to find the settings you need, what to do with them once discovered, and how to undo their handiwork if they make things worse.

One word of caution: Some settings can be changed only by the person holding the almighty Administrator account — usually the computer's owner. If Windows refuses to flip a switch, call the PC's owner for help.

Finding the Right Switch

NEW

Windows 11 continues Microsoft's migration to the Settings app, which now sports hundreds if not thousands of switches. The Control Panel bundled with earlier Windows versions still lurks in Windows 11, but you'll encounter it far less than before.

To find the right switch to flip, let Windows help you. Follow these steps to find the setting you need:

1. **Click the taskbar's Search icon (shown in the margin), click inside the Search box that appears atop the Search window, and type a word describing the setting you want to find.**

   When you type the first letter, every setting containing that letter appears in a list above the Search box. If you don't know the exact name of your setting, begin typing a keyword: **display, troubleshoot, mouse, user, privacy,** or something that describes your need.

TIP

   Don't see the right setting? Press the Backspace key to delete the letters you've typed and then try again with a different word.

   The Search box, described in Chapter 7, lists other matches for your keyword: files on your computer, apps from Microsoft Store, and even items found on websites. If you see too much clutter, filter the results: Type the word **settings:** into the Search box, followed by a space and your search term. For example, to search for camera settings, type this into the Search box and press Enter:

   ```
   settings: camera
   ```

2. **Click your desired setting on the list.**

   Windows takes you directly to that setting.

When searching for a setting, always try clicking the taskbar's Search icon first. That brings up a Search box that often saves a lot of time when searching for set-tings, among other things. Spending a few minutes with the Search box often yields better results than scouring the hundreds of settings haphazardly stuffed elsewhere in Windows.

Looking for the settings inside a particular *app*, rather than inside Windows itself? Look in the app's upper-right corner for an icon containing either three dots in a row or three stacked lines. Click that icon, and a drop-down menu appears, almost always listing an entry for Settings.

Flipping Switches with the Windows Settings App

Windows 11 tosses more settings than ever into the ever-expanding Settings app. Most Windows settings live there now, sparing you a trip to the old Control Panel found in previous Windows versions.

To open the Settings app, click the Start button and click the Settings icon (a little gear) near the bottom of the Start menu's left pane.

The Settings app appears, as shown in Figure 12-1. In keeping with the new, standardized look in Windows 11, the Settings app looks identical whether you're viewing it on a desktop PC, tablet, or laptop.

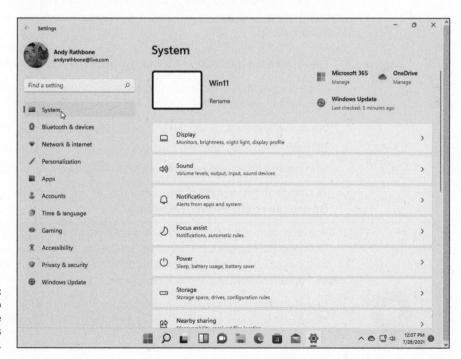

FIGURE 12-1:
The Settings app lets you change your computer's behavior.

The Settings app breaks its settings down into 11 categories, each covered in the rest of this chapter.

Adjusting the System settings

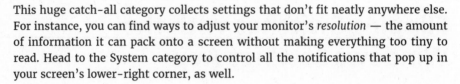

This huge catch-all category collects settings that don't fit neatly anywhere else. For instance, you can find ways to adjust your monitor's *resolution* — the amount of information it can pack onto a screen without making everything too tiny to read. Head to the System category to control all the notifications that pop up in your screen's lower-right corner, as well.

The rest of this section covers the most important things you'll eventually need to tweak in the System category.

Changing the screen resolution

One of the many change-it-once-and-forget-about-it options in Windows, *screen resolution* determines how much information Windows can cram onto your computer screen. Changing the resolution either shrinks everything to pack more stuff onscreen, or it enlarges everything at the expense of desktop real estate.

To find your most comfortable resolution — or if a program or game mutters something about you having to change your *screen resolution* or *video mode* — follow these steps:

1. Click the Start button, click the Settings icon, and click the System icon.

The Settings app normally opens to the System page, so you may not need to click the System icon.

2. When the System page appears, click the word Display from the right pane.

The Display settings appear, as shown in Figure 12-2.

3. To change the screen resolution, click the Display Resolution drop-down list and select your desired resolution.

The drop-down menu lists a variety of resolutions, all sorted by number. The larger the numbers, the higher the resolution, and the more information Windows can pack onto your computer screen. Unfortunately, packing more information onto your screen shrinks the text and images.

Unless you have a good reason not to, choose the resolution with the word (*Recommended*) next to it. That's the highest resolution your computer supports.

Choosing the Windows-recommended setting makes for the clearest text and images.

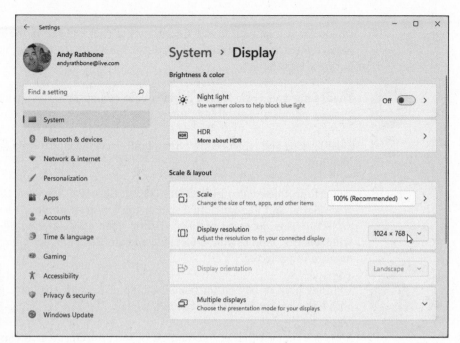

FIGURE 12-2:
The Settings app's
System page
opens to show
the Display
settings.

4. **When Windows immediately changes to the new resolution, click the Keep Changes button to authorize the change. If you don't like the new resolution, or it makes your display illegible, just wait for the screen to return to its previous setting.**

TIP

When Windows makes changes your display's resolution, it gives you 15 seconds to approve the change by clicking the Keep Changes button. If a technical glitch renders your screen unreadable, you won't be able to see or click the onscreen button.

Windows notices that you didn't approve the changes, so it quickly reverts to your original, viewable display settings. Whew!

After you change your video resolution once, you'll probably never return here unless you buy a new monitor or upgrade your computer's video. You might also need to revisit this window if you plug a second computer screen into your PC, which I describe in the following section.

Adding a second monitor or projector

Have you been blessed with an extra computer screen, perhaps a leftover from a deceased PC? Connect it to your PC or tablet, and you've doubled your Windows desktop: Windows stretches your workspace across both computer screens. That lets you view the online encyclopedia in one computer screen while writing your term paper in the other.

Or you can mirror your laptop's screen with what you see on the second monitor, handy when connecting to a projector at meetings, or holding video chats with business associates.

TIP

These same steps also let you connect your computer to most widescreen TVs for viewing photos and watching movies.

Most laptops and tablets come with a built-in video port for plugging in a nearby monitor.

To perform these video gymnastics on a desktop PC, however, the PC needs *two* video ports, and one port must match the *connector* on your second monitor or projector. This poses no problem if they're only a few years old. Most modern Windows PCs, laptops, and tablets include an HDMI port for plugging in a second monitor or projector.

TIP

You may need to buy an inexpensive adapter or cable that matches the ports of both your desktop PC and the second display.

After you connect the second monitor or the projector to your computer and turn it on, follow these steps on your PC:

1. **Click the Start button, and click the Settings icon. When the Settings app appears, click the System icon.**

2. **When the Settings app opens to its System page, click Display from the right pane.**

   The Settings app then shows its Display settings, which depict one monitor with two numbers in it, as shown in Figure 12-3.

3. **Choose how Windows should display itself on the two monitors.**

   At first, Windows assumes you want to duplicate your display on both monitors. However, you can choose how Windows should behave on the second monitor with the options provided in the drop-down menu shown in Figure 12-3. The drop-down menu offers these options, each handy for different scenarios:

   - *Duplicate These Displays:* This option, shown in Figure 12-3, duplicates your desktop on both screens, which is helpful when you want to project an image of your desktop onto a wall or screen for presentations.

   - *Extend These Displays:* This stretches Windows to fit across both screens, giving you an extra-wide desktop. This works best when you like to view *lots* of open windows simultaneously.

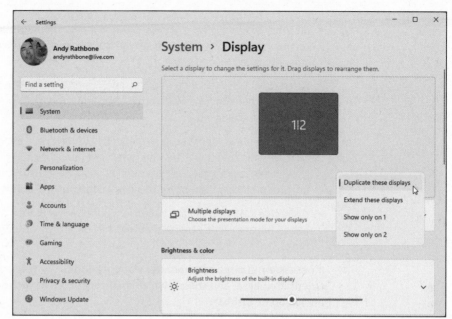

FIGURE 12-3:
FIGURE 12-3:
The Display
settings page
opens to show
that your display
is duplicated on
each monitor.

- *Show Only on 1:* Choose this before you're ready to show off your presentation; it blanks the screen on the second monitor. When you're ready for action, switch to Duplicate These Displays so that your second screen duplicates your first.

- *Show Only on 2:* Choose this option to show only the second display, which is useful when hooking up a PC to a TV for watching movies in a dark room.

Each time you choose one of the preceding options, a small window appears onscreen. Click the Keep Changes button to change to your new display settings. Click the Revert button if you don't like it. If changing the display makes the screen illegible, just wait a few seconds: If you don't click Keep Changes, Windows assumes something is wrong, and it reverts to your earlier setting.

4. **Click the Multiple Displays section to choose the presentation mode for your monitors.**

This section, useful for both troubleshooters and people who frequently plug in a second monitor, holds some extra settings, each described in the following list:

- *Remember Window Locations Based on Monitor Connection:* Selecting this check box tells Windows to remember all the work you did setting up your extra monitors. Keep this checked unless you constantly connect to different monitors in different situations.

- *Minimize Windows When a Monitor Is Disconnected:* This check box normally remains checked, which automatically minimizes any open windows when you unplug the second monitor.

- *Detect Other Display:* Handy when troubleshooting, this option lets you know whether Windows even recognizes the second monitor, projector, or TV that you've plugged in.

- *Identify:* Windows identifies its monitors by numbers, but sometimes you can't tell which monitor is assigned which number. Click this button, located beneath the picture representing your two monitors, and each monitor physically displays its assigned number on the center of its screen.

- *Connect to a Wireless Display:* Useful for connecting without a cable, this option fetches a little window that searches for any wireless TVs within range.

5. **If necessary, change your monitor's orientation in the Display Orientation area, and choose which monitor should have the Start button on its taskbar.**

Windows assumes your monitor is in *landscape* mode, where the monitor's display is wider than it is tall. (Most monitors and all TV sets are set up this way.) If you have a swiveling monitor or tablet that's set up vertically, visit the Display Orientation section to tell Windows how you've rotated your monitors.

The Display Orientation section lets you choose the default Landscape mode or Portrait mode if you've turned a monitor or tablet sideways, perhaps to better display a full page of reading material.

Finally, decide which of the two monitors listed onscreen should reveal the Start menu when you press the Windows key. Click the desired onscreen monitor, and then select the Make This My Main Display check box.

6. **If necessary, drag and drop the onscreen computer screens to the right or left until they match the physical placement of the *real* computer screens on your desk. Then choose your main display.**

The Display section window of the Settings app shows your two monitors as little onscreen squares. Drag and drop the onscreen monitors until they match the placement of your *real* monitors.

Any Settings changes you make take place immediately; as soon as you click the Keep Changes button, you're through.

Running Windows with two (or more) monitors may need a few other settings tweaks, as well:

>> To adjust the screen resolution of your two monitors, follow the directions given in the previous section, "Changing the screen resolution." This time,

however, the Advanced Display Settings window shows *both* monitors. Click the monitor you want to change, and the Resolution drop-down list applies to that monitor alone.

>> If you move the physical position of either of your two monitors, return to the first step and start over. You need to tell Windows of their new positions so that it places the correct display on the correct monitor.

>> Windows normally extends the taskbar along the bottom of your second monitor, which looks odd when connecting to TVs or during presentations. To turn it off, open the Personalization category in the Settings app, and choose Taskbar Behaviors from the right column. There, click the toggle switch called Show My Taskbar on All Displays. This toggle lets you either limit your taskbar to your main display or extend it across the other connected displays as well.

Cutting back on notifications and ads

What Windows calls *Notifications*, other people call "Nags." Notifications are the little informational blurbs that appear for a few seconds in your screen's bottom corner and then hunker down in the Notifications pane for later reading.

Some people like to stay instantly up to date, glancing at the notifications to see the latest headline, for example, or the subject line of an incoming email. Others find the unexpected messages to be an intrusion. To control them, visit the Notifications settings in the Systems category by following these steps:

1. **Click the Start button, click the Settings icon, and click the System icon.**

2. **When the System page appears, click Notifications from the right pane.**

   The Settings app displays the Notifications settings, as shown in Figure 12-4. All the settings apply to the Notifications pane — the information-filled strip that appears when you click the Time and Date area, located on the taskbar's right edge.

3. **Adjust the following settings as needed:**

NEW

   - *Notifications:* Click this single toggle switch to stop *all* your apps from bugging you with notifications. (Click the toggle switch back to On if you miss your apps' notifications.)

   - *Focus Assist:* Designed for the meticulous, this setting lets you designate the hours when notifications may appear. This way, you can give yourself uninterrupted time for work or video games. You can also choose to keep notifications from appearing on a second monitor, preventing the board room from seeing your reminder to pick up more kitty litter. You can also designate which specific apps may send notifications, and silence the rest.

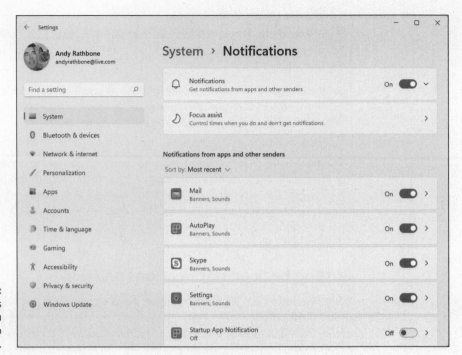

FIGURE 12-4:
The Notifications settings let you turn off pop-up announcements.

- *Notifications from Apps and Other Senders:* The most often-used setting, Notifications from Apps and Other Senders lets you pick and choose which apps may send notifications. This setting offers a great way to stop the obnoxious ones, but preserve the important. The apps are sorted automatically, with the last one to bug you appearing at the top of the list.

- *Offer Suggestions on How I Can Set Up My Device:* Designed for people who rush through setting up their computer's user accounts, this check box lets Windows remind you to finish customizing Windows 11. Turn it off after a month or so, or when you're reasonably happy with how your computer works.

- *Get Tips and Suggestions When I Use Windows:* Although helpful at first, these notifications may turn into a nuisance after you've used Windows for a few months. At that point, toggle them off with a click inside this check box.

By carefully flipping the toggle switches listed above, you can remove most of the nags from the Notifications pane. Miss the notifications? Reverse your decision by clicking the missed setting's toggle.

TIP

To turn off other pop-up ads, head to the Personalization category in the Settings app, and choose Device Usage from the right pane. There, turn off every toggle switch you spot.

Connecting and adjusting Bluetooth and other devices

 In Windows Land, *devices* are physical things such as your mouse, keyboard, printer, memory cards, and scanner. Accordingly, the Devices category of the Settings app contains settings to adjust your mouse's scroll wheel, as well as how your computer reacts when you insert a memory card. In short, device settings are a hodgepodge that you can locate most easily by searching from the Start menu's Search box, as described in this chapter's first section, "Finding the Right Switch."

After you find this hidden spot in the Settings app, you can use it to make all the adjustments covered in the next few sections.

Adding a Bluetooth gadget

Bluetooth technology lets you connect nearby gadgets wirelessly to your computer, removing clutter from your desktop. On a tablet, Bluetooth lets you add a wireless mouse and keyboard, external speaker, and other gadget without hogging any of your computer's coveted USB ports — those rectangular or oval holes where you plug in flash drives and other gadgetry.

Most tablets, laptops, and new desktop PCs come with built-in Bluetooth; you can add it to an older PC by plugging a tiny Bluetooth module into a vacant USB port.

Bluetooth can also connect your computer, laptop, or tablet with some smartphones for wireless internet access — if your wireless provider allows it – in a trick known as "tethering."

To add a Bluetooth item to a computer, laptop, or tablet, follow these steps:

1. **Make sure that your Bluetooth device is turned on and ready to pair.**

Most Bluetooth devices include a simple On/Off switch. Telling the device to begin pairing is a little more difficult. Sometimes you can simply flip a switch. Other devices make you hold down a button until its little light begins flashing.

When you spot the flashing light, the device is ready to pair with another Bluetooth device including, you hope, your computer.

 2. **Click the Start button, click the Settings icon, and in the Settings app, click the Bluetooth and Devices icon.**

The Settings app opens to show the Devices category, which conveniently opens to Bluetooth and Devices, shown in Figure 12-5.

If your computer's Bluetooth toggle is set to Off, click it to turn it On. Then click the Add Device button, just beneath it.

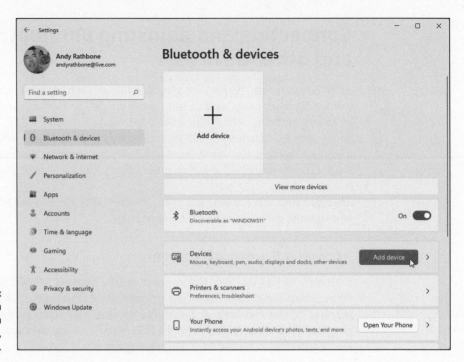

FIGURE 12-5:
To add a
Bluetooth
wireless gadget,
click Add Device.

3. **Click the Add Device button from the right side of the Bluetooth and Devices page, and then click the Bluetooth option from the Add a Device window.**

   Your computer quickly begins searching for any nearby Bluetooth devices that want to connect, known in Bluetooth parlance as *pair*.

   If your device doesn't appear, head back to Step 1 and make sure that your Bluetooth gadget is still turned on and ready to pair. (Many impatient gadgets give up and turn off after 30 seconds of waiting for a connection.)

4. **When your device's name appears below the words Add a Device, click its name.**

5. **Type in your device's code if necessary, and, if asked, click the Pair button.**

   Here's where things get tricky. For security reasons, some devices make you prove that you're sitting in front of your *own* computer and that you're not a stranger trying to break in. Unfortunately, devices employ slightly different tactics when making you prove your innocence.

   Sometimes you need to type a secret string of numbers called a *passcode* into both the device and your computer. (The secret code is usually hidden somewhere in your device's manual.) But you need to type quickly before the other gadget stops waiting.

On some gadgets, particularly Bluetooth mice, you hold in a little push button on the mouse's belly at this step.

Cellphones sometimes make you click a Pair button if you see matching passcodes on both your computer and phone.

TIP

When in doubt, type 0000 on your keyboard or press the Enter key. That's often recognized as a universal passcode for frustrated Bluetooth device owners who are trying to connect their gadgets.

Make sure your computer's Bluetooth isn't turned off: The toggle switch beneath the word Bluetooth, shown earlier in Figure 12-5, should be turned On. (Turning it off extends the battery life on tablets and laptops; on desktop PCs, always leave it turned on.) Don't see the Bluetooth toggle? Then your computer doesn't have built-in Bluetooth. You need to buy a Bluetooth adapter, an inexpensive little box that plugs into your computer's USB port.

After a gadget successfully pairs with your computer, its name and icon appear when you click View More Devices, shown on the right side of Figure 12-5.

To add a Bluetooth device from the Windows desktop, click the taskbar's Bluetooth icon (shown in the margin), choose Add a Bluetooth Device, and then jump to Step 3 in the preceding list. Don't see the taskbar's Bluetooth icon? Then click the upward-pointing arrow that lives a few icons to the left of the taskbar's clock. The Bluetooth icon appears in the pop-up menu, ready for your click.

To disconnect a Bluetooth gadget, follow the first two steps in this section. Then, when you spot your gadget listed atop Figure 12-5, click the three vertical dots (shown in the margin) and choose Disconnect from the pop-up menu. Don't click the other option, Remove Device, or you'll need to go through the bother of pairing it again with your computer.

Adding a printer or scanner

Quarrelling printer manufacturers couldn't agree on how printers and scanners should be installed. As a result, you install your printer in one of two ways:

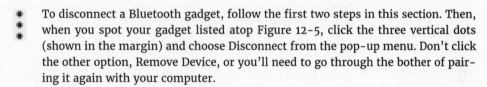

>> Some manufacturers say simply to plug in your printer or scanner by pushing its rectangular-shaped connector into a little rectangular-shaped USB port on your PC. Windows automatically notices, recognizes, and embraces your new device. Stock your printer with any needed ink cartridges, toner, or paper, and you're done.

>> Other manufacturers take an uglier approach, saying you must install their bundled software *before* plugging in your device. And if you don't install the software first, the printer or scanner may not work correctly.

Unfortunately, the only way to know how your printer or scanner should be installed is to check the bundled manual. (Usually, this information appears on a colorful, one-page Quick Installation sheet packed in the printer's box.)

No manual? Most manufacturers now offer them online at their website.

If your printer lacks installation software, install the cartridges, add paper to the tray, and follow these instructions to put it to work:

1. **With Windows up and running, plug your printer into your PC and turn on the printer.**

Windows may send a message saying that your printer is installed successfully, but follow the next step to test it.

2. **Click the Start button, click the Settings icon, and in the Settings app, click the Bluetooth and Devices icon.**

The Settings app opens to show the Bluetooth and Devices category, shown previously in Figure 12-5.

3. **From the right side of the Settings app, choose Printers and Scanners.**

The Settings app displays any printers and scanners attached to your PC. If you spot your printer listed by its model or brand name, click its name, click the Manage button, and click the words "Print a Test Page" when the Managing Your Device window appears. If the test page prints correctly, you're finished. Congratulations.

Test page *didn't* work? Check that all the packaging is removed from inside your printer and that it has ink cartridges. If it still doesn't print, your printer may be defective. Contact the store where you bought it, and ask who to contact for assistance.

The Managing Your Device window for your printer often contains a Printer Properties button as well. A click on that button lets you access the settings of your printer or scanner so that you can change their behavior.

That's it. If you're like most people, your printer works like a charm. If it doesn't, see the tips and fix-it tricks in the printing section of Chapter 8.

>> To remove a printer you no longer use, click its name in Step 3 and choose Remove Device from the pop-up menu. That printer's name no longer appears as an option when you try to print from a program. If Windows asks to uninstall the printer's drivers and software, click Yes — unless you think you may install that printer again sometime.

TIP

» You can change printer options from within many programs. Choose File in a program's menu bar (you may need to press Alt to see the menu bar), and then choose Print Setup or choose Print. The window that appears lets you change things such as paper sizes, fonts, and types of graphics.

» When you create a network, which I describe how to do in Chapter 15, you can share your printer with other PCs on your network. Your printer will be listed as available for all the computers on your network.

» If your printer's software confuses you, try clicking the Help buttons in its menus. Many buttons are customized for your particular printer model, and they offer advice not found in Windows.

» To print from your tablets and phones, buy and install a Wi-Fi printer. After it's hooked up to your network and shared, it should appear as a print option in most popular Wi-Fi devices.

» I cover both printers and scanners in Chapter 8.

Connecting your phone

NEW

The Settings app in Windows 10 contained a separate entry called Phone for linking your phone with your PC. Windows 11 now melts that information into the Bluetooth and Devices category in a section called Your Phone.

However, Windows 11 should really call it "Your Android Phone." Owners of iPhones miss out on the vast majority of the app's features found in the newly improved Your Phone app. (I cover the app more in Chapter 17.) The app only works with Android phones running Android version 7.0 or later, and to take advantage of *all* the app features, you need one of the newest versions of Samsung's Galaxy smartphones.

Why bother connecting your Android phone to your PC? Well, once connected, the Your Phone app in Windows 11 lets you do the following things:

» Read your phone's notifications on your PC.

» Send and read your phone's text messages from your PC.

» Easily view your phone's photos on your PC's monitor.

» Run your phone's apps on your PC.

» Make calls with your phone.

But before you can do any of those things, you must connect your Android phone with Windows 11 by following these steps:

1. **Click the Start button, click the Settings icon, and from the left pane of the Settings app, click the Bluetooth and Devices icon.**

   The Settings app opens to the Bluetooth and Devices page.

2. **Click the Open Your Phone button on the Settings app's right pane and, when the Use Your Android Phone from Your PC window appears, click the Get Started button.**

   The Get Started window appears, inviting you to use your Android phone from your PC.

3. **If asked, click the Sign In button to connect your Android phone with your Microsoft account.**

   When prompted, sign in with your Microsoft account.

   If you're already logged on to your PC with a Microsoft account, jump to the next step.

4. **On your Android phone, visit the link listed on the Pair Devices window, and follow the instructions.**

   The instructions here differ according to your type of phone. You may need to use your phone to scan a QR code on your computer's screen, for example, or input a number displayed on your phone into your computer.

   If you're having trouble, visit the Google Play app and download the Your Phone Companion – Link to Windows app. Sometimes the app itself makes the linking process easier.

   Windows connects with your phone, allowing you to access it from your PC, as shown in Figure 12-6.

Even with Windows 11, the link between Windows and your phone is still a work in progress. Some features work only on certain phone models, for example, and the required Your Phone app may drain your phone's battery more quickly than usual. (For an easier way to access your phone's photos, install the OneDrive app: It automatically places *all* your phone's photos wirelessly onto OneDrive, where they can be viewed on your PC as well.)

Still, if you hate typing text messages on your phone's tiny keyboard, the app may be worth your time. I describe how to view, download, or delete your Android phone's photos in Chapter 17.

FIGURE 12-6:
Connect Windows
with your phone
to view photos,
send messages,
and make phone
calls from
your PC.

Connecting to nearby Wi-Fi networks and internet

 For most people, the Wi-Fi settings listed in the Network and Internet category contains only one useful item: A way to find and connect with nearby Wi-Fi networks.

 To bypass the Settings app and leapfrog directly to those settings, click the Wi-Fi icon in the taskbar, that strip along the bottom of your screen. When the Quick Action panel menu pops up, click the little right-pointing arrow next to the Wi-Fi icon in the menu's upper-left corner. Finally, when the list of nearby Wi-Fi networks appears, click the name of your desired network. (The strongest network always appears atop the list.) Flip back to Chapter 9 for more details.

The other items in the Settings app's Network and Internet category apply mostly to techies and can be safely ignored. Here, geeks can tweak their VPN (Virtual Private Network), and old-schoolers can create dial-up internet connections.

I devote Chapter 15 completely to networking, and the internet gets its due in Chapter 9.

Personalizing your PC's look and feel

 One of the most popular categories in the Settings app is the Personalization category, which lets you change the look, feel, and behavior of Windows in a wide variety of ways. On the Personalization page await these nine icons:

>> **Background:** Paydirt for budding interior designers, the Background settings let you choose a particular color or photo (sometimes called *wallpaper*) for your desktop. I cover changing wallpaper in the next section.

>> **Colors:** When you're satisfied with your background, choose Colors from the left pane to choose the color of the frames around your Start menu, windows, apps, and taskbar. Click a color from the presented grid, and you're through. (To mix your own favorite color, click the View Colors button below the color grid.)

>> **Themes:** After you've chosen your favorite background, colors, and lock screen, visit here to save them as a *theme* — a collection of your embellishment touches that can be easily slipped on or removed. The Get More Themes in Microsoft Store link takes you to the Microsoft Store, where you can download dozens of free themes that change the look of Windows.

>> **Lock Screen:** Normally, Windows chooses from its own bundled photos to place on the *lock screen* — the image that appears when you first turn on your PC. Here, you can choose your own photo.

>> **Touch Keyboard:** Handy only for touchscreen owners, this lets you splash different colors across the onscreen keyboard. More important, it lets you change the onscreen keyboard's size, handy mostly for thumb-typers and owners of wide-screen tablets and laptops.

>> **Start:** Visit here to control the look and feel of the Start menu itself. (I describe these settings in Chapter 2, which covers the Start menu in detail.)

>> **Taskbar:** Head here to customize the behavior of your *taskbar,* the thin, icon-filled strip living along your desktop's bottom edge. I cover this topic in Chapter 3. (To jump quickly to the taskbar's Settings window, right-click the taskbar and choose Properties. The window that appears also lets you change your Start menu's settings.)

>> **Fonts:** A relatively new entry aimed at graphic designers and greeting card fans, this lets you install new fonts. To install a new font, just drag and drop it from File Explorer or your desktop onto the Fonts page's Add Fonts box. (To add more fonts to your PC, click the Get More Fonts in the Microsoft Store link.)

>> **Device Usage:** Confused about Windows 11? Click here and toggle on all the ways you plan on using your computer: Gaming, Family, Creativity, School, Entertainment or Business. Windows then tosses up suggestions about how to manage those tasks more easily.

In the next few sections, I explain the Personalization tasks that you'll reach for most often and how to handle the settings that appear.

Changing the desktop background

A *background*, also known as wallpaper, is simply the picture covering your desktop. To change it, follow these steps:

1. **Click the Start button, choose the Settings icon, and open the Personalization category.**

   Windows quickly kicks you over to the Settings app's Personalization category, open to the Theme setting.

TIP

   You can visit the Personalization category more quickly by right-clicking the desktop and choosing Personalize from the pop-up menu. The Personalization category opens directly to the Theme setting.

2. **Click the Background category from the right pane, and choose Picture from the Personalize Your Background drop-down menu shown in Figure 12-7.**

   The Background menu lets you create a background from a picture, a solid color, or a *slideshow* — a combination of photos that automatically changes at preset intervals.

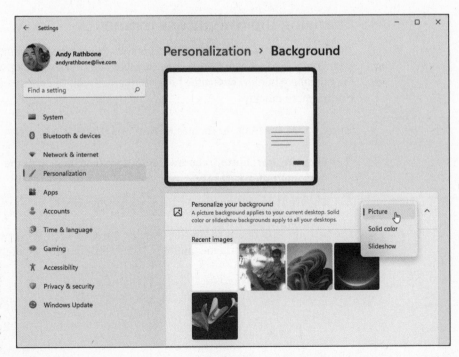

FIGURE 12-7:
The Personalization category lets you control how Windows looks on your PC.

3. **Click a new picture for the background.**

Microsoft lists a few pictures to choose from. If you don't like Microsoft's offerings, click the Browse Photos button, listed in the Choose a Photo section, to search your computer's Pictures folder for potential backgrounds.

When you click a new picture, Windows immediately places it across your desktop and shows you a preview at the top of the Personalization page. If you're pleased, jump to Step 4; otherwise, keep browsing the available photos.

4. **Decide whether to fill, fit, stretch, tile, center, or span the picture.**

Although Windows tries to choose the best-looking setting, very few pictures fit perfectly across the desktop. Small pictures, for example, need to be either stretched to fit the space or spread across the screen in rows like tiles on a floor. When tiling and stretching make your background look odd or distorted, visit the Choose a Fit drop-down menu. There, you can try the Fill or Fit option to keep the perspective. Or try centering the image and leaving blank space around its edges. Choose the Span option only if you've connected your PC to two monitors and want the image to fill both screens.

As you choose different options, Windows immediately changes the background to show your new choice. Like what you see? Close the Settings window, and you're done. Windows automatically saves your new background across your screen.

Changing the computer's theme

Themes are simply collections of settings to spruce up your computer's appearance: You can save your favorite screen saver and desktop background as a *theme*, for example. Then, by switching between themes, you can change your computer's clothes more quickly.

To try one of the built-in themes in Windows, follow these steps:

1. **Click the Start button, choose the Settings icon, and open the Personalization category.**

2. **Choose Themes from the Settings app's right side.**

The Settings app opens to display themes bundled with Windows, as shown in Figure 12-8. Click any theme, and Windows tries it on immediately.

CHOOSING A SCREEN SAVER

In the dinosaur days of computing, computer monitors suffered from *burn-in:* permanent damage when an oft-used program etched its image into the screen. To prevent burn-in, people installed a screen saver that replaced the static image with a blank screen or moving lines. Today's computer screens no longer suffer from burn-in problems, but some people still use screen savers because they look cool and add a layer of privacy.

Changing your screen saver requires a return to the Control Panel of yesteryear by following these steps:

1. **Click in the Search box next to the taskbar's Start button, type** screen saver, **and press Enter.**

   The Control Panel's Screen Saver Settings window appears.

2. **Click the downward-pointing arrow in the Screen Saver box, and select a screen saver. Then click the Preview button for an audition. View as many candidates as you like before making a decision.**

   Be sure to click the adjacent Settings button, as well, because some screen savers offer options, letting you specify the speed of a photo slideshow, for example.

3. **If desired, add security by selecting the On Resume, Display Logon Screen checkbox.**

   This safeguard keeps both people and cats away from your keyboard while you're fetching coffee. It makes Windows ask for a password after waking up from Screen Saver mode. (I cover passwords in Chapter 14.)

4. **When you're done setting up your screen saver, click OK.**

   Windows saves your changes.

If you *really* want to extend the life of your display (and save electricity), don't bother with screen savers. Instead, put your computer to sleep before stepping away: Right-click the Start button, click Shut Down or Sign Out, and choose Sleep from the pop-up menu. To wake your PC, tap any key on the keyboard.

Instead of choosing from the built-in themes, feel free to make your own by clicking the words Save Theme for saving your currently assigned desktop background, window color, sounds, screen saver, and mouse cursor. Type a name for your theme, and it appears as a choice in this section.

You can also download new themes from the Microsoft Store.

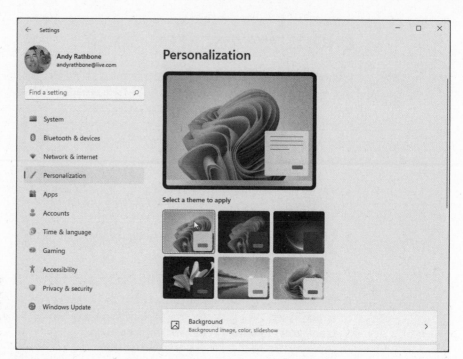

FIGURE 12-8:
Choose a
preconfigured
theme to change
how Windows
looks and sounds.

Fixing and removing apps

 The Settings' App category lets you uninstall unwanted apps and reset malfunctioning ones. You can also choose *default* apps — for example, the app you want to begin playing music when you open a music file. You can also choose which apps may open automatically as soon as you start Windows. That lets you open the apps more quickly, but makes Windows load a little more slowly. (I cover apps more completely in Chapter 6.)

Removing an app from your Start menu doesn't take much effort. Right-click the app's icon from the Start menu, and choose Unpin from Start from the pop-up menu.

That doesn't physically remove the app though. The app lives on in the Start menu's alphabetical list and on your computer. To permanently remove an app or program from your PC, follow these steps:

 1. Click the Start button, click the Settings icon from the Start menu, and choose the Apps icon from the left pane.

2. When the Apps category appears, click Apps and Features from the window's left pane.

The Apps and Features window appears, listing your currently installed apps and programs sorted alphabetically.

TIP

To sort the programs by their installation date, click the Sort By option and choose Sort By Install Date from the drop-down menu. This makes it easy to find the misbehaving app you installed yesterday.

The same menu lets you view programs installed on different drives. This comes in handy on small tablets, where you may want to store programs on memory cards rather than their main memory.

The final menu option, Sort by Size, helps find and remove oversize apps when you're running out of storage space.

3. **Click the More menu to the left of the unloved program, and click its Move or Uninstall button.**

Click the More menu (shown in the margin) next to a listed program, and several options appear below it:

- *Advanced Options:* Mostly technical stuff appears in this menu area, but if the app isn't working correctly, try the Repair option. (If the app still misfires, choose Reset. The app deletes its data and reinstalls itself.)

- *Move:* When you're running out of storage space, choose this option, if available. It lets you move an app or program onto another drive in your PC or onto your tablet's memory card, freeing up space for your files.

- *Uninstall:* Click this button — as well as the confirmation button that follows — to completely remove the app or program from your PC.

Depending on which option you've clicked, shown in Figure 12-9, Windows either boots the program off your PC or moves it to another disk drive or memory card.

After you delete a program, it's gone for good unless you kept its installation CD. Unlike other deleted items, deleted programs don't linger inside your Recycle Bin. Mistakenly deleted apps, however, can almost always be relocated and reinstalled from the Microsoft Store. (The Microsoft Store remembers which apps you've downloaded or purchased, making them easy to reinstall for free.)

WARNING

Always use the Settings app to uninstall unwanted programs. Simply deleting their files or folders doesn't do the trick. In fact, doing so often confuses your computer into sending bothersome error messages.

INSTALLING NEW APPS AND PROGRAMS

Today, most programs install themselves automatically as soon as you download them from the Microsoft Store, double-click their downloaded installation file, or slide their discs into your PC's drive.

If you're not sure whether a program has installed, go to the Start menu and look for its name. If it appears in the All Apps alphabetical list, the program has installed.

But if a program doesn't automatically leap into your computer, here are some tips that can help:

- You need an Administrator account to install programs. (Most computer owners automatically have an Administrator account.) That keeps the kids, with their Standard or Child accounts, from installing programs and messing up the computer. I explain user accounts in Chapter 14.

- Downloaded a program? Windows saves downloaded files in your Downloads folder. To find the Downloads folder, open any folder and click the word *Downloads* in the folder's Quick Access area, located at the top of its left pane. When the Downloads folder appears, double-click the downloaded program's name to install it.

- Many eager, newly installed programs want to add a desktop shortcut, a Start menu icon, *and* a Quick Launch toolbar shortcut. Say "yes" to all. That way you can start the program from the desktop, avoiding a trip to the Start menu. (Changed your mind? Right-click any unwanted shortcuts and choose either Delete or Unpin to remove them.)

- It never hurts to create a restore point before installing a new program. (I describe creating restore points in Chapter 13.) If your newly installed program goes haywire, use System Restore to return your computer to the peaceful state of mind it enjoyed before you installed the troublemaker.

Microsoft doesn't let you delete many of the apps bundled with Windows 11, unfortunately. You're simply stuck with them. (But you can still remove them from the Start menu by right-clicking their icons and choosing Unpin from Start from the pop-up menu.)

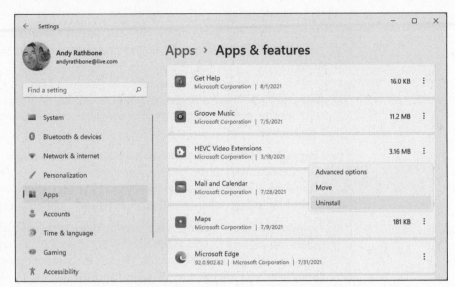

FIGURE 12-9:
Click an
unwanted app or
program, and
click the Uninstall
button.

Creating and changing accounts for others

Head to the Accounts category to create or change accounts for people who can use your computer, a chore I cover in Chapter 14, as well as to delete accounts for those no longer welcome. This category also lets you change your password or account picture. If you work on more than one PC, visit the category's Sync Your Settings section to control what settings should link to your Microsoft account. Those settings then appear on any Windows device you log in to with your Microsoft account.

Changing date, time, and language settings quickly

Visited mostly by frequent fliers, this set-it-once-and-forget-it category lets you change your time zone, adjust the time and date formats to match your region, and tweak other settings relating to your language and geographic location.

Laptop and tablet owners will want to drop by here when visiting different time zones. Bilingual computer owners will also appreciate settings allowing characters from different languages.

To visit here, click the Start button, click the Settings icon from the menu, and click the Settings app's Time and Language category. Four entries appear on the left pane:

>> **Date and Time:** These settings are fairly self-explanatory. (Right-clicking your taskbar's date and time area and choosing Adjust Date and Time lets you visit here as well.)

>> **Language and Region:** Moved to a new country? Update your change here; your computer then passes on the new country to any apps that require that information. If you're bilingual or multilingual, visit here when you're working on documents that require entering characters from different languages.

>> **Typing:** A plethora of options await to control how Windows interprets your typing. Toggles here let you decide whether Windows should automatically correct or highlight misspelled words. You can also visit your corrections history to change any mistakes Windows has made.

>> **Speech:** If Windows doesn't recognize your voice well, visit here to fine-tune its speech recognition settings. (You may also need to buy and install a better microphone to take advantage of speech-recognition programs.)

Setting up for video games

The Gaming category lets you control how you record video games on Windows. It also lets you check your PC's connection to Microsoft's Xbox gaming consoles and activate the Xbox Game Bar.

Adapting Windows for your special physical needs

Nearly everybody finds Windows to be challenging, but some people face special physical challenges as well. To assist them, the Settings app's Accessibility category offers a variety of welcome changes.

TIP

If your eyesight isn't what it used to be, for example, you may appreciate the ways to increase the text size on your computer screen.

Follow these steps to modify the settings in Windows:

TIP

1. **Load the Windows Settings app.**

   You can fetch the Settings app either of two ways:

- **Mouse:** Click the Start button, and then click the Settings icon from the Start menu.

- **Keyboard:** From the desktop, press ▦+I.

2. **When the Settings app appears, select the Accessibility icon.**

   The Accessibility area appears, as shown in Figure 12-10.

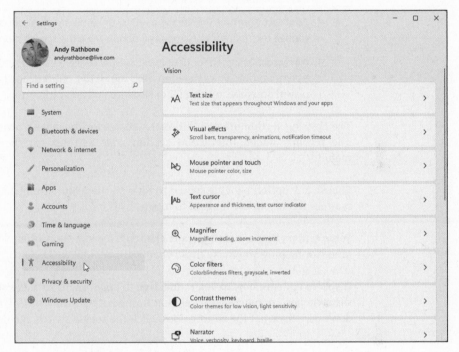

FIGURE 12-10:
The Ease of Access Center provides help for users with physical limitations.

3. **Change the settings according to your needs.**

   To make your computer easier to control, the Ease of Access window offers three groups of settings: Vision, Hearing, and Interaction. Each offers ways to help you see, hear, or control your PC. To turn a feature on or off, click its toggle button in these categories:

   - **Text Size:** Perhaps the most frequently accessed section, this lets you enlarge text in Windows and its apps.

   - **Visual Effects:** The first toggle switch in here makes the scroll bars more visible. It's my first stop after installing Windows 11.

   - **Mouse Pointer and Touch:** Visit here to change the size, color, and shape of the mouse pointer, making it easier to spot in a sea of text.

- **Text Cursor:** This area lets you change the cursor, the little bar that appears when you type words.

- **Magnifier:** When turned on, this enlarges the area around the mouse pointer when moved, making it easier to point and click in the right locations.

- **Color Filters:** This setting helps color-blind PC owners adjust the colors to make them easier to distinguish.

- **Contrast Themes:** This lets you adjust or eliminate most onscreen color, a change that helps vision-impaired people view the screen more clearly.

- **Narrator:** Designed for people with visual challenges, this setting activates a computerized voice that describes the words, buttons, and bars displayed onscreen, making them easier to find and click.

The Hearing section offers additional settings for those with hearing difficulties. The recently added Interaction section adds settings for those with limited mobility.

Choose any option's toggle switch to turn on the feature immediately. If it makes matters worse, choose it again to toggle it off.

Some centers that assist physically challenged people may offer software or assistance for helping you make these changes.

If you're not sure how to begin, feel free to experiment with the settings. Most of the switches are toggle switches that immediately turn a setting on or off. If you don't care for what the setting does, click the toggle switch again to turn it off.

Managing your privacy and security

 There's very little privacy left today when it comes to the internet. Nonetheless, this category lets you see the controls that Windows offers to limit the amount of information that apps and websites can gather about you. For example, you can control which apps can access your location and control your camera, as well as which apps can see your list of contacts in the People app.

Remember, though, that if you deny apps access to your information, they won't be as helpful. The Maps app, for example, needs to know your physical location before it can give you directions.

When you're done here, think about calling your bank, as well as your credit card and insurance companies. They, too, are often guilty of selling or sharing your information with other companies.

THE DESKTOP'S VANISHING CONTROL PANEL

Each update to Windows considerably beefs up the Settings app, but Windows occasionally drops you into a relic of the past: the desktop's Control Panel. You'll probably never need to visit here; if you do find yourself wandering its corridors, it's probably because the Settings app dropped you there to access an uncommon switch.

If you need to visit there out of nostalgia, however, take note that Windows 11 removed the Control Panel from the Start button's right-click pop-up menu.

To find the Control Panel, type **control panel** into the Start menu's Search box and press Enter. The Control Panel appears, ready for you to wax nostalgic at the look of yesteryear.

Staying current and safe with Windows Update

Windows 10 contained a slew of security and backup tools. Windows 11 whittles it all down to one: Windows Update. Since Windows Update runs automatically, receiving security patches in the background every few weeks, you'll probably never have to visit here anymore.

TIP

But here's one tip: If you hear that Microsoft has released an emergency security patch to counter some evilness traveling through the internet, drop by this section and click the Check for Updates button.

That tells your PC to check in with Microsoft immediately and grab any waiting security updates.

As for the old tools that used to be here, I cover them in Chapter 13. There, you discover how to speed up Windows, free up hard drive space, back up your data, and create a safety net called a restore point.

For information about the security settings that once lived here, flip back to Chapter 11.

Chapter **13**

Keeping Windows from Breaking

I f Windows seems desperately broken, hop ahead to Chapter 18 for the fix; Windows 11 offers more quick fix tricks than ever. But if your computer seems to be running reasonably well, stay right here. This chapter explains how to keep it running that way for the longest time possible.

This chapter is a checklist of sorts, with each section explaining a fairly simple and necessary task to keep Windows running at its best. You discover how to set up and turn on the automatic backup program in Windows called *File History,* for example.

If somebody says your computer has a bad driver, it's not a personal insult. A *driver* is a little program that helps Windows talk to your computer's various parts. This chapter explains how to remove bad drivers by placing an updated driver behind the wheel.

TECHNICAL STUFF

CREATING A RESTORE POINT

Windows is moving away from restore points to its newer Reset system, covered in Chapter 18. But old-school System Restore fans can still create and use the trusty Windows restore points to return a PC to a time when it was feeling better. Restore points behave a bit like a time capsule, saving your PC's settings at a specific point in time. If those settings become damaged later, returning to an earlier restore point can sometimes solve the problem.

To create a restore point, follow these steps:

1. **Click the taskbar's Search icon, type** Create a Restore Point **into the pop-up Search box, and click the Create a Restore Point link from the Search results.**

   The System Properties window appears, opened to the System Protection tab, which lists options for System Restore. Look for the Configure and the grayed-out Create buttons near the window's bottom edge.

2. **In the Available Drives window, click your Local Disk C: (System) drive. Then click the Configure button and, when the System Protection for Local Disk (C:) window appears, click the Turn On System Protection button and click OK.**

   That turns on System Protection for your C: drive, which is required before you can use System Restore. When you click OK, the window closes, returning you to the System Properties window. Note how your handiwork now lets you select the Create button.

3. **Click the Create button to fetch the System Protection window, type a name for your new restore point, and then click the window's Create button to save the restore point.**

   Choose a name that describes your computer's condition, such as "Created just before installing new bowling app," so you'll remember it better. Windows creates a restore point with your chosen name, leaving you some open windows to close.

By creating and labelling your own restore points on good days, you'll know which ones to use on bad days. I describe how to resuscitate your computer from a restore point in Chapter 18.

Backing Up Your Computer with File History

Your computer's hard drive will eventually die, unfortunately, and it will take everything down with it: years of digital photos, music, letters, financial records, scanned memorabilia, and anything else you've created or stored on your PC.

That's why you must back up your files on a regular basis. When your hard drive finally walks off the stage, your backup copy lets you keep the show on the road.

NEW

Windows 11 continues to push people to use OneDrive, Microsoft's rental space on the internet, for storing their computer's backups. To that end, Windows 11 now hides File History from its former spot in the Settings app.

But if you know where to find it, and I describe that secret here, Windows 11 still includes the free, automatic backup program called *File History*. After you turn it on, File History backs up every file in your main folders every hour. The program is easy to turn on, is simple to figure out, runs automatically, and backs up your most important files.

Before File History can go to work, you need two things:

>> **An external hard drive:** For dependable, automatic backups, you need a portable hard drive, which is a relatively inexpensive hard drive in a little box. A cord connects from the box to one of your computer's USB ports, and when the drive is plugged in, Windows recognizes the drive immediately. Keep the drive plugged in to your computer, and File History gives you completely automatic backups.

TIP

It's difficult to keep a portable hard drive constantly plugged in to a laptop or tablet because they're moved around so often. A safer but slightly more expensive option is to buy a Wi-Fi hard drive that stays at home. When you walk in the front door, Windows will find the wireless drive and automatically back up your files.

>> **Flip the On Switch:** The File History program still comes free in Windows 11. But the program can't do anything until you find it and tell it to begin running.

Follow these steps to tell your computer to start backing up your work automatically every hour:

1. **Plug your portable drive's cable into your USB port.**

The rectangular-shaped plug on the end of the drive or its cable plugs in to the rectangular-shaped USB port on your computer. (If the plug doesn't fit in the first time, flip it over.) Some newer computers also include smaller *USB-C* ports, which are oval. Those push into the computer's matching oval slot in either direction. Somebody finally made computers simpler!

Using a wireless drive? Then install it according to its instructions so that Windows will recognize it. (Unfortunately, I can't give you exact instructions because different brands and models work slightly differently.) Some models plug into a USB port on your router, that box that turns your internet signal into a Wi-Fi hotspot in your home.

2. **Click the taskbar's Search button, type** File History, **and press Enter.**

The File History settings area jumps to the screen, shown in Figure 13-1, and begins searching for a plugged-in hard drive or memory card.

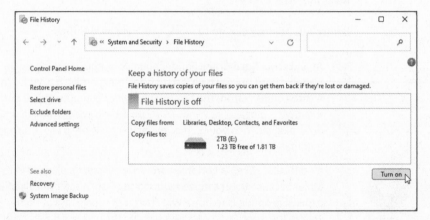

FIGURE 13-1:
Click the Turn On button to start File History.

3. **If necessary, select a drive for File History by clicking Add a Drive and choosing your drive from the drop-down window.**

Usually, File History finds your plugged-in portable drive and selects it automatically. If yours did, jump to Step 4.

If your computer contains more than one portable drive, the Select a Drive window appears, listing the available storage spaces. Click the one you want, and click OK.

If your drive isn't listed, then Windows isn't recognizing it. Try unplugging it, restarting your computer, and then plugging it back in to a different USB port.

Once you've successfully added a drive, the Turn On button at the window's bottom becomes clickable.

TECHNICAL STUFF

To choose a networked location, click the Select a Network Drive link in File History's opening window. Networked drives work well as backup locations for portable PCs, such as tablets and laptops. (I explain how to create a home network in Chapter 15.) If you try to save to a networked drive on another PC, Windows asks you to enter a username and password from an Administrator account on the other PC.

4. **Click the Turn On button.**

   Click the Turn On button to start the backup process rolling.

When you turn on File History, Windows immediately starts its backup — even if one isn't scheduled yet. That's because the ever-vigilant Windows wants to make sure it grabs everything right now, before something goes wrong. The first backup can take a *long* time.

After backing up everything, though, Windows backs up only the *changed* files every hour, which takes much less time. It keeps the first batch of backed up files, thankfully, in case you ever want to retrieve those down the road.

Although File History does a remarkable job at keeping everything easy to use and automatic, it comes with a few bits of fine print, described here:

>> File History backs up everything in your main folders: Documents, Music, Pictures, Videos, Desktop, Favorites, Downloads, and a few others. To exclude some (perhaps exclude your Videos folder if you already store backup copies of your videos elsewhere), click the Exclude Folders link from the File History window's left pane. There, you can remove some folders and even add others.

>> Windows normally backs up changed files automatically every hour. To change that schedule, click the Advanced Settings link from File History's left pane. Then choose the backup frequency. (You can choose between every 10 minutes to once a day.) You can also tell File History how long to keep backups. (I choose Until Space is Needed.)

>> When you turn on File History, it only backs up *your* files and settings. Other people with accounts on your PC must turn on File History while logged in to their own accounts, too.

TECHNICAL STUFF

CREATING A SYSTEM IMAGE BACKUP

Windows 7 introduced a popular way to back up a computer. Instead of backing up *files*, it copies *all* your hard drive's contents into one compressed file and then stores that file on a second hard drive. System images such as this come in handy for two main reasons:

- **Efficiency:** When your computer's hard drive eventually dies, you can replace the hard drive, restore the system image backup, and have all your files and programs back. It's a quick way to be up and running again.

- **Completeness:** File History backs up only files in your main folders, and the Microsoft Store backs up only your apps and settings. A system image backs up those things as well, but it also backs up your Windows *desktop programs* and their information. For example, File History won't back up your email from the desktop version of Microsoft Office. A system image will, though, because it backs up *everything*.

Windows 11 offers the same system image backup method introduced in Windows 7. You can even store a system image on the same portable drive you use for File History. (Make sure your portable drive is large enough to hold *all* the information on your computer's C: drive.)

To create a system image in Windows 11, click the Start button, type **Control Panel** into the Search box, and press Enter. Then, in the Control Panel's System and Security section, choose Backup and Restore (Windows 7). When the Backup and Restore Your Files window appears, click the words Create a System Image from the left pane. Follow the steps to tell Windows 11 to create a system image backup of your computer.

You should do this daily, if possible; if not, do it weekly or monthly. Then, if you ever need to take your computer to a repair shop, take in your portable hard drive and tell the technician you have a "system image backup." The techie can use that backup to rescue all your computer's files and programs from the date of your last system image backup.

TIP

>> File History also provides a handy way to move your files from an old Windows 10 PC to a new Windows 11 PC, a tiresome chore I describe in Chapter 20.

>> I describe how to restore files from the File History backup in Chapter 18. That section is worth looking at now, though: Not only does File History work in emergencies, but it enables you to compare current files with versions you

created hours or days before. It lets you revive better versions of files that you've changed for the worse.

WARNING

>> Windows saves your backup in a folder named FileHistory on your chosen drive. Don't move or delete that folder, or else Windows may not be able to find it again when you choose to restore it.

Finding Technical Information about Your Computer

If you ever need to look under the Windows hood, heaven forbid, head for the Settings app by clicking the Start button and choosing the Settings icon shown in the margin.

When the Settings app appears, select the System category and choose About from the bottom of the right column. Shown in Figure 13-2, the System window offers a technical briefing about your PC's viscera:

>> **Device Specifications:** This area lists your PC's type of *processor* (its brains, so to speak) along with its amount of memory, known as RAM. You can upgrade memory fairly easily on a PC or laptop, but not on a tablet.

>> **Windows Specifications:** Windows comes in several editions and versions. In this section, Windows lists the edition that's running on your particular computer, as well as the version of that edition. Chances are, you'll see Windows 11 Home or Pro listed here under Edition. The version number usually changes once a year, because that's how often Microsoft updates Windows 11 with menu changes and new features. (Microsoft updated Windows 10 twice a year, much to the dismay of the techies in charge of business PCs.)

TECHNICAL STUFF

>> **Related Settings:** Aimed at techies, this section offers a few links to little-used settings found inside the aging Windows Control Panel.

>> **Help from the Web:** Clicking this section's Get Help link takes you to Microsoft's Virtual Agent, a robot that gives you a mechanical run-around when you're looking for help. For better — and human-supplied — answers, visit Microsoft's Answer's Forum at https://answers.microsoft.com.

WARNING

Most of the stuff listed in the Settings app's System window is fairly complicated, so don't mess with it unless you're sure of what you're doing or a technical support person tells you to change a specific setting.

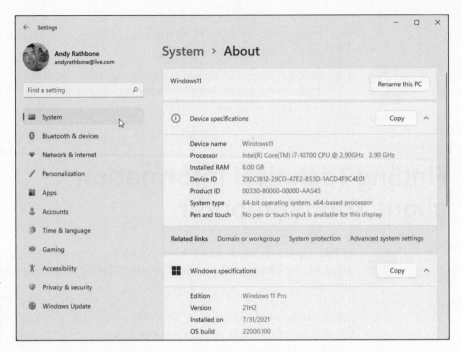

FIGURE 13-2:
Clicking the
System category
provides
technical
information
about your PC.

Freeing Up Space on Your Hard Drive

If Windows begins whining about running out of storage space, you can tell it to fix the problem itself. You just need to turn on *Storage Sense*, a Windows feature that tells Windows to take out its own trash.

To turn on Storage Sense, which makes Windows automatically empty its Recycle Bin and delete temporary files left behind by your apps and programs, follow these steps:

1. **Click the Start button and click the Settings icon shown in the margin.**

   The Settings app appears.

2. **Click the System category, and click the word Storage from the left column of the System page.**

   The Storage section appears, as shown in Figure 13-3.

3. **Click the Storage Sense toggle switch to On.**

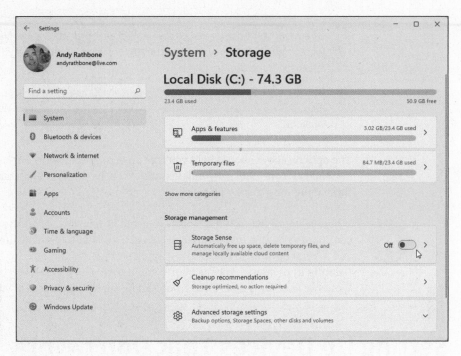

FIGURE 13-3:
The Storage
section offers
many ways to
increase storage
space on your PC.

After you complete the preceding steps, Windows begins taking care of its own housekeeping automatically. To fine-tune how Windows manages its storage space, click the Storage Sense link itself. There, the Settings app's Storage section offers several other options:

>> **Cleanup of Temporary Files:** This option lets you choose how often Windows deletes temporary files that it created in the background for its own house-keeping tasks. You never see these files, as they're all created without your knowledge. Chances are good that you'll never miss them.

>> **Automatic User Content Cleanup:** Here, you can make Windows free up storage space every day, every week, every month, or only when your disk space runs low. You can also tell it how often to empty your Recycle Bin. Don't tell it when to delete the content of your Downloads folder unless you're diligent about moving those downloaded files to another folder.

>> **Locally Available Cloud Content:** When you access files stored on OneDrive, Windows saves copies on your PC. Here, you can tell Windows to delete those downloaded copies if you haven't opened them for a certain amount of time.

>> **OneDrive:** When you access a file stored on OneDrive, Windows downloads a copy to your PC for you to open. If you haven't touched that copy for a while, Storage Sense will delete it, leaving an identical copy safely stored on

OneDrive. To free up space by deleting those extraneous extra files, open any folder, right-click OneDrive from the folder's left pane, and choose Free Up Space from the pop-up menu.

>> **Run Storage Sense Now:** Meant for people who need extra space immediately, this option works like much like Disk Cleanup did in older Windows versions.

The options above should help you free up enough space to continue working. But if Windows continually complains about not having enough room, you can try these more long-term options:

WARNING

If you've upgraded to Windows 11, your old Windows version usually remains on your hard drive in a folder called `Windows.Old`. That folder consumes *lots* of space, and several options in the Settings app's Storage section offer to let you delete it. Deleting it, of course, means your computer won't be able to return to that older Windows version, a last-ditch troubleshooting task I cover in Chapter 18.

Setting Up Devices That Don't Work (Fiddling with Drivers)

Windows comes with an arsenal of *drivers* — software that lets Windows communicate with the gadgets you plug in to your PC. Normally, Windows automatically recognizes your new part, and it simply works. Other times, Windows heads to the internet and fetches some automated instructions before finishing the job.

In fact, the newest version of Windows now lets you download drivers automatically from Windows Update, a refreshing tact that saves you the time of tracking down drives.

But occasionally, you'll plug in something that's either too new for Windows to know about or too old for it to remember. Or perhaps something attached to your PC becomes cranky, and you see odd messages grumble about "needing a new driver."

In these cases, it's up to you to track down and install a Windows driver for that part. The best drivers come with an installation program that automatically places the software in the right place, fixing the problem. The worst drivers leave all the grunt work up to you.

If Windows doesn't automatically recognize and install your newly attached piece of hardware — even after you restart your PC — follow these steps to locate and install a new driver:

1. **Visit the part manufacturer's website, and download the latest Windows driver.**

   You often find the manufacturer's website stamped somewhere on the part's box. If you can't find it, search for the part manufacturer's name on Google (www.google.com) and locate its website.

   Look in the website's Support, Downloads, or Customer Service area. There, you usually need to enter your part's name, its model number, and your computer's operating system (Windows 11) before the website coughs up the driver.

   No Windows 11 driver listed? Try downloading a Windows 10, 8.1, 8, or 7 driver, instead — they sometimes work just as well.

2. **Run the driver's installation program.**

   Sometimes clicking your downloaded file makes its installation program jump into action, installing the driver for you. If so, you're through. If not, head to Step 3.

    If the downloaded file has a little zipper on the icon, right-click it and choose Extract All to *unzip* its contents into a new folder that contains the files. (Windows names that new folder after the file you've unzipped, making it easy to locate.)

3. **Right-click the Start button, and choose Device Manager from the pop-up menu.**

   The Device Manager appears, listing an inventory of every part inside or attached to your computer. A yellow triangle with an embedded exclamation point icon appears next to the troublemaking part.

4. **Click your problematic device listed in the Device Manager window. Then click Action from the Device Manager's menu bar, and choose Add Legacy Hardware from the drop-down menu.**

   The Add Hardware Wizard guides you through the steps of installing your new hardware and, if necessary, installing your new driver. Beware, though: This last-ditch method of reviving problematic parts can frustrate even experienced techies.

Luckily, you need to install drivers only in either of these two cases:

>> You've just bought and installed a new piece of hardware, and it's not working correctly. The drivers packaged with newly bought computer gadgets are usually old. Visit the manufacturer's website, download the latest driver, and install it. Chances are good that the new driver fixes problems with the first set of drivers.

>> You've plugged in a new gadget that Windows doesn't recognize. Tracking down and installing the latest driver can often fix the problems.

If you're not having trouble with a piece of hardware, don't bother updating its driver, even if you find a newer one online. Chances are good that newer driver adds support only for newer models of the gadget you own. And that new driver might throw a glitch into something that was already working fine.

Finally, don't bother signing up for a service that claims to keep your computer up to date with the latest drivers. They can do more harm than good.

TIP

If your newly installed driver makes things even worse, there's a solution: Head back to Device Manager, double-click the troublesome part's name, and click the Driver tab in the Properties window. Keep your breathing steady. Then click the Roll Back Driver button. Windows ditches the newly installed driver and returns to the previous driver.

Chapter **14**

Sharing One Computer with Several People

Windows allows several people to share one computer, laptop, or tablet without letting anybody peek into anybody else's personal files.

The secret? Windows grants each person their own *user account,* which neatly isolates that person's files. When a person types in their user account name and password, the computer looks tailor-made just for them: It displays their personalized desktop background, menu choices, programs, and files — and it forbids them from seeing items belonging to other users.

This chapter explains how to set up a separate user account for everybody in your home, including the computer's owner, family members, and roommates.

It also explains how to create accounts for children, which allows you to monitor their computer activity and set limits where you feel necessary.

Understanding User Accounts

Windows wants you to set up a *user account* for everybody who uses your PC. A user account works like a cocktail-party name tag that helps Windows recognize who's sitting at the keyboard. Windows offers two types of user accounts: Administrator and Standard. (It also offers a special Standard account for children.)

To begin playing with the PC, people click their account's name when the Windows Sign In screen first appears, as shown in Figure 14-1.

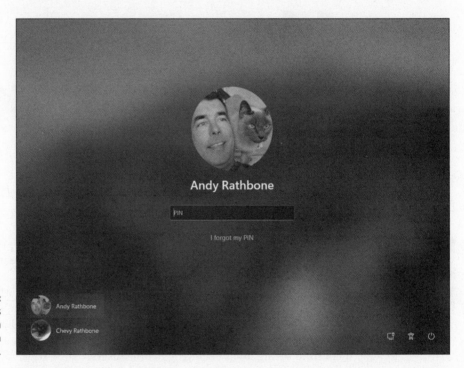

Who cares? Well, Windows gives each type of account permission to do different things on the computer. If the computer were a hotel, the Administrator account would belong to the desk clerk, and each tenant would have a Standard account. Here's how the different accounts translate into computer lingo:

>> **Administrator:** The administrator controls the entire computer, deciding who gets to play with it and what each user may do on it. On a computer running Windows, the owner usually holds the almighty Administrator account. He or

she then sets up accounts for each household member and decides what they can and can't do with the PC.

>> **Standard:** Standard account holders can access most of the computer, but they can't make any big changes to it. They can't run or install new programs, for example, but they can run existing programs.

>> **Child:** The Child account setting is actually just a Standard account with the Microsoft Family Safety settings automatically turned on. I cover Microsoft family controls in Chapter 11.

>> **Guest:** Like Windows 10, Windows 11 no longer offers guest accounts. Microsoft removed them because most visitors now arrive toting their own smartphones, tablets, laptops, or all three.

Here are some ways accounts are typically assigned when you're sharing the same computer under one roof:

>> In a family, the parents usually hold Administrator accounts, and the kids usually have Standard accounts.

>> In a dorm or shared apartment, the computer's owner holds the Administrator account, and the roommates have Standard accounts, depending on their trustworthiness level (and perhaps how clean they've left the kitchen that week).

To keep others from signing in under your user account, you must protect it with a password. (I describe how to choose a password for your account in this chapter's later "Setting Up Passwords and Security" section.)

TIP

Sometimes somebody will be signed in to their account, but the computer will go to sleep if they haven't touched the keyboard for a while. When the computer wakes back up, only that person's user account and photo will show up onscreen. Windows lists the other account holders' names in the screen's lower-left corner, though, letting them sign in with a click on their names.

TECHNICAL STUFF

You may run across a reference for a Local account. A *Local account* is simply an Administrator or Standard account that isn't a Microsoft account. Local accounts are tied to a specific computer. They don't require an email address, and they lack the perks of a Microsoft account.

Changing or Adding User Accounts

Windows offers two slightly different ways to add user accounts. It separates them into the two types of people you're most likely to add to your computer:

>> **Family members:** By choosing this type of account, you can automatically set up controls on your children's accounts. Any adults you add here can automatically monitor your children's computer usage. All family members must have Microsoft accounts; if they don't already have them, the process helps you create them.

>> **Other members:** This type of account works best for roommates or other long-term guests who will use your computer but don't need monitoring or the ability to monitor children.

The next two sections describe how to create both types of accounts, as well as how to change existing accounts.

REMEMBER

Only Administrator accounts can add new user accounts to a computer. If you don't have an Administrator account, ask the computer's owner to upgrade your account from Standard to Administrator.

Adding an account for a family member or friend

Adding a family member adds an important distinction to the account. If you add a child, the child's activity is curtailed according to the limits you set. And if you add an adult, that person also has the ability to monitor the activity of any added children.

If you want to add an account that's not involved in these family matters, choose the other option, called Adding an Account for Someone Else. There, you can create an account for a roommate or long-term guest.

Administrator account holders can create either type of account by following these steps:

1. **Click the Start button, and click the Settings icon.**

2. **When the Settings app appears, click the Accounts icon.**

   The Accounts screen appears, as shown in Figure 14-2, offering ways to change your own account, as well as add accounts for other people.

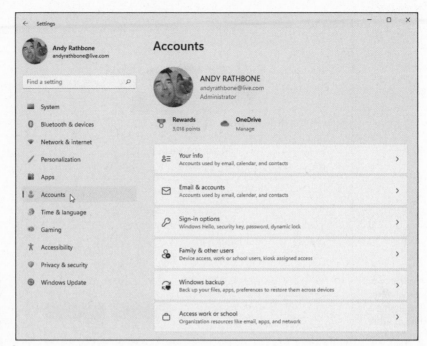

FIGURE 14-2:
Click the words
Family and Other
Users to begin
creating a new
user account.

TIP

3. **Click the words** `Family & Other Users` **from the right pane.**

The right pane of the Family and Other Users screen lets you create either of two accounts: one for a family member, or one for someone else. If you're creating an account for a family member, move to Step 4. If you're *not* adding a relative, jump ahead to Step 5.

4. **In the Add a Family Member section, click the Add Account button, and follow the steps to send the person an invitation.**

A window appears, shown in Figure 14-3, asking for you to enter the person's email address. You have several options:

- If you already know the person's email address, type it into the Enter Their Email Address box and click Next. (If the email address isn't already a Microsoft account, it will be turned into one.)

- If the person doesn't have an email account, Microsoft assumes you're adding a child as a family member. In that case, click the Create One For a Child link. That takes you to a page where you can sign them up for an email address that also serves as a Microsoft account.

No matter which option you choose, your invited family member, either a child or adult, will receive an email saying they've been invited to have a family account on your computer. After they accept the offer, they automatically appear as an account on your computer.

FIGURE 14-3:
Choose whether
you're adding a
child or adult
family member.

At this point, you've finished adding a family member. To add somebody who's not a relative, move to Step 5.

5. **Choose Add Someone Else to This PC.**

    Microsoft immediately complicates matters by displaying the How Will This Person Sign In window, shown in Figure 14-4, which asks for the new account holder's email address.

    Microsoft is trying to say that you can choose either of two types of accounts for your new account holder:

    - *Microsoft account:* A Microsoft account is required for many Windows tasks and features. Described in Chapter 2, a Microsoft account is simply an email address that links to Microsoft, its computers, and its billing department. Only Microsoft account holders can download apps from the Microsoft Store app, store and retrieve files on an internet storage space called OneDrive, and access other perks offered by a Microsoft account. To create a Microsoft account, go to Step 6.

    - *Local account:* Select this option for people not interested in Microsoft accounts and their perks. It lets the person use your computer with an account tied only to your computer. To create a Local account, jump to Step 7.

FIGURE 14-4:
Enter the email
address of the
person you want
to add.

TIP

Can't decide which type of account to create? Creating a Local account is always a safe bet. (Local account holders who want or need the advantages of a Microsoft account can upgrade to one at any time.)

6. **Type the email address of the new account holder's Microsoft account into the Email Address text box, click Next, and then click Finish.**

The account will be waiting on the Sign In screen shown back in Figure 14-1.

When the person wants to use the computer, he chooses the account bearing his email address and then types in his Microsoft account password. Windows visits the internet, and if the email address and password match, the account is ready for action. You've finished.

7. **Click the words I Don't Have This Person's Sign-In Information, shown at the bottom of Figure 14-4.**

Alarmed that you'd consider choosing a lowly Local account over the wondrous Microsoft account, Microsoft tries to make you create a Microsoft account for the new account.

8. **Click the Add a User Without a Microsoft Account link.**

This tells Microsoft that yes, you really do want a Local account. (After all, Local account holders can always turn their account into a Microsoft account at any time.)

A new screen appears, asking for a name for the account (username), the account's password, and a password hint in case you forget the password.

9. **Enter a username, password, and password hint, and then click Next.**

Use the person's first name or nickname for the username. Choose a simple password and hint; the user can change them after they sign in.

Before you forget, tell the person their new username and password. (Or write them down and keep them in a secure place.) Their username will be waiting at the Sign In screen's lower-left corner for them to begin using the computer.

TIP

Windows normally creates Standard accounts for all new users whether or not they've signed in with a Microsoft or Local account. If at a later time you want to change this, you can upgrade the Standard account to an Administrator account, as described in the next section.

Changing existing accounts

The Windows Settings app lets you create a new account for a friend or family member, as described in the previous section. And it lets you tweak your own account, changing your account password or switching between a Microsoft or a Local account.

Administrators can even modify other accounts, changing them to Standard or Administrator accounts, or even deleting them completely.

But if you want to have more control than that — the ability to change an existing Local account's name or password — you need the power of the desktop's Control Panel.

REMEMBER

You can't change or reset Microsoft accounts with these steps — those account holders must go online to do that — but you *can* change a Local account.

To change an existing user's Local account, follow these steps:

1. **Click the Start button on the left side of the taskbar, type** Control Panel **in the Search box, and press the Enter key.**

2. **Click to open the Control Panel's User Accounts category.**

3. **Click the User Accounts link, and then click the Manage Another Account link.**

TIP

The Manage Accounts window appears, as shown in Figure 14-5, listing all the accounts on your computer.

FIGURE 14-5:
The Manage
Accounts window
lets you change
the settings of
other account
holders on the
computer.

4. **Click the account you'd like to change.**

   Windows displays a page with the account's photo and lets you tweak the account's settings in any of these ways:

   - *Change the Account Name:* Here's your chance to correct a misspelled name on a Local account. Or feel free to jazz up your own Local account name, changing Jane Smith to Crystal Powers.

   - *Create a Password:* Every Local account should have a password to keep out other users. Here's your chance to add one. If the account already has a password, this link changes to Change the Password, giving you a chance to change it.

   - *Change the Account Type:* Head here to promote a Standard user of high moral character to an Administrator account or bump a naughty administrator down to Standard.

   WARNING

   - *Delete the Account:* Don't choose this option hastily, because deleting somebody's account also deletes all of that person's files. If you *do* choose it, also choose the subsequent option that appears: Keep Files. That option places all of that person's files in a folder on your desktop for safekeeping.

   - *Manage Another Account:* Save your current crop of changes and begin tweaking somebody else's account.

5. **When you're through, close the window by clicking the X in its upper-right corner.**

   Any changes made to a user's account take place immediately.

Switching Quickly between Users

Windows enables an entire family, roommates, or employees in a small office to share a single computer or tablet. The computer keeps track of everybody's programs while different people use the computer. Mom can be playing chess and then let Jerry sign in to check his email. When Mom signs back in a few minutes later, her chess match is right where she left it, pondering the sacrifice of her rook.

Known as *Fast User Switching*, switching between users works quickly and easily. When somebody else wants to sign in to their account for a moment, perhaps to check email, follow these steps:

1. **Open the Start menu.**

   To open the Start menu, click (or tap) the Start button or press the keyboard's Windows key ( ).

2. **Click your user account photo from along the screen's left edge.**

   A menu pops up, as shown in Figure 14-6.

3. **Choose the name of the user account holder who wants to sign in.**

   Windows leaves you signed in but immediately fetches the other person's account, letting them type in their password.

When that person finishes with the computer, they can sign out just as you did in
Step 2 — by clicking their user account photo in the Start menu's left pane. This
time, however, they'll choose Sign Out. Windows closes down their session, letting you sign back in with your own password. And when Windows reappears, so
does your work, just as you left it.

TIP

Keep these tips in mind when juggling several people's accounts on a single PC:

>> With all this user switching, you may forget whose account you're actually
using. To check, open the Start menu. The current account holder's picture
appears in the menu's bottom left pane. (Hover your mouse over the picture
to see the name.)

>> To see other accounts currently signed in, open the Start menu and click the
current account holder's name. A pop-up menu lists the other user accounts
but places the words Signed In beneath the name of each account holder
who's currently signed in.

WARNING

>> Don't restart the PC while another person is still signed in, or that person
will lose any work they haven't saved. (Windows warns you before restarting
the PC, giving you a chance to ask the other person to sign back in and save
their work.)

>> If a Standard account owner tries to change an important setting or install software, a window appears, asking for Administrator permission. If you want to approve the action, just step over to the PC and type your password into the approval window. Windows lets you approve the change, just as if you'd done it while signed in with your own account.

Changing a User Account's Picture

Okay, now the important stuff: changing the boring picture that Windows automatically assigns to your user account. For every newly created user account, Windows chooses a generic silhouette. Feel free to change the picture to something more reflective of the Real You: You can snap a photo with your computer's webcam or choose any photo in your Pictures folder.

To change your user account's picture, head for the Start menu and click your picture along the menu's left edge. When the menu drops down, choose Change Account Settings. Windows presents the screen shown in Figure 14-7.

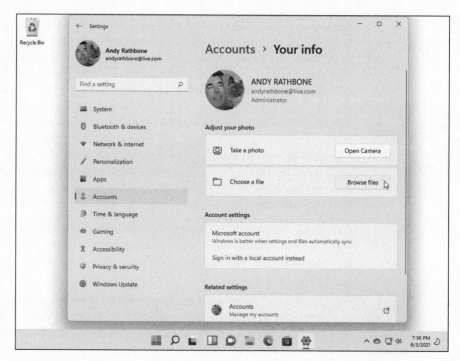

FIGURE 14-7:
Windows lets each user choose an account picture.

The Accounts page lets you change your picture two main ways:

>> **Take a Photo:** Click the adjacent Open Camera button, shown only for people with a camera connected to their laptops, tablets, or computers, to take a quick *selfie*, slang for a self-shot portrait, for your account photo.

TIP

WHAT DOES MY MICROSOFT ACCOUNT KNOW ABOUT ME?

A Microsoft account is simply an email address and a password that lets Microsoft identify you. By logging in with a Microsoft account, you can access many Microsoft services: OneDrive, for example, gives you an online cubbyhole for storing and sharing files across your PC, tablet, and phone, even if it's from Apple or Android. You also need a Microsoft account to download and run many Windows apps.

In short, Windows works much better when you log in with a Microsoft account. I use one; I keep my shopping list on my PC, but thanks to OneDrive, I can read and update the same list on my Android phone while at the grocery store.

Like just about every company these days, Microsoft collects information about you, which is made easier when you use a Microsoft account. That really shouldn't be a surprise. Google, Facebook, Apple, and every website you visit gathers information about you as well. Most banks, internet service providers, credit card companies, and insurance companies also stockpile and sell information about their customers.

To help combat your erosion of privacy, Microsoft lets you see what information it has stored about you and lets you delete portions you aren't comfortable seeing listed.

To do that, visit the Microsoft Privacy Center at https://account.microsoft.com/privacy and sign in with your Microsoft account. There, you can view information about your billing and payments; renew, cancel, or subscribe to Microsoft services like OneDrive, Office 365, and Xbox Live; find your lost Windows devices on a map; clear your Bing search history; and change your marketing preferences. Plus, you can check your kids' computer activity, provided you've set them up with a Microsoft account.

You should also visit the Settings app's Privacy and Security page, which lets you access similar information.

It's worth taking a look in both places to see what sort of information Microsoft stores and making sure there aren't any surprises. If only your bank, insurance, and credit card companies made it as easy to see how much of your information they're selling.

>> **Choose a File:** To assign a picture already on your computer, click the Browse Files button. A new window appears, showing photos in your Pictures folder. Click a desired picture, and click the Choose Picture button. Windows quickly slaps that picture atop your Start menu.

TIP

Here are a few more tips for choosing your all-important account photo:

>> After you've chosen an account photo, it attaches to your Microsoft account and anything you sign in to with that account: Microsoft websites, programs, and apps, as well as any Windows computer you sign in to with your Microsoft account.

>> You can grab any picture off the internet and save it to your Pictures folder. Then click the Browse Files button in the Choose a File section, mentioned earlier in this section, to locate the picture and assign it as your account photo. (Right-click the internet picture and, depending on your web browser, choose Save Image As or a similar menu option.)

>> Don't worry about choosing a picture that's too large or too small. Windows automatically shrinks or expands the image to fit the circular space.

Setting Up Passwords and Security

There's not much point to having a user account if you don't have a password. Without one, a snoop from the neighboring cubicle or even another family member can click your account on the Sign In screen and peek through your files.

People with administrator accounts, especially, should have passwords. If they don't, they're automatically letting anybody wreak havoc with the PC: When a permission's screen appears, asking for a protective password, anybody can just press Enter to gain entrance.

Microsoft account holders must change their passwords online by visiting https://account.microsoft.com. Local account holders can create or change a password by following these steps:

1. **Click the Start button, and click the Settings icon from the Start menu.**

2. **When the Settings app appears, click the Accounts icon.**

   The familiar Accounts window appears, shown earlier in Figure 14-2, where you can add other accounts, change your own, and perform other account-related chores.

3. **Choose the Sign-in Options link from the Accounts window's right edge.**

The Sign-In Options screen appears, listing all the ways you may log into your computer.

4. **Click the Password option on the window's right side; when the menu drops down, click the Change button.**

People who haven't created a password should instead click the Create a Password button.

5. **Make up an easy-to-remember password, and type it into the New Password text box. Then retype the same characters into the Retype Password text box below it, and click Next.**

Retyping the password eliminates the chance of typos.

TIP

CREATING A PASSWORD RESET DISK

A Password Reset Disk serves as a key, letting you back in to your own computer in the event you've forgotten the password to your Local account. (You can't create a Password Reset Disk for a Microsoft account.) To create a Password Reset Disk, follow these simple steps:

1. **Log in to your PC with your Local account, insert a flash drive into a USB port, and wait for Windows to recognize it.**

2. **Click the Start button, then click in the Start menu's Search box, type** password reset disk, **and press Enter.**

3. **Click the Create a Password Reset Disk option that appears below the Search box.**

The Forgotten Password Wizard appears and walks you through the process of creating a Password Reset Disk from a memory card or a USB flash drive.

When you forget your password on that particular computer, you can insert your Password Reset Disk as a key. Windows lets you in to choose a new password, and all will be joyous. Hide your Password Reset Disk in a safe place because it lets *anybody* into your account on that computer.

No matter how many times you change your password, your original Password Reset Disk still works, always providing a backup key to get into your account.

Changing an existing password works slightly differently: The screen shows a Current Password box where you must first type your existing password. (That keeps pranksters from sneaking over and changing your password during lunch hours.)

You can find out more about passwords in Chapter 2.

Signing in with Windows Hello

Password-protected accounts help keep your account secure, both from seedy strangers on the internet and from people nearby. But very few people enjoy stopping their flow to type in a password — if they can even remember it.

Windows tries to solve that problem with its Windows Hello technology. Windows Hello lets you skip bothersome passwords and log in securely in less than a second. By attaching either a compatible camera or a fingerprint reader to your computer, you can log in with the swipe of a finger or a glance at the camera.

Many new laptops and PCs now include built-in Windows Hello compatible readers and cameras; if yours doesn't, you can buy one that plugs in to your computer's USB port.

To set up Windows Hello, follow these steps:

1. **Click the Start button, click the Settings icon (shown in the margin), and choose Accounts.**

   The Settings app's Accounts page appears.

2. **Click Sign-In Options from the left pane.**

   The screen shows your options for signing in to your account, shown in Figure 14-8. If you don't see an option to set up Windows Hello, make sure your compatible fingerprint reader or camera is plugged in to your computer and fully installed.

3. **Click the Set Up button for either the fingerprint reader or camera, and follow the instructions.**

   Windows walks you through scanning either your fingerprint (any finger will do, as long as you use that finger consistently when you want to sign in to your account), iris, or face. You may need to create a *PIN,* a four-digit number that adds an additional layer of security for special circumstances.

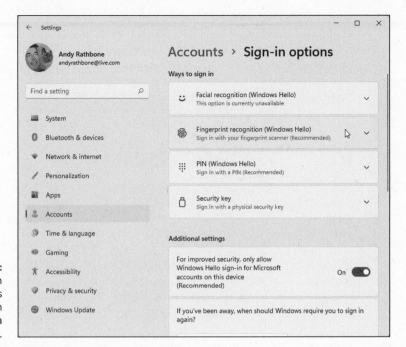

FIGURE 14-8:
Choose an option
from Windows
Hello to sign in
without a
password.

TIP

Windows Hello may seem more like science fiction than reality, but don't write it off too quickly. You'll appreciate Windows Hello for several reasons:

>> Fingerprint readers are fairly inexpensive and easy to install. You can find several models selling on Amazon for around $30, and they work amazingly well. I love mine.

>> Many new laptops come with fingerprint readers already installed near the keyboard area. Some tablets, too, include built-in fingerprint readers.

>> Windows recognizes most compatible fingerprint readers as soon as they're plugged in to your computer's USB port. You rarely need to install any bundled software.

>> Whenever Windows asks you to sign in, just slide your finger across the reader. The screen quickly clears, and you're ready for work. You don't need to remember or type in a complicated password. There's nothing to forget.

>> Windows Hello not only lets you sign in to your device, but lets you buy things in the Microsoft Store, all without typing in a password.

>> As the Windows Hello technology grows, Windows Hello may eventually let you enter your favorite password-protected websites, as well.

Chapter **15**

Connecting Computers with a Network

B uying yet another PC can bring yet another computing problem: How can two or more PCs share the same internet connection and printer? And how do you share your files between your two PCs?

The solution involves a *network.* When you connect two or more computers, Windows introduces them to each other, automatically letting them swap information, share an internet connection, and print through the same printer.

Today, most computers can connect without anybody tripping over cables. Known as *Wi-Fi* or *wireless,* this option lets your computers chatter through the airwaves like radio stations that broadcast and take requests.

This chapter explains how to link a houseful of computers so that they can share things. After you've created a wireless network, you can share your internet connection with not only your Windows PCs but also smartphones, tablets, and other computerized gadgets. And, if you choose to give the password to your visitors, they can connect to the internet, as well.

Be forewarned, however: This chapter contains some pretty advanced stuff. Don't tread here unless you're running an Administrator account and you don't mind doing a little head-scratching as you wade from conceptualization to actualization to "Hey, it works!"

Understanding a Network's Parts

A *network* is simply two or more computers that have been connected so they can share things. Although computer networks range from pleasingly simple to agonizingly complex, they all have three things in common:

>> **A router:** This little box works as an electronic traffic cop, controlling the flow of information between computers, as well as between your network and the internet. Today's routers support both wired and wireless networks.

>> **A network adapter:** Every computer needs its own *network adapter* — an electronic mouthpiece of sorts. A *wired* network adapter lets you plug in a cable; the cable's other end plugs into your router. A *wireless* network adapter translates your computer's information into radio signals and broadcasts them to the router. Most computers and laptops today include both adapters.

>> **Network cables:** Computers connecting wirelessly don't need cables, of course. But computers without wireless adapters need cables to connect them to the router.

When you plug a modem into the router, the router quickly distributes the internet signal to every computer on your network. (Some modems come with built-in routers, sparing you from having to connect the two.)

Most home networks resemble a spider, as shown in Figure 15-1, with some computers' cables connecting to the router in the center. Other computers, laptops, tablets, and gadgets connect wirelessly to the same router.

The router divides its attention among networked computers efficiently, letting every computer simultaneously share a single internet connection.

Windows lets every computer share a single printer as well. If two people try to print something simultaneously, Windows stashes one person's files until the printer is free and then sends them automatically when the printer is ready for more work.

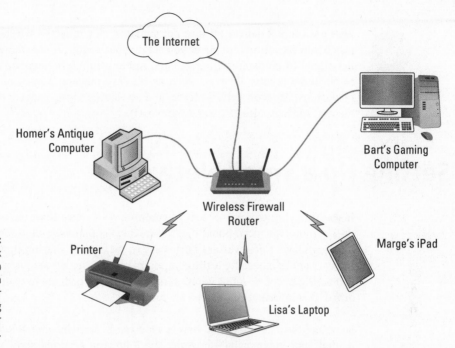

FIGURE 15-1:
A network resembles a spider, with each computer communicating with a router near the center.

The Internet

Homer's Antique Computer

Wireless Firewall Router

Bart's Gaming Computer

Printer

Marge's iPad

Lisa's Laptop

TIP

CHOOSING BETWEEN WIRED AND WIRELESS NETWORKS

You can easily string cables between computers, routers, and gadgets that sit on the same desk or live within one room. Beyond that, though, cables quickly become messy. To cut the clutter, most computers today include *wireless (Wi-Fi)* adapters, which let the computers chatter through the air.

But just as radio broadcasts fade as you drive out of the city, wireless signals also fade. The more they fade, the slower the connection becomes. If your wireless signals pass through more than two or three walls, your computers may not be able to communicate. Wireless networks are also more difficult to set up than wired networks.

Although wireless connections are popular, wired connections work more quickly, efficiently, securely, and inexpensively than wireless. But if your spouse wants the cables removed from the hallways, wireless may be your best option. For best results, combine the two: Connect adjacent computers and devices with cables and use wireless for the rest.

REMEMBER

Wireless routers deliver an internet signal to *all* connected wireless gadgets, not just Windows computers. After you set up your router, it also delivers your internet signal to iPads and other tablets, Apple computers, smartphones, and even some home theater devices (such as Blu-ray players, game consoles, "smart" televisions, Amazon Echo gadgets, and streaming video gadgets such as a Chromecast, Amazon Fire TV, and Roku boxes).

Setting Up a Small Network

If you're trying to connect lots of computers — more than ten — you probably need a more advanced book, like *Networking For Dummies All-in-One*, 8th Edition, by Doug Lowe. Networks are fairly easy to set up, but sharing their resources can be scary stuff, especially if the computers contain sensitive material. But if you're just trying to set up a few computers and wireless gadgets in your home or home office, this information may be all you need.

So without further blabbing, here's a low-carb, step-by-step list of how to set up a small and inexpensive network. The following sections show how to buy the three parts of a network, install the parts, and make Windows create a network out of your handiwork.

Buying parts for a network

Visit the computer store across town or online, buy this stuff, and you're well on your way to setting up your network:

» **Network adapters (optional):** Because most new computers and laptops include both wired *and* wireless adapters, you can probably cross this off your shopping list. But if you need to add an adapter, pick up an inexpensive wired or wireless adapter that plugs into the computer's USB port. (Mobile devices like laptops, tablets, and smartphones *all* include built-in wireless adapters.)

» **Network cable (optional):** Not using wireless? Then buy *Ethernet* cables, which resemble phone cables but with slightly thicker jacks. Buy a cable for each computer you want to connect. The cables must be long enough to reach from the computer to the router, described next.

» **Router:** This little box does all the magic. Most routers today include built-in wireless; many also include a broadband modem for internet access. Wireless routers usually include four jacks to accommodate up to four nearby computers relying on cables.

TIP

Some Internet Service Providers (ISPs) supply you with a wireless router or modem, and they even send a techie to your home to set up your network for you. It never hurts to ask.

Setting up a wireless router

Wireless connections bring a convenience felt by every smartphone owner. But with computers, a wireless connection also brings complication. You're basically setting up a small radio transmitter that broadcasts to tiny radios inside your computers. You need to worry about signal strength, finding the right signal, and even entering passwords to keep outsiders from eavesdropping.

Unfortunately, different brands of wireless routers come with different setup software, so there's no way I can provide step-by-step instructions for setting up your particular router.

However, every router requires you to set up these three things:

>> **Network name (SSID):** Enter a short, easy-to-remember name here to identify your particular wireless network. Later, when connecting to the wireless network with your computer, smartphone, tablet, or other wireless gadget, you'll select this same name to avoid accidentally connecting with your neighbor's wireless network.

>> **Infrastructure:** Of the two choices, choose Infrastructure instead of the rarely used alternative, Ad Hoc.

>> **Security:** To keep out snoops, this option uses a password to encrypt your data as it flies through the air. Most routers offer at least three types of password options: WEP is barely better than no password, WPA is better, and WPA2 is better still. Choose the strongest security option available, and create a memorable password with mixed characters, such as **Five&Three=8!**.

Some routers include an installation program to help you change these settings; other routers contain built-in software that you access with your web browser in Windows.

REMEMBER

As you set each of the preceding three settings, write them on a piece of paper: You must enter these same three settings when setting up the wireless connection on each of your computers and other wireless gadgets, a job tackled in the next section. You also need to pass out that information to any houseguests who want to piggyback on your internet connection while they visit.

Setting up Windows computers to connect to a network

First, a word to the wired crowd: If you've chosen to connect a computer to your router with a cable, plug one end of the cable into your computer's network port. Plug the cable's other end into one of your router's network ports. (The ports are usually numbered; any number will do.) To connect other computers to the same router, connect cables between those computers' network ports and the router's other empty network ports.

If your internet company didn't do it for you, plug a cable from your broadband modem's LAN or Ethernet port into your router's WAN port. (Those ports are almost always labeled, and if your router and modem live together in one box, you can skip this step.) Turn on your router, and you've finished: You've discovered how easy it is to create a wired network.

Wireless is a different story. After you set up your router to broadcast your network wirelessly, you must tell Windows how to receive it. Chapter 9 offers the full course in connecting to wireless networks, both your own and those you find in public, but here's an abbreviated version for connecting to your own network:

1. **Click the Start button, and choose the Settings icon from the Start menu.**

2. **When the Settings window appears, click the Network and Internet icon.**

    At the top of the Network and Internet page, Windows lists whether you're connected to the internet and, if you're connected, lists the name of the Wi-Fi network that your computer uses to slurp its data.

3. **Click the page's Wi-Fi section and make sure the Wi-Fi toggle at the page's top is turned on. Then click the Show Available Networks button.**

    When you click the Show Available Networks button, Windows quickly sniffs the airwaves for nearby wireless networks and a list drops down, shown in Figure 15-2, listing of all the wireless networks within range of your computer. With any luck, your own network will be at the list's top. Your network will have the name — the *SSID* — that you chose when setting up your router, described in the previous section.

4. **Choose the desired wireless network by clicking its name, clicking the Connect Automatically button, if desired, and then clicking the Connect button.**

    The closest wireless network is usually the strongest, so you'll probably spot your own wireless network at the top of the list.

TIP

    If you select the adjacent Connect Automatically checkbox before clicking the Connect button, Windows automatically connects to that network the next time you're within range, sparing you from repeating all these steps.

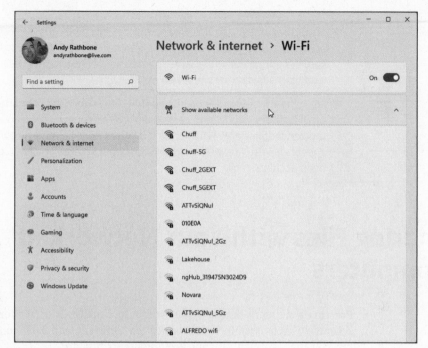

FIGURE 15-2:
Windows places
the strongest
available
network at
the top
of the list.

5. **Enter a password, and click Next.**

Here's where you type in the same password you entered into your router when setting up your wireless network. (To confuse things, Windows 11 refers to your password as a "Network Security Key.")

At this point, Windows treats your newly joined wireless network as a *public* network, the same as one you'd find in a coffee shop or airport. You won't be able to find or access your other networked computers until you make some changes, covered in the next section.

If Windows asks to make your computer "discoverable," choose Yes: You're in your own home, and you want your other computers to be able to swap files. But if you're connecting to somebody *else's* network — a public network, for example, click No. You want your PC to be discoverable only when on your *own* network.

TIP

If you're still having problems connecting, try the following tips:

>> Head back to Step 2, and click the Troubleshoot button. Windows performs some basic diagnostics and resets your networking equipment. If the troubleshooter can't fix the problem, it offers clues as to the connection-robbing culprit.

» Cordless phones and microwave ovens can interfere with wireless networks, oddly enough. If you're having trouble with signal strength, try to keep your cordless phone out of the same room as your wireless computer, and don't heat up that sandwich when web browsing.

 » From the Windows desktop, the taskbar's Wi-Fi icon (shown in the margin) provides a one-click way to see available wireless networks. If your desktop's taskbar contains a Wi-Fi icon, click it, click the right-pointing arrow that appears next to the wireless icon in the pop-up menu, and jump to Step 3 in the preceding steps.

Sharing Files with Your Networked Computers

Creating a network between your computers makes it easier for them to share resources, such as an internet connection, printers, and even your files. But how can you share some files while keeping others private?

Microsoft's solution used to be called a *Homegroup*. It was an automatic way of flipping networking switches so Windows PCs could see each other, as well as share their files, folders, and printers.

Windows 10 eventually removed the ability to create Homegroups, and Homegroups are still missing from Windows 11. That means you need to flip your computer's networking switches manually.

The following sections explain which switches to flip so that Windows 11 can still share files with other computers and devices on your network.

Setting your home network to private

In Windows 7, 8, 8.1, and some earlier versions of Windows 10, Homegroup provided a fairly easy way to share your files. With a few clicks, it automatically let other people on your network share your Music, Pictures, and Videos folders. And it conveniently left out the folder most people *don't* want to share: Documents.

Now, with Homegroup support dropped, Windows 11 doesn't share *any* files or folders: It treats your home network as a *public* network. Public networks work fine in coffee shops and airports, where you don't want strangers to know about your connected computer, much less access its private files.

SWITCHING FROM PUBLIC TO PRIVATE

TIP

When you first open File Explorer's Network area, Windows displays some banners that can be confusing. Here's the correct way to click all the pop-up messages and banners so Windows will quickly switch your network from Public to Private and turn on File Sharing.

If you're not sure you clicked everything correctly, following the steps in the next three sections will make sure all the switches are flipped in the right direction. If you'd like to, try an easy way to set up a private network by clicking through these pop-up messages and banners.

1. **Open File Explorer, and click Network in the left pane.**

2. **When the Network Discovery Is Turned Off window appears, click OK.**

3. **Click the yellow banner atop File Explorer that says, `Network Discovery and File Sharing Are Turned Off. Click to Change.`**

4. **When the pop-up menu appears below the banner, choose Turn On Network Discovery and File Sharing.**

5. **When the Network Discovery and File Sharing window appears, choose the first option, No, Make the Network that I Am Connected to a Private Network.**

This does two things: It lets your PC see other PCs on your network, and it lets those PCs see your PC. When anybody on your network clicks your computer's name, they can see any files, folders, or printers you've shared with the network. If your network still isn't working correctly, then follow the rest of the steps in this section to complete the setup process.

However, you want a *private* network at home so you can share files, as well as a printer, among all your computers. To switch your network to private, follow these steps:

1. **Click the Start button, click the Settings icon, and click Network and Internet from the left pane.**

   The Network and Internet section appears, shown in Figure 15-3, letting you double-check your Network settings on the top of the page.

2. **Change the network to Private, if necessary.**

   Make sure that the network says the words Private Network beneath the word Properties, as shown in Figure 15-3. If it says Public Network, click the Properties button. When the Properties page appears, click the Private button from a drop-down menu near the top of the Properties page.

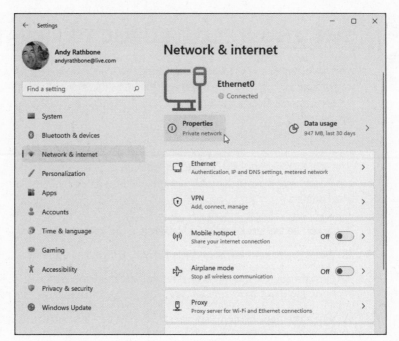

FIGURE 15-3:
The Network and
Internet page lets
you toggle your
network between
Public and
Private.

Making a network Private prevents your PC from appearing to wandering internet strangers, and limits access to those PCs on your own private network.

3. **Click the Start button, and, in the Search box along the Start menu's top, type** Manage Advanced Sharing Settings **and press Enter, and confirm that these settings are correct:**

The age-old Control Panel's Advanced Sharing Settings page appears, shown in Figure 15-4. The settings it displays may already be correct, but they're the first place to look if your network isn't behaving correctly. You can open each of the three sections listed below by clicking the downward-pointing arrow next to the section's name.

Private: Make sure the network is set to Private (Current Profile). If it says Public, repeat Steps 1 and 2. When a network is set to Private, Windows should automatically toggle Network Discovery to On, which allows your PCs to see each other. If necessary, toggle on the Turn on File and Printer Sharing option.

Guest or Public: Everything in this section should be toggled off. That keeps your computer safer when connected to a public network.

All Networks: Make sure that a dot appears next to these settings:

- Turn off Public Folder Sharing

- Use 128-bit Encryption to Help Protect File Sharing Connections

- Turn On Password Protected Sharing

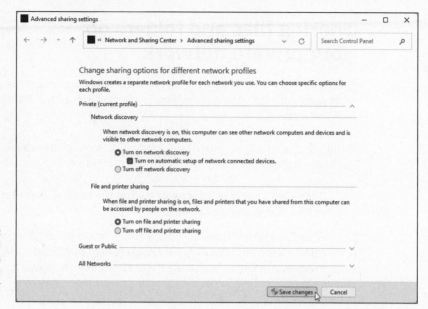

FIGURE 15-4:
The Advanced
Sharing settings
page lets you
fine-tune your
network settings.

4. **Click the Save Changes button.**

   Windows takes the necessary background steps that begin sharing your printer and allow you to start choosing which files and folders to share.

Most people need to follow these steps only once, when first setting up their *home* network. As you travel with laptops and tablets, Windows automatically treats every newly encountered network as public, adding the tighter security controls that go along with it.

After you set up your home network as private, several things happen:

» Your networked computers show up in File Explorer's Network area, located on the bottom of File Explorer's left pane. (Your other computers should now be able to see your computer as well.)

» You can see any files shared by other PCs on your network.

» Any printer installed on one of your Windows PCs will appear as an option in the other PC's printing menus.

» You can begin sharing files and folders on your Windows computer, a task I describe in the next section.

Sharing files and folders on your private network

After you make your network private, as described in the previous section, other computers on your network can finally see your computer. But they can't access its files or folders.

Before they can do that, you must manually share your files and folders by following these steps:

1. **Open File Explorer by clicking its icon on the taskbar, and find the folder or files that you want to share.**

   When File Explorer appears, click the This PC link in its left pane; your most popular folders appear along File Explorer's right side. From there, you can navigate to the folder containing the items you want to share.

   I explain how to navigate File Explorer and select items in Chapter 5.

2. **Right-click the folder or files you want to share, and from the pop-up menu that appears, choose Show More Options. When the full menu appears, click Give Access To, and then click the option labeled Specific People from the pop-out menu.**

   The Choose People to Share With window appears, as shown in Figure 15-5. There, you can add people who should be allowed to access those files or folders on your home network.

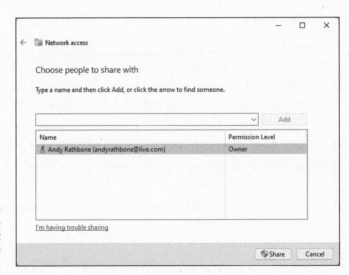

FIGURE 15-5:
Choose the people you want to access those folders.

3. **Add the names of people who should be able to access those files or folders, and click the Add button.**

   Add the people on your network who should be able to access those files and folders. You can do this in several ways, with these being the easiest:

   - *Microsoft accounts:* If your network holders use Microsoft accounts, just type the email address linked to their Microsoft account.

   - *Everyone:* To add everyone on your network, simply add the word **Everyone.**

4. **Click an added person's name and choose what type of access to grant that person.**

   You have three options here, as shown in Figure 15-6: Read, Read/Write, and Remove:

   - *Read:* The most popular option, this allows the person to view the contents of the file or folder, but not make any changes. If they want to make changes, they can copy the file or folder to their own computer and make changes there. But they won't be able to alter the copy on your own PC.

   - *Read/Write:* This lets people not only view, read, and copy the items, but to *change* them as well. That means they can also delete them, so be careful when granting this power, especially if you've shared that item with Everyone, as described in Step 3.

   - *Remove:* Choose this option to remove a listed person's access to the items, handy when somebody can no longer be trusted with access to your files.

5. **Click the Share button to put your changes in motion.**

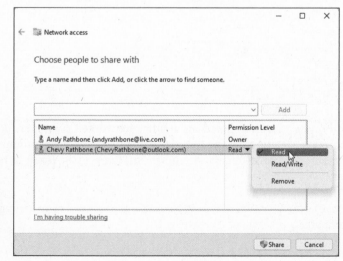

FIGURE 15-6: Choose the people who should have access to your shared items, as well as their type of access.

When you're through sharing items, the next section explains how to access items shared on the network.

Accessing what others have shared

To see the shared folders of other people on both your PC and home network, click the File Explorer icon (shown in the margin), found on the taskbar that runs along the bottom of every Windows screen.

When File Explorer appears, click Network, found in the Navigation pane along File Explorer's left edge. The right side of the window, shown in Figure 15-7, promptly lists the names and icons of every computer on your network that offers shared files.

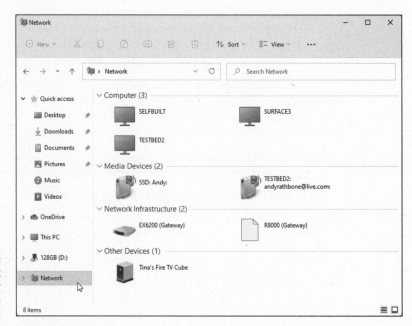

FIGURE 15-7: Click Network to see other accessible PCs on your network.

To browse the files shared on another networked computer, double-click that computer's name from the Network window. The window promptly displays that computer's shared folders, as shown in Figure 15-8, ready to be browsed as if they were your own.

If it asks for a password, type in a name and password of an account holder on that computer.

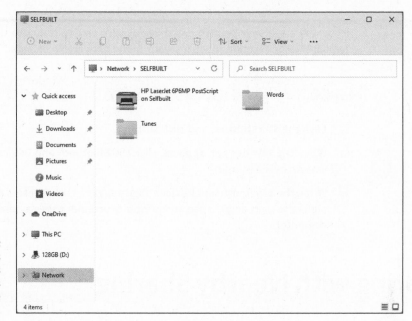

FIGURE 15-8:
Click a computer's
name, and its
available files
appear to the
right.

You can do more than browse those files, as described here:

>> **Opening:** To open a file on a shared folder, double-click its icon, just as you would any other file. The appropriate program opens it. If you see an error message, the sharing person created the file using a program you don't own. Your solution? Buy or download the program or app, or ask the person to save the file in a format that one of your programs can open.

>> **Copying:** To copy a file from another networked PC, drag it into your own folder. Or right-click the file's icon and choose Copy from the pop-up menu; then right-click inside the destination folder, and choose Paste from the pop-up menu.

Sharing a printer on the network

If you've created a network, covered earlier in this chapter, Windows makes sharing a printer quite easy. After you plug a USB printer — the kind with the connector shown in the margin — into one of your networked Windows PCs, you're set: Windows automatically recognizes the newly plugged-in printer as soon as it's turned on.

Plus, your Windows PC quickly spreads the news to all the PCs in your network. Within minutes, that printer's name and icon appear on all those PCs and in all their programs' print menus.

If you don't see your printer listed, make sure you've followed the steps in this chapter's earlier section, "Setting your home network to private."

To see that shared printer on your other networked Windows PCs, follow these steps:

1. **Click the Start button, and click Settings.**

2. **When the Settings app appears, click the Bluetooth and Devices icon (shown in the margin).**

3. **When the Bluetooth and Devices page appears, click Printers & Scanners along the right edge to see any printer or scanner that's available to your computer.**

Sharing with Nearby Sharing

Creating a network makes it easier to share files with other PCs in your home. It's the best way to share an internet connection, as well as printers.

NEW

But a network isn't the only way to share files:

>> You can attach files to email and send them to people with the Mail app or any other email program, as I cover in Chapter 10.

>> You can share your OneDrive files and folders with anybody on the internet, as I explain in Chapter 5.

Plus, you can share files between nearby computers with the Nearby Sharing feature. Nearby Sharing works with Bluetooth or your computer's Wi-Fi, which come built-in to nearly every portable computer and device. (If your PC doesn't have Bluetooth, you can add it by buying a Bluetooth adapter and plugging it into one of your PC's USB ports.)

Nearby Sharing isn't the fastest way to send a file, so don't use it for sending large videos. It's mainly used for sending a small file or two to adjacent laptops. To be safe and save battery life on laptops and tablets, turn off Nearby Sharing after sharing your files.

TIP

If you're an Apple fan, Nearby Sharing works much like the AirDrop feature found on Apple devices like iPads, iPhones, and Macs.

TIP

The next two sections explain how to turn on Nearby Sharing, as well as how to use it for sharing files with nearby devices.

Turning on Nearby Sharing

Before you can share files with Nearby Sharing, you must first turn on the feature by following these steps:

1. **Click the Start button, choose the Settings icon, and choose the System category.**

The Settings app opens to show its System settings.

2. **Choose Nearby Sharing from the right pane.**

The Nearby Sharing settings appear, shown in Figure 15-9.

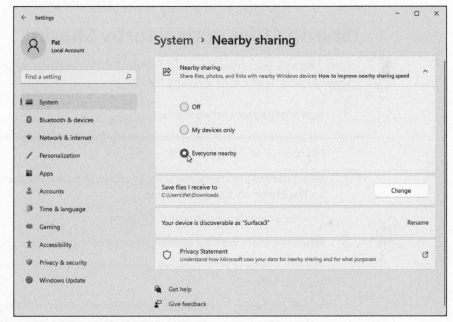

FIGURE 15-9:
Click the Nearby Sharing toggle to My Devices Only or Everyone Nearby.

3. **Choose who to can send you files.**

Nearby Sharing offers three options:

- *Off:* Choose this setting if you've already set up a private home network, and you're at home. You don't need Nearby Sharing.

- *My Devices Only:* Choose this only if you want to restrict the Nearby Sharing to your own PCs.

- *Everyone Nearby:* The most popular option, this allows anybody with a Windows 10 or Windows 11 computer to both receive and send items through Nearby Sharing. It's a handy way to send somebody a file during a meeting in a boardroom or coffee shop. (If a stranger tries to send you an unwanted file, simply ignore the message that pops up on your PC; the transfer won't take place.)

Your changes take place immediately. If it's not working, make sure you've turned on Bluetooth; Nearby Sharing needs that to work. (I explain how to turn on Bluetooth in Chapter 3.)

After you've turned on Nearby Sharing, you don't need to revisit this setting unless you want to turn it off.

Sharing files with Nearby Sharing

After you and your friend have turned on Nearby Sharing, follow these steps to share a file or folder with a nearby friend:

1. **Find the file you want to share.**

File Explorer offers the easiest way to share things with Nearby Sharing, but a few other apps also support the new feature.

2. **Select the item or items you want to share, and click the app's Share icon on File Explorer's top row of icons.**

Click the Share icon option atop File Explorer.

3. **When the Share window appears, choose how you wish to share the file.**

The Share window in File Explorer, shown in Figure 15-10, offers three ways to share your items:

- *Nearby Sharing:* This area lists any nearby computers with Nearby Sharing turned on. Click a computer's name to start sending copies of the files to that computer. It also offers a quick way to turn Nearby Sharing on or off, saving you some time.

- *Email a Contact:* Frequently contacted people appear as a row atop the window. Click a person's name, and choose their preferred email address to email them the files. This works best for fairly small files, not videos or a large number of photos.

- *Share with App:* Choose an app listed from this group to send the file to that app on your own PC.

Share 1 item

Nearby sharing   Everyone nearby ⌄

Testbed2

Email a contact   Find more people

AR   TR   AR   BS
Me   Tina Rathbone Andy Rathbone Bob Soulages

Share with app   Find more apps

Feedback Hub   OneNote for   Snip & Sketch   Mail

Discoverable as Surface3   ⚙ Nearby sharing settings

FIGURE 15-10:
Click the name of
the computer
that should
receive the file.

4. **Have the other person approve the transfer.**

When you choose a computer's name in the previous step, a message pops up
on the receiving computer. That lets the owner accept the transfer and, just as
important, decline unwanted or unexpected file transfers.

After the recipient approves the transfer by clicking the Save button, the
incoming files appear in their Downloads folder.

5

Music, Photos, and Videos

Chapter 16

Playing and Copying Music

Built for minimalists, the Windows Groove Music app sticks to the essentials. With a few clicks, it plays music stored on your computer.

For some, that's plenty. But the Groove Music app lacks more robust features. Stuck in a world of digital music files, the Groove Music app can't copy music CDs onto your computer. It can't create CDs from your music files. It can't even *play* a music CD you've slipped into your PC's disc drive. And it can't play music stored on OneDrive unless that music is also downloaded to your PC.

In short, Groove Music is now a bare-bones player for music stored on your own computer. That's fine for Windows tablets and many new laptops; they lack disc drives, so their owners naturally embrace digital music.

On a desktop PC, however, you may want to stick with the music program from yesteryear, Windows Media Player. Windows Media Player works much like it did in earlier Windows versions with one big exception: It can no longer play DVDs. (It can still play CDs, however.)

This chapter explains how and when to jump between the Groove Music app and Windows Media Player. It also explains when you might want to jump ship with the standard Windows offerings and download a more full-featured app to meet your music needs.

Playing Music with the Groove Music App

In keeping with the music of today's youth, the Windows Groove Music app recognizes music files only if they're stored on either your PC, or, when told, a flash drive you've pushed into your computer's USB port. The Groove Music app turns up its nose at playing those old-fashioned CDs or DVDs, so don't even try.

But if you simply want to play your own digital music collection, the Groove Music app handles the job fairly simply and easily. When first opened, as shown in Figure 16-1, the program shows the music stored on your own PC. (You'll only see your OneDrive music if you've told OneDrive to store your music on your PC as well as on OneDrive, a chore I cover in Chapter 5.)

To launch the Groove Music app and begin listening to music, follow these steps:

1. **Click the Start menu's Groove Music icon.**

   Fetch the Start menu with a click of the Start button on the left edge of the taskbar, the strip that runs along the bottom of your screen. When the Start menu appears, click the Groove Music app's icon, shown in the margin.

   If you don't spot the Groove Music app's icon, click the Start menu's All Apps button to see all your installed apps. Then choose Groove Music from the list of alphabetically sorted apps.

   When launched, the Groove Music app appears onscreen, as shown in Figure 16-1, showing tiles representing your albums, artists, or songs. (When opened for the first time, you may need to click through some welcome screens.)

2. **View your music by album, song, or artist.**

   The Navigation pane along the left edge of the Groove Music app offers these options for viewing your music:

   - *Search:* Type an artist's name, song, or album title into this box, and the app reveals any matches stored on your PC.

   - *My Music:* Click My Music from the Navigation pane, and the app displays your music. Click the Songs, Artists, or Albums links beneath the words My Music, on the app's right pane, to see your music grouped by song, artist, or album.

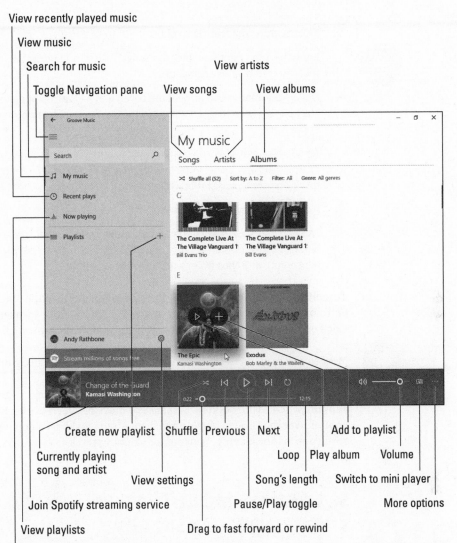

View recently played music
View music
Search for music
Toggle Navigation pane
View songs
View artists
View albums

Create new playlist
Currently playing song and artist
View settings
Join Spotify streaming service
View playlists
View currently playing music

Shuffle
Previous
Next
Loop
Play album
Volume
Song's length
Switch to mini player
Pause/Play toggle
Drag to fast forward or rewind
Add to playlist
More options

FIGURE 16-1:
The Groove Music app plays music stored on your PC.

- *Recent Plays:* Recently played music appears here, making it easy to hear a replay.

- *Now Playing:* Choose this to see your currently played song, as well as a list of songs that are queued to play next.

- *Playlists:* Playlists *you* create appear here, ready to be played again with a click of their names. Or create your own playlist by clicking the adjacent plus sign icon.

3. Tell the app what music to play.

TIP

From the app's right side, click the Songs, Artists, or Albums tabs to view your music sorted by those categories.

Hover your mouse over any album cover, and a Play icon appears. Click it to start playing everything contained in the tile, be it a single album or an artist's entire work.

An adjacent plus sign icon lets you quickly add that item to the current playlist or a new playlist. By hovering over items and clicking the plus sign, you can quickly create a playlist that will keep you listening to music for hours.

4. Adjust the music while it plays.

The App bar, shown along the bottom of Figure 16-1, offers you several icons to control your music: Shuffle, Loop, Previous (to move to the previous song), Pause/Play, and Next (to move to the next song).

To adjust the volume, click the little speaker on the App bar in the screen's bottom-right corner. Or, from the desktop, click the little speaker icon next to the clock on the taskbar, that strip along the desktop's bottom edge.

TIP

Most touchscreen tablets include a volume rocker switch along one of their edges.

The Groove Music app keeps playing music even if you begin working with other apps or switch to the desktop. To pause or move between tracks, hover your mouse pointer over the Groove Music app's icon on the taskbar; a pop-up menu appears, with controls for playing, pausing, or skipping tracks.

SQUEEZING MORE FEATURES FROM THE GROOVE MUSIC APP

TIP

The Groove Music app doesn't do much more than play your music. But you can stretch it to its minimalist limits with these tips:

- **Create playlists:** A playlist is simply a list of songs arranged in a certain order. To create one, hover your mouse pointer over any tile, and a plus sign icon appears either next to a song or atop a list of songs. Click the plus sign icon, and a pop-up list of playlists appears. Click the desired playlist, and the Groove Music app copies that song or songs to the list. If you haven't created any playlists yet, the words New Playlist appear in a box; change those words to a term that describes your list of songs, and you've created your first playlist. Microsoft account owners receive a perk: Playlists created on your PC also appear on your Windows tablet or Xbox One.

- **OneDrive access:** The Groove Music app can't play songs stored exclusively on OneDrive. When you try to play a song or album stored on OneDrive, the app quickly downloads the music to your computer. That means you need an internet connection to access them. I describe how to keep your OneDrive music stored both on your PC and OneDrive in Chapter 5.

- **Pin to Start menu:** Right-click a favorite album in Groove Music, and choose Pin to Start from the pop-up menu. Click Yes at the confirmation screen for quick, one-click Start menu access.

- **Buying music:** The app no longer lets you buy music or listen to online radio stations. Instead, it asks you to subscribe to the Spotify streaming service. If you don't see Spotify on the Start menu's All Apps section, then you need to download Spotify from the Microsoft Store app.

- **Try another app:** If you like the simplicity of apps but want a little more power, look for VideoLAN's VLC app, or try some of the other alternatives available in the Microsoft Store.

Handing Music-Playing Chores Back to Windows Media Player

Microsoft hopes that the Groove Music app will meet all your musical needs. Accordingly, Windows tries to shoehorn you into using the Groove Music app. Open a music file from your desktop's Music folder, for example, and the Groove Music app automatically jumps in to play the file.

With its large and simple controls, the Groove Music app works fine on touch-screen tablets. However, when you switch to the desktop, you may prefer a more full-featured music program. Luckily, Windows 11 still includes Windows Media Player, a Windows desktop staple for more than a decade.

Follow the steps in this section to hand your music-playing chores back to Windows Media Player and to make the program easier to find.

1. **Click the Start button, and type** windows media player **into the Search box, located at the top edge of the Start menu.**

   The Start menu's Search window lists Windows Media Player.

 2. **Choose Pin to Start from the list of options on the right side of the Search window.**

This places the Windows Media Player icon on your Start menu for easy access. (The same menu lets you select Pin to Taskbar; that places a second link to Windows Media Player on your taskbar, the strip that runs along the bottom of the screen.)

3. **Open your Music folder, and right-click a song you want Windows Media Player to play.**

   A pop-up menu appears.

4. **Click Open With, and then, when the second pop-up menu appears, click Choose Another App.**

   You may see Windows Media Player listed on the first pop-up menu, but don't click it. If you do, Windows Media Player will only play that one song, but Groove Music will still play all of the others.

5. **When the How Do You Want to Open this File window appears, shown in Figure 16-2, choose Windows Media Player and click the checkbox called Always Use This App to Open MP3 Files.**

   This step tells Windows Media Player to play your music instead of the Start menu's Groove Music app. If you store your music in file formats besides MP3, you may need to repeat these steps for those other files.

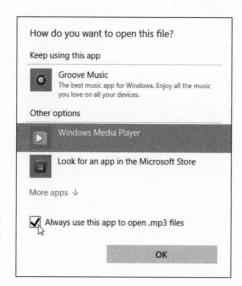

FIGURE 16-2:
Choose Windows
Media Player to
let it play your
music.

After you follow these steps, Windows Media Player jumps into action whenever you double-click a music file on the desktop. You can also launch Windows Media Player directly by clicking its icon (shown in the margin) on the Start menu or on your taskbar.

REMEMBER

These steps don't permanently disable or uninstall the Start menu's Groove Music app; it still works fine. To open the Groove Music app, just click its icon from the Start menu. When the Groove Music app appears, it still displays and plays all your music.

However, when you click a song from the desktop's File Explorer program, Windows Media Player pops up and begins playing your song.

Follow these same steps to choose which other programs should open your favorite files. You're not limited to the choices Microsoft set up with Windows 11.

TIP

RUNNING WINDOWS MEDIA PLAYER FOR THE FIRST TIME

The first time you open the desktop's Windows Media Player, an opening screen asks how to deal with the player's settings for privacy, storage, and the music store. The screen offers two options:

- **Recommended Settings:** Designed for the impatient, this option loads Windows Media Player with Microsoft's chosen settings in place. Windows Media Player sets itself up as the default player for most of your music and video. Windows Media Player sweeps the internet to update your songs' title information, and it tells Microsoft what you're listening to and watching. Choose Recommended Settings if you're in a hurry; you can always customize the settings some other time.

- **Custom Settings:** Aimed at the fine-tuners and the privacy-conscious folks, this choice lets you micromanage Windows Media Player's behavior. A series of screens lets you choose the types of music and video that the player can play, and you can control how much of your listening habits should be sent to Microsoft. Choose this option only if you have time to wade through several minutes of boring option screens.

If you later want to customize any Windows Media Player settings — either those chosen for you in Recommended Settings setup or the ones you've chosen in Custom Settings setup — click Windows Media Player's Organize button in the upper-left corner and choose Options.

Stocking the Windows Media Player Library

 You can load Windows Media Player by clicking its icon in the Start menu or taskbar, that strip along the desktop's bottom edge. No icon in the Start menu or taskbar? The previous section explains how to put it there.

When you run Windows Media Player, the program automatically sorts through your computer's stash of digital music, pictures, and videos, automatically cataloging everything it finds.

But if you've noticed that some of your PC's media is missing from the Windows Media Player Library, you can tell the player where to find those items by following these steps:

1. Click Windows Media Player's Organize button (in the program's upper-left corner), and choose Manage Libraries from the drop-down menu to reveal a pop-out menu.

The pop-out menu lists the four types of media that Windows Media Player can handle: Music, Videos, Pictures, and Recorded TV.

2. From the pop-out menu, choose the name of the type of files you're missing.

A window appears, as shown in Figure 16-3, listing your monitored folders. For example, the player normally monitors the contents of your Music folder, so anything you add to your Music folder automatically appears in the Media Player Library as well.

But if you're storing items elsewhere — perhaps on a portable hard drive, flash drive, or network location — here's your chance to give the player directions to that other media stash.

3. Click the Add button, select the folder or drive containing your files, click the Include Folder button, and click OK.

Clicking the Add button brings the Include Folder in Music window to the screen. Navigate to the folder you'd like to add — the folder on your portable hard drive, for example — and click the Include Folder button. Windows Media Player immediately begins monitoring that folder, adding the folder's music to its library.

FIGURE 16-3:
Click the Add
button and
browse to a new
folder you want
Windows Media
Player to monitor.

To add music from even more folders or drives — perhaps a folder on another networked PC or a flash drive — repeat these steps until you've added all the places Windows Media Player should search for media.

To stop the player from monitoring a folder, follow these steps, but in Step 3, click the folder you no longer want monitored and then click the Remove button shown in Figure 16-3.

When you run Windows Media Player, the program shows the media it has collected (shown in Figure 16-4), and it continues to stock its library in the following ways:

» **Monitoring your folders:** Windows Media Player constantly monitors your Music, Pictures, and Videos folders, as well as any other locations you've added. Windows Media Player automatically updates its library whenever you add or remove files from your folders. (You can change what folders Windows Media Player monitors by following the three preceding steps.)

» **Adding played items:** Anytime you play a music file on your PC or from the internet, Windows Media Player adds the song or its internet location to its library so you can find it to play again later. Unless specifically told to, Windows Media Player *doesn't* add recently played items residing on other people's PCs, USB flash drives, or memory cards.

FIGURE 16-4:
Click an item
from the left to
see its contents
on the right.

>> **Ripped music from CD:** When you insert a music CD into your CD drive, Windows may offer to *rip* it. That's computerese for copying the CD's music to your PC, a task described in the "Ripping (Copying) CDs to Your PC" section, later in this chapter. Any ripped music automatically appears in your Windows Media Player Library. (Windows Media Player won't copy DVD movies to your library, unfortunately, nor does it play the discs.)

>> **Downloaded music from online stores:** When you buy a song and place it in your Music folder, Windows Media Player automatically stocks its library with your latest purchase.

TIP

Feel free to repeat the steps in this section to search for files whenever you want. Windows Media Player ignores the files it has already cataloged and adds any new ones.

TECHNICAL
STUFF

Windows Media Player doesn't offer an advanced editor for changing a song's *tags*, which are described in the nearby sidebar. Instead, the player edits them for you automatically from an online database.

TECHNICAL STUFF

WHAT ARE A SONG'S TAGS?

Inside every music file lives a small form called a *tag* that contains the song's title, artist, album, and other related information. When deciding how to sort, display, and categorize your music, Windows Media Player reads those tags — *not* the songs' filenames. Nearly every digital music player, including the iPod, also relies on tags.

Tags are so important, in fact, that Windows Media Player visits the internet, grabs song information, and automatically fills in the tags when it adds files to its library.

Many people don't bother filling out their songs' tags, but other people update them meticulously. If your tags are already filled out the way you prefer, stop Windows Media Player from messing with them: Click the Organize button, choose Options, click the Library tab, and deselect the checkbox next to Retrieve Additional Information from the Internet. If your tags are a mess, by contrast, leave that checkbox selected so the player will clean up the tags for you.

If Windows Media Player makes a mistake, fix the tags yourself: Right-click the song (or, in the case of an album, the selected songs), and choose Find Album Info. When a window appears listing the player's guess as to the song or album, choose the Edit link. In the new window that appears, you can fill in the album, artist, genre, tracks, title, contributing artist, and composer. Click Done when you're through tidying up the information.

Browsing the Windows Media Player Libraries

The Windows Media Player Libraries are where the behind-the-scenes action takes place. There, you organize files, create playlists, burn or copy CDs, and choose what to play.

When first loaded, Windows Media Player displays your Music folder's contents, appropriately enough. But Windows Media Player actually holds several libraries, designed to showcase not only your music but also photos, video, and recorded TV shows.

All your playable items appear in the Navigation pane along the window's left edge, shown in Figure 16-5, where they can be accessed with a click. The pane's top half shows your own media collection, appropriately listed with your name at the top.

FIGURE 16-5:
Click the type of media you're interested in browsing from the Navigation pane along the left.

Windows Media Player organizes your media into these categories:

>> **Playlists:** Do you enjoy playing albums or songs in a certain order? Click the Save List button atop your list of songs to save it as a playlist that shows up in this category. (I cover playlists in this chapter's later "Creating, Saving, and Editing Playlists" section.)

>> **Music:** All your digital music appears here. Windows Media Player recognizes most major music formats, including MP3, WMA, and WAV. (It even recognizes non-copy-protected AAC files, sold by iTunes.) And Windows 11 also includes support for FLAC, a format that compresses the music without losing any sound quality.)

>> **Videos:** Look here for videos you've saved from a camcorder or digital camera, smartphone, or for videos you've downloaded from the internet. Windows Media Player recognizes AVI, MPG, WMV, ASF, DivX, some MOV files, and a few other formats. Windows 11 also adds support for MKV files, a relatively new video format used by some smartphones for taking high-definition videos.

>> **Pictures:** Windows Media Player can display photos individually or in a simple slideshow, but your Pictures folder and Photos app, both covered in Chapter 17, handle photos better. (Windows Media Player can't correct upside-down photos, for example, a feat done easily from within your Pictures folder of the Photos app.)

>> **Other Libraries:** Here you can find media appearing on other PCs in your home *network* — a private way of connecting PCs that I describe in Chapter 15.

After you click a category, Windows Media Player's Navigation pane lets you view the files in several different ways. Click Artist in the Navigation pane's Music category, for example, and the pane shows the music arranged alphabetically by artists' first names.

Similarly, clicking Genre in the Music category separates songs and albums by different types of music, shown earlier in Figure 16-5. Instead of just showing a name to click — blues, for example — the player arranges your music into piles of covers, just as if you'd sorted your albums or CDs on your living room floor.

TIP

To play anything in Windows Media Player, right-click it and choose Play. Or, to play all your music from one artist or genre, right-click the pile and choose Play All.

TIP

YES, WINDOWS SPIES ON YOU

Just like your bank, credit card company, smartphone, and grocery store club card, the Groove Music app and Windows Media Player both spy on you. Microsoft's 5,000-word online Privacy Statement boils down to this: Both players tell Microsoft every song, file, or movie you play. Some people find that creepy, but if Microsoft doesn't know what you're playing, Windows can't retrieve that artist's profile information and artwork from the internet.

If you don't care that Microsoft hums along to your music, don't bother reading any further. If you *do* care, choose your surveillance level in Windows Media Player: Click the Organize button in Windows Media Player's top-left corner, choose Options, and click the Privacy tab. Here's the rundown on the Privacy tab options that cause the biggest ruckus:

- **Display Media Information from the Internet:** If this option is selected, Windows Media Player tells Microsoft what CD you're playing and retrieves doodads to display on your screen: CD covers, song titles, artist names, and similar information.

- **Update Music Files by Retrieving Media Info from the Internet:** Microsoft examines your files, and if it recognizes any, it fills in the songs' tags with the correct information. (For more information on tags, see the "What are a song's tags?" sidebar.)

(continued)

(continued)

- **Send Unique Player ID to Content Providers:** Known in the biz as *data mining,* this option lets other corporations track how you use Windows Media Player when playing copy-protected music.

- **Cookies:** Like many other programs and websites, Windows Media Player tracks your activity with little files called *cookies.* Cookies aren't necessarily bad, as they help the player keep track of your preferences.

- **Customer Experience Improvement:** When enabled, this feature gives Microsoft your "player usage data," a generic term that could mean anything. I turn mine off.

- **History:** Windows Media Player lists the names of your recently played files for your convenience — and for the possible guffaws of your coworkers or family. To keep people from seeing the titles of music and videos you've recently played, remove *all* the check marks from this section and click the two buttons called Clear History and Clear Caches.

For more information about your privacy settings, visit Microsoft's privacy center online at http://www.microsoft.com/privacy.

Playing Music Files in a Playlist

Windows Media Player plays several types of digital music files, but they all have one thing in common: When you tell Windows Media Player to play a song or an album, Windows Media Player immediately places that item on your *Now Playing list* — a list of items queued up for playing one after the other.

You can start playing music through Windows Media Player in a number of ways, even if Windows Media Player isn't currently running:

>> Click the File Explorer icon (shown in the margin) on your taskbar, right-click an album or a music-filled folder, and click Play with Windows Media Player. The player jumps to the screen and begins playing your choice.

>> While you're still viewing your own Music folder, right-click items and choose Add to Windows Media Player List. Your computer queues them up in Windows Media Player, ready to be played after you've heard your currently playing music.

>> Place a music CD in your computer's CD drive tray, and push the tray into your computer. Click the Select to Choose What Happens with Audio CDs pop-up message. When the second pop-up menu appears, choose Play Audio CD, and Windows automatically plays future audio CDs as soon as you insert them.

>> Double-click a song file, whether it's sitting on your desktop or in any folder. Windows Media Player begins playing it immediately.

To play songs listed within Windows Media Player's own library, right-click the song's name and choose Play. Windows Media Player begins playing it immediately, and the song appears in the Now Playing list.

Here are other ways to play songs within Windows Media Player:

>> To play an entire album in Windows Media Player's library, right-click the album from the library's Album category and choose Play.

>> Want to hear several files or albums, one after the other? Right-click the first one, and choose Play. Right-click the next one, and choose Add to Now Playing List. Repeat until you're done. Windows Media Player queues them all up in the Now Playing list.

>> To return to a recently played item, right-click Windows Media Player's icon in the taskbar. When the list of recently played items appears, click your item's name.

>> No decent music in your music folder? Then start copying your favorite CDs to your computer — a process called *ripping,* which I explain in the "Ripping (Copying) CDs to Your Computer" section, later in this chapter.

Controlling Your Now Playing Items

You can play music directly from the Windows Media Player Library: Just right-click a file, album, artist, or genre, and choose Play. Windows Media Player begins playing the music, but the program stays put, often filling the screen.

 To summon a smaller, more manageable player, click the Library/Player toggle button shown in the margin and summon the Now Playing window shown in Figure 16-6. (The Library/Player toggle button lives in the library's lower-right corner.) Don't see the controls? Hover your mouse pointer over the Media Player window, and the controls appear along the window's bottom edge.

The minimalist Now Playing window shows what's currently playing, be it a video or artwork from your currently playing song. Onscreen controls let you adjust the volume, skip between listed songs or videos, or pause the action.

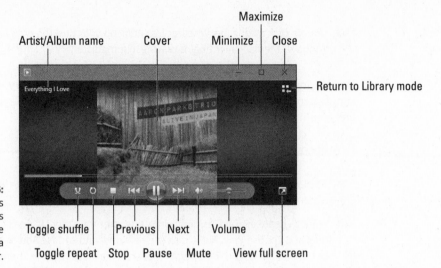

Artist/Album name   Cover   Minimize   Maximize   Close

Return to Library mode

FIGURE 16-6:
The window's
bottom buttons
work much like
the buttons on a
CD player.

Toggle shuffle   Previous   Next   Volume

Toggle repeat   Stop   Pause   Mute   View full screen

Windows Media Player offers the same basic controls when playing any type of file, be it a song, video, CD, or photo slideshow. Figure 16-6 shows Windows Media Player open to its Now Playing window as it plays an album. The labels in the figure explain each button's function. Or rest your mouse pointer over an especially mysterious button, and Windows Media Player displays a pop-up explanation.

The buttons along the bottom work like those found on any CD player, letting you play, stop, rewind, fast-forward, and mute the current song or movie. For even more controls, right-click anywhere in the Now Playing window. A menu appears, offering to perform these common tasks:

>> **Show List:** This shows the playlist along the right side, which is handy for jumping directly to different songs.

>> **Full Screen:** This enlarges the window to fill the screen.

>> **Shuffle:** This plays songs randomly.

>> **Repeat:** This loops the same song.

>> **Visualizations:** Choose between showing the album cover, wavy lines, groovy spirals, dancing waves, or other freaky eye games.

>> **Enhancements:** This opens an equalizer, balance adjuster, playback speed, volume balancer, and other sound options.

>> **Lyrics, Captions, or Subtitles:** Display these items, if they're available, which come in handy when practicing for Karaoke night.

>> **Always Show Now Playing on Top:** This keeps the window above your other windows on the desktop.

>> **More Options:** This brings up the Options page, where you can tweak Windows Media Player's habits when ripping CDs, stocking your Windows Media Player Library, and other tasks.

>> **Help with Playback:** This fetches the Help program to deal with head-scratchers.

TIP

The Now Playing controls disappear from the screen when you haven't moved the mouse for a while. To bring them back, move your mouse pointer over the Now Playing window.

To return to the Windows Media Player Library, click the Library/Player toggle icon in the window's upper-right corner.

TIP

When you minimize Windows Media Player to the desktop's taskbar, hover your mouse pointer over the player's icon: A control pops up, letting you pause or jump between songs.

Playing CDs

As long as you insert the CD in the CD drive correctly (usually label-side up), playing a music CD is one of Windows Media Player's easiest tasks. Start by pushing the drive's Eject button, a rarely labelled button that lives next to or on the disc drive on the front of your computer.

When the drive tray emerges, drop the CD (label-side up) into your CD drive and push the tray back into the drive. Windows Media Player jumps to the screen to play it, usually identifying the CD and its artist immediately. In many cases, it even tosses a picture of the cover art on the screen.

The controls along the bottom, shown previously in Figure 16-6, let you jump from track to track, adjust the volume, and fine-tune your listening experience.

If for some odd reason Windows Media Player doesn't start playing your CD, look at the Library item in Windows Media Player's Navigation pane along the left side of the window. You should spot either the CD's name or the words *Unknown Album.* When you spot the listing, click it and then click the Play button to start listening.

TIP

Press F7 to mute Windows Media Player's sound and pick up that phone call. Pressing Ctrl+P toggles the pause/play mode.

Want to copy that CD to your PC? That's called *ripping,* and I cover ripping in the "Ripping (Copying) CDs to Your PC" section, later in this chapter.

Playing DVDs

And now for a bit of bad news: Windows Media Player can't play DVDs. That news comes as a bit of a shock, considering that the Media Player in Windows 7 *could* play DVDs. What gives?

According to Microsoft, DVDs are old-school technology that's no longer needed. Today's ultrathin laptops and tablets don't even have DVD drives. Most people watch movies by streaming them to their computers over the internet, Microsoft says. Or they watch their discs on a DVD player or gaming console connected to a TV.

TECHNICAL STUFF

Also, Microsoft no longer wanted to pay licensing fees to the companies owning the patents required for playing DVDs.

But although Windows Media Player can no longer play DVDs, Windows can still play DVDs if you buy some DVD-playing software. Microsoft and other companies sell DVD-playing software through the Microsoft Store app. (I cover the Microsoft Store app and its digital shelves full of apps in Chapter 6.)

Playing Videos and TV Shows

Many digital cameras and smartphones can capture short videos as well as photos, so don't be surprised if you find several videos in the Video library of Windows Media Player.

Playing videos works much like playing a digital song. Click Videos in the Navigation pane along Windows Media Player's left side. Double-click the video you want to see, and start enjoying the action, as shown in Figure 16-7.

FIGURE 16-7:
Move the mouse over the video to make the controls appear along the bottom.

Windows Media Player lets you watch videos in several sizes. Make it fill the screen by holding down Alt and pressing Enter, for example. (Repeat those key-strokes to return to the original size.)

>> To make the video adjust itself automatically to the size of your Windows Media Player window, right-click the video as it plays, choose Video from the pop-up menu, and select Fit Video to Player on Resize.

>> You can also toggle full-screen mode by clicking the Full Screen toggle in the video's lower-right corner, shown in Figure 16-7.

>> When choosing video to watch on the internet, your connection speed determines its quality. Broadband connections can usually handle high-definition videos, but slower connections and slower computers often have problems. You won't damage your computer by choosing the wrong quality of video; the video just skips and pauses while playing.

TECHNICAL STUFF

PLAYING INTERNET RADIO STATIONS

Windows Media Player doesn't offer an easy way to play internet radio stations. However, Windows offers you several ways to listen to music over the internet:

- Head to Google (www.google.com), and search for *Internet radio station* to see what turns up. When you find a station broadcasting in MP3 or Windows Media Audio (WMA) format, click the website's Tune In or Listen Now button to load Windows Media Player and start listening.

- I like the stations at SomaFM (www.somafm.com). It offers more than two dozen stations in a variety of genres, all playable through either your browser or Windows Media Player.

- Install a music streaming app, such as Pandora or Spotify, which lets you tune in to thousands of stations from around the world. Both are available through the Microsoft Store app.

Creating, Saving, and Editing Playlists

A *playlist* is simply a list of songs (and/or videos) that play in a certain order. So what? Well, the beauty of a playlist comes with what you can *do* with it. Save a playlist of your favorite songs, for example, and they're always available for play-back with a single click.

You can create specially themed playlists to liven up long-distance drives, parties, special dinners, workouts, and other events.

To create a playlist, follow these steps:

1. Open Windows Media Player, and find the Playlist pane.

TIP

Don't see a playlist hugging Windows Media Player's right edge? Click the Play tab near the upper-right corner. Or, when the player is in Now Playing mode, right-click a blank part of the Windows Media Player window and choose Show List from the pop-up menu: The list of currently playing items appears along Windows Media Player's right edge.

2. Right-click the album or songs you want, choose Add To, and select Play List.

Alternatively, you can drag and drop albums and songs onto the Playlist pane along Windows Media Player's right edge, as shown in Figure 16-8. Either way, Windows Media Player begins playing your playlist as soon as you add the first song. Your song choices appear in the right pane in the order you've selected them.

FIGURE 16-8:
Drag and drop albums and songs onto the Playlist pane.

3. Fine-tune your playlist to change the order or remove songs.

Added something by mistake? Right-click that item in the playlist, and choose Remove from List. Feel free to rearrange your playlist by dragging and dropping items up or down the list.

Check the line at the bottom of the playlist to see how many items you've added to the playlist as well as your playlist's duration in minutes.

4. When you're happy with your playlist, click the Save List button at the list's top, type a name in the highlighted box, and press Enter.

Windows Media Player lists your new playlist in the library's Playlists section, ready to be heard when you double-click it.

After you save a playlist, you can burn it to a CD with one click, as described in the next tip.

TIP

Make your own Desert Island Disc or Greatest Hits playlists, and then burn them to a CD to play in your car or on your home stereo. After you create a playlist of less than 80 minutes, insert a blank CD into your CD burner and click the Burn tab. Take up the player's offer to import your current playlist, and click the Start Burn button.

TIP

To edit a previously created playlist, double-click the playlist's name in the Library's Playlists area. Rearrange, add, or delete items in the playlist, and click the Save List button.

Ripping (Copying) CDs to Your PC

In a process known as *ripping*, Windows Media Player can copy your CDs to your PC as MP3 files, the industry standard for digital music. But until you tell the player that you want MP3 files, it creates *WMA* files — a format that won't play on iPads, most smartphones, nor many other music players.

TIP

To make Windows Media Player create songs with the more versatile MP3 format instead of WMA, click the Organize button in the upper-left corner, choose Options, and click the Rip Music tab. Choose MP3 instead of WMA from the Format drop-down menu, and nudge the audio quality over a tad from 128 to 256 or even 320 for better sound. (For even better sound, choose FLAC instead of WMA or MP3; however, the files will consume much more storage space.) If you plan to move the music to a portable music player, be sure to choose a format that player supports. When in doubt, choose MP3.

To copy CDs to your PC's hard drive, follow these instructions:

1. Open Windows Media Player, insert a music CD, and click the Rip CD button.

You may need to push a button on the front or side of your computer's disc drive to make the tray eject.

Windows Media Player connects to the internet; identifies your CD; and fills in the album's name, artist, and song titles. Then the program begins copying the CD's songs to your PC and listing their titles in the Windows Media Player Library. You're through.

If Windows Media Player can't find the songs' titles automatically, however, move ahead to Step 2.

2. **Right-click the first track, and choose Find Album Info, if necessary.**

   If Windows Media Player comes up empty-handed, right-click the first track and choose Find Album Info.

   If you're connected to the internet, type the album's name into the Search box and then click Search. If the Search box finds your album, click its name, choose Next, and click Finish.

   If you're not connected to the internet, or if the Search box comes up empty, right-click the first song, click Edit, and manually fill in the song title. Repeat for the other titles, as well as the album, artist, genre, and year tags.

Here are some tips for ripping CDs to your computer:

» Normally Windows Media Player copies every song on the CD. To leave Tiny Tim off your ukulele music compilation, however, remove the check mark from the box next to Tiny Tim's name. If Windows Media Player has already copied the song to your PC, feel free to delete it from within Windows Media Player. Click the Library button, right-click the song sung by the offending yodeler, and choose Delete.

» Windows Media Player automatically places your ripped CDs into your Music folder. You can also find your newly ripped music there, as well as in the Windows Media Player Library.

Burning (Creating) Music CDs

To create a music CD with your favorite songs, create a playlist containing the CD's songs, listed in the order you want to play them; then burn the playlist to a CD. I explain how to do that in the "Creating, Saving, and Editing Playlists" section, earlier in this chapter.

But what if you want to duplicate a CD, perhaps to create a disposable copy of your favorite CD to play in your car? No sense scratching up your original. You'll want to make copies of your kids' CDs, too, before they create pizzas out of them.

Unfortunately, neither Windows Media Player nor Windows 11 offers a Duplicate CD option. Instead, you must jump through the following five hoops to create a new CD with the same songs in the same fidelity as the original CD:

1. **Rip (copy) the music to your hard drive.**

   Before ripping your CD, change your burning quality to the highest quality: Click Organize, choose Options, click the Rip Music tab, and change the Format box to a lossless format like WAV, ALAC, or FLAC. Click OK.

2. **Insert a blank CD into your computer's disc drive.**

3. **In Windows Media Player's Navigation pane, click the Music category and choose Album to see your saved CDs.**

4. **Right-click the newly ripped album in your library, choose Add To, and choose Burn List.**

   If your Burn List already had some listed music, click the Clear List button to clear it; then add your CD's music to the Burn List.

5. **Click the Start Burn button.**

Now for the fine print. Unless you change the quality to a lossless format when copying the CD to your PC, Windows Media Player compresses your songs as it saves them on your hard drive, throwing out some audio quality in the process. Burning them back to CD won't replace that lost quality. If you want the most accurate duplicates Windows Media Player can handle, change the Ripping Format to WAV (Lossless).

REMEMBER

If you do change the format to WAV (Lossless) in order to duplicate a CD, remember to change it back to MP3 afterward, or else your hard drive will run out of room when you begin ripping lots of CDs.

A simpler solution might be to buy CD-burning software from Amazon or your local office supply or computer store. Unlike Windows Media Player, most CD-burning programs have a Duplicate CD button for one-click convenience.

THE WRONG PLAYER KEEPS OPENING MY FILES!

TIP

Windows Media Player isn't the only Windows program for playing songs and viewing movies. Many people use iTunes for managing their songs and movies because it conveniently drops items into their iPads and iPhones for on-the-road enjoyment.

But when your computer includes more than one media player, the players start bickering over which one handles your media-playing chores.

Windows settles these arguments with its Defaults area in the Settings area. To choose the player that should open each format, head for this chapter's earlier section, "Handing Music-Playing Chores Back to Windows Media Player." That section explains how to choose which player should handle which types of media files.

Chapter **17**

Fiddling with Photos, Videos, and Phones

For years, Windows graciously offered to import your photos as soon as you plugged in your camera. When Windows 10 arrived, though, that feature fell by the wayside. To make up for past mistakes, Windows 11 now offers at least five ways to import photos from your camera and smartphone.

This chapter walks you through the easiest ways to copy your digital photos and videos from your phone or camera to your computer. From there, you can show them off to friends and family, email them to distant relatives, and save them in places where you can easily relocate them.

One final note: After you've begun creating a digital family album on your computer, please take steps to back it up properly by turning on File History or OneDrive, the automatic backup features in Windows that I describe in Chapter 13. Computers come and go, but your family memories can't be replaced.

Dumping Photos from a Phone or Camera to Your Computer

Most digital cameras come with software that grabs your camera's photos and places them onto your computer. That software can be complicated and unwieldy, though. Thankfully, Windows can easily fetch photos from nearly any make and model of digital camera, as well as most phones. In keeping with the Windows march away from desktop programs, Windows now lets the Photos app handle the job of importing and organizing your photos.

These steps work for most digital cameras and smartphones; iPhone owners may have better luck going through iTunes to copy their photos to their computer.

To import photos from your camera or phone into your computer, follow these steps:

1. Plug the phone or camera's cable into your computer.

Many cameras come with two cables: one that plugs into your TV set for viewing and another that plugs into your computer. You need to find the one that plugs into your computer for transferring photos. (With phones, your USB charging cable usually handles the job.)

Plug the transfer cable's small end into your camera or phone, and plug the larger end (shown in the margin) into your computer's *USB port,* a rectangular-looking hole about ½-inch long and ¼-inch high. USB ports live on the back of the older computers, along the front of newer computers, and along the sides of laptops and tablets.

TIP

If the USB plug doesn't want to fit into the port, turn over the plug and try again.

If you plug in an Android phone, be sure to tell it to connect in "Camera Mode" mode rather than "Media Device" mode. That lets Windows recognize your phone as a simple camera rather than a complicated phone.

If Windows doesn't recognize your digital camera, make sure that the camera is set to *display mode* — the mode where you can see your photos on the camera's display. If you still have problems, unplug the cable from your computer, wait a few seconds, and then plug it back in.

2. Turn on your phone or camera (if it's not already turned on), click the Start menu, and open the Photos app with a click on its icon.

The Photos app appears onscreen. If by chance you have two devices containing photos, perhaps your smartphone with a memory card, choose your camera from the pop-up menu.

3. **Click the Import button on the Photos app's upper-right corner, and choose From a Connected Device from the pop-up menu.**

The pop-up menu, shown in Figure 17-1, offers two options depending on what you've plugged into your USB port:

- *From a Folder:* Choose this to import photos from a folder. That folder may be on a portable hard drive or flash drive you've plugged into your PC, or perhaps a folder from another PC you've connected through a network. You need to choose this only once; when opened, the Photos app will subsequently import any photos it finds in that folder. The photos will quickly appear in the Photos app.

- *From a Connected Device:* Choose this to import photos stored on a camera or phone that you've plugged into your USB port in the prior two steps. (If a pop-up menu appears, choose your camera's name from the pop-up menu.)

TIP

If you prefer importing photos through File Explorer, you still can. Open File Explorer, and click This PC from the pane along File Explorer's left edge. When you spot your camera's name listed on File Explorer's right side, right-click the camera's icon. When the pop-up menu appears, choose Import Pictures and Videos. The old Import Pictures and Videos program appears, ready to import your photos, just as it did in previous Windows versions.

FIGURE 17-1:
When Windows recognizes your camera, it offers to copy its photos to your computer.

4. **Click the Select menu and decide which photos to import.**

The Photos app immediately searches your camera for new digital photos and videos, and then displays them, shown in Figure 17-2. The app sorts your photos by the month you snapped them.

Click the Select menu, and a drop-down menu lists three options:

- *None:* Click this only if you've changed your mind about importing, perhaps because you've connected the wrong camera.

- *All Items:* Choose this to import *all* your camera's photos, even if they've been imported before.

- *Items Since Last Import:* Select this option to import only your new photos. Windows quickly selects only the photos you haven't yet imported.

You can also cherry-pick just a few photos; just click the box in the thumbnail of the photos you want to import.

If you don't want to import a selected photo, click to remove the check mark from the unwanted photo's upper-right corner. To see more photos, use the scroll bar shown along the right edge of Figure 17-2. (I cover scroll bars in Chapter 4.)

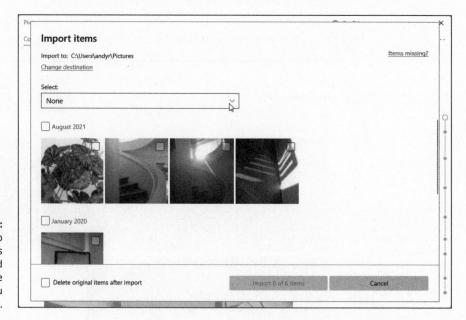

FIGURE 17-2:
The Photos app displays groups of pictures based on the time and date you took them.

5. **Review your selected photos, and click the Import Selected button.**

   Windows begins importing your selected photos, leaving the original copies on your camera. Windows places copies of your photos into your computer's Pictures folder, separating the photos into groups named after their year and month. For example, photos snapped in January 2020 appear in a folder named 2020–01.

When Windows finishes importing your photos, the Photos app remains onscreen to display your newest pictures. Your newest photos always appear at the top of the app. As you scroll down the app's list of photos, you go back in time, seeing older photos organized by month and day. I walk you through the rest of the Photos app later in this chapter.

Making Photos and Videos with the Camera App

Most tablets, laptops, and some desktop computers come with built-in cameras, sometimes called *webcams.* These tiny cameras can't take high-resolution close-ups of that rare bird in the neighbor's tree, but they work fine for their main purpose: snapping a quick headshot photo for use as an account photo on your computer, Facebook, or other websites.

The cameras can also shoot video, making them perfect for holding internet video chats through Zoom or the built-in Teams Chat app covered in Chapter 10.

To snap a photo or shoot video through your computer's camera with the Camera app, follow these steps:

1. **From the Start menu, click the Camera icon to open the app.**

   If you don't spot the Camera icon on the Start menu, click the Start menu's All Apps button to see an alphabetical list of every app on your computer.

2. **If the app asks permission to use your camera and microphone or location, decide whether to click Yes or No.**

   As a security precaution, Windows may ask permission to turn on your camera. That helps prevent sneaky apps from spying on you without your knowing. If you're using the camera app, click the Yes button to give it permission.

   The program might also ask for permission to access your precise location. That lets the program stamp your photo with its location information. That's handy to have when traveling, but it can be an invasion of privacy when at your house or that of a friend.

   After you decide whether to allow access to your location, the camera window turns into a giant viewfinder, showing you exactly what the camera sees: your face.

   If your computer or tablet includes two cameras (usually one in front and one in back), you can toggle between them by clicking the Change Camera icon, shown in the upper-right corner of Figure 17-3.

3. **Click the Camera icon to snap a photo, or click the Video icon to begin recording a movie. (Click the Video icon again to stop recording.)**

When the camera detects a face, it places a square around the face, letting you know where the camera will focus. Yes, it's a little creepy.

TIP

The Camera app saves all your snapped photos and videos in a folder named `Camera Roll` inside your `Pictures` folder. That folder is backed up by File History, which I cover in Chapter 13.

TIP

Planning to chat with friends or coworkers through Zoom or Teams Chat? Fire up the camera app, and you can see your background, as well as your lighting, before the meeting. That lets you spend some time decluttering your space and adjusting the lights before going "live" with friends or coworkers.

FIGURE 17-3:
Choose your camera's options, and click the Camera icon for a snapshot or the Video icon for a movie.

Grabbing Photos from Your Android Phone through the Your Phone App

NEW

Most cameras don't have Wi-Fi, so their photos can move to your computer only through cables or memory cards. Today's smartphones, by contrast, live and die by the airwaves. That makes it much easier to copy their photos and videos onto your computer:

>> To grab a quick photo or two from your phone, email them to yourself or your friends.

>> To grab all your phone's photos and videos automatically, install Microsoft's OneDrive app, available for both Android and Apple phones. The app automatically uploads your phone's latest photos and videos onto OneDrive whenever you connect to a Wi-Fi connection. To see them, click OneDrive in the File Manager app, as I describe in Chapter 5; your phone's photos and videos await in a folder called Camera Roll inside OneDrive's Pictures folder.

To fill in the middle ground between all or a few, Microsoft recently updated its old Your Phone Companion app. It now lets you browse through two thousand of your phone's latest photos, and then grab only the ones you want.

TIP

With Windows 11 and a fairly new Android phone, though, the newly updated app does a lot more than that. As I describe in Chapter 12, the app lets you send and receive your phone's text messages from your PC, run your phone's apps in an onscreen window, view your phone's notifications, and, with a microphone and speaker, send and receive phone calls. It's an easy way to harness the power of your phone from your laptop or desktop PC. (Currently, the app only lets you view and copy photos, not videos.)

To copy photos from your phone with the app, follow these steps:

1. **Install the Microsoft Your Phone app onto your Android smartphone, and link the phone with your PC.**

   From your phone, visit the Microsoft Store app, and install the Your Phone app by Microsoft. Run the app on your phone, and follow the instructions to link it with your Windows PC.

   I describe the process of connecting your Android smartphone with your PC in more detail in Chapter 12.

2. **From your PC, open the Your Phone app.**

   Click the Start button, and click the Your Phone app near the bottom of the Start menu's list. The app appears onscreen and displays your photos, as shown in Figure 17-4.

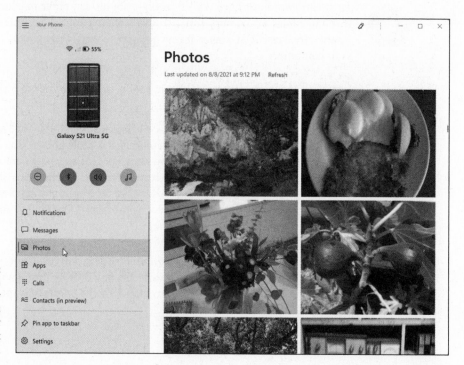

FIGURE 17-4:
When linked with your PC, the Your Phone app opens to display your phone's latest 2,000 photos.

3. **To grab a photo, right-click it and choose from the pop-up menu's options.**

   The pop-up menu offers these options:

   - *Open:* The most-used option, this opens the photo for viewing with your default photo viewing app, usually Photos.

   - *Open With:* This lets you choose which app should open that photo, handy when you want to open a photo *editor* rather than a viewer.

   - *Copy:* Choose this to copy the photo to the clipboard for pasting later, handy for pasting it into an email or graphics-editing program.

SEEING YOUR PHONE ON YOUR PC

You can do quite a bit with your newer model Samsung smartphone and Windows newly updated Your Phone app. Here's the rundown:

- **View settings:** Just open the app, as shown earlier in Figure 17-4, and the top of the left pane shows your phone's wireless strength and battery level, as well as a way to toggle its Bluetooth, sound, music player, and Do Not Disturb settings.

- **Notifications:** If you're not bugged enough with your PC's incessant notifications, you can turn on this option to see the notifications coming from your phone, as well.

- **Messages:** This handy feature lets you read and respond to your phone's messages using your PC's full-sized keyboard. No more thumb-typing!

- **Photos:** Another handy feature, this displays your phone's photos on your PC, as I describe earlier in this chapter.

- **Apps:** You can run your phone's apps on your PC, as long as you don't mind seeing them in a small phone-sized window. (It might be easier just to run them on your phone.)

- **Calls:** If you connect a microphone to your PC, this option lets you send and receive your phone's calls directly from your PC. Call your friends and tell them their car warranty has expired!

Although the Your Phone app gains new features and stability with each release, some of the features still seem a bit half-baked. It's worth an install, though, if you own a Samsung Galaxy phone that's new enough to take advantage of them. To see the currently supported models, open the Microsoft Store app, and view the fine print for the Your Phone app.

- *Save As:* Choose this to save the photo to your PC for later reference.

- *Share:* This setting fetches your email program with the photo attached, ready for emailing to a friend.

- *Delete:* Weed out bad photos by choosing this option and quickly deleting them.

When you're through viewing or grabbed the photos you need, close the app by clicking the X in its upper-right corner.

The Your Phone app offers several other features as well, as described in the sidebar, "Seeing your phone on your PC." Microsoft seems to be actively adding new features, so don't be surprised to see the app grow more powerful in the months to come.

Viewing Photos with the Photos App

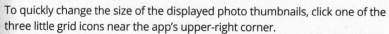

Microsoft constantly updates Windows to add new features. But some features also disappear: The desktop's Photo Viewer, a Windows staple for nearly a decade, no longer appears on the Start menu.

When you want to view photos and videos, Microsoft clearly plans for you to reach for the newer Photos app, shown previously in Figure 17-1. It's a quick way to view your memories in different ways:

>> **Collection:** When opened from the Start menu, the Photos app appears in Collection mode. It displays *all* your photos and videos, sorted by the order you shot them. Although it leaves nothing out, it's often overkill unless you're ready to sit down and weed out the bad ones. (Right-click an unwanted photo and click Delete from the pop-up menu to ditch it for good.)

TIP

To quickly change the size of the displayed photo thumbnails, click one of the three little grid icons near the app's upper-right corner.

>> **Albums:** The Photos app takes a more curated approach here, automatically breaking down your photos into groups named after the day they were shot. It automatically weeds out duplicates, making for a short but sweet way to show off your highlights. To create your own album, select some photos, right-click any one of them, and choose Add to Album from the pop-up menu. Then you can add those photos to an existing album or create your own new album.

>> **People:** If you click Accept when first opening this category, the Photos app constantly scans your incoming photos for faces. A click on the People link displays a headshot of every face it recognizes, grouped by person. Click that person's headshot to see every photo featuring their face. (If this sounds creepy, turn it off by clicking the Photo app's More icon, choosing Settings, and clicking the toggle switch in the People section.)

>> **Folders:** This simply lets you view your photos by their folders, which can be a handy way to view photos stored on a newly inserted thumb drive.

>> **Video Editor:** This switches to the Video Editor app, where you can trim existing videos or create your own.

The next four sections explain how to make the most of the Photos app.

Viewing your photo collection

When opened, the Photos app automatically grabs your computer's photos and videos and places them on the screen in large thumbnails, sorted by the date you took them. That makes it easy to show off the latest vacation photos on a tablet, phone, or even a computer that's hooked up to a TV or large monitor.

To launch the Photos app and start showing off your photos, follow these steps:

1. **From the Start menu, click the Photos icon.**

The Photos app quickly appears, shown in Figure 17-5. The Photos app searches for photos and videos in your computer's Pictures folder, as well as your OneDrive folders, and displays them as one group, all in the order they were taken.

The Photos app also appears when you open a photo from the desktop's File Explorer. (I explain how to browse your files with File Explorer in Chapter 5.)

2. **Scroll down to the photo you want to view or edit.**

The Photos app displays your photos in one long stream, without folders. Called simply *Collection*, the scrolling display places your most recently shot photos at the top, with the oldest ones at the bottom.

Scroll down with a mouse by using the scroll bar along the app's right edge. On a touchscreen, just slide your finger up or down the screen to see newer or older photos.

TIP

The app shows a scrollable list of years next to the scrollbar, letting you slide down quickly to see photos taken in a particular year.

3. **Click a photo to see it fullscreen, and choose any menu option to view, navigate, manipulate, or share your pictures.**

When a photo fills the screen, shown and labelled in Figure 17-6, the menus appear along the top. Each menu option lets you control the app and photos in a different way:

- *Next/Previous photo:* Move your mouse to the photo's left or right edge, and arrows appear along the edge. Click the right arrow to see older photos, or click the left arrow to see newer photos.

- *Zoom:* Click this button, and a sliding control appears, letting you zoom in or out of the photo.

- *Delete:* If you spot a blurred photo, click this icon to delete it immediately. Weeding out the bad photos makes it easier to relocate the good ones.

- *Add to favorites:* Click here to add the photo to an album called Favorites, making it easier to find again later.

- *Rotate:* Clicking this icon rotates your photo clockwise by 90 degrees; to rotate in the opposite direction, click it three times.

- *Crop:* A click on this icon places a resizable square around your photo. Drag the square's edges in or out to frame the photo so it looks its best.

- *Edit and Create:* This fetches a large drop-down menu with options for editing, adding effects, adding text, turning it into a video, and using other photo manipulation tools.

- *Share:* A click here lets you share your photo through any means your PC has to offer, including mail and Near Sharing, a convenient way to pass files to other PCs described in Chapter 15.

- *Print:* A click on this icon sends your photo to your printer.

- *Return to previous view:* Return to viewing thumbnails of your photos by clicking the left-pointing arrow in the photo's upper-left corner. (You may need to click or tap the currently displayed photo before the little arrow appears.)

- *See More:* A click on these three dots fetches a new drop-down menu. This menu lets you start a slideshow, copy the photo, save it in a new format, open it in a new program, set it as your computer's lock screen or background, and see details such as the photo's name, size, date taken, and resolution. (It also holds any extra menu items that don't fit along the top, like Print.)

4. **To exit the Photos app, click the X in its upper-right corner.**

The app clears itself from the screen.

FIGURE 17-5:
The Photos app displays photos stored on your computer and on OneDrive.

Zoom in or out

Add photo to album or video

More options

Add to favorites   Crop   Print

Return to thumbnail view

Delete   Rotate   Edit   Share

Previous

View fullscreen

Next

FIGURE 17-6:
Click any of these places to do different tasks while viewing a photo.

Viewing photo albums

Everybody likes to take pictures, but only a meticulous few like to spend hours organizing them, weeding out the bad ones, and sorting them into easily accessible folders.

That's where the Photos app's robotically curated Albums view comes in handy. When you switch to Album view, the Photos app turns its robotic eye on all your photos (including those on OneDrive), weeds out the duplicates, finds a splashy one for the cover, and names it by the date of the photo session. When you open the Albums view, the app automatically turns your photos into a slideshow.

To view the Photos app's albums, follow these steps:

1. From the Start menu, click the Photos icon.

The Photos app quickly appears, shown previously in Figure 17-5, to show its Collection mode: a string of photos sorted by the order you shot them.

2. From the Photos app's top menu, choose Albums.

The Photos app sorts your photos into albums that represent the best of your session and displays them, shown in Figure 17-7.

The app sorts each collection of photos by date or name. Click an album, and the Photos app shows you the best of that session's photos, shown in Figure 17-8.

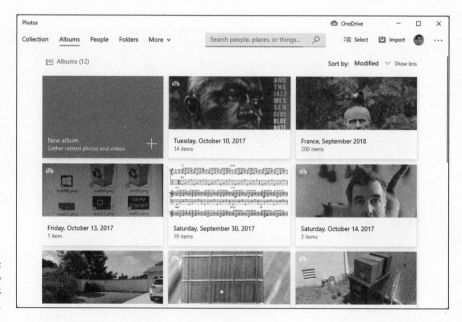

FIGURE 17-7:
Click Albums to see your photos sorted by session.

FIGURE 17-8:
Click a date to see your best photos from that day's photo-shooting session.

3. **Click any photo to view it, or click the Watch button to view an automated slideshow.**

   The Photos app fills the screen with the photo; to see more, click the Next or Previous arrows along the photo's left and right edges.

The Photos app takes its best guess as to which photos work best for each session. Taking mercy on the vacation-photo-saturated relatives sitting on your couch, the app leaves out some of your photos. That's usually a good thing, as it's smart enough to remove duplicates and blurry photos.

You can also click the Save in OneDrive button to save your album to OneDrive, where you can view it with any of your devices with a OneDrive app. (That includes most popular phones, tablets, and some smart TVs these days.)

Clicking the Watch button, shown in the bottom of Figure 17-8, plays a slideshow with music and a splashy title page. You can change the music and adjust the slideshow by clicking the adjacent Edit button, which drops you into the Video Editor to make the changes.

Viewing a slideshow

Windows offers several ways to display your photos as a slideshow. They're a great way to show photos to friends crowding around your computer screen.

To see a slideshow of all the pictures in a File Manager folder, open one of the folder's photos. When the photo opens in the Photos app, click the app's More icon and choose Slideshow from the drop-down menu: The Photos app will display a slideshow with all the photos in that folder.

Here are more tips for successful on-the-fly slideshows:

> Before starting the slideshow, rotate any sideways pictures, if necessary, so they all appear right-side up.

> The slideshow includes only photos in your currently viewed folder or that you've selected. It doesn't dip into folders *inside* that folder and show their photos too.

Help!

IN THIS PART . . .

Put the Windows 11 repair tools to work.

Understand error messages.

Move from your old PC to your new PC.

Find help for Windows 11.

Chapter **18**

The Case of the Broken Window

Sometimes you just have a vague sense that something's wrong. Your computer displays an odd screen that you've never seen before, or Windows starts running more slowly than Congress.

Other times, something's obviously gone haywire. Programs freeze, menus keep shooting at you, or Windows constantly nags you with an incomprehensible error message every time you turn on your computer.

Many of the biggest-looking problems are solved by the smallest-looking solutions. This chapter points you to the right one.

TRY THIS FIRST

Sometimes a vague sense of frustration keeps growing stronger. Your wireless internet isn't working right. The printer won't connect. A website takes forever to load. A program just won't cooperate. Dozens of problems start with small irritations like these.

Oddly enough, sometimes the simplest fix is to restart your computer:

1. Right-click the Start button, choose Shut Down or Sign Out, and choose Restart from the pop-up menu.

Your programs begin closing by themselves. If a program asks you whether you want to save your work, be sure to save it. Then your computer turns itself off. A few seconds later, it rises from the dead to leave you at the lock screen, ready for another round.

Whether restarting your computer gives *you* a much-needed cooling off period or it really fixes the problem, a restart often works wonders. Give it a try before spending too much time on the more strenuous fixes.

The Magic Fixes in Windows

For years, System Restore was the Windows go-to fix when your computer began running roughly. System Restore lives on in Windows 11, as I describe in this chapter's later sidebar, "Restoring from a restore point." But Windows offers several other powerful tools that bring an ailing computer back to health.

The following sections explain each tool, when to reach for it, and how best to make it work its magic.

Resetting your computer

When dealing with a particularly sick computer, sometimes reinstalling Windows is the only cure. In the past, reinstalling Windows took *lots* of time and effort. And after reinstalling Windows, you still needed to copy your files and programs back onto your computer. It could take hours — even if you had up-to-date backups.

Windows aims to solve that problem. By pushing a few buttons, you can tell Windows to reinstall itself onto your computer. And while installing a fresh copy of itself, Windows preserves everybody's user accounts and personal files.

For Microsoft account holders, Windows preserves any apps they've downloaded from the Microsoft Store, as well as some of their most important computer settings.

TECHNICAL STUFF

Performing a reset saves settings from your wireless network connections as well as from your cellular connection, if you have one. The Reset tool also remembers any BitLocker and BitLocker-To-Go settings, drive letter assignments, and personalization settings, including your lock screen background and desktop wallpaper.

When your computer wakes up feeling refreshed with its new copy of Windows, you only need to reinstall your desktop programs. (The program politely leaves a handy list of those programs on your desktop, complete with website links, if available, so you know exactly what to reinstall.) Missing apps can easily be installed from the Microsoft Store: Open the Microsoft Store app from the Start menu, and click the Library icon from the app's left edge. A list of your previously downloaded apps appears, with an Install button next to them.

TIP

The Reset tool can go one step further, if you like, by wiping your computer completely clean of *everything*: user accounts, data, and personal files. Then Windows reinstalls itself, just as if it were on a new PC. That lets you either start from scratch or simply give away or sell your computer without worrying about leaking your personal information.

To reset your ailing PC, follow these steps:

1. **Click the Start button, choose the Settings icon from the Start menu, and click the System category.**

   The Settings app opens to the System page.

2. **From the System page, click the Recovery setting from the right pane, and then click Reset PC.**

   Windows displays the Reset This PC window shown in Figure 18-1, offering two ways to reset your computer:

   • *Keep My Files:* The choice used by nearly *everyone*, this reinstalls Windows, but preserves everybody's user accounts and files. The only things you lose are *desktop programs*, which must be reinstalled from their original discs or installation files. If you choose this option, jump to Step 4.

   • *Remove Everything:* Choose this only when you want to wipe *everything* away from your computer, including everybody's user accounts and files, and reinstall Windows. Then you can start from scratch or safely sell or give your computer to others. If you choose this, move to Step 3.

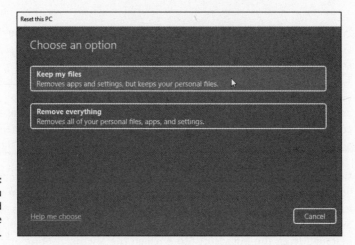

FIGURE 18-1:
Unless you have a very good reason, choose Keep My Files.

3. **Choose whether to just remove your files or to remove files *and* clean the drive.**

   Windows offers you several choices:

   - *Just Remove My Files:* Select this option only when your computer will stay within your family. Although this option is relatively secure, somebody with the right tools may be able to extract some previously erased information. (If your computer contains more than one drive, Windows asks whether you want to remove the files from both drives or just the drive where Windows is installed.)

   - *Remove Files and Fully Clean the Drive:* Select this option when you intend to sell or donate your computer to strangers. This more time-consuming option removes your data and scrubs the hard drive *extra* clean. That keeps out everybody but the most dedicated specialists who own expensive data recovery equipment.

   - *Which Drive:* A third option appears to people who have spread Windows across two disk drives, perhaps by storing their File History backups on a second drive. Choose All Drives to fully clean both drives; choose Only the Drive Where Windows Is Installed to preserve your File History backup.

   When you click an option and click the Reset button, Windows removes everything from your computer, fully cleaning the drive, if requested, and then reinstalls itself to leave your computer with a "like new" copy of Windows. At that point, you're finished, and your computer's ready to start afresh or be given away safely.

4. **Take note of what desktop programs (and, possibly, drivers) need to be reinstalled, click Next, and then click the Reset button.**

   Windows asks how you'd like to reinstall Windows.

5. **Choose how to reinstall Windows.**

Windows offers two ways to reinstall:

- *Cloud Download:* Built for people with a fast broadband connection, this reloads Windows directly from Microsoft's own computers. It's a handy option if you don't have a backup copy of Windows or if the other option fails.

- *Local Reinstall:* Try this option first to save time. Windows looks for a backup copy of itself, either stashed in secret on your hard drive or stored on a flash drive or DVD.

When you choose your option, Windows asks for final approval and then carries out your bidding.

Windows reinstalls itself on your computer, which takes anywhere from 15 minutes to an hour. When your computer wakes up, it should feel refreshed and ready to work again. Expect any or all of the following things to take place when resetting your computer:

>> When your computer wakes up and you sign in, you find a shortcut called Removed Apps waiting on your desktop. Click it, and your web browser displays a page with links to any available removed desktop programs and drivers that you need to reinstall — if you decide you miss them, that is. (And if you *do* miss them, you need the program's installation discs to reinstall them.)

>> Shortly after Windows wakes up, it visits Windows Update to download and install oodles of security patches, as well as updated copies of its bundled apps. Grab a good novel.

>> After resetting your computer, reinstall your desktop programs one by one, restarting your computer after each new install. That gives you the best chance to weed out any misbehaving programs that may have caused the problems that messed things up.

>> If you're connected to a network, you may need to tell Windows whether you're on a *private* (home) network or a *public* network. I describe that process in Chapter 15.

WARNING

>> If you inserted a Windows DVD into your computer in Step 5, be careful when your computer restarts. As it restarts, your computer may ask you to "Press any key to boot from disc." *Don't* press any key; instead, wait a few seconds until the message disappears. Then Windows loads itself from your computer's newly refreshed *hard drive* rather than the Windows installation DVD.

>> If you've wiped your hard drive completely clean, you can use a File History backup, described in the next section, to restore the files that once lived in your Documents, Music, Pictures, and Videos folders.

Restoring backups with File History

The Windows backup program, File History, saves the files that *you've* created. It doesn't back up your apps and programs. After all, apps and programs can always be reinstalled. But many of the moments that inspired so many of your photos, videos, and documents can *never* be re-created.

To keep your files safe, File History automatically makes a copy of *every* file in your Documents, Music, Photos, and Videos folders. It copies all the files on your desktop as well. And File History automatically makes those copies *every hour*.

File History makes your backups easy to see and restore, letting you flip through different versions of your files and folders, comparing them with your current versions. Should you find a better version, a press of a button brings that older version back to life.

REMEMBER

File History doesn't work until you turn it on, a process I describe in Chapter 13. Please, *please* flip back a few chapters and turn it on now. The earlier you turn it on, the more backups you'll have to choose from when you need them. Your portable hard drive also needs to be plugged into your PC in order for your PC to access the files.

To browse through your backed-up files and folders, restoring the ones you want, follow these steps:

1. **Click the taskbar's Search button, type** File History, **and press Enter.**

   The age-old Control Panel appears, open to the File History section.

2. **Click the Restore Personal Files link from the section's left side.**

   The File History program appears, shown in Figure 18-2. The program looks much like a plain old folder, but it's actually showing the folders you've backed up: your main folders, your desktop, your contacts, your favorite websites, as well as your Music, Documents, Videos and Music folders, among others.

   Feel free to open the folders inside the File History window. You can also peek inside the files you find there to see their contents.

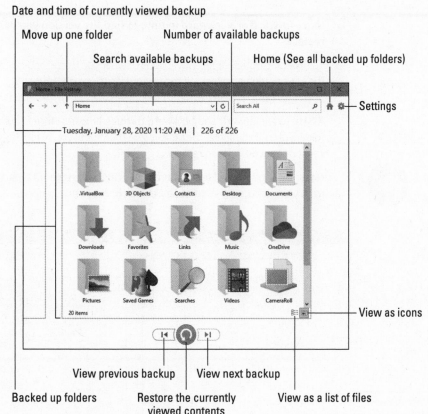

Date and time of currently viewed backup

Move up one folder

Number of available backups

Search available backups

Home (See all backed up folders)

Settings

Tuesday, January 28, 2020 11:20 AM | 226 of 226

View as icons

View previous backup

View next backup

View as a list of files

Backed up folders

Restore the currently viewed contents

FIGURE 18-2:
The File History program lets you restore backups from any of your main folders.

3. **Choose what you'd like to restore.**

Point and click your way through the libraries, folders, and files until you spot the item or items you'd like to restore:

- *Folder:* To restore an entire folder, open it so you're viewing its contents.

- *Files:* To restore a group of files, open the folder containing them, so the files' icons are onscreen.

- *One file:* To restore an earlier version of a file, open that file from inside the File History window. File History displays that file's contents.

When you've found the file or folder you want to restore, move to the next step.

4. Move forward or backward in time to find the version you'd like to restore.

To browse through different versions of what you're currently viewing, choose the left-pointing arrow along the bottom, as shown in Figure 18-3. To see a newer version, choose the right-pointing arrow.

As you move forward and backward through time, feel free to click open folders or individual files, peeking inside them until you're looking at the version that you want to retrieve.

TIP

Not sure whether a folder contains your sought-after item? Type a word or two from your document into the Search box in File History's upper-right corner.

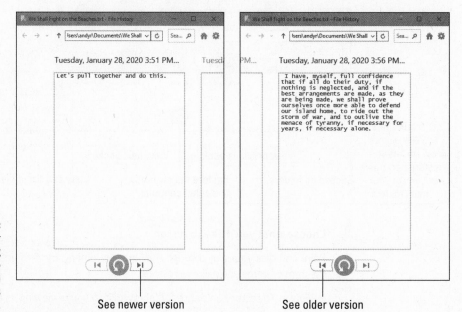

See newer version

See older version

FIGURE 18-3:
Click the left or right arrow along the bottom to see newer and older versions of the file.

5. Click the Restore button to restore your desired version.

Whether you're looking at an individual file, a folder, or an entire library's contents, clicking the Restore button (shown in the margin) places that item back in the place where it used to live.

That brings up a potential problem, however: What happens if you try to restore an older file named Notes into a place that already contains a file named Notes? Windows warns you of the problem with the window in Figure 18-4, which brings you to Step 6.

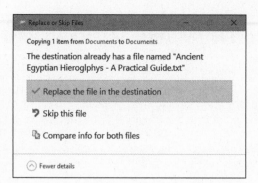

FIGURE 18-4:
Choose whether
to replace the
existing file, skip
the file, or which
file to keep.

6. **Choose how to handle the conflict.**

   If Windows notices a naming conflict with the item you're trying to restore, File History offers you three ways to handle the situation, as shown in Figure 18-4.

   - *Replace the File in the Destination.* Click this option only when you're *sure* that the older file is better than your current file.

   - *Skip This File.* Click this if you don't want to restore the file or folder. This option returns you to File History, where you can browse other files.

   - *Compare Info for Both Files.* Often the best choice, this option lets you compare the files' sizes and dates before choosing which one to keep, the replacement file or the currently existing file. Or, if you want, this choice also lets you keep *both* files: Windows simply adds a number after the name of the incoming file, naming it Notes (1), for example.

7. **Exit File History by closing the window.**

   You close the File History window just as you close any other window: Click the X in its upper-right corner.

Want to know more about File History? Read on:

>> In addition to backing up everything in your main folders and on your desktop, File History stores a list of your favorite websites, listed earlier in Figure 18-2 as Favorites.

>> I explain how to use File History to move an old computer's files to a new computer in Chapter 20.

TIP

>> Don't become too dependent on the File History program. Microsoft is phasing it out as it pushes everybody toward storing their backups on OneDrive, its rental storage service on the internet. You may want to invest in a third-party backup program to take File History's place.

RESTORING FROM A RESTORE POINT

The new Recovery programs in Windows work wonders in resuscitating an ailing computer, and they're more powerful than the older System Restore technology. But in case you've come to rely on the System Restore programs built into earlier Windows versions, Windows 11 still includes System Restore — if you know where to find it.

To send your computer back to a restore point when it was working much better, follow these steps:

1. **Click the Start button, type** System Restore **in the Search box, and press Enter. When the System Properties window appears, click the System Restore button.**

   The System Restore window appears.

2. **Click the Next button at the System Restore window.**

   The System Restore Point lists available restore points.

3. **Click a listed restore point.**

4. **Click the Scan for Affected Programs button to see how your chosen restore point will affect programs.**

   A handy touch, this feature lists programs you'll probably need to reinstall.

5. **Click Next to confirm your chosen restore point. Then click Finish.**

   Your computer grumbles a bit and then restarts, using those earlier settings that (hopefully) worked fine.

If your system is *already* working fine, feel free to create your own restore point, as I describe at the beginning of Chapter 13. Name the restore point something descriptive, such as Before Installing Tax Software. (That way, you know which restore point to use if things go awry.)

Windows Keeps Asking Me for Permission

Like earlier Windows versions before it, Windows 11 offers both Administrator and Standard user accounts. The Administrator account, meant for the computer's owner, holds all the power. Holders of mere Standard accounts, by contrast, aren't allowed to do things that might change the computer or its settings.

But no matter which of the two accounts you hold, you'll occasionally brush up against the Windows version of a barbed-wire fence. When a program tries to change something on your computer, Windows pokes you with a message like the one shown in Figure 18-5.

FIGURE 18-5:
The Windows permission screen pops up when a program tries to change something on your PC.

Standard account holders see a slightly different message that commands them to fetch an Administrator account holder to type a password.

Of course, when screens like this one pop up too often, most people simply ignore them and give their approval — even if that means they've just allowed a virus to settle comfortably inside their PC.

BRINGING IN A TROUBLESHOOTER

Windows offers a wide variety of automated troubleshooters: little robots that examine both Windows and your PC in order to diagnose problems, flip switches, and occasionally even solve the problem. To find them, open the Settings app's System page, and choose the Troubleshoot section from the right pane.

If you don't see a recommended troubleshooter waiting to solve your current problems, click the Other Troubleshooters section. The right pane shows almost two dozen troubleshooting programs that aim to fix problems with printers, Windows Update, sound, program compatibility, and more.

Just click the Run button next to the troubleshooter you want, and the Troubleshooter appears, trying various fixes, and asking you if the problem is fixed before moving on to the next potential fix. It's worth a visit before calling in a professional or packing up your PC and taking it to the shop.

So when Windows sends you a permission screen, ask yourself this question: "Is Windows asking permission for something *I* did or requested?" If your answer is yes, give your approval so Windows can carry out your bidding. But if Windows sends you a permission screen out of the blue when you haven't done anything, click No or Cancel. That helps keeps potential nasties from invading your PC.

If you don't have time for this bothersome security layer, and you're willing to suffer the consequences, you can find out how to turn off user account permissions by reading Chapter 11.

I Need to Retrieve Deleted Files

Everybody who's worked on a computer knows the agony of seeing hours of work go down the drain: You mistakenly delete a file.

The Windows File History backup program, described earlier in this chapter, is a lifesaver here. But if you never turned on File History — an easy task I explain in Chapter 13 — Windows offers another way to retrieve your deleted files: the Recycle Bin.

 The Recycle Bin works because Windows doesn't *really* destroy your deleted files. Instead, Windows slips those files into your Recycle Bin (shown in the margin), which lives on your desktop.

Open the Recycle Bin with a double-click, and you find every file or folder you've deleted within the past few weeks. I cover the Recycle Bin in Chapter 3, but here's a tip: To restore a file or folder from the Recycle Bin, right-click the file and choose Restore. The deleted item magically reappears in its former home.

I Need to Fix Broken Apps

Windows makes it fairly easy to repair apps, which are almost always downloaded from the Microsoft Store. If an app no longer seems in good health and you'd like to reset it and start from scratch, follow these steps:

 1. **Click the Start button, and choose the Settings icon from the Start menu.**

The Settings app appears, open to the System page.

2. **From the right pane of the System app, click the Apps icon (shown in the margin). When the Apps window appears, click the Apps and Features section from the window's right edge.**

   The Apps and Features page appears, listing your apps alphabetically along the bottom.

3. **Click the More button (shown in the margin) next to the malfunctioning app's name, and, when the menu drops down, click Advanced Options.**

4. **When the Advanced Options settings appear, click the Repair button.**

   This tells Windows to repair the app, if possible, preserving your settings and data.

5. **If Repair doesn't fix the problem, click the adjacent Reset button.**

When you choose Reset, Windows deletes and reinstalls the app from scratch, taking any of your preference settings and sign-in details along with it. This isn't a big deal with, say, the Calculator app. But more elaborate apps like Mail and Calendar may take some time to bring back up to speed with the right settings.

My Settings Are Messed Up

Sometimes you want to return to the way things were *before* you started messing around with them. Your salvation lies in the Restore Default button, which awaits your command in strategically placed areas throughout Windows. A click of that button returns the settings to the way Windows originally set them up.

Here are a few Restore Default buttons you may find useful:

» **Apps:** Windows includes a Repair and a Reset button that restores malfunctioning apps back to their original working condition. I describe how in the previous section, "I Need to Fix Broken Apps."

» **Firewall:** If you suspect foul play within Windows Firewall, bring back its original settings and start over. (Some of your programs may need to be reinstalled.) Click the Start button, and type **firewall and network protection** in the Search box. When the Windows Security window appears, choose Firewall and Network protection from the left pane. In the right pane, click Restore Firewalls to Default. (Be careful with this one, as you may need to reinstall some apps and programs.)

WARNING

>> **Media Player:** When the age-old Media Player Library contains mistakes, tell it to delete its index and start over. In Media Player, right-click the Forward or Backward arrows in the top menu, click Tools, choose Advanced from the pop-out menu, and choose Restore Media Library. (Or if you've accidentally removed items from the Media Player Library, choose Restore Deleted Library Items instead.)

>> **Colors:** Windows lets you tweak your desktop's colors and sounds, sometimes into a disturbing mess. To return to the default colors and sounds, right-click the Start button and choose Settings. Open the Personalization category, choose Themes from the right pane, and choose the Windows them from the Current Theme section.

>> **Fonts:** Have you tweaked your fonts beyond recognition? Return them to normal by clicking the Start menu, typing **Control Panel** into the Search box and pressing Enter. When the Control Panel appears, click Appearance and Personalization, and then clicking Fonts. In the left pane, click Font Settings and then click the Restore Default Font Settings button.

>> **Libraries:** In Windows 11, libraries are hidden by default. (I explain how to turn them on in Chapter 5.) When turned on, libraries appear in every folder's Navigation pane. But if one of your libraries is missing (say, the Music library), you can put it back. From within File Explorer, right-click the word Libraries along the right side of any folder, choose More Options from the pop-up menu, and choose Restore Default Libraries. Your default libraries — Documents, Music, Pictures, and Videos — all reappear.

>> **Network adapters:** This one-click solution removes and reinstalls your network adapters and switches your network to its original settings. To reset your network, click the Start button, choose Settings, and choose the Network and Internet category from the left pane. From the right pane, click the Advanced Network Settings section, and then click the Network Reset option. Finally, click the Reset Now button. To restore your network to working order when this process finishes, you'll need to complete the steps I describe in Chapter 15 that show how to share files with your networked computers.

>> **Folders:** Windows hides a slew of switches relating to folders, their Navigation panes, the items they show, how they behave, and how they search for items. To mull over their options or return them to their default settings, open any folder and click the More icon shown in the margin. When the drop-down list appears, choose Options. The Folder Options window appears, which lists a Restore Defaults button on each of its tabs: General, View, and Search. (Click Apply after each change to make it stick.)

Finally, don't forget the Reset option in Windows, described at the beginning of this chapter. Although it's overkill for many problems, it resets most of your settings to the default.

I Forgot My Password

When Windows won't accept your password at the Sign In screen, you may not be hopelessly locked out of your own computer. Check all these things before letting loose with a scream:

» **Check your Caps Lock key.** Windows passwords are *case-sensitive,* meaning that Windows considers *OpenSesame* and *opensesame* to be different passwords. If your keyboard's Caps Lock light is on, press your Caps Lock key again to turn it off. Then try entering your password again.

» **Use your Password Reset Disk.** I explain how to create a Password Reset Disk for a Local account holder in Chapter 14. (The disk doesn't work for Microsoft account holders.) When you've forgotten the password to your Local account, insert that disk to use as a key. Windows lets you back into your account, where you can promptly create an easier-to-remember password. (Flip to Chapter 14 and create a Password Reset Disk now if you haven't yet.)

» **Let another user reset your password.** Anybody with an Administrator account on your computer can reset your password. Have that person head for the desktop's Control Panel (see Chapter 12), click User Accounts, and then click User Accounts again. There, they can click the Manage Another Account link to see a list of every account. They can click your account name and click the Change the Password link to create a password you can remember more easily.

Note: If you've forgotten the password to your *Microsoft account,* none of the preceding suggestions will work. Instead, open any web browser and visit www.live.com. Enter your Microsoft account email, and click the Forgot Password? link. The site then leads you through the steps to reset your password.

If none of these options works, you're in sad shape, unfortunately. Compare the value of your password-protected data against the cost of hiring a password recovery specialist. You can find a specialist by searching for *recover windows password* on Google (www.google.com). Look for one with good reviews and who's been in business for a few years.

MY PROGRAM IS FROZEN!

TIP

Eventually, one of your apps or programs will freeze up solid, leaving you in the cold with no way to reach its normal Close command. Should you find yourself facing this icy terrain, these steps will extricate the frozen program from your computer's memory (and the screen as well):

1. **Right-click the Start menu, and select the Task Manager option from the pop-up menu.**

   The Task Manager program appears, and its Apps section lists the names of currently running programs.

2. **Click the name of the frozen app or program.**

   If you don't spot your program's name, clicking the More Details link reveals everything currently running on your PC.

3. **Click the End Task button, and Windows whisks away the frozen program.**

   If your computer seems a bit groggy afterward, play it safe by restarting it.

My Computer Is Frozen Solid

Every once in a while, Windows just drops the ball and wanders off somewhere to sit under a tree. You're left looking at a computer that just looks back. None of the computer's lights blink. Panicked clicks don't do anything. Randomly tapping the keyboard does nothing, or worse yet, the computer starts to beep at every key press.

When nothing onscreen moves (except, perhaps the mouse pointer), the computer is frozen up solid. Try the following approaches, in the following order, to correct the problem:

>> **Approach 1:** Press Esc twice.

- This action rarely works, but it's a quick first salvo that can't hurt anything.

>> **Approach 2:** Press the Ctrl, Alt, and Delete keys simultaneously, and choose Start Task Manager from the menu that appears.

- If you're lucky, the Task Manager appears with the message that it discovered an unresponsive application. The Task Manager lists the names of currently running programs, including the one that's not responding. On the Processes tab, click the name of the program that's causing the mess and then click the End Task button. You lose any unsaved work in that program, of course, but you should be used to that. (If you somehow stumbled onto the Ctrl+Alt+Delete combination by accident, press Esc to quit Task Manager and return to Windows.)

- If that still doesn't do the trick, press Ctrl+Alt+Delete again and click the Power icon (shown in the margin) in the screen's lower-right corner. Choose Restart from the pop-up menu, and your computer shuts down and restarts, hopefully returning in a better mood.

>> **Approach 3:** If the preceding approaches don't work, turn off the computer by pressing its power button. (If that merely brings up the Turn Off the Computer menu, choose Restart, and your computer should restart.)

>> **Approach 4:** If you keep holding down your computer's power button long enough (usually about 4 to 5 seconds), it eventually stops resisting and turns off.

Chapter **19**

Strange Messages: What You Did Does Not Compute

Error messages in *real* life are fairly easy to understand. A blinking digital clock means you need to set the time. A parked car's beep means that you've left your keys in the ignition. A spouse's stern glance means that you've forgotten something important.

But Windows error messages may have been written by a Senate subcommittee, if only the messages weren't so brief. The error messages rarely describe what you did to cause the event or, even worse, how to fix the problem.

In this chapter, I've collected some of the most common Windows error messages, notifications, and just plain confusing attempts at conversation. Find a message that matches what you're experiencing and then read how to handle the situation as gracefully as Windows will allow.

Add Your Microsoft Account

Meaning: Although the messages in these windows may be worded slightly differently, they all mean the same thing: You must sign in with a Microsoft account to perform your desired task. If you don't have a Microsoft account, you see the message in Figure 19-1. As described in Chapter 2, Microsoft accounts let you reap the most benefits from Windows.

FIGURE 19-1:
To take advantage of some Windows features, you must create a Microsoft account.

Probable causes: You may have tried to buy an app from the Microsoft Store, access OneDrive from the internet, or activate the Windows Family Safety controls, which all require a Microsoft account.

Solution: Sign up for a free Microsoft account, as I describe in Chapter 2.

Calendar Notifications

Meaning: When your upcoming appointment is happening soon, Windows sends the message in Figure 19-2.

Probable cause: You've entered an appointment into the built-in Calendar app, and Windows is reminding you that it's coming up soon. This is one of many notifications that pop up in the screen's lower-right corner.

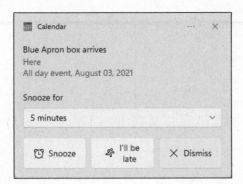

FIGURE 19-2:
Choose between
the offered
options.

Solutions: Most people prefer seeing reminders about their appointments. But if the sheer number of notifications begins disturbing you after a while, feel free to turn them off. I explain how to pick and choose which apps can send notifications in Chapter 12.

Choose What Happens with This Device

Meaning: Windows wants to know what to do with the device you've just plugged into your computer, so the message shown in Figure 19-3 appears in your screen's lower-right corner.

FIGURE 19-3:
Click to tell
Windows how to
react whenever
you connect that
device with your
computer.

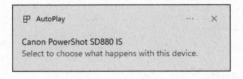

When you click the window in Figure 19-3, the window in Figure 19-4 appears in the screen's *upper*-right corner.

Probable causes: You just slid a *flash drive* (a stick of memory) into your computer's USB port, attached a phone or camera, or connected another device to your computer.

Solution: Choose how you want Windows to react when you reconnect that device in the future. You can always change this decision by visiting the Settings app's Bluetooth and Devices page and choosing AutoPlay from the right pane. Click any listed device, and a drop-down menu lists all your choices. (I prefer the Ask Me Every Time option, when it's available, so I can choose the action I prefer at each particular moment.)

FIGURE 19-4:
Tell Windows
what to do with
the item you've
just inserted into
your computer.

Deleted Files Are Removed Everywhere

Meaning: When you delete a file from OneDrive, your online storage space, it will no longer be available to your other devices. To remind you, Windows sends the message in Figure 19-5.

FIGURE 19-5:
Deleting files
from OneDrive
removes them
from the
OneDrive folder
of all your
devices.

Probable cause: You're deleting a file that's stored on OneDrive.

Solutions: Feel free to delete the file from OneDrive if you no longer need it there. Just be sure to keep a copy on the PCs that need to have it. I explain the intricacies of OneDrive in Chapter 5. (If you delete a OneDrive file, it goes to the OneDrive Recycle Bin, where it stays for 30 days.) To retrieve a mistakenly deleted file, click the message's Open OneDrive's Recycle Bin button, select the mistakenly deleted file, and click the Restore button.

Did You Mean to Switch Apps?

Meaning: Your currently viewed app is trying to open another app. Windows shows you the message in Figure 19-6 to make sure the app isn't trying to do anything evil.

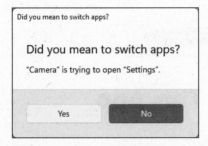

FIGURE 19-6: Click Yes unless you think the app is trying something sneaky.

Did you mean to switch apps?

Did you mean to switch apps?

"Camera" is trying to open "Settings".

Yes   No

Probable cause: You've clicked a link inside one app that requires another app to handle the job.

Solution: Unless you think the app is trying to install a virus or do something bad, click the Yes button to approve the job.

Do You Want to Allow This App to Make Changes to Your Device?

Meaning: Are you sure that this software is free from viruses, spyware, and other harmful things?

Probable cause: A window similar to the one shown in Figure 19-7 appears when you try to install downloaded software or a driver for one of your computer's parts. In this case, Microsoft's security program simply wants to open a program to see if it's safe.

Solutions: If you're sure the requested action is safe, click the OK, Yes, or Install button. But if this message appears unexpectedly or you think it may not be safe, click the Cancel, No, or Don't Install button. I cover safe computing in Chapter 11.

FIGURE 19-7:
Do you think this
software is safe?

Do You Want to Pin This App to the Taskbar?

Meaning: An app is trying to pin itself to the taskbar, that strip of icons along the bottom of your screen.

Probable cause: Some newly installed apps aren't content to simply add themselves to the Start menu. They want to hog some space on the taskbar, as well. So Windows asks for your approval by displaying the window shown in Figure 19-8 before allowing that to happen.

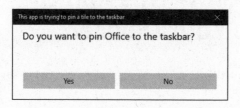

FIGURE 19-8:
Should this app
be allowed to
appear on the
taskbar?

Solutions: If you think you'll be using the app frequently, and there's room for it on the taskbar, click Yes. Otherwise, click No. You can always pin the app there later, as I describe in Chapter 3.

Do You Want to Save Changes?

Meaning: You haven't saved your work in a program, the program is about to close, and your work is about to be lost.

Probable causes: The window in Figure 19-9 appears when you're trying to close an application, sign out, or restart your computer before telling a program to save the work you've created.

FIGURE 19-9:
Do you want to
save your work?

Solutions: Click the Save button to save your work and let the program close. I cover saving files in Chapter 6. Don't want to save the file? Then click Don't Save to discard your work and move on. Or, if the cat stepped on the keyboard, click Cancel to stymie the cat's mischief and return to normalcy.

Enter Network Credentials

Meaning: Windows isn't letting you access a particular file or folder, so it sends Figure 19-10.

FIGURE 19-10:
Enter your user
account and
password to
continue.

Probable cause: You're trying to access a file or folder on a network or another user account where you don't have permission.

Solutions: Ask the owner of that user account or networked computer to give you permission to access the file, a process I cover in Chapter 15. Then, when you enter your user account and password, Windows will let you see the folder or file. Still see the message? Double-check to make sure you've entered your username and password correctly.

How Do You Want to Open This File?

Meaning: The window in Figure 19-11 appears when you need to give an app permission to carry out an action.

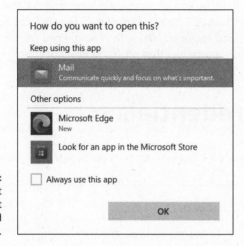

FIGURE 19-11: Windows doesn't know what program should open this file.

Probable cause: Windows apps and programs often fight over the right to open your files. To make sure that the right program is opening your file, Windows displays this message for you to confirm that the correct program is handling the job.

Solutions: If the correct program is listed as opening your file, click the Always Use This App checkbox, and then click the OK button. Windows won't bug you the next time you open that type of file. The message reappears the next time you open a *different* type of file, however. If the wrong program is trying to open the file, click or tap the correct program from the message's list.

If Windows doesn't offer any valid suggestions, however, click the Look for an App in the Store option. (I cover this problem in Chapter 6.) To open the file, you may need to download or buy an app from the Microsoft Store.

Keep These Display Settings?

Meaning: Are you able to view what you see onscreen, and does it look the way you want?

Probable cause: Windows sends up Figure 19-12 as a safeguard when you change your display settings, perhaps to change the resolution so that more information will fit onto the screen.

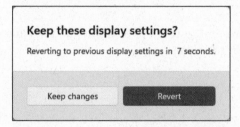

FIGURE 19-12: Windows wants to make sure your recent display changes worked correctly.

Solutions: If everything looks fine onscreen, click Keep Changes, and Windows sticks with the newly changed display settings. If you don't click anything, Windows assumes the changes have made your display unreadable, so it jumps back to the last settings that worked.

Let's Finish Setting Up

Meaning: Figure 19-13 is Microsoft's way of making sure you know about all the new features in Windows 11. And that includes some features you may have to pay for down the road.

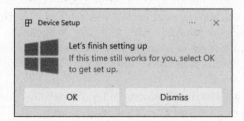

FIGURE 19-13: Windows 11 wants to finish introducing its new features.

Probable cause: Owners of new or recently upgraded computers see this a lot.

Solutions: Click Remind me Later to put off the task; click Continue to run through the screens. I click the No Thanks button at each screen. You can always turn on the features later if and when you need them. If you want to revisit them, click the Get Started app from the Start menu's All Apps section.

No Usable Drive Found

Meaning: The message in Figure 19-14 tells you that the Windows backup program, File History, isn't working.

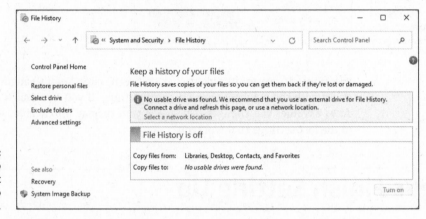

FIGURE 19-14:
Your backup drive or card isn't plugged in to your computer.

Probable cause: File History was saving your files on a portable hard drive, flash drive, or memory card that's no longer plugged in to your computer.

Solutions: This message appears most often on laptops and tablets after you've taken them on the road, leaving your backup drive at home. So find your portable hard drive, flash drive, or memory card, and plug it back into your computer. (If File History doesn't begin working again, revisit the File History section in Chapter 13 to make sure the settings are correct.)

After you plug the drive back into your computer, File History thoughtfully makes a fresh backup of everything that hasn't yet been saved.

Save to OneDrive

Meaning: Windows wants to store your files automatically on OneDrive, so it sends the message in Figure 19-15.

FIGURE 19-15: Do you want to save your screenshots to OneDrive?

Probable cause: You've pressed ▦+PrtScrn to take a *screenshot* — a picture of what's on the screen. Normally, Windows stores the screenshot file in the `Screenshot` folder that resides within your `Pictures` folder. But Windows wants you to store them instead on OneDrive, your online storage space.

Solutions: Click Yes if you need to access those screenshots from any devices or web browser. But click No if you'll only access them from your own PC. That prevents OneDrive from eventually running out of room, and Microsoft from asking you to pay for more storage.

Select to Choose What Happens with Removable Drives

Meaning: Windows sends the message shown in Figure 19-16 when it wants to know what to do when you plug a hard drive or flash drive into your computer's USB port.

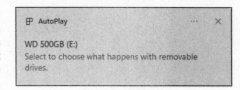

FIGURE 19-16:
Windows wants
to know what
to do with
a new drive.

Probably cause: You've plugged a new hard drive or flash drive into your computer's USB port.

Solution: You can just ignore the message, and it will go away with no harm done. If you click it, Windows lets you choose between three actions:

» **Configure Storage Settings:** This opens the Settings app's Storage settings, few of which have to do with portable drives. (Previously, Windows would offer to let you use the drive as a backup device.)

» **Open Folder to View Files:** The most likely choice, this lets you view the contents of your newly plugged-in drive.

» **Take No Action:** Choose this, and Windows stops sending you pointless messages like this. Then, when you want to see what's inside the drive, you can open File Explorer to view the drive's contents.

Threats Found

Meaning: When the built-in Windows antivirus program finds a potentially dangerous file on your computer, it lets you know with the message in Figure 19-17. Windows then removes the file so it can't harm your computer or files.

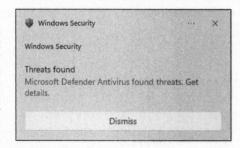

FIGURE 19-17:
Microsoft
Defender
Antivirus has
found and
removed a
potentially
dangerous file on
your computer.

Like most notifications, this one always appears in the screen's lower-right corner.

Probable cause: A potentially dangerous file — *malware* — probably arrived through email, a flash drive, a networked computer, or an evil website. Windows is removing the file so it can't do any harm.

Solutions: Microsoft Defender Antivirus is already removing the offender, but try to remember what action forced Microsoft Defender Antivirus to clean up the problem. Then, if possible, try not to repeat that action. It wouldn't hurt to tell Microsoft Defender Antivirus to give your computer a full scan and to scan any storage device you just connected. (I explain Microsoft Defender Antivirus in Chapter 11.)

Then click the Dismiss button, breathe a sigh of relief, and continue with your work.

USB Device Not Recognized

Meaning: When you see the message in Figure 19-18, it means Windows can't figure out what's been plugged into your computer's USB port.

FIGURE 19-18:
Windows doesn't recognize what's in your PC's USB port.

Probable cause: Unfortunately, many culprits could be responsible here, ranging from a broken device to a bad driver to bad luck.

Solutions: First, try unplugging the device, waiting 30 seconds, and then plugging it into a different USB port. If that doesn't work, visit the device's support page on the internet: You may need to download and install some software before Windows can recognize the device. Or the device might simply be broken. Before assuming it's broken, though, try restarting your computer by right-clicking the Start button, clicking Shut Down or Sign Out from the pop-up menu, and clicking Shutdown from the next menu.

Verify Your Identity on This PC

Meaning: Windows sends the message in Figure 19-19 when it wants to make sure you're really you before letting you do something important.

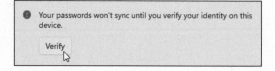

Probable cause: This usually appears when you or somebody else has created a new user account on a PC. Until you can access everything normally, you need to prove your identity.

Solutions: Clicking the Verify button and entering your account password at this point almost always tells Windows to open the gates and let you work in peace.

We're Not Allowed to Find You

Meaning: The Maps app in Windows wants to know your current physical location, as shown in Figure 19-20; Windows, in turn, wants to know whether you will allow that.

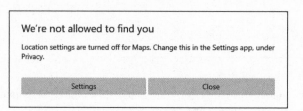

Probable cause: A particular app needs your location to do something. In this case, the Maps app wants to know your location so it can display that information on the map.

Solutions: If you trust the app and feel comfortable letting it know where you're currently sitting or standing, click Settings, which opens the app's section in the Settings app. There, you can allow the app to access your location without it having to ask again. If you think the app is being too nosy, click Close or No. However, the app will probably ask for permission again the next time you open it.

You Don't Currently Have Permission to Access This Folder

Meaning: If you spot the window in Figure 19-21, it means Windows won't let you peek inside the folder you're trying to open. A similar message appears when Windows won't let you peek inside a file.

FIGURE 19-21:
Find somebody with an Administrator account to open the folder or file.

Probable cause: The file or folder belongs to somebody with a different user account.

Solutions: If you hold an Administrator account, you can open files and folders from other people's user accounts by clicking Continue. If you don't have an Administrator account, however, you're locked out.

Your Privacy Settings Blocked Access to Your Location

Meaning: Something in Windows is asking permission to know your current physical location, as shown in Figure 19-22, and Windows wants to know whether you want to allow that.

FIGURE 19-22:
Click Settings and give the app permission to know your location.

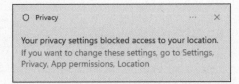

Probable cause: Your Privacy settings in Windows 11 are set so that no apps at all are allowed to know your location.

Solutions: To change your Privacy settings, open the Settings app from the Start menu. Then head for the Privacy and Security section. There, you can pick and choose between what apps can access information that many people consider private. I cover the Settings app in Chapter 12.

settings into your new PC

» **Transferring files and settings with a program or technician**

» **Transferring files and settings yourself with a portable hard drive**

Chapter **20**

Moving from an Old PC to a New Windows 11 PC

When you bring home your exciting new Windows 11 computer, it lacks the most important thing of all: the stuff from your *old* computer. How do you copy your files from that dusty old PC to that shiny new Windows PC? How do you even *find* everything you want to move?

This chapter explores your options, and compares their degrees of difficulty.

TIP

Here's a timesaver: If you're just *upgrading* your relatively new Windows 10 PC to Windows 11, you can skip this chapter. When you upgrade, Windows 11 leaves your personal files, apps, and desktop programs in place. Older versions of Windows are probably running on older PCs; those PCs won't be powerful enough to upgrade to Windows 11, unfortunately.

Moving to Windows 11 the Microsoft Way

The reason Microsoft removed and hid backup programs from Windows 11 boils down to one word: *OneDrive*, the built-in storage space on the internet that comes baked into Windows 11.

Windows makes it easier than ever to store all your files on OneDrive. As soon as you create a file or import a digital photo, Windows practically begs you to begin saving it in your 5GB of OneDrive space. Throughout Windows 11, pop-up ads and suggestions all tout OneDrive's benefits.

Actually, OneDrive works *really* well as a backup plan. If you store the contents of your PC's Documents, Music, Pictures, and Videos folders on OneDrive, they'll automatically be waiting for you on your new Windows 11 PC.

When you step over to your new computer and sign in with your Microsoft account, all your files, folders, *and* settings automatically travel to your new PC. Any apps you downloaded from the Microsoft Store automatically pour into your new PC, as well.

In short, there's no work on your part. You don't need to pick and choose what to back up, nor do you need to spend hours finding and copying all your data into a backup. If you told Windows to use OneDrive, it automatically backed up every-thing on your old PC while you worked. Just as effortlessly, it will automatically drop that information into your new Windows 11 PC.

OneDrive warrants a few caveats, though:

>> OneDrive works only with PCs running Windows 8, Windows 8.1, or Windows 10. Windows 7 PCs couldn't use apps, and most Windows 7 PC owners didn't use OneDrive.

>> Restoring all those files and folders from OneDrive to your new PC can take time. That's why it's faster to keep them on OneDrive and just grab them as you need them.

>> Windows offers only 5GB of free OneDrive storage space, which isn't enough to back up most PCs. To bump that online shoebox size to 100GB, you must pay Microsoft $1.99 each month. If your PC has a large collection of music, videos, or photos, you may need 1TB (1,000GB) of space, available for $6.99 a month or $70 a year.

In short, OneDrive is the easiest way to transfer your files, apps, and settings to your new Windows 11 PC. But unless you barely use your PC, you'll be paying a monthly or yearly fee for that convenience.

Hiring a Third Party to Make the Move

For years, Windows came with the Windows Easy Transfer program that simplified moving your files from one PC to another. Unfortunately, Microsoft discontinued the program.

Microsoft may have walked out on the automated PC file transfer business, but third-party vendors are happy to do the job. You basically have two options: using computer upgrade software or taking your PC to a professional.

The following sections cover the pros and cons of each.

Buying Laplink's PCmover program

The PCmover software suite of programs from Laplink (www.laplink.com) transfers not only your old PC's files and settings but some of its programs as well. That's more work than Microsoft's old Easy Transfer program ever attempted. The PCmover suite works on every Windows version from Windows XP to Windows 11.

However, the powerful transfer programs come with a staggering array of potential complications, which isn't surprising: Moving from one PC to another is fraught with possible mishaps. (On the positive side, Laplink helps you move by offering free, 24-hour tech support in the United States, Canada, Australia, New Zealand, and the United Kingdom.)

The free PCmover Windows Store Edition is available from the Microsoft Store app, but it only transfers 500MB of files (and no settings, apps, programs, or user profiles), and then lets you know you should buy the Home or Professional versions to finish the job.

Instead, you should choose between PCmover Home or PCmover Professional. Both let you transfer information only from *one* old PC to *one* new PC. That's usually not a problem, but keep in mind that you can't give the program to a friend after you've transferred your files.

>> **PCmover Home:** This minimalist package moves files, settings, and user profiles to your new PC. However, it won't move apps and programs.

>> **PCmover Professional:** The more popular (and more expensive) option, this software copies apps and programs to the new PC, as well as your files, settings, and user profiles.

Both programs copy your old PC's files, settings, and some programs to your new PC, as shown in Figure 20-1. However, neither package guarantees to copy *all* your programs. Because of technical reasons, some programs can transfer, but others won't. (The reasons behind those potential problems come with their own fine-print section too detailed to list here.)

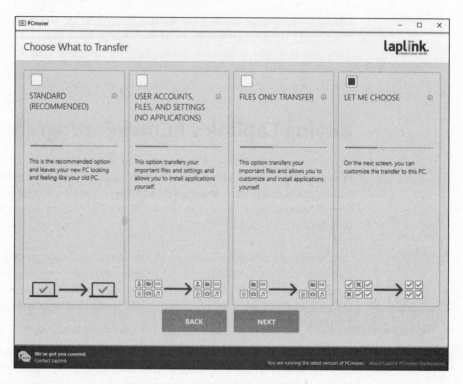

FIGURE 20-1:
Laplink's PCmover helps you move from an old PC to a new one.

If you plan to transfer your files over a network, you can buy and download your chosen PCmover program from Laplink's website. Most people, however, find a better deal by buying the PCmover Ultimate boxed program from Amazon (www.amazon.com). That package includes PCmover Professional *and* a transfer cable, and it costs less than the version on Laplink's website.

The PCmover programs are copy-protected, so you need a working internet connection before you can begin using them. Also, depending on the amount of information on your old PC — and the way you connect your two computers — the transfer process can take several hours.

In short, the PCmover software works best for somebody who's not only patient but also experienced enough with computers to know how to talk with tech support people if something goes wrong. (Tech support people usually speak very, well, *technically*.)

ZINSTALL WINWIN PRO

TIP

PCmover may be the least expensive third-party file transfer solution, but it's not the most comprehensive. Zinstall WinWin costs more than twice as much as the competition. Depending on your situation, though, it might do a more thorough job, especially when transferring desktop programs from your old PC to your new one.

For more information about products from Zinstall, visit the company's website at www.zinstall.com.

Visiting a repair shop

Most local computer repair shops can move your old PC's information to your new PC. (Call first to see whether they want the PC alone, or the PC, monitor, keyboard, and mouse.) Repair shops that make house calls are even better because you won't have to unplug any cables and drop off your PCs at the shop.

Check with your neighbors — they've probably already found a favorite local computer shop or technician.

The prices at local computer repair shops vary widely, and they probably charge more than the price of buying file-transfer software. But if something goes wrong, *they're* the ones talking to tech support, not you.

A repair shop can probably transfer your files even if your old computer no longer turns on or has trouble running. Chances are good that your old computer's hard drive still works, and it still has all your files. Techies at the repair shop can usually transfer your files from your old computer's hard drive directly to your new PC.

Even if you hate throwing in the towel and calling a professional, remember, you need to transfer your old PC's information only *once*. And, if the techie who does the job seems friendly and competent enough, grab a business card. It may come in handy down the road.

Transferring Files Yourself

You can transfer files yourself if you're moving from a Windows 8, 8.1, or 10 PC. You can do this with a combination of a Microsoft account and the built-in File History backup program in Windows. You tell the program to back up the files on your old PC, and then you tell File History on your new Windows 11 PC to restore those files.

However, you need a portable hard drive for this to work. Portable hard drives are fairly inexpensive, usually costing less than $100. And there's a bonus: When you're through transferring the files, the drive works perfectly for backing up your *new* computer.

To transfer files from an old Windows 8, 8.1, or 10 computer to a new Windows 11 computer, follow these steps:

1. **If you've already been using File History on your old PC, jump to Step 5. Otherwise, move to Step 2.**

2. **Sign in with your Microsoft account on your old PC.**

   When you sign in with a Microsoft account, Microsoft remembers many of your settings and services so it can duplicate them on other PCs you sign in to.

   If you've been using a local account on your old Windows PC, convert it to a Microsoft account, a fairly simple chore I describe in Chapter 14.

3. **Plug the portable hard drive into your old PC, and set up File History to save your files onto the portable hard drive.**

   File History comes built in to Windows 8, 8.1, and 10. I describe how to set it up and turn it on in Chapter 13. Figure 20-2 shows how to tell Windows 11 about your new backup drive. Once Windows finds the drive, it could take anywhere from a few minutes to a few hours to back up your files for the first time.

FIGURE 20-2:
Tell Windows to use your new drive to back up your files.

While File History backs up your files, it shows the statement, Backing up your data.

When File History has finished backing up your files to the portable drive, those words change to say, Last Backup, followed by the date and time it finished backing up your files. At that point, move to Step 4.

4. **Sign in to your new Windows 11 PC with the same Microsoft account you used on your old PC. Then plug the portable hard drive into your new computer.**

   By signing in with your Microsoft account, your settings automatically transfer to your new PC. Any files you've stored on OneDrive will be available, too.

5. **Sign in with your Microsoft account on your new PC, open File History, and direct your new Windows 11 PC toward your old File History backup.**

   On your new Windows 11 PC, click the Start button and type **file history** into the Search box. Then click Restore Your Files with File History. When the File History window appears, click Configure File History Settings.

   The Settings app's File History window appears, as shown in Figure 20-3.

   If you spot a checkbox labeled I Want to Use a Previous Backup on this File History Drive, click it. A window drops down, listing the backup you've made on your old PC. Click its name, and click the Turn On button.

   Your new PC begins backing up its files for the first time, but these incoming files won't damage your old PC's backup.

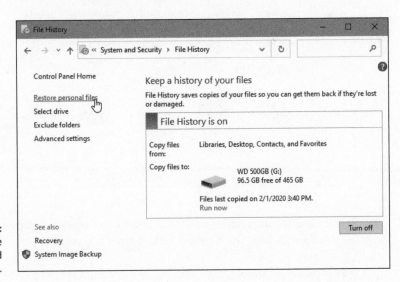

FIGURE 20-3: Choose the backup you'd like to restore.

6. Choose Restore Personal Files from the File History window's left pane.

The window shown in Figure 20-4 appears.

7. Choose the files and folders to restore, and click the green Restore button.

Click the Forward or Back arrows next to the big green button along the window's bottom until you find the date and time of the files you'd like to restore.

For example, if you used File History on your old PC for the first time in Step 4, click the Back arrow (on the left) until you're at the Number 1 backup.

If you've been using File History on your old PC all along, click the Forward arrow (on the right) to move to your most recent backup.

When you're viewing the files or folders you want to restore, click the green button found on the window's bottom edge, shown in Figure 20-4. File History begins copying your old PC's files and folders onto your new PC.

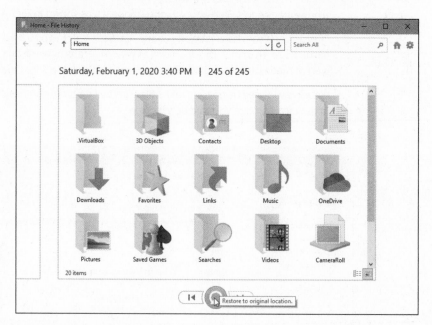

FIGURE 20-4:
Click the green button to restore the files and folders.

If there are no complications and your new PC has enough storage space, your new PC should soon have the files and folders from your old PC.

➤➤ If you've already been using File History on your old PC, all your old PC's backups should still be available to you on your new PC.

>> Your new PC will continue to back up your new computer's files to your portable hard drive. Keep the hard drive plugged in permanently. (Or, if you bought a new laptop or tablet, plug it in frequently so your computer can keep your backups current.)

>> If you've just borrowed a friend's portable hard drive, you can unplug it at this point and give it back. But you should really have your own portable hard drive so you can begin backing up your new Windows 11 PC.

>> Your Microsoft account and File History can transport your settings and files to your new PC. However, you must still install all your old desktop *programs* onto your new PC.

>> If you're moving to Windows 11 from a Windows 10, 8.1, or 8 PC, you can find your apps waiting for you in the Microsoft Store app: Click your icon near the Microsoft Store app's upper-right corner, and choose My Library from the drop-down menu. There you can find and download your old apps to your new PC.

>> Microsoft no longer updates the File History program, so if these instructions no longer work, then File History may have been pushed aside to make way for OneDrive's backup system.

» **Understanding Microsoft's support policies**

» **Finding help for a particular problem or program**

Chapter **21**

Help on the Windows Help System

D on't bother plowing through this whole chapter for the nitty-gritty. What you find here are the quickest ways to make Windows dish out helpful information when something on the desktop leaves you stumped:

» **Press F1 when on the desktop:** Press the F1 key from within Windows or any desktop program.

» **Start menu:** Click the Start button, and click the Get Help icon.

 » **Question mark:** If you spot a little question mark icon within a window's upper-right corner, pounce on it with a quick click.

In each case, Windows fetches help, either by going online, fetching built-in instructions, or leading you to a built-in tutorial.

This chapter explains how to take advantage of the help Windows 11 has to offer.

Getting Started with Windows 11

The bundled Tips app offers a short guided tour to Windows 11. It appeals mostly to the same people who enjoy reading book introductions that set the mood for what's coming.

 To open the app, click the Start button and click the Tips icon (shown in the margin) from the Start menu. The app appears, as shown in Figure 21-1.

FIGURE 21-1:
The new Tips app offers a short introduction to Windows 11.

The Tips app presents a grid of large tiles, each offering tips about a different subject. Click the See What's New button, shown in Figure 21-1, to see a quick explanation of the biggest additions to Windows 11.

Feel free to click any of the other categories and browse the offered tips. However, the Tips app serves as a very brief introductory guide to Windows 11. It's definitely not a problem solver.

Contacting Support

Windows 11 comes with an app that hopes to simplify finding the type of help you need for your particular problem. Called simply Get Help, the app works much like those phone robots that make you press different numbers on your phone until you're finally routed to the proper department.

In fact, the Get Help app needs some help of its own: It works only when you're connected to the internet. If you're not connected, the app simply displays an error message.

To summon the Get Help app and begin routing yourself to somebody or something that can help you with your computer's particular problem, follow these steps:

1. **Click the Start button, click the All Apps icon, and click Get Help (the icon is in the margin).**

   The Get Help program appears, shown in Figure 21-2, and fetches a Virtual Assistant (a robot) to answer your problem.

2. **Type your question into the box along the app's bottom edge.**

   The robot searches Microsoft's online stash of answers for any matches and presents the results. If any of the results answers your question, you're through!

If you still have questions, though, the next two sections explain your options.

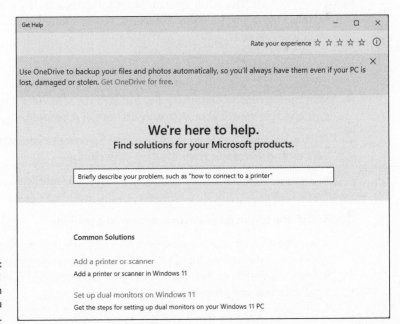

FIGURE 21-2:
The Windows 11 Get Help program tries to guide you to an answer.

Microsoft's support options

If you've purchased your computers directly from Microsoft's online or retail stores, Microsoft offers extended service and warranty plans. By paying in advance, you can take advantage of Microsoft's support plans without having to pay extra down the road.

Microsoft changes its support plans often, though, so to hear the latest on Microsoft's paid support plans, open the Get Help app, choose Chat, and ask what support plans Microsoft currently offers.

Note: Microsoft closed all its Microsoft Store retail locations in June 2020. Microsoft now offers only online support.

Microsoft's free support options

For free support, your best bet is the Microsoft Community website. It's an online gathering place for confused owners, knowledgeable tech enthusiasts, and an occasional Microsoft employee.

You visit the website, choose your category, type your question, and wait. Sometimes a Microsoft employee will answer, but more often than not, somebody with a similar problem will chime in. The more people who respond, the more likely everybody will find a solution to a common problem.

Remember, though: The forums are for Microsoft products. If you're having problems with software from another company, you're limited to that other company's technical support.

To visit the free Microsoft Answers forum, follow these steps:

1. **Visit the Microsoft Community website at** https://answers.microsoft.com, **and sign in with your Microsoft account, if prompted.**

2. **Choose your product from the first page, then choose your Windows version and your topic from the drop-down boxes.**

   You may even be able to narrow down your search by subtopic, as shown in Figure 21-3.

3. **Search the forum for previously answered questions.**

   If something about your computer isn't working correctly, it probably isn't working for others either. To search, click the little magnifying glass icon in the screen's upper-right corner, type a few key words describing your problem into the Search box, and press Enter.

When the website lists the results, spend some time browsing them to see if any solutions work for your computer's particular problem. If not, move to Step 4.

4. **Click the** `Ask a Question` **link at the page's top. When the form appears, type your question, and fill out a title, problem description, and category. Then click the Submit button.**

    To ask a question, click the `Ask a Question` link. The website presents a form, shown in Figure 21-4, for you to fill in a subject and details about your computer's problem.

    Don't forget to fill out the Category drop-down lists at the bottom of the form. They let you choose your Windows version, as well as narrow down your question by topic. Those little chores help others find your question, and possibly provide answers, when they visit later on.

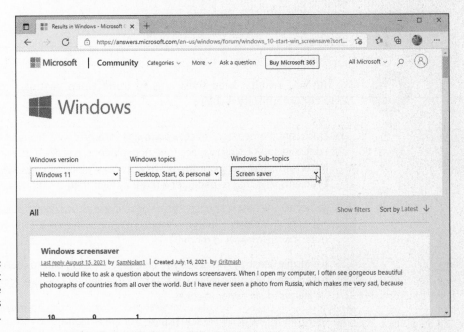

FIGURE 21-3:
The Microsoft Answers online forum provides free tech support.

And then you wait. When somebody responds, a notice appears in your email with a link to your posted message and the response. Click the emailed link to revisit the forum, where you can begin a correspondence that may solve your problem.

The Microsoft Community website is free, and although it's not guaranteed to provide an answer, it's definitely worth a try. I've found quite a few solutions just by browsing the answers to previously asked questions.

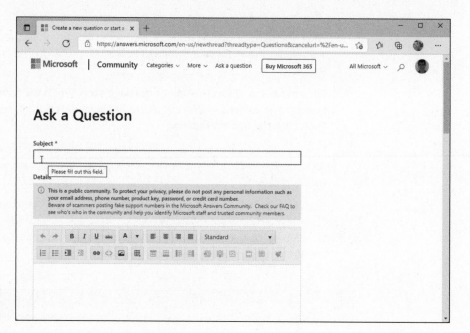

FIGURE 21-4:
Type a subject for
your question.

TIP

For the best results, keep these tips in mind when posting a message on the Microsoft Community website:

>> Don't rant. Remember, most website visitors aren't paid. Many of them are confused souls trying to piece together solutions, just like you. Many computer nerds also hang out there. They're actually interested in solving problems, and they're persuaded more by logic than emotions.

>> To attract the best responses, be as descriptive as possible. If you see an error message, list it in its entirety, without typographical errors. Type your computer's exact make and model.

>> If possible, list the exact steps you take on your computer to reproduce the problem. If your problem is reproducible on other people's computers, it's always *much* easier to solve.

>> Most of the best answers don't come from Microsoft's paid technicians. They come from strangers who have your same problem, perhaps even the same make and model of computer, and who want to swap tips to make things better for you both.

>> Keep an eye on your email Inbox, and respond to people who try to help. The information you're exchanging will live on inside the forum for years. Even if you're not able to solve your immediate problem, you're leaving a trail that can help others solve that problem down the road.

7

The Part of Tens

Chapter **22**

Ten Things You'll Hate about Windows 11 (and How to Fix Them)

You may find yourself thinking Windows 11 would work better if only . . . (*insert your pet peeve here*).

If you find yourself thinking (or saying) those words frequently, read this chapter. Here, you find not only a list of ten of the most aggravating things about Windows 11 but also the best ways you can fix them.

Knowing Whether Your PC Can Upgrade to Windows 11

Just as it does with every new Windows version, Microsoft touts Windows 11 as being the most secure Windows version ever. This time, however, they're probably right: Windows 11 will only run on computers with a special TPM 2.0 (Trusted Platform Module) chip. This chip adds an extra layer of security over how Windows performs, making it much more secure than the past.

Plus, Windows 11 requires an extra speedy CPU (Central Processing Unit) that keeps it zipping along speedily. These requirements make Windows 11 run faster and more securely than ever before.

However, most older PCs don't meet these requirements. Chances are, your old Windows 10 PC won't make the grade.

But how do you know if your computer is up to snuff with the new requirements? Microsoft released a free PC Health Check app that runs on your PC and lets you know if it's up to snuff. You can download the app `https://aka.ms/GetPCHealth` `CheckApp` and run it on your own PC to find out if it meets the rigorous requirements.

If your PC, laptop, or tablet passes the test, you're in luck: Windows 11 is a free upgrade.

If it doesn't pass, you have two options:

>> Buy a new PC with Windows 11 already installed. It will be faster than your old PC, and I explain how to move your old PC's data to your new PC in Chapter 20.

>> Stick with your old PC. Microsoft will keep supporting Windows 10 until October 2025. That's almost four more years. And by then, Windows 12 may be just around the corner.

There's No Backup Program!

Actually, Windows 11 includes several backup programs. But Microsoft is making them increasingly difficult to find. File History, the backup program used in Windows 10, is no longer being developed and could disappear soon. The Windows 7 system image backup still exists in Windows 11, but its future is even more doubtful.

No, Microsoft's vision of a backup program in Windows 11 is OneDrive. In theory, OneDrive is great: It lets you store 5GB of files on the internet for free. That's enough of a taste to hook many people.

OneDrive is convenient, easy to use, and transparent: You probably won't even know that you're storing your files on the internet rather than your own PC. I use OneDrive all the time.

The problem lies when you eventually outgrow that tiny 5GB of free space. At that point, Microsoft wants you to pay a recurring monthly or annual fee for storage.

I pay the annual fee. I use a lot of different computers, and I like being able to access my same batch of files from my Apple iPad, my Android phone, and my Windows PCs and tablets.

If you don't have those needs, though, you may be better served by paying once for a third-party backup program and forgetting about Microsoft's solution in the clouds.

I Want the Start Button and Menu in the Lower-Left Corner!

To make Windows 11 look new and exciting, Microsoft centered all the icons on the taskbar, that strip along the bottom of your desktop. That breaks tradition with every version of Windows dating back to the nineties. Many people don't like it.

Luckily, you can put the Start button and taskbar icons back where they belong by following these steps:

1. **Right-click a blank portion of the taskbar and choose Taskbar Settings from the pop-up menu.**

   The Settings app opens to show the taskbar settings.

2. **From the right pane, click the Taskbar Behaviors section.**

3. **In the Taskbar Alignment section, choose Left instead of Center from the drop-down menu.**

The taskbar moves back to the far left, placing the Start button where it's lived for the past 30 years.

TIP

If you prefer that Windows 11 looked more like your old, familiar version of Windows, check out the Stardock website (www.stardock.com). There, you'll find an inexpensive way to ditch the Windows 11 menu in favor of something more like older Windows versions.

Windows 11 Keeps Changing!

Microsoft sends a big update to Windows 11 every year, a welcome relief from the two annual updates sent to Windows 10. Each update contains hundreds of changes; many are simply "under-the-hood" bug fixes, others are subtle changes to the wording in menus, and others add big new features.

Yet, even when Windows 11 doesn't change noticeably, its bundled apps do. Microsoft constantly tweaks its apps such as Mail and Calendar, Photos, Camera, Groove Music, and others. To see a list of changes, open the Microsoft Store app, click the three dots in its upper-right corner, and choose Downloads and Updates from the drop-down menu.

The Microsoft Store subsequently lists all your installed apps, and the last time they've been updated behind your back. (Click the Library icon from the left pane, then click the Get Updates button at the page's top to download the app's latest versions.) Chances are good that you'll see that many of your apps have been updated within the past week.

In short, Windows 11 changes constantly, and there's no way for you to stop it. Menus may change their names overnight; the Start menu sometimes sprouts new icons in new locations. Some apps gain new features or names, and others drop features. Some apps disappear altogether.

Rapid change is the price you pay for Microsoft's "always up-to-date" vision for Windows 11. Unfortunately, there's no way to lock Windows 11 in place and say, "Stop changing!"

I Don't Want a Microsoft Account

Microsoft wants *everybody* to sign in with a Microsoft account. To Microsoft's credit, Windows 11 is much easier to use with a Microsoft account. Many services require one. Without a Microsoft account, you miss out on the benefits of OneDrive's online storage space. Your *child* even needs to sign in with a Microsoft account if you want to track their computer usage.

But if you don't want a Microsoft account, you don't need one. Just sign up for a Local account instead. Local account holders limit themselves to the "old school" world of life on the desktop. For many people, the desktop works just fine.

A Local account lets you use your desktop and desktop programs, just as they've worked on Windows 7 and earlier Windows versions.

I explain how to create both Local and Microsoft user accounts in Chapter 14.

Windows Makes Me Sign in All the Time

The power-conscious Windows normally blanks your screen when you haven't touched a key for a few minutes. And, when you belatedly press a key to bring the screen back to life, you're faced with the lock screen.

To move past the lock screen, you need to type your password to sign back in to your account. Some people prefer that extra level of security. If the lock screen kicks in while you're spending too much time at the water cooler, you're protected: Nobody can walk over and snoop through your email.

Other people don't need that extra security, and they simply want to return to work quickly. Here's how to accommodate both camps:

To keep Windows from asking for a password whenever it wakes back up, local account holders can follow these steps:

1. **Click the Start button, and click the Settings icon.**

   The Settings app appears.

2. **Click the Accounts category from the Settings app's left pane, and then click Sign-in Options from the right pane.**

3. **Click Password from the Sign-in Options window, and then click the Change button that appears.**

4. **Type your current password into the Current Password box, and click Next. Then leave the New Password, Confirm Password, and Password Hint boxes blank.**

5. **Click Next, and then click Finish at the next screen.**

That resets your password to nothing, leaving you with a more easy-going Windows. When your computer wakes up from sleep, you're left at the same place where you stopped working, and you don't have to enter your password anymore.

Unfortunately, it also leaves you with a less-secure Windows. Anybody who walks by your computer will have access to all your files.

To return to the safer-but-less-friendly Windows, follow these same steps, but in Step 4, create a new password instead of leaving the boxes blank.

If you hate signing in, you're a perfect candidate for Windows Hello. Instead of having to type a name and password, you simply slide your finger over a fingerprint reader. Windows immediately greets you and lets you in. I describe how to set up Windows Hello in Chapter 14.

I Can't Line Up Two Windows on the Screen

With its arsenal of dragging-and-dropping tools, Windows simplifies grabbing information from one window and copying it to another. You can drag an address from an address book and drop it atop a letter in your word processor, for example.

However, the hardest part of dragging and dropping comes when you're lining up two windows on the desktop, side by side, to swap information between them.

Windows offers a simple way to align windows for easy dragging and dropping:

1. **Drag one window against a left, right, top, or bottom edge.**

   When your mouse pointer touches the screen's edge, the window reshapes itself to fill half the screen.

   Windows also lets you drag windows to corners, which is your way of telling the windows to reshape themselves to fill one-quarter of the screen. By dragging a window into each corner, you can align four windows neatly on the screen.

2. **Drag the other window against the opposing edge.**

   When your mouse pointer reaches the other edge, the two windows are aligned side by side.

You can also minimize all the windows except for the two you want to align side by side. Then right-click a blank spot on the taskbar and choose Show Windows Side By Side. The two windows line up on the screen perfectly.

Try dragging windows to each position on the desktop, including the corners, so you'll be prepared when you need to view several files onscreen simultaneously.

It Won't Let Me Do Something Unless I'm an Administrator!

Windows gets really picky about who gets to do what on your computer. The computer's owner gets the Administrator account. And the administrator usually gives everybody else a Standard account. What does that mean? Well, only the administrator can do the following things on the computer:

>> Install programs.

>> Create or change accounts for other people.

>> Start an internet connection.

>> Connect some gadgetry.

>> Perform actions affecting other people on the PC.

People with Standard accounts, by nature, are limited to fairly basic activities. They can do these things:

>> Run previously installed programs.

>> Change their account's picture and password.

If Windows says only an administrator may do something on your PC, you have two choices: Find an administrator to type their password and authorize the action, or convince an administrator to upgrade your account to an Administrator account, a simple task I cover in Chapter 14.

I Don't Know What Version of Windows I Have

Windows 11 comes in several versions. Not sure exactly what version of Windows lives on your computer? Windows doesn't really shout it out, but a little probing forces it to reveal that information. Specifically, you need to look at the System window.

Follow this step to see what version of Windows is installed:

1. **Right-click the Start button, and choose Settings from the pop-up menu.**

   The Settings app opens to the System category; scroll down to the About section on the right edge, and open it. There, in the right pane's Windows Specifications section, you can see what version of Windows lives on your PC. Chances are good that it's Windows 11 Home or Pro version. (Windows 11 only comes in a 64-bit version, if anybody needs to know.)

If you're running an earlier version of Windows, follow these steps:

1. **From the Desktop, click the Start button.**

2. **Right-click the menu item named either Computer or My Computer, and choose Properties from the pop-up menu.**

   When the System Properties window appears, read the information to discover your version of Windows and whether it's 32-or 64-bit.

If your desktop doesn't have a Start button, you're still running Windows 8, and you should think about upgrading. (Microsoft will stop supporting Windows 8 in January 2023.) And, if you haven't heard yet, Microsoft no longer supports Windows 7, meaning it no longer receives security updates. That leaves it vulnerable to viruses, ransomware, and other cybertrouble.

My Print Screen Key Doesn't Work

Contrary to its name, the Print Screen key doesn't shuttle a picture of your screen to your printer. Instead, the Print Screen key (usually labeled PrintScreen, PrtScr, or PrtSc) sends the screen's picture to the Windows Clipboard.

From there, you can paste it into a graphics program, such as Paint, letting the graphics program send the picture to the printer.

If you want to capture an image of the entire screen and quickly save it as a file, press ▦+PrtScr.

That shortcut tells Windows to snap a picture of your current screen and save it as a file. Windows saves those pictures in your computer's Pictures folder within a folder called *Screenshots*. Screenshot files are in the PNG format, a favorite with many graphics programs. (The screenshot doesn't include your mouse pointer.) Subsequent screenshots include a number after the name, as in Screenshot (2) and Screenshot (3).

When saved, your screenshot can head for your printer when you right-click the file and choose Print from the pop-up menu.

Some tablets can also take and save a screenshot if you hold down the volume down toggle and press the tablet's built-in Windows key. Other tablets require different key combinations, so check your tablet's manual to see how it takes screenshots.

When something on your computer screen looks confusing or broken, take a screenshot. Sending the screenshot file to a tech support person lets them see exactly what you're seeing, which increases their chance of fixing it.

Chapter **23**

Ten or So Tips for Tablet and Laptop Owners

For the most part, everything in this book applies to deskbound PCs, laptops, *and* tablets. Windows 11 offers some exclusive settings for the portable crowd, however, and I cover those items here.

Designed for travelers, it explains how to toggle Airplane mode in a hurry, connect to yet another Wi-Fi hotspot, and toggle an uncooperative tablet's autorotate feature.

Since so many portable PCs include touchscreens, I explain the new touchscreen gestures offered by Windows 11, as well as how to tweak them to do your will.

WHERE'S TABLET MODE?

Windows 8, 8.1 and 10 included something called Tablet mode, which made Windows switch to its finger-friendly mode. When in Tablet mode, the Windows Start menu would fill the entire screen, for example; the currently running app would fill the screen as well. Because tablets are often smaller than desktop monitors, seeing one program at a time made it easier to focus on essential information.

Tablet mode never really caught on, though, and it often confused desktop PC owners. So Windows 11 ditched Tablet mode completely. Instead, Windows 11 always adds extra space to menu items, making them easier to poke with a fingertip.

Plug in a keyboard, and Windows 11 knows to stop displaying its onscreen keyboard; that gives you back half of your onscreen real estate, letting you more easily see what you're doing onscreen.

Chances are, you won't miss the extra layer of complication Tablet Mode added to the mix.

If nothing else, please read the section on backing up your laptop or tablet before traveling. It's more essential than ever.

Using the New Touchscreen Gestures

NEW

Touchscreens, found on tablets and some laptops, let you substitute your fingertips for the traditional mouse and keyboard. Instead of clicking a button to push it, for example, you tap it.

Windows has supported touchscreens for years, but Windows 11 introduces some new ways to manipulate interacting with a touchscreen display. For example, Windows 11 displays a handy grid when you slide a window into a corner; the grid lets you see different ways to snap the rest of your open windows into place. (Flip back to Chapter 4 for the details.)

Windows 11 also supports *haptic* feedback with pens, a complicated way of saying you feel slight vibrations when writing, much like the feeling of a normal pen. That lets you *feel* what you're doing, much like writing on textured paper. (You tablet or laptop must support haptic feedback, however.)

NEW

Finally, Windows 11 introduces several new ways to drag your fingers across the screen to do certain tasks, each described in the following list:

>> Slide a finger inward from the left edge to open the Widgets panel. (I explain the information-filled Widgets panel in Chapter 3.)

>> Slide a finger inward from the right edge to see the current month's calendar and the Notifications pane.

>> Slide three fingers down the screen, and all your open apps minimize themselves to icons on the taskbar, leaving you with an empty desktop.

>> Slide three fingers back up the screen to place your minimized windows back onto the desktop.

>> Slide three fingers to the left or right to switch quickly between open apps.

>> Slide four fingers to the left or right to switch between any open virtual desktops. (I explain virtual desktops in Chapter 3.)

If your laptop includes a trackpad rather than a touchscreen, many of these same gestures work there, as well.

TIP

To adjust your trackpad's settings, choose Settings from the Start menu, and choose Bluetooth and Devices from the left pane. Choose Touchpad from the right pane, and all the available options appear, ready to be toggled on or off, or subtly tweaked to your liking.

TIP

To adjust your touchscreen settings, choose Settings from the Start menu, and choose Bluetooth and Devices from the left pane. Choose Touchscreen from the right pane to see your options, including turning them on or off.

Switching to Airplane Mode

Most people enjoy working with their tablets or laptops during a long flight. Portable devices are great for watching movies and playing games while pretending to catch up on some work.

But most airlines make you turn off your wireless connection while the plane is in flight, referred to in airport lingo as *Airplane mode*.

To turn on Airplane mode on a tablet or laptop, follow these steps:

1. **Click or tap the Wi-Fi icon near the clock in the screen's lower-right corner.**

An icon-filled panel appears, including the Airplane Mode toggle icon.

2. **Click or tap your Airplane Mode icon (shown in the margin).**

When the icon's surrounding button is highlighted, Airplane mode is on, which turns off your tablet's radios: Wi-Fi, Bluetooth, and GPS.

To turn off Airplane mode and reconnect to the internet, repeat these steps. This time, however, you toggle *off* Airplane mode, which reactivates your Wi-Fi, Bluetooth, and GPS.

TIP

Airplane mode not only puts your tablet and laptop in compliance with airline safety rules, but it conserves battery life as well. If you're running short on battery life and don't need the internet, feel free to keep your computer in Airplane mode.

If your laptop or tablet has a wireless cellular data plan, Airplane mode turns that off as well. It's a handy way to shut *off* all your computer's radio activity with one switch.

If you're using Bluetooth earphones, though, feel free to turn on your laptop or tablet's Bluetooth. (The Bluetooth icon lives right next to the Airplane mode icon.) Airlines don't mind Bluetooth, just Wi-Fi.

Connecting to a New Wireless Internet Network

Every time you connect to a wireless network, Windows stashes its settings for connecting again the next time you visit. But when you're visiting a wireless network for the first time, you need to tell your computer that it's time to connect.

I explain wireless connections more thoroughly in Chapter 15, but here are the steps for quick reference:

1. **Turn on your laptop's wireless adapter if necessary.**

Most adapters stay on continuously unless your computer is in Airplane mode. If so, turn off Airplane mode, as described in the preceding section.

2. **When the panel appears, click the arrow to the right of the panel's wireless network icon, shown in the margin.**

Windows lists any wireless networks it finds within range.

3. **Connect to a wireless network by clicking its name and clicking the Connect button.**

At many places, clicking the Connect button connects your laptop to the internet immediately. But if your laptop asks for more information, move to Step 4.

WARNING

Never connect to a wireless network listed as an *ad hoc* connection. Those connections are usually set up in public places by thieves hoping to rip off unsuspecting visitors.

4. **Enter the wireless network's name and security key/passphrase if asked.**

Some secretive wireless networks don't broadcast their names, so Windows lists them as Hidden Network. If you spot that name or Windows asks for the network's security key, track down the network's owner and ask for the network's name, known as its *SSID* (Service Set Identifier) and security key or passphrase to enter here.

When you click the Connect button, Windows announces its success. (You may also need to click through a disclaimer when connecting at some public places.) Be sure to select the adjacent checkbox labeled Connect Automatically. That tells your computer to remember the password and connect automatically the next time you come within range.

If you sign in with a Microsoft account, your Wi-Fi passwords travel with your account. If you log in to a Wi-Fi network with your laptop, you can automatically log into the same Wi-Fi network with your tablet as well.

Toggling Your Tablet's Screen Rotation

Most Windows tablets are meant to be held horizontally. But when you pick them up, they automatically rotate to keep your work right-side up. Turn your tablet vertically, for example, and your desktop becomes long and narrow.

Autorotation comes in handy when you're reading a digital book, for example, because the longer, thinner pages more closely resemble a printed book. It's also a convenient way to rotate photos on a tablet when showing them off to friends. But when the screen rotates unexpectedly, autorotate becomes a bother.

TIP

Most tablets come with a rotation lock button along one edge. (The rotation button is usually near the power button for some reason.) Pressing that toggle button either locks the screen in place or lets it rotate freely.

You can also toggle autorotation directly from Windows by following these steps:

1. Tap the Start button and then tap Settings. When the Settings window opens, tap the System setting from the left pane, and then tap the Display section from the right side.

Windows 11 shows its settings for adjusting all aspects of your display.

2. Tap the toggle switch in the Rotation Lock setting.

When the button says On, Windows stops the screen from rotating automatically. Tap it, and the button says Off, forcing the tablet stay right-side up no matter how you move the tablet.

Repeat these steps to toggle autorotate on or off.

Adjusting to Different Locations

PCs don't move from a desktop, making some things pretty easy to set up. You need to enter your location only once, for example, and Windows automatically sets up your time zone, currency symbols, and similar things that change over the globe.

But the joy of a tablet or laptop's mobility is tempered with the annoyance of telling the thing exactly where it's currently located. This section supplies the steps you need to change when traveling to a different area.

Follow these steps to let your laptop know you've entered a new time zone:

1. From the desktop, right-click the Date and Time area in the taskbar's lower-right corner.

A pop-up menu appears.

2. Click Adjust Date and Time.

The Settings app appears, open to the Time and Language page.

3. Click the Time Zone option, and then select your current time zone from the drop-down list.

That changes your time zone, which is all most travelers need. Extended-stay travelers may opt to change region-specific items — the region's currency symbol, for example, or the date, time, and number formats — or to add foreign characters to their keyboard.

If you travel often, turn on the Set Time Zone Automatically toggle switch.

If you're deeply embedded in a foreign zone, move to Step 4.

4. **Change your date and time formats, as well as regional and language preferences to match your current country's customs.**

   The options on the Time and Language page of the Settings app let you change all the regional settings in Windows:

   - *Date and Time:* This is the section you changed in Step 3. There's no need to revisit unless you erred in that step.

   - *Language and Region:* Choose this option to tell your apps what country you're visiting. (This lets the apps display local content that matches your location.) You can also add another language here so you can read and type in that language. You can also change your keyboard layout to match other country's keyboards as well.

   - *Sync Now:* Clicking this tells Windows to check in with Microsoft's server and automatically set your PC's time and date.

5. **Close the Settings app, if desired.**

   Your changes take place immediately. To exit the Settings app, click the Close icon in the app's upper-right corner.

Turning on the Traffic Widget

NEW

Windows 11 introduces a panel of *Widgets* — little information–filled boxes that can be called up with a quick click on a taskbar icon or, on a touchscreen, a finger swipe inward from the screen's left edge.

Although I explain Widgets in Chapter 3, a handy one to add when traveling is the Traffic Widget. It places a small, localized map in the Widget panel that constantly shows the state of your nearby traffic flow.

Click or tap the little map, and your browser fills the screen with a map of your immediate area and its current traffic situation. (While it's there, you can also find directions to nearby locations.)

The Traffic Widget is quick to fetch, updates automatically, and can help you decide if it's worth leaving the hotel at that particular moment, or waiting until the traffic dies down.

Make sure the Weather Widget is added and set to update automatically. No sense grabbing that coffee until the hurricane passes.

Backing Up Your Laptop Before Traveling

I explain how to back up a PC in Chapter 13, and backing up a laptop or tablet works just like backing up a desktop PC. Please, please remember to back up your laptop before leaving your home or office. Thieves grab laptops and tablets much more often than desktop PCs. Your laptop and tablet can be replaced, but the data inside them can't.

Keep the backed-up information at *home* or in the *cloud* — not in your laptop's bag.

Theft is why I don't recommend storing any sort of backup memory card inside your tablet or in your tablet's carrying case. When the thief takes your tablet, he takes your backup as well.

Microsoft's OneDrive, built in to Windows 11, lets you store your information on the internet quite easily, providing an automatic backup. I explain how to set up OneDrive in Chapter 5.

Accessing the Mobility Center

Introduced in Windows 7, the Mobility Center lives on in Windows 11. It's a collection of frequently accessed settings for portable devices.

To access the Mobility Center, right-click the Start button and choose Mobility Center from the pop-up menu. The Mobility Center appears, as shown in Figure 23-1.

Different manufacturers offer different settings, but most of them offer quick ways to toggle screen brightness, sound volume, rotation, battery plans, and ways to connect to monitors and projectors.

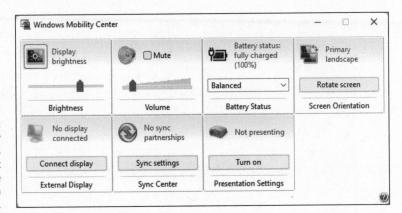

FIGURE 23-1:
The Mobility
Center places
laptop and tablet
settings in one
easy-to-reach
location.

Turning Calculator into a
Road Warrior Tool

When it burst onto the computing scene in the mid-eighties, Windows included a basic calculator with the usual arithmetic functions. Today the calculator sports many new features that help not only math students, but world travelers.

Specifically, the calculator now includes a wide variety of converters, letting you calculate currency exchange rates, metric values, and a variety of other measurements.

To access Calculator's different conversion modes, follow these steps:

1. **Click the Start menu, type Calculator into the Search box, and press Enter.**

The Calculator app appears, shown in Figure 23-2.

2. **Click the Menu icon in Calculator's upper-left corner.**

A menu drops down, listing all the modes the Calculator app can display.

3. **From the menu's Converter section, choose what you want to convert.**

Choose Currency, for example, to convert from dollars to Euros.

4. **Enter the amount you want to convert and the currency of your currently visited country.**

To convert $100 into Euros, for example, enter 100 into Calculator's type pad by clicking (or touching) the calculator buttons. Beneath that, use the drop-down menu to choose Euros, or the type of currency you'd like to convert. Calculator offers a wide variety of currency, from Afghanistan's Afghani to Zambia's Kwacha.

As soon as you choose the type of currency, Calculator looks up the current exchange rate and lists how far that much money will go in the country you're visiting.

In another boon for travelers, Calculator converts volume, temperature, and speed measurements. It's worth a look when traveling in unfamiliar countries or when you've finished a trip and need to itemize receipts.

Index

B

back-arrow icon, Edge browser, 187
backups
  in File History backup, 271–275
  laptop best practices, 432
  migrating files using File History backup, 401–405
  system image, 273
Backward button, 74
BD-RE drives, 108
BD-ROM drives, 108
Best Match category, Search box, 155
Bing, 11, 193
BitLocker, 365
BitLocker-To-Go settings, 365
Bluetooth
  adding devices, 249–251
  module, 249
  notification icon for, 60
  taskbar icon for, 56
Bluetooth earphones, 428
Blu-Ray drives, 91, 95
borders, 80
browser
  adding favorite pages, 191–192
  address bar, 187
  Address bar, 190
  clicking links, 189
  defaults in, 11
  defined, 33
  downloading files, 197–198
  finding more information on websites, 194–195
  history list, 192
  home page, 190
  Internet Explorer and, 183
  menu icons, 186–188, 190
  moving from one web page to another, 188–190
  opening, 186
  opening favorites, 190–191

overview, 179, 186–188
  phishing scams, avoiding, 233–234
  printing in, 173
  refreshing, 187
  saving picture, 196–197
  saving text, 196
  saving web page, 195–196
  search engine, 193–194
  settings, 188
  SmartScreen Filter, 233
  syncing, 188
  tabs, 186–187
  typing addresses in Address bar, 190
burn-in, 259
burning CDs, 108, 341, 342–343

C

Calculator app, 33, 433–434
Calendar app
  adding appointments to, 217–218
  defined, 33
  notifications, 382–383
  overview, 199, 216
Camera app
  defined, 33
  making photos and videos with, 349–350
  shooting videos with, 349–350
  taking photos with, 349–350
Camera Roll folder, 351
cameras
  Camera app overview, 33
  Camera Roll folder, 351
  "choose what happens with this device" message, 383–384
  copying photos to computer, 92
  display mode, 346
  icon, 92

Caps Lock key, 377
captions, 336
CD drives, 91, 95
CD-R drives, 108
CD-RW drives, 108
CDs (compact discs), 107–108
  burning music playlist to, 341
  buying blank, 108–109
  duplicating, 111
  playing, 337
  ripping from, 330
  ripping music from, 341–342
  saving files to, 109–111
cellular data plan, 428
central processing unit (CPU), 17, 275, 416
Chat. See Teams Chat
Cheat Sheet, 6
Child account, 283
children, safety for, 234–236
"choose what happens with this device" message, 383–384
Chrome browser, 181
clicking links, 189
cloud storage
  About tab, 118
  accessing from Internet, 122–123
  Account tab, 117
  ads on, 11
  Backup tab, 118
  Camera Roll folder, 351
  changing status of files or folders, 121
  defined, 34, 87
  "deleted files are removed everywhere" message, 384
  Files on Demand feature, 117, 120–122
  files to sync, 114
  freeing up space on, 277–278
  Groove Music access to, 325
  icon for, 57
  Network tab, 118

About the Author

Andy Rathbone started geeking around with computers in 1985 when he bought a 26-pound portable CP/M Kaypro 2X. Like other nerds of the day, he soon began playing with null-modem adapters, dialing computer bulletin boards, and working part-time at Radio Shack.

He wrote articles for various techie publications before moving to computer books in 1992. He's written the *Windows For Dummies* series, *Microsoft Surface For Dummies*, *Upgrading & Fixing PCs For Dummies*, and many other computer books.

Today, he has more than 15 million copies of his books in print, and they've been translated into more than 30 languages. You can reach Andy at his website, www.andyrathbone.com.

Author's Acknowledgments

Special thanks to Dan Gookin, Matt Wagner, Tina Rathbone, Steve Hayes, Kristie Pyles, Mary Corder, Colleen Diamond, and Ryan Williams.

Thanks also to all the folks I never meet in editorial, sales, marketing, proofreading, layout, graphics, and manufacturing who work hard to bring you this book.

Publisher's Acknowledgments

Executive Editor: Steve Hayes

Project Editor: Colleen Diamond

Copy Editor: Colleen Diamond

Technical Editor: Ryan C. Williams

Proofreader: Debbye Butler

Production Editor: Mohammed Zafar Ali

Cover Image: © Russian Labo/Getty Images;
Screen capture courtesy of Andy Rathbone